THE EARLY MARRIAGES OF STRAFFORD COUNTY NEW HAMPSHIRE 1630-1870

SUPPLEMENT

Robert Sayward Canney

HERITAGE BOOKS
2008

HERITAGE BOOKS
AN IMPRINT OF HERITAGE BOOKS, INC.

Books, CDs, and more—Worldwide

For our listing of thousands of titles see our website
at
www.HeritageBooks.com

Published 2008 by
HERITAGE BOOKS, INC.
Publishing Division
100 Railroad Ave. #104
Westminster, Maryland 21157

Copyright © 1997 Robert Sayward Canney

Other books by the author:
The Early Marriages of Strafford County, New Hampshire, 1630-1850
The Early Marriages of Strafford County, New Hampshire, 1630-1860
The Early Marriages of Strafford County, New Hampshire, Supplement, 1630-1870
The Early Marriages of Strafford County, New Hampshire, Second Supplement, 1630-1870

All rights reserved. No part of this book may be reproduced or transmitted in any form or by any means, electronic or mechanical, including photocopying, recording or by any information storage and retrieval system without written permission from the author, except for the inclusion of brief quotations in a review.

International Standard Book Numbers
Paperbound: 978-0-7884-0681-2
Clothbound: 978-0-7884-7188-9

INTRODUCTION

This supplemental volume presents a combination of previously unrecorded marriages and updated entries from the previous edition. The updated information within the old entries is designated by underlining.

The material has been gathered from town records, Piscataqua Pioneer files, census records, private manuscripts, and published town histories. The marriages are arranged, first, by the groom's surname and then chronologically by marriage date. Parentage, birth and death dates, and the official performing the ceremony are included when available.

While most recorded marriages occurred in Strafford County, a small number took place in southern York County, Maine, and northern Rockingham County, New Hampshire, but are included due to their connection with Strafford County families.

ABBOTT, John, 3rd, b. Aug. 3, 1758, d. May 1837, m. Dec. 21, 1780, by Rev. Matthew Merriam, Martha Twombly, b. in 1759, d. in 1835, dau. of Ezekiel, both of Berwick, Me.

ABBOTT, Jedediah, m. Jan. 2, 1792, in Berwick, Me., Rachel Twombly, dau. of Ezekiel.

ABBOTT, Rev. Edward F., d. June 17, 1886, aged 71, m. Sept. 7, 1846, in Milton, Charlotte Cushing Jones, d. Jan. 13, 1882, aged 64, both of Milton.

ABBOTT, John H., m. Oct. 29, 1861, by Rev. James Rand, Mrs. Eliza A. (Dexter) Lane, wid. of George W., dau. of George G.

ABBOTT, Sylvester, m. July 25, 1862, in Dover, Elizabeth Westman.

ABBOTT, Isaac F., b. Nov. 1, 1842, d. Jan. 14, 1895, m. Oct. 10, 1867, in Dover, Lizzie J. Cushman, b. July 14, 1843, d. Mar. 18, 1892.

ABBOTT, George F., m. Aug. 15, 1868, in Dover, Sarah S. Tuttle.

1) **ADAMS**, John, d. 1701, m. Avis -----, d. Oct. 6, 1699.

2) ADAMS, Rev. Hugh, son of John, b. May 7, 1676, d. Oct. 1748, m. early as 1701, Susannah Winburn, dau. of Rev. John.

3) ADAMS, Capt. Nathaniel, son of Matthew, b. 1726, d. Oct. 18, 1768, m. (1) in 1752, Deborah Knight, dau. of Capt. John, m. (2) in 1755, Elizabeth Parker, of Portsmouth, dau. of William.

(4) ADAMS, Nathaniel, son of Nathaniel, b. 1756, m. (1) Eunice Woodman, d. Sept. 1794, m. (2) Martha Church.

ADAMS, John, b. Aug. 7, 1759, d. Aug. 1, 1837, m. Nov. 12, 1786, by Rev. Jeremiah Shaw, Hannah Paine, b. May 8, 1760, d. Apr. 11, 1847.

ADAMS, Benjamin, of Barnstead, m. Oct. 2, 1798, by Rev. Isaac Smith, Elizabeth Rand, of Pittsfield.

ADAMS, Ebenezer, of Milton, d. Apr. 4, 1855, aged 62, m. May 2, 1819, in Wakefield, Betty Sanborn, of Wakefield, d. Apr. 30, 1852, aged 57.

ADAMS, Solomon, of Middleton, Mass., m. July 20, 1823, by Rev. Joseph Haven, Ruth Haven, of Rochester, d. 1826, aged 34, dau. of Rev. Joseph.

6) ADAMS, Samuel, son of John, b. June 20, 1810, d. Apr. 3, 1892, m. Sept. 21, 1836, Mary Jane Moulton, (lived in Portsmouth).

ADAMS, James, of Barnstead, m. Nov. 14, 1840, by Rev. Nathaniel Berry, Hannah Hurd Varney, of Farmington.

ADAMS, John J. J., of Durham, m. May 26, 1852, in Newmarket, Helen M. Branscomb, of Newmarket.

ADAMS, Jacob, son of Ebenezer, b. 1828, d. 1901, m. Jan. 1855, in Milton, Sarah E. Hayes, b. 1824, d. 1874.

ADAMS, John Q., son of Mark, d. Sept. 6, 1918, aged 83, m. July 9, 1859, in Gilmanton, Mary O. Freeman, both of Alton.

8) **ADAMS**, Joseph, M. R., son of Rev. John, b. May 10, 1838, m. Jan. 1, 1860, Olive Esther Libbey.

AKERMAN, James D., d. Apr. 28, 1904, aged 69, m. (pub. Jan. 17, 1854, in Portsmouth), Anna Dearborn, dau. of Jonathan.

ALLARD, James, of New Durham Gore, m. Mar. 20, 1794, by Rev. Isaac Smith, Elizabeth Watson, of Gilmanton.

ALLARD, Benjamin, m. July 29, 1796, in New Durham, Elizabeth Sherburne.

ALLARD, Daniel, Jr., m. Aug. 3, 1850, by Elder Elias Hutchins, Caroline H. Haskell, d. July 1855.

ALLEN, James, m. Apr. 29, 1784, by Rev. Isaac Smith, Dorcas Judkins.

ALLEN, Elisha, m. May 15, 1800, by Rev. Joseph Hilliard, Polly Pray, d. Nov. 17, 1863, aged 82.

ALLEN, John, m. May 14, 1812, by Rev. Isaac Smith, Deborah Sweatt.

ALLEN, William, of Rochester, son of Samuel, b. 1794, d. May 25, 1848, m. Nov. 27, 1817, by Rev. Joseph Haven, Sarah Nute, of Milton, b. Oct. 18, 1794, d. Mar. 28, 1887, aged 92, dau. of Jotham.

ALLEN, Charles, of Lee, son of Samuel, d. Oct. 26, 1890, aged 85, m. int. Oct. 29, 1829, in Lee, Hannah Gilman, of Gilford.

ALLEN, Asa, of Lee, son of Samuel, d. Dec. 5, 1861, aged 53, m. (pub. Jan. 29, 1839, in Wakefield), Patience O. Piper, of Tuftonboro, d. Sept. 3, 1853, aged 38.

ALLEN, Levi W., of Rochester, son of William, b. in 1823, d. Jan. 22, 1899, m. Sept. 3, 1846, Sarah Ann Furbish.

ALLEN, William H., m. Sept. 6, 1869, by Rev. Asa Piper, Elizabeth B. Nichols, both of Wakefield.

ALLEY, Samuel, m. Dec. 19, 1867, by Rev. Robert S. Stubbs, Sarah C. (Leighton) Quimby, wid. of Joseph C., b. 1817, d. Mar. 12, 1907.

AMAZEEN, Henry C., of Farmington, son of William, d. Apr. 29, 1897, m. Jan. 11, 1849, in Farmington, Abigail Wentworth, of Milton, d. Mar. 19, 1905, aged 75, dau. of William.

AMBROSE, Nathaniel, of Moultonboro, son of Nathaniel, d. Jan. 18, 1874, aged 81, m. Mar. 10, 1814, by Rev. Jeremiah Shaw, Irena Brown, of Wolfeboro, d. Mar. 23, 1884, aged 89.

AMES, Fisher, m. Apr. 6, 1867, in Dover, Nancy A. Webster.

ANDERSON, James, m. (pub. Apr. 24, 1827, in Salmon Falls), Mary Ann Griffith.

ANDREWS, Joshua, son of Elisha, b. Aug. 7, 1720, m. in 1744, in Berwick, Me., Olive Emery.

ANDREWS, Samuel, b. 1754, d. 1849, m. July 5, 1779, by Rev. Matthew Merriam, Hannah Dunnell, both of Berwick, Me.
ANDREWS, Elisha, m. Mar. 24, 1799, in Berwick, Me., Olive Hayman.
ANDREWS, Howard, m. Nov. 22, 1867, by Rev. Alden Sherwin, Mary J. Hatch.
ANDREWS, Frank B., m. Dec. 25, 1868, by Rev. Robert Stubbs, Anna V. Cook.
ANDREWS, Abram P., m. Aug. 11, 1869, in Dover, Harriet Curtis.
ANNABLE, George W., of Portsmouth, son of Robert W., d. May 6, 1894, aged 73, m. (pub. Oct. 5, 1847, in Providence, R.I.), Anna Twombly, of Dover.
APPLEBEE, Thomas, son of Hawley, d. Mar. 2, 1841, aged 84, m. (1) June 9, 1785, by Rev. Matthew Merriam, Molly Goodwin, m. (2) Judith Rines, b. 1769, d. Nov. 23, 1859, dau. of Henry
APPLEBEE, James, son of Thomas, b. Mar. 17, 1801, d. Oct. 30, 1880, m. Nov. 20, 1825, in Alton, Sally Rines, b. Mar. 2, 1803, d. May 14, 1897, dau. of Henry.
APPLEBEE, John, son of Thomas, b. 1809, d. 1853, m. Nov. 13, 1834, in Acton, Me., Mary Buzzell, b. 1805, d. 1875.
APPLEBEE, William, of Milton, d. May 10, 1873, aged 42, m. Nov. 20, 1855, in Milton, Susan Miller, of Acton, Me., b. Apr. 24, 1827, d. Oct. 22, 1898, dau. of John.
APPLEBEE, Theodore S., m. Aug. 6, 1864, in Dover, Augusta Leighton.
APPLEBEE, Oliver H., m. Sept. 22, 1866, by Rev. James Rand, Ellen C. Rains.
ARCHIBALD, Reuben, of Wakefield, m. Oct. 5, 1875, by Rev. Asa Piper, Elzira Davis, of Limerick, Me.
ARNOLD, M. P., of Salem, Mass., m. Aug. 18, 1873, in Great Falls, Mrs. Priscilla S. French, of Great Falls.
ASH, Thomas, Jr., son of Thomas, m. early as 1730, Eleanor -----.
ASHTON, Benjamin F., m. Dec. 21, 1864, in Dover, Lizzie Porcher.
ATKINS, Ephraim B., m. (pub. July 10, 1873, in Dover) Abbie E. Pickering, both of Great Falls.
ATKINSON, Theodore, son of William King Atkinson, b. July 5, 1794, d. Aug. 24, 1822, m. Nov. 3, 1816, by Rev. J. W. Clary, Anna Louisa Tufts, d. Nov. 25, 1845, aged 52, dau. of Asa, both of Dover.
ATWATER, Constant L.T., m. Feb. 20, 1864, in Dover, Ellen M. Langley.
AUSTIN, Elijah, of Madbury, d. Feb. 8, 1857, m. Aug. 6, 1835, by Rev. Isaac Willey, Sarah C. Hayes, of Farmington.
AUSTIN, Albert, m. May 20, 1866, in Dover, Amanda Downs.

AUSTIN, Jacob K., m. July 21, 1866, in Dover, Mary C. Witham.

AVERY, Thomas, d. Sept. 6, 1744, m. Oct. 8, 1697, by Rev. John Pike, wid. Abigail Coomes.

AVERY, Moses, b. 1759, d. Nov. 5, 1825, m. in 1779, by Rev. Joseph Buckminster, Elizabeth Colbath.

AVERY, John, m. Aug. 3, 1779, by Rev. Isaac Smith, Mary French.

AVERY, Samuel, Jr., m. Jan. 27, 1780, by Rev. Isaac Smith, Prudence Lock.

AVERY, Samuel, Jr., of Barnstead, m. Apr. 3, 1783, by Rev. Isaac Smith, Anna Evans, of Gilmanton.

AVERY, Jonathan, m. Dec. 16, 1784, by Rev. Isaac Smith, Dorothy Dudley, both of Gilmanton.

AVERY, Samuel, Jr., m. Aug. 11, 1785, by Rev. Isaac Smith, Anne Chase, both of Gilmanton.

AVERY, Robert, m. Mar. 15, 1792, by Rev. Isaac Smith, Catron Buzzy.

AVERY, Daniel, of Gilford, d. 1826, m. Mar. 12, 1823, by Rev. Noah Piper, Betsey Piper, of Stratham.

AVERY, James C., d. Aug. 3, 1829, aged 29, m. June 28, 1829, by Rev. Hubbard Winslow, Nancy Rundlett, both of Dover, d. May 25, 1883, aged 82.

AVERY, David, b. Mar. 18, 1815, d. Feb. 24, 1904, m. June 1, 1836, by Rev. Nathaniel Berry, Sally L. Holmes, d. Oct. 29, 1861, aged 89, both of Strafford.

AVERY, Henry C., m. Nov. 21, 1860, in Alton, Emma R. Sawyer, d. Dec. 17, 1908, aged 79, dau. of Rev. Seth, both of Alton.

AVERY, George W., son of Daniel E., d. June 8, 1811, aged 72, m. Nov. 18, 1862, in Dover, Eliza G. Trickey, d. Feb. 17, 1916, aged 78, dau. of Lemuel G.

AVERY, Solomon, m. Aug. 28, 1866, in Dover, Ellen L. McDuffee.

AYERS, Levi, m. Jan. 6, 1813, by Rev. Isaac Smith, Susan -----, both of Gilmanton.

AYERS, Thomas, m. Jan. 10, 1813, by Rev. Isaac Smith, Sally Gale, both of Gilmanton.

AYERS, John H., m. Sept. 13, 1866, by Rev. James Rand, Emma A. Fogg.

BABB, Thomas, m. Mar. 17, 1757, by Rev. Amos Main, Meribah Locke, of Barrington.

BABB, William, of Barrington, d. June 20, 1846, aged 81, m. Mar. 17, 1789, Sarah Leighton, b. Feb. 5, 1762, d. May 18, 1847, dau. of James.

BABB, Sampson, of Barrington, d. May 25, 1877, aged 92, m. (1) Nov. 27, 1806, by Rev. Joseph Haven, Abigail Hammett, d. Aug.

25, 1808, aged 26, m. (2) Elizabeth -----, d. Nov. 27, 1850, aged 60.
BABB, Joel, of Strafford, m. June 18, 1829, by Rev. John Winkley, Charlotte Babb, of Barrington.
BABB, Asahel, d. Aug. 5, 1886, aged 74, m. Jan. 29, 1835, by Elder Enoch Place, Lydia Berry, d. Jan. 24, 1887, aged 78, both of Strafford.
BABB, Sampson, of Barnstead, b. Dec. 30, 1820, d. Dec. 7, 1910, m. Nov. 27, 1850, by Rev. Nathaniel Berry, Almira Evans, of Strafford, b. July 27, 1824, d. Feb. 24, 1909.
BABB, John A., m. Jan. 4, 1866, by Rev. Francis E. Abbott, Mary E. Bickford.
BABB, Leonard P., m. Oct. 24, 1866, in Dover, Rachel Rothwell.
BACON, Samuel, m. Mar. 14, 1754, in Dover, Anna Orne.
BACON, Charles E., b. Mar. 11, 1832, d. June 10, 1898, m. June 15, 1856, in Dover, Susan Clark, b. Sept. 29, 1838, d. Aug. 4, 1908, both of Dover.
BADGER, William, m. May 1, 1803, by Rev. Isaac Smith, Martha Smith, d. Jan. 30, 1810, aged 30, dau. of Rev. Isaac.
BADGER, William, m. Jan. 15, 1827, by Rev. John Osborne, Mary S. Joy, b. Jan. 22, 1811, dau. of Timothy, both of Newmarket.
BADGER, John P., m. Oct. 26, 1870, in Dover, Adelaid Hussey.
BAILEY, Frank P., m. June 26, 1865, in Dover, Ellen J. Gray.
BAILEY, J. H., m. Aug. 10, 1867, by Rev. Robert S. Stubbs, Fanny W. Beacher.
2) **BAKER**, Charles, b. 1721/2, d. Sept. 26, 1784, m. (1) before 1749, Love Downs, dau. of Thomas, m. (2) Mary (Carr) Roberts, wid. of Francis, b. Feb. 4, 1721/2, d. Oct. 21, 1807, dau. of John, of Newbury, Mass.
3) BAKER, John, son of Col. Otis, b. Dec. 12, 1762, d. Feb. 24, 1815, m. Oct. 9, 1808, in Gilmanton, Lois (Twombly) Baker, wid. of Otis, d. Nov. 30, 1820.
BAKER, Charles W., of Brookfield, m. July 4, 1824, in Wolfeboro, Hannah A. Whitten, of Wolfeboro, b. Jan. 23, 1799, d. Dec. 1874, dau. of Jesse.
BAKER, James W., d. Nov. 28, 1880, m. (1) Jan. 15, 1846, by Elder Enoch Place, Mary E. Place, d. Aug. 13, 1890, aged 67, dau. of Elder Enoch, both of Strafford, m. (2) ? Nov. 13, 1891, in Dover, Lydia E. O'Conner.
BAKER, Asa S., son of Sharanton, d. June 19, 1911, aged 80, m. (1) June 15, 1852, in Dover, Frances R. Buzzell, m. (2) May 1, 1865, Sarah F. Meader.
BAKER, George E., m. Dec. 24, 1862, by Rev. James Rand, Mrs. Fannie E. Baker.

BAKER, Eben F., m. Jan. 1, 1865, in Dover, Darinda A. Hill.
BALCH, Rev. Benjamin, b. Feb. 12, 1743, d. May 4, 1815, m. May 4, 1764, in Barrington, Joanna O'Brien.
BALCH, Capt. George Washington, m. (pub. Sept. 29, 1804, in Portsmouth), Dorothy Noble.
BALL, Charles G., m. Mar. 6, 1864, in Dover, Lizzie P. Hammett.
BALLENTINE, Hugh, m. Nov. 19, 1857, in Milton Mills, Emily W. Brackett, d. Feb. 13, 1913, aged 74, dau. of John, both of Great Falls.
BANFIELD, Nathaniel, of Wolfeboro, m. (1) (pub. Nov. 20, 1827, in Brookfield), Lois Giles, of Brookfield, d. Sept. 25, 1843, aged 38, m. (2) Jan. 29, 1844, in Wolfeboro, Mary Ann Young, of Milton, d. Apr. 29, 1888, aged 68, dau. of Isaac.
BANFIELD, Enoch, of Boston, Mass., d. July 26, 1848, aged 39, m. (pub. Nov. 19, 1844, in Tuftonboro), Elizabeth L. Place, of Milton, d. Jan. 21, 1915, aged 91, dau. of David.
BARBER, William H., m. Nov. 12, 1864, in Dover, Maria D. Cole.
BARKER, Deac. Benjamin, of Somersworth, b. Oct. 16, 1799, d. Dec. 18, 1873, m. (1) Aug. 13, 1827, by Rev. Isaac Willey, Eliza W. March, of Rochester, b. June 19, 1796, d. Jan. 14, 1836, aged 30, dau. of Jonas C., m. (2) Charity Tibbetts, b. Dec. 5, 1800, d. Sept. 1, 1874, aged 73, dau. of James.
BARKER, John H., m. Sept. 17, 1873, in Rochester, Lucinda T. Leighton, both of Farmington.
BARNARD, Moses, m. Oct. 1, 1831, by Rev. John Winkley, Hannah Foss, both of Strafford.
BARNES, Benjamin, b. Feb. 25, 1799, d. Sept. 16, 1878, m. (1) Oct. 20, 1825, by Rev. J. W. Clary, Pamelia Hanson, b. Mar. 23, 1801, d. Mar. 5, 1828, dau. of Stephen, m. (2) int. Mar. 9, 1834, in Dover, Martha Knight Knapp, of Newburyport, Mass., b. 1808, d. Mar. 27, 1856.
BARNES, Benjamin, Jr., m. Apr. 4, 1864, by Rev. James Rand, Mary E. Meader, d. Mar. 25, 1928, aged 84, dau. of Isaac.
BARTLETT, Joseph, m. Dec. 6, 1801, by Rev. Isaac Smith, Peggy Brown.
BARTLETT, James, of Dover, b. Aug. 14, 1792, d. July 17, 1837, m. (1) June 28, 1820, Lydia Ballard, of Durham,. b. Jan. 3, 1793, d. Jan. 10, 1828, dau. of Joshua, m. (2) June 23, 1831, Jane M. Andrews, d. June 21, 1858, dau. of George.
BARTLETT, Alfred, son of Josiah, b. Aug. 30, 1820, d. Aug. 16, 1887, aged 66, m. (1) Nov. 14, 1844, by Rev. Mr. Thompson, Mary M. Furber, of Lee, dau. of John, d. Nov. 24, 1857, aged 34.
BARTLETT, Jared, m. int. Apr. 15, 1847, in Lee, Mrs. Elizabeth C. Mathews, both of Lee.

BARTLETT, Edward St. John, son of Josiah, b. Jan. 31, 1825, d. Feb. 11, 1915, m. Jan. 9, 1849, by Rev. James Pike, Almira F. Sawyer, b. Dec. 4, 1824, d. Apr. 18, 1896, both of Lee.

BARTLETT, Israel, m. May 5, 1849, in Lee, Elizabeth C. Mathes, both of Lee.

BARTLETT, John, of Lee, b. 1823, m. int. Dec. 13, 1856, in Lee, Abby A. Haley, of Epping, b. 1827.

BARTLETT, John C., son of Jonathan, b. 1839, m. (1) May 13, 1863, in Dover, Elizabeth A. Scales, of Nottingham, b. 1840, both of Lee, m. (2) Mar. 6, 1890, in Dover, Jennie (Richardson) Seavey, dau. of James.

BARTLETT, Thomas, of Lee, m. int. Apr. 16, 1864, in Lee, Elizabeth W. Titcomb, of Sanford, Me.

BASSETT, Alanson C., m. June 27, 1870, in Dover, Abbie P. Hanson.

BATCHELDER, Jacob, of Pittsfield, m. Oct. 8, 1789, by Rev. Isaac Smith, Mehitable Cleveland, of Gilmanton.

BATCHELDER, Nathan, of Loudon, m. Mar. 10, 1811, by Rev. Isaac Smith, Peace Clifford, of Gilmanton.

BATCHELDER, Ransom, of Northwood, m. int. Sept. 20, 1828, in Lee, Hannah Furber, of Lee.

BATCHELDER, William, of Nottingham, m. int. Nov. 18, 1837, in Lee, Mrs. Mary Randall, of Lee.

BATCHELDER, Augustus E., m. Feb. 2, 1874, in Alton, Mattie E. Ayers, both of New Durham.

BATCHELDER, Justice, of Salmon Falls, m. June 8, 1874, by Rev. Asa Piper, Sarah O. Grant, of Acton, Me.

BATEMAN, John H., m. Dec. 16, 1868, in Dover, Sarah E. Foss.

BEAN, George, m. Sept. 24, 1776, by Rev. Isaac Smith, Sarah Robinson, of Meredith.

BEAN, Gideon, m. Jan. 28, 1777, by Rev. Isaac Smith, Margaret Friend Folsom, d. Oct. 1807.

BEAN, Levi, m. Oct. 14, 1784, by Rev. Isaac Smith, Elizabeth Folsom.

BEAN, Durrel, m. Jan. 20, 1791, by Rev. Isaac Smith, Hannah Moulton.

BEAN, John, 3rd, m. Nov. 7, 1800, by Rev. Isaac Smith, Anna Folsom.

BEAN, Samuel, m. Nov. 11, 1800, by Rev. Isaac Smith, Polly Gunnison.

BEAN, Stephen, Jr., m. Dec. 28, 1801, by Rev. Isaac Smith, Sally Elkins.

BEAN, George W., m. May 28, 1829, in Gilmanton, Betsey Moody.

BEAN, Enos, m. Sept. 15, 1866, by Rev. James Rand, Mrs. Mary Lunt.
BECK, Samuel, d. Nov. 1823, aged 62, m. (1) near 1785, Mary (Randall) Jones, wid. of Ebenezer, d. Dec. 15, 1811, aged 69, dau. of Nathaniel, m. (2) in 1812, by Rev. John Osborne, Lovey Clough, of Lee.
BECK, Henry, m. (pub. June 16, 1804, in Portsmouth), Fanny Simpson.
BECKETT, William R., of Newfield, Me., m. Dec. 25, 1869, by Rev. Asa Piper, Helen Dunnels.
BEEDE, Daniel, son of Nathan, of Sandwich, b. June 15, 1771, d. Apr. 1799, m. Nov. 29, 1792, in Strafford, Lydia Hoag, b. June 17, 1772, d. 1817, dau. of Enoch.
BEMIS, Henry, m. June 4, 1867, by Rev. Robert S. Stubbs, Emma Vedion.
BEMIS, George, m. Aug. 22, 1871, by Rev. Asa Piper, Fanny Ridley, both of N. Shapleigh, Me.
3) **BENNETT**, Benjamin, son of John, b. 1687, d. July 18, 1723, m. Dec. 16, 1714, Penelope Cook.
3) BENNETT, Arthur, son of John, killed 1722, m. early as 1715, Dorcas Rollins, dau. of Thomas.
BENNETT, John, m. Aug. 23, 1727, in Rochester, Sarah Clark.
4) BENNETT, Deac. John, of Newmarket, son of Arthur, b. 1716, d. 1789, m. near 1739, Lydia Durgin, dau. of Francis.
BENNETT, John, m. Aug. 16, 1781, by Rev. Isaac Smith, Lydia Gilman.
BENNETT, Thomas, of New Durham Gore, m. Jan. 2, 1794, by Rev. Isaac Smith, Martha Willey, of New Durham.
BENNETT, Samuel, of Northwood, b. Feb. 13, 1787, d. Apr. 25, 1852, m. Mar. 5, 1808, Susan Demeritt, b. Oct. 4, 1789, d. Sept. 23, 1858, dau. of John.
BENNETT, Ebenezer L., of Northwood, d. June 10, 1883, aged 87, m. Aug. 30, 1820, by Rev. John Osborne, Catherine T. Stevens, of Lee, d. Apr. 6, 1860, aged 68.
BENNETT, Nathaniel, m. int. June 10, 1832, in Lee, Sally Mathes, of Lee.
BENNETT, Stephen A., of Wakefield, d. Dec. 10, 1896, aged 81, m. Apr. 3, 1844, in Milton, Sarah A. Berry, of Milton.
BENNETT, George Kittredge, of Newmarket, b. May 28, 1828, d. May 26, 1876, m. (1) int. July 28, 1850, in Lee, Maria J. Rollins, of Lee, m. (2) Mar. 7, 1855, by Elder Elias Hutchins, Loretta Sullivan Chesley, of Durham, b. Apr. 9, 1836.
BENNETT, Edward, m. Dec. 28, 1850, in Newmarket, Sarah Rances, both of Durham.

BENNETT, Thomas A., b. 1832, m. Aug. 8, 1858, by Rev. Samuel Sherburne, Sarah Jane Whiting, b. 1835, both of Lee.
BENNETT, Seth C., m. Dec. 8, 1864, in Dover, m. Belle Wiggin.
BENNETT, David S., of Lee, son of Ebenezer L., b. 1835, d. 1906, m. May 31, 1866, in Lee, Mrs. Rebecca P. Durrell, of Newmarket, b. 1836, d. 1913.
BENNETT, Andrew B., m. Dec. 25, 1869, in Dover, Jenny L. Poor.
BENNETT, George W., m. June 27, 1870, in Dover, Coridle Young.
BENSON, Ephraim C., m. Aug. 17, 1865, in Dover, Florence E. Caverly.
BERRY, Jeremiah, b. 1721, d. 1785, m. (1) Oct. 3, 1745, in Rye, Hannah Locke, d. July 1, 1770, aged 47, m. (2) Sept. 8, 1771, in Rye, Eleanor Brackett, wid. of Samuel.
BERRY, George, d. Feb. 26, 1820, aged 69, m. (1) Oct. 1779, Abigail Hall, d. July 11, 1791, aged 33, both of Barrington, m. (2) Mar. 4, 1792, by Rev. Joseph Haven, Sarah Frost, of Rochester.
BERRY, John Bickford, m. Mar. 25, 1782, in New Durham, Martha Bickford.
BERRY, Benjamin, m. in 1790, in New Durham, Susannah Bickford.
BERRY, John, d. Apr. 3, 1851, aged 73, m. Jan. 11, 1798, by Rev. Benjamin Randall, Susannah McNeal, d. Apr. 27, 1856, aged 78, dau. of Daniel, both of Barrington.
BERRY, William, m. Nov. 26, 1801, by Rev. Isaac Smith, Polly Osgood.
BERRY, William, d. May 16, 1878, aged 91, m. Oct. 30, 1806, by Rev. Benjamin Randall, Sarah Hall, d. Sept. 3, 1845, aged 62, both of Barrington.
BERRY, Benjamin, Jr., of Barrington, d. Sept. 12, 1844, aged 62, m. Apr. 16, 1807, by Rev. Joseph Haven, Sarah Hayes, of Farmington, d. Sept. 18, 1854, aged 70, dau. of Samuel.
BERRY, Ira L., m. July 12, 1808, in Alton, Lavina Drew.
BERRY, Levi, son of Benjamin, b. in 1787, m. Oct. 26, 1809, in Barrington, Margaret F. Moulton.
BERRY, Joseph, m. May 9, 1813, in New Durham, Hannah Runnels.
BERRY, Ezra, of Barrington, m. Feb. 9, 1819, by Elder Enoch Place, Elizabeth Pearl, of Rochester, d. 1832, aged 33, dau. of Ebenezer.
BERRY, Francis, Jr., d. Dec. 25, 1866, aged 72, m. (1) July 2, 1820, Adah Libbey, d. Aug. 12, 1828, aged 32, m. (2) Temperance Wiggin, b. Aug. 9, 1804, d. Sept. 20, 1878, dau. of David.
BERRY, Nathaniel, d. 1839, aged 58, m. Nov. 28, 1822, by Elder Enoch Place, Sally Tuttle, both of Strafford.
BERRY, Jonathan N., m. Mar. 9, 1828, Eliza Berry, d. Oct. 23, 1847, aged 42, both of Milton.

BERRY, William, d. Feb. 22, 1894, aged 88, m. Nov. 6, 1828, by Rev. John Winkley, Mary Brown, d. Aug. 5, 1883, aged 75, both of Strafford.

BERRY, Hosea, d. Nov. 14, 1879, aged 76, m. int. Jan. 4, 1829, in Dover, Susan Perkins, d. Mar. 21, 1876, aged 72.

BERRY, Deac. Edward, b. July 16, 1787, m. May 20, 1830, Anne Coe, b. June 28, 1792, d. Apr. 1, 1864, dau. of Rev. Curtis.

BERRY, Jonathan, d. Jan. 13, 1892, aged 85, m. Sept. 11, 1831, by Rev. John Winkley, Tamson Brewster, d. Mar. 3, 1880, aged 66, both of Strafford.

BERRY, Stephen F., m. int. Sept. 25, 1831, in Dover, Hannah Bunker, dau. of John.

BERRY, Lt. William, m. Dec. 1832, by Rev. John Winkley, Polly Hayes, both of Strafford.

BERRY, Capt. James Neal, d. Oct. 1, 1881, aged 78, m. (pub. Oct. 1, 1833, in Milton), Eliza G. Bennett, d. Aug. 6, 1884, aged 81, both of Milton.

BERRY, Edward, m. Nov. 27, 1834, by Rev. John Winkley, Jane Foss, both of Strafford.

BERRY, David H., son of David, d. Sept. 7, 1875, aged 65, m. Oct. 25, 1835, by Elder Enoch Place, Betsey D. Brock, d. Feb. 3, 1882, aged 72, both of Strafford.

BERRY, Benjamin, m. Apr. 22, 1838, by Rev. John Winkley, Mary Foss, both of Strafford.

BERRY, James M., m. Mar. 31, 1839, by Rev. John Winkley, Sarah C. Hayes, both of Strafford.

BERRY, Jesse C., son of George, d. Jan. 11, 1891, aged 77, m. (pub. Nov. 12, 1839, in Strafford), Jane H. Sanders, d. July 23, 1867, aged 48, both of Strafford.

BERRY, Samuel, m. June 11, 1840, by Rev. John Winkley, Margaret Berry, both of Strafford.

BERRY, James H., d. Dec. 29, 1898, aged 80, m. Nov. 25, 1841, by Rev. John Winkley, Rachel Akerman, d. Apr. 18, 1881, aged 61, both of Somersworth.

BERRY, Ezekiel H., m. Dec. 11, 1841, by Rev. John Winkley, Mary Hayes, both of Strafford.

BERRY, George 2nd, of Strafford, m. Dec. 22, 1842, by Elder Enoch Place, Mary Danforth, of Somersworth, d. Mar. 28, 1888, aged 63, dau. of Coleman.

BERRY, Ezekiel H., son of Stephen, d. Mar. 24, 1849, aged 30, m. (1) Nov. 14, 1844, by Rev. Nathaniel Berry, Syrena O. Hilton, both of New Durham, m. (2) Mary Hayes, b. Oct. 7, 1818, d. Apr. 17, 1891.

BERRY, Joshua, m. June 25, 1848, in Durham, Love Bunker, d. Oct. 15, 1878, aged 53, dau. of John.

BERRY, Jonathan, son of James, b. Nov. 26, 1817, d. July 20, 1907, m. (1) Oct. 6, 1852, in Milton, Eliza W. Hussey, b. Aug. 3, 1822, d. Aug. 4, 1853, m. (2) Sarah E. Cloutman, b. Mar. 27, 1827, d. Nov. 22, 1904, dau. of Joshua.

BERRY, Stephen B., m. Apr. 26, 1853, by Rev. John Winkley, Eliza Brewster, both of Barnstead.

BERRY, David S., of Strafford, b. May 28, 1831, d. Apr. 27, 1866, aged 34, m. Aug. 11, 1854, in Strafford, by Rev. John Winkley, Eliza A. Smith, of Barrington, b. Aug. 22, 1832, d. Feb. 18, 1905, dau. of David B..

BERRY, Samuel, m. May 21, 1856, by Rev. John Winkley, Lavina Winkley, both of Strafford.

BERRY, George G., of Strafford, m. Mar. 25, 1862, by Rev. John Winkley, Mary F. Scruton, of Farmington.

BERRY, Edwin E., m. Feb. 2, 1864, in Dover, Emma J. Hurd.

BERRY, Alonzo J., m. Nov. 25, 1866, in Dover, Anabel Gerrish.

BERRY, Frank J., m. May 20, 1868, by Rev. Robert S. Stubbs, Sarah H. Ross.

BERRY, Joseph F., m. Aug. 25, 1868, in Dover, Josephine M. Reynolds, d. July 14, 1925, aged 82.

BERRY, Francis W., m. July 20, 1870, in Dover, Lucy A. Holt.

BERRY, Eben C., m. Oct. 6, 1870, in Dover, Celissa A. Buzzell.

BERRY, Josiah W., m. July 11, 1874, by Rev. Asa Piper, Lena Dearborn, both of Hollis, Me.

3) **BICKFORD**, John, son of Thomas, b. in 1690, m. near 1715, Deborah -----.

BICKFORD, Thomas, of Portsmouth, son of Henry, d. Dec. 18, 1772, aged 68, m. Oct. 4, 1727, by Rev. Jos. Adams, Elizabeth Furber, of Newington, dau. of Jethro.

BICKFORD, John, of Durham, son of Benjamin, m. (1) Apr. 4, 1750, by Rev. Jos. Adams, Mary (Gamble) Trickey, of Newington, wid. of Thomas, m. (2) Elizabeth -----.

4)BICKFORD, Benjamin, son of Joseph, m. Nov. 19, 1750, Mary Bennett, dau. of Lt. Abraham.

BICKFORD, Benjamin, son of Benjamin, m. Dec. 26, 1751, by Rev. John Adams, Sarah Pitman, dau. of Zachariah.

5) BICKFORD, Reuben, son of Joseph, d. near 1797, m. Nov. 29, 1753, Elizabeth Kent, bpt. Apr. 18, 1729, dau. of John.

4) BICKFORD, John, son of John, m. Jan. 1, 1754, Joanna Stevenson.

BICKFORD, Henry, m. Jan. 9, 1755, by Rev. Amos Main, Abigail Tibbetts, of Lebanon, Me., dau. of Capt. Benjamin.

NEW HAMPSHIRE MARRIAGES SUPPLEMENT

BICKFORD, Daniel, son of Joseph, m. Aug. 7, 1755, by Rev. Jos. Adams, Elizabeth Hodgdon, both of Portsmouth.

4) BICKFORD, Winthrop, son of John, b. 1731, d. Mar. 1, 1811, m. (1) Nov. 30, 1756, Love Cromwell, dau. of Samuel, m. (2) May 16, 1780, by Rev. Jos. Adams, Esther (Ross) Langley, wid. of Thomas, both of Durham.

5) BICKFORD, Jonathan, Jr., son of John, b. Jan. 2, 1730, d. May 11, 1818, m. May 26, 1757, by Rev. James Pike, Sarah Wilmot, of Somersworth, d. Mar. 23, 1824, aged 85, dau. of James.

BICKFORD, Solomon, son of Benjamin, b. 1734, d. Feb. 3, 1830, m. Nov. 23, 1758, Susan Fox, d. Oct. 25, 1817, aged 91.

BICKFORD, Ephraim, d. May 31, 1823, aged 80, m. Mar. 22, 1772, by Dr. Belknap, Sarah Bickford, d. 1829, aged 76.

BICKFORD, Henry, son of Thomas, d. Jan. 6, 1798, aged 47, m. Apr. 30, 1774, Elizabeth Gerrish.

BICKFORD, Benjamin, of New Durham, son of Reuben, m. Sept. 27, 1781, Hannah Langley, dau. of Thomas, Jr.

BICKFORD, Joseph, m. Jan. 26, 1784, by Rev. Isaac Hasey, Debby Tebbets.

BICKFORD, Ebenezer, m. Aug. 12, 1789, in New Durham, Miriam Berry.

BICKFORD, Benjamin, m. Oct. 7, 1792, Peggy Mitchell.

BICKFORD, Isaac, b. Mar. 19, 1760, d. Mar. 14, 1819, m. Dec. 5, 1793, by Rev. Joseph Haven, Comfort Chamberlain, b. 1771, d. Apr. 9, 1848, dau of Ephraim.

BICKFORD, George, of Parsonfield, Me., son of George, m. Mar. 21, 1795, by Rev. Benjamin Randall, Sarah Thomas, of New Durham.

BICKFORD, Reuben, d. Oct. 12, 1838, aged 78, m. Apr. 21, 1795, Deborah Durgin, d. Nov. 15, 1855, aged 78, dau. of Trueworthy.

5) BICKFORD, Robert, son of Winthrop, b. Oct. 21, 1780, d. Sept. 25, 1838, aged 68, m. Nov. 10, 1799, Hannah M. Dame, b. Apr. 12, 1776, d. Dec. 4, 1863, dau. of John.

BICKFORD, Moses, of Durham, b. June 16, 1780, m. July 6, 1802, by Rev. John Osborne, Sarah Ellison, of Barrington.

BICKFORD, Andrew, m. Nov. 17, 1803, Susannah Follett, d. Apr. 13, 1836.

BICKFORD, Moses, of Rochester, m. Mar. 1805, in Dover, Mary Bickford, of Dover.

BICKFORD, Aaron, of Rochester, b. 1790, d. Oct. 15, 1852, m. (1) May 12, 1814, by Rev. Enoch Place, Temperance Thompson, of Wakefield, d. June 21, 1823, aged 28, m. (2) Patience Jenness, b. 1803, d. Apr. 1, 1890, dau. of William.

5) BICKFORD, Thomas, son of Ephraim, of Dover, b. Aug. 8, 1791, d. Oct. 9, 1865, m. (1) Sept. 14, 1815, in Newmarket, Olive Ann

Estes, b. May 30, 1794, d. July 14, 1856, both of Dover, m. (2) July 28, 1857, by Rev. Thomas G. Salter, Eliza Cushing, d. July 5, 1887, aged 83, dau. of Jonathan.

BICKFORD, Daniel, m. Nov. 28, 1816, by Rev. Paul Jewett, Betsey Ricker, b. Oct. 3, 1787, dau. of Ezekiel.

BICKFORD, Ephraim L., m. Aug. 20, 1820, by Rev. William Demeritt, Sally Davis.

6) BICKFORD, Robert, son of Robert, b. Mar. 3, 1805, d. Apr. 11, 1876, m. Dec. 15, 1831, Elizabeth -----.

BICKFORD, Ira Lucas, son of Isaac, b. Dec. 16, 1825, d. Feb. 20, 1900, m. Apr. 14, 1849, in Lowell, Mass., Charlotte Howe, b. 1830, d. Sept. 8, 1896, dau. of Charles.

BICKFORD, Charles D., m. June 16, 1862, Judith Davis, b. Mar. 15, 1842, d. Nov. 18, 1906, dau. of Samuel.

BICKFORD, Merrill D., m. Mar. 7, 1866, in Dover, Clara A. Davis.

BILLINGS, George G., m. May 11, 1867, by Rev. James Rand, Harriet I. Blaisdell.

BLAISDELL, Ezra, m. Dec. 31, 1776, by Rev. Isaac Smith, Deborah Batchelder, of Loudon.

BLAISDELL, Thomas, m. Mar. 11, 1784, in Lebanon, Me., Elizabeth Varney.

BLAISDELL, John C., m. Mar. 4, 1869, by Rev. Robert S. Stubbs, Mary J. Clark.

BLAISDELL, Herbert H., m. Sept. 4, 1875, in Rochester, Ida M. Rust.

1) **BLAKE**, William, son of John, b. 1741, in Epsom, d. Feb. 24, 1829, m. (1) early as 1770, Sarah Taylor, dau. of John, m. (2) ---- - -----.

BLAKE, Stephen, m. July 14, 1782, by Rev. Isaac Smith, Judith Sargent.

BLAKE, William, m. Sept. 10, 1809, in Dover, Abigail Libbey.

BLAKE, John, Jr., m. Nov. 25, 1810, by Rev. Isaac Smith, Polly Sanborn, both of Gilmanton.

BLAKE, Samuel, m. June 3, 1838, in Barrington, Abigail Stanton Babcock.

BLAKE, Charles H. d. July 11, 1898, aged 68, m. (1) (pub. July 22, 1851, in Great Falls), Mary C. Webster, d. Feb. 28, 1868, aged 34, both of Rochester, m. (2) Harriet D. -----, d. Aug. 25, 1908, aged 65.

BLUNT, Ephraim, m. Nov. 21, 1776, by Rev. Isaac Smith, Martha Ordway, both of Loudon.

BLUNT, Capt. William, d. 1823, m. Sept. 1786, Mary Fernald, d. Sept. 4, 1859, dau. of Simeon.

BOARDMAN, Benjamin, b. Oct. 27, 1757, d. July 7, 1846, m. Nov. 7, 1785, in Wakefield, Hepzibath Martin.

BOCOCK, William, of Great Falls, m. Feb. 18, 1861, in Rochester, Mrs. Agnes Hoy, of Berwick, Me.

1) **BODGE**, Henry, d. 1696, m. (1) Elizabeth -----, m. (2) Rebecca (Wilson) Barnes, wid. of Henry, dau. of Gowen.

4) BODGE, Benjamin, son of Ichabod, b. Oct. 11, 1755, d. 1802, m. Oct. 17, 1780, Maribah Hall.

BODGE, Josiah, of Lee, d. Dec. 20, 1851, aged 89, m. Nov. 1787, Molly Edgerly, of Barrington, d. Nov. 3, 1846, aged 82.

4) BODGE, Daniel, son of Ichabod, of Newmarket, m. Oct. 22, 1789, by Rev. Nathaniel Ewer, Polly Cram, of Newmarket.

BODGE, Aaron, of Lee, m. int. Mar. 12, 1837, in Lee, Ann Clark, of Dover.

BODGE, Jeremiah, of Madbury, m. int. Oct. 22, 1842, in Lee, Mary Ann Gear, of Lee.

BODGE, John, of Barrington, b. 1810, d. 1879, m. May 1, 1852, by Elder Samuel Sherburne, Eliza Daniels, of Nottingham, b. 1827, d. Jan. 6, 1908, dau. of Samuel.

BODGE, Daniel W., of Dover, m. 1855, in Newmarket, Sarah Smith, of Newmarket.

BOODEY, Ira, of Barrington, b. 1801, d. 1895, m. Nov. 11, 1824, by Elder Enoch Place, Joanna Seaward, of Strafford, b. 1800, d. 1890.

BOODEY, John, b. Apr. 26, 1795, d. May 25, 1874, m. Apr. 6, 1826, in Middleton, Sally Langley, b. Sept. 16, 1796, d. July 23, 1849, both of New Durham.

BOODEY, Daniel, m. int. Jan. 25, 1834, in Lee, Sally G. Higgins, both of Lee.

BOODEY, George S., of Strafford, son of Ira, b. 1839, d. 1869, m. Apr. 1, 1860, by Rev. John Winkley, Eliza J. Carter, of Barrington, b. 1842, d. 1906.

BOODEY, John O., b. 1842, d. 1914, m. Nov. 27, 1863, in Dover, Orissa O. Hanson, b. Mar. 24, 1845, d. Jan. 31, 1909.

BOOTHBY, Johnson, m. Dec. 24, 1861, in Dover, Abbie Haines.

BOOTHBY, C. S., m. Mar. 29, 1866, in Dover, Lillie G. Remick.

BOOTHBY, G. F., m. Mar. 29, 1866, in Dover, Ellen D. Cobb.

BOSTON, James C, m. Dec. 14, 1849, in Newmarket, Lois C. Hutchins, both of Somersworth.

BOSTON, Oliver, m. Nov. 21, 1866, by Rev. James Rand, Mary E. Cooper.

BOSTON, William, m. May 14, 1869, in Dover, Bell Hanks.

BOSTON, Henry, of New Durham, m. Oct. 20, 1875, by Rev. Asa Piper, Susan A. Drew, of Brookfield.

BOYCE, Antipas, m. Jan. 24, 1660, in Boston, Mass., Hannah Hill, b. Mar. 17, 1638, dau. of Valentine.

BOYNTON, William, m. Oct. 22, 1787, by Rev. Isaac Smith, Molly Huckins, of Gilmanton.

BOYNTON, John Jr., of New Hampton, m. Feb. 5, 1789, by Rev. Isaac Smith, Lydia Dow, of Gilmanton.

BOYNTON, Capt. David, of Meredith, m. July 18, 1793, by Rev. Isaac Smith, Lydia Sibley, of Gilmanton.

BRACEWELL, John, m. Feb. 11, 1864, by Rev. Theodore Edson, Mary Hope.

BRACKETT, James, Jr., son of James, b. 1748, d. 1831, m. Dec. 23, 1773, by Rev. Matthew Merriam, Anna Stillings, both of Berwick, Me.

BRACKETT, Nathaniel, b. 1751, d. 1842, m. Sept. 12, 1776, by Rev. Matthew Merriam, Sarah Chadbourne, b. Mar. 10, 1756, dau. of Humphrey, both of Berwick, Me.

BRACKETT, Nathan, b. 1754, d. 1842, m. Aug. 6, 1778, by Rev. Matthew Merriam, Mary Heard.

BRACKETT, Samuel, 3rd, b. 1757, d. 1849, m. Apr. 26, 1781, by Rev. Matthew Merriam, Molly Wentworth.

BRACKETT, Jacob, b. Aug. 14, 1760, d. Sept. 30, 1829, m. May 1, 1796, Hannah Wentworth, b. Feb. 25, 1777, d. Aug. 3, 1866, dau. of Gershom.

BRACKETT, Levi, m. Aug. 18, 1808, in Berwick, Me., Patience Hall.

BRACKETT, Heard, m. int. Apr. 5, 1813, in Lebanon, Me., Betsey Ricker.

BRACKETT, Samuel, m. Oct. 15, 1818, in Berwick, Me., Joanna Hall.

BRACKETT, David, of Newmarket, m. Nov. 8, 1846, in Newmarket, Elizabeth B. Francis, of Durham.

BRACKETT, John S., m. Apr. 6, 1864, in Dover, Bessie E. Tuttle.

BRACY, John, of York, Me., m. Feb. 13, 1728/29, Mary Drew, dau. of Francis.

BRACY, Abraham, m. May 31, 1868, in Dover, Sylvinia J. Hinman.

BRADBURY, John, m. July 30, 1776, by Rev. Isaac Smith, Susanna Hutchinson.

BRADBURY, John, m. Dec. 28, 1783, by Rev. Isaac Smith, Anna Emerson, both of Gilmanton.

BRADEEN, Andrew S., m. Oct. 21, 1871, in Rochester, Annie M. Morse.

BRAGDON, Samuel, of Milton, d. Dec. 11, 1840, aged 69, m. (1) Betsey Clements, of Somersworth, d. Sept. 12, 1812, m. (2) Lydia Walker, b. 1779, d. July 10, 1826, dau. of Richard, m. (3) Susan Nute, of Milton, d. Jan. 18, 1833, m. (4) (pub. Dec. 24, 1833, in Somersworth), Lydia Clements, of Somersworth, d. Oct. 23, 1855, aged 75.

BRAGDON, John, d. Sept. 16, 1860, aged 59, m. (pub. Feb. 13, 1838, in Great Falls), Mrs. Lydia J. (Horn) Varney, d. Jan. 28, 1857, aged 56, dau. of Richard, both of Milton.

BRAGDON, Charles, of Rochester, son of Amos, d. June 14, 1893, aged 77, m. (1) July 14, 1844, by Rev. Nathaniel Barker, Susan Adams, of Milton, d. Mar. 11, 1845, aged 23, m. (2) Dec. 17, 1846, by Elder Elias Hutchins, Rosamond P. Adams, d. Oct. 28, 1847, aged 23.

BRAGDON, George A., of Shapleigh, Me., m. Sept. 21, 1874, by Rev. Asa Piper, Sarah E. Nason, of Acton, Me.

BRAGG, Samuel, son of Samuel, d. Feb. 3, 1813, in Barnstead, aged 68, m. (1) early as 1770, Mary Kinsman, d. July 1801, aged 59, wid. of Samuel, of Ipswich, m. (2) 1802, Abigail (Tasker) Nelson, wid. of Samuel, d. 1830, dau. of John.

BRASBRIDGE, Staats M., d. Sept. 11, 1877, aged 76, m. Sept. 12, 1821, by Rev. Joseph Boodey, Sally Danielson, d. Sept. 3, 1868, aged 65, both of Strafford.

BREWER, Dexter, of Dover, m. June 24, 1818, in Portland, Me., Jane Frost, of Portland, Me.

BREWSTER, Paul L., of Dover, m. (1) in 1825, in Barrington, Temperance Spinney, of Dover, d. May 7, 1826, aged 28, m. (2) Dec. 22, 1827, by Rev. John Osborne, Susannah C. Wiggin, of Lee.

BREWSTER, Joseph, of Ossipee, m. (pub. Sept. 8, 1829, in Wakefield), Mrs. Nancy C. Moulton, of Wakefield, b. 1799, d. 1867, wid. of Jonathan.

BREWSTER, George W., son of Paul, d. July 4, 1897, aged 85, m. Apr. 16, 1840, by Elder Enoch Place, Phebe L. Ham, d. Dec. 23, 1853, aged 41, both of Strafford.

BREWSTER, John L., m. Jan. 1, 1850, by Rev. John Winkley, Comfort Caverly, both of Strafford.

BREWSTER, Daniel J., m. Jan. 9, 1864, in Dover, Georgio A. (Lord) Hall, wid. of George W.

BREWSTER, Timothy M., m. Mar. 29, 1864, by Rev. James Rand, Mary Ann Libbey, d. Oct. 25, 1887, aged 69, dau. of Jeremiah.

BREWSTER, Eli V., m. Oct. 3, 1867, by Rev. Robert S. Stubbs, Freelove J. Hayes, d. Jan. 27, 1908, aged 82, dau. of Joseph.

BRIER, Simeon, of Canterbury, m. Oct. 22, 1816, by Rev. Isaac Smith, Sally Davis, of Gilmanton.

BRIGHTMAN, George E., of Fall River, Mass., m. Feb. 6, 1855, by Rev. Alvin Tobey, Lydia A. Snell, of Lee.

BROCK, John, d. July 17, 1869, aged 86, m. Jan. 28, 1802, by Rev. Benjamin Randall, Lydia Neal, d. Apr. 22, 1861, aged 78, both of Barrington.

BROCK, Nathaniel, m. (1) Jan. 28, 1802, by Rev. Isaac Hasey, Abigail Critchet, m. (2) int. July 28, 1870, in Lebanon, Me., Nancy Kelley.

BROCK, James T., of Durham, son of Ezra, d. Jan. 30, 1848, aged 42, m. (pub. Sept. 11, 1827, in Portsmouth), Lavina Furber, of Northwood.

BROCK, Elijah, b. June 3, 1816, d. Dec. 7, 1900, m. June 4, 1838, by Rev. John Winkley, Lucy Hannah Berry, b. May 29, 1819, d. May 2, 1903, both of Strafford.

BROCK, John W., d. 1862, aged 53, m. int. Jan. 13, 1839, in Dover, Lucy W. Young.

BROCK, John F., m. Jan. 5, 1863, in Dover, Susan M. Evans.

BROOKS, Al, m. July 15, 1870, in Dover, Mrs. M. A. Peterson.

BROWN, Joseph, m. Nov. 27, 1746, in Rye, Abigail Goss, b. Oct. 2, 1724, dau. of Richard.

BROWN, John, son of Charles, d. Mar. 7, 1773, m. near 1751, Hannah Wallingford, b. May 5, 1720, dau. of Col. Thomas.

BROWN, Jonathan, b. Dec. 22, 1825, m. near 1755, Mary -----, b. Apr. 27, 1729.

BROWN, Moses, of Tuftonboro, d. Aug. 3, 1809, aged 51, m. Feb. 1790, by Rev. Jeremiah Shaw, Dolly Fitts, of Moultonboro.

BROWN, Daniel, of No. 2 District of Maine, m. Feb. 27, 1810, by Rev. Isaac Smith, Elizabeth Folsom, of Gilmanton.

BROWN, Nathaniel, of Nottingham, m. int. Aug. 30, 1823, in Lee, Nancy Rollins, of Lee.

BROWN, Nathan, m. Nov. 16, 1828, Sophia Demeritt, dau. of Robert.

BROWN, Edmond, of Somersworth, m. Nov. 21, 1830, in Lebanon, Me., Mary Butler, of Sanford, Me.

BROWN, Samuel, b. 1813, d. 1890, m. Sept. 8, 1831, by Elder Enoch Place, Louisa Davis, b. 1810, d. 1884, both of Strafford.

BROWN, John P., of Strafford, m. Apr. 27, 1835, by Rev. John Winkley, Nancy Twombly, of Barrington.

BROWN, Solomon, m. int. Apr. 12, 1838, in Lee, Mrs. Mary Wentworth, both of Lee.

BROWN, Benjamin, of New Hampton, m. Dec. 7, 1839, in Lee, Mary Chesley, of Lee, dau. of Lemuel.

BROWN, William P., son of James, d. July 26, 1891, aged 80, m. (pub. Mar. 10, 1840, in Great Falls), Hannah J. Gilman.

BROWN, George W., of Somersworth, m. Oct. 25, 1840, in Lebanon, Me., Nancy L. Dolloff.

BROWN, Daniel, of Strafford, d. Nov. 22, 1856, m. May 17, 1842, by Rev. John Winkley, Mrs. Lydia Ann Caverly, of Barrington, wid. of Joshua, d. Mar. 22, 1904, aged 90.

BROWN, Isaac Badger, b. 1808, d. May 31, 1879, m. (1) May 26, 1842, Sophronia Dame, b. Apr. 19, 1806, d. June 5, 1843, dau. of Benjamin, m. (2) Susan E. -----, b. 1818, d. Apr. 6, 1900.

BROWN, Eli, son of Moses, d. Aug. 27, 1897, aged 83, m. Nov. 6, 1842, by Rev. Nathaniel Berry, Mehitable Berry, d. May 20, 1903, aged 86, dau. of Isaac, both of Alton.

BROWN, Asa, m. Feb. 22, 1845, in Moultonboro, Harriet N. Wiggin.

BROWN, Daniel, m. Nov. 25, 1847, by Rev. John Winkley, Huldah D. Emerson, both of Northwood.

BROWN, Joseph, of Northwood, m. June 1, 1849, by Rev. John Winkley, Melissa Ann Berry, of Strafford.

BROWN, Andrew, m. May 15, 1853, by Rev. John Winkley, Catherine L. Smith, both of Barrington.

BROWN, Calvin, m. int. May 5, 1855, in Lebanon, Me., Olive Goodwin.

BROWN, Nathaniel J., b. Oct. 17, 1827, d. July 30, 1864, m. Sept. 6, 1855, by Elder Elias Hutchins, Lucinda J. Rollins, b. Dec. 14, 1831, d. Mar. 3, 1905, dau. of Eliphalet, both of Dover.

BROWN, John, m. Jan. 5, 1856, by Rev. James Rand, Lois E. Kennison, of Rumford.

BROWN, George H., b. 1833, d. 1896, m. Dec. 11, 1856, by Rev. John Winkley, Elvira Johnson, b. 1840, d. 1913, both of Strafford.

BROWN, Isaac, son of Joseph, d. Mar. 23, 1919, aged 82, m. (1) Aug. 23, 1857, in Barrington, Sarah A. F. Hall, both of Barrington, m. (2) Mar. 15, 1893, in Dover, Jane Ayers, of New Durham.

BROWN, Edmond K., son of Adam T., d. July 10, 1865, aged 39, m. (1) July 4, 1859, in Great Falls, Sarah Jane Dore, d. May 14, 1861, aged 32, both of Ossipee, m. (2) July 14, 1862, by Rev. James Rand, Abbie K. Ayers, d. Oct. 13, 1872, aged 46.

BROWN, James E., of Barrington, son of Joseph, d. Mar. 3, 1896, aged 60, m. Oct. 8, 1860, in Barrington, Lizzie W. Crosby, of Brownfield, Me.

BROWN, John Frank, of Moultonboro, d. Aug. 1, 1887, aged 53, m. Sept. 11, 1862, in Dover, Elizabeth J. Roberts.

BROWN, Philander, m. Dec. 21, 1867, by Rev. Francis E. Abbott, Mrs. Mary J. Taylor.

BROWN, Emerson L., m. Feb. 27, 1870, in Dover, Charlotte W. Mason.

BROWN, James L., m. Nov. 5, 1870, in Rollinsford, Ida E. Jordan.

BROWN, Woodman W., of Dover, m. May 3, 1874, in Dover, Emma M. Daniels, of Barrington.

BRYANT, John S., m. int. Sept. 18, 1824, in Lee, Mary Willey, both of Lee.

BRYANT, Edwin A., m. Mar. 21, 1866, in Dover, Isabella (Drew) Bryant, wid. of Perley B.

BUCK, Reuben, son of Dr. Reuben, d. Feb. 2, 1854, aged 40, m. Dec. 29, 1841, Adaline Dore, d. Oct. 9, 1904, aged 87, dau. of Robert.

BUCK, Dr. Jeremiah C., of Acton, Me., d. Mar. 15, 1885, aged 63, m. Jan. 16, 1850, in Milton, Eunice C. Swasey, of Milton, d. Aug. 5, 1893, aged 66, dau. of Deac. Charles.

BUNCE, Charles, d. Jan. 30, 1887, aged 62, m. Feb. 28, 1866, in Dover, Mary E. Bickford, d. June 3, 1883, aged 62.

BUNCE, George F., m. Apr. 18, 1870, in Dover, Sarah E. Wentworth.

3) **BUNKER**, Clement, of Durham, son of James, m. Mar. 24, 1738/9, Rebecca Drew, b. Apr. 24, 1716, dau. of Sergt. John.

BUNKER, Eli, son of Jonathan, b. Apr. 22, 1760, d. Aug. 3, 1842, m. Jan. 30, 1783, Anna Gordon, of New Hampton.

BUNKER, Jonathan, son of Jonathan, b. 1768, m. Mar. 29, 1787, Betsey Rand.

BUNKER, Enoch, m. Sept. 1, 1793, in Barnstead, Sally Wiggin.

BUNKER, Valentine, son of Benjamin, m. Sept. 30, 1794, Hannah Phillips, of Kittery, Me.

5) BUNKER, Aaron, son of Benjamin, d. Jan. 10, 1838, aged 56, m. in 1806, by Rev. John Osborne, Sarah Fernald, d. Oct. 7, 1861, both of Durham.

5) BUNKER, Rememberance, son of Zachariah, m. in 1807, by Rev. John Osborne, Rachel Pendergast, of Durham, d. Aug. 28, 1858, dau. of John.

BUNKER, Joseph, son of Benjamin, m. (pub. Jan. 27, 1807) Betsey Hawkins, of Barrington.

BUNKER, John, m. Nov. 23, 1809, in Barrington, Mary Babb.

BUNKER, Benjamin F., son of Aaron, m. Nov. 2, 1834, Abigail F. Chesley, d. Jan. 23, 1879, dau. of Capt. Joseph.

BUNKER, Richard, of Durham, son of John, m. Feb. 12, 1835, in Strafford, Judith Berry, of Strafford.

BUNKER, Jacob, of Durham, son of Samuel, b. May 23, 1812, d. May 10, 1908, aged 96, m. (pub. May 17, 1836, in York, Me.), Hannah Carlisle, d. Apr. 7, 1898, aged 79.

BUNKER, Nathaniel P., son of Remembrance, b. July 10, 1811, m. Apr. 30, 1837, in Newmarket, Susan L. Hilton.

6) BUNKER, Timothy, son of Zechariah, m. Aug. 31, 1842, by Rev. Alvin Toby, Augusta M. Tuttle, dau. of Levi, both of Newmarket.

BUNKER, Charles, son of Aaron, m. Jan. 1, 1846, Rebecca Elkins, of Newmarket.

BUNKER, William Henry, of Durham, b. 1825, m. int. Nov. 23, 1854, in Lee, Abby Jane Augusta Thompson, of Lee, b. 1835.

BUNKER, James M., son of William, b. Aug. 18, 1830, d. July 12, 1905, aged 74, m. Aug. 10, 1855, in Strafford, Eliza Jane Clark, d. July 6, 1907, aged 71, dau. of James V.

BUNKER, John Johnson, son of Ephraim, b. Dec. 19, 1834, d. 1918, m. June 17, 1860, in Durham, Louisa Victoria Clough, b. Oct. 17, 1838, d. Oct. 31, 1899, dau. of Benjamin, both of Durham.

BUNKER, George F., m. Feb. 12, 1866, in Dover, Nancy S. Thompson.

BUNKER, Thomas R., m. June 9, 1866, Joanna Wentworth.

BURLEIGH, Benjamin L., m. June 3, 1804, by Rev. Isaac Smith, Hannah Pulsifer, both of Gilmanton.

BURLEIGH, John B., son of James, d. May 25, 1900, aged 92, m. Oct. 26, 1828, by Rev. John Osborne, Lydia Caverly, d. Feb. 24, 1855, aged 45, both of Newmarket.

BURLEY, William, of Wakefield, son of Jonathan, d. July 19, 1872, aged 78, m. (1) Sept. 24, 1815, Lydia Ames, b. 1796, d. 1833, m. (2) Lydia S. Glidden, b. 1814, d. 1893.

BURLEY, Daniel, of Lee, d. Nov. 16, 1852, aged 63, m. int. Nov. 21, 1823, in Lee, Mehitable B. Locke, of Greenland, d. Apr. 8, 1882, aged 89.

BURLEY, William Porter, of Wakefield, son of William, d. Oct. 23, 1887, aged 71, m. (1) Dec. 2, 1834, by Rev. Isaac Willey, Lydia Glidden, of Newmarket, b. 1796, d. 1853, m. (2) Lydia S. Ames, b. 1814, d. 1893.

BURLEY, Oliver P., d. Nov. 8, 1848, aged 33, m. Apr. 17, 1841, by Rev. Elihu Scott, Mary Jane Demeritt, dau. of Samuel.

BURLEY, Nathaniel A., b. 1822, d. 1875, m. (pub. Apr. 14, 1843, in Boston, Mass.), Susan A. Mordough, b. 1822, d. 1903, both of Wakefield.

BURLEY, Col. William R., of Wakefield, son of William, b. 1816, d. 1887, m. Jan. 1, 1852, in Wakefield, Sarah A. Pike, of Brookfield, d. Aug. 12, 1897, aged 66, dau. of Dudley.

BURLEY, Daniel W., m. int. Dec. 26, 1852, in Lee, Margaret Ann Lock, both of Lee.

BURLEY, Charles Henry, son of John, d. Oct. 29, 1915, aged 85, m. (1) (pub. Sept. 12, 1854, in Newmarket), Olive Russell, m. (2) Feb. 21, 1867, in Dover, Dora J. Thompson. m. (3) Sept. 9, 1894, in Dover, Sarah Jane Morrill, of Moultonboro, b. 1827.

BURLEY, Charles, m. June 26, 1862, in Dover, Mary McGough.

BURLEY, Joseph F., m. Nov. 28, 1867, in Dover, Mary E. Wade.

BURLEY, Samuel D., m. Dec. 24, 1867, by Rev. Robert S. Stubbs, Clara Styles.

3) **BURNHAM**, John, son of Lt. Jeremiah, m. Jan. 9, 1717/18, Lydia Chesley, dau. of Philip.
4) BURNHAM, Rev. Jeremiah, son of John, d. Aug. 21, 1784, m. (1) Apr. 21, 1749, by Rev. J. Adams, in Newington, Elizabeth Adams, d. June 2, 1753, aged 22, dau. of Matthew, both of Oyster River, m. (2) Mar. 14, 1756, Abigail Emerson, dau. of Timothy.
BURNHAM, Samuel, of Moultonboro, m. Jan. 1778, by Rev. Isaac Smith, Jane Rogers, of Gilmanton Gore.
BURNHAM, John, m. near 1780, Elizabeth Burnham, d. Aug. 3, 1797, dau. of Jeremiah.
5) BURNHAM, Jacob, son of Samuel, b. Oct. 20, 1748, m. Feb. 24, 1785, Polly McDaniel.
5) BURNHAM, Silas, son of Samuel, b. 1760, d. Dec. 31, 1835, m. (1) Mar. 2, 1785, Judith Hoitt, dau. of Richard, m. (2) Jan. 5, 1792, Anna Wallace, of Nottingham, b. 1770, d. Aug. 25, 1852, dau. of William.
5) BURNHAM, Robert, of Durham, son of Joseph, m. Jan. 3, 1793, by Rev. Nathaniel Ewer, Nancy Doe, of Newmarket, d. Nov. 9, 1807, dau. of Reuben.
6) BURNHAM, Moses, son of John, b. Mar. 26, 1781, d. Apr. 15, 1848, m. Mar. 30, 1815, Elizabeth Merrill.
BURNHAM, Joseph Pinder, Jr. b. Apr. 19, 1795, d. Apr. 11, 1872, aged 76, m. Apr. 22, 1815, by Rev. John Osborne, Esther Varney, b. Oct. 29, 1788, d. Oct. 1857, aged 68, both of Durham.
6) BURNHAM, Joseph, son of John, b. Sept. 14, 1789, d. Dec. 4, 1867, m. Dec. 7, 1815, Lydia Hodgdon, of Dover, b. Oct. 7, 1788, dau. of Peter.
BURNHAM, Elliot G., b. Aug. 1, 1796, d. Apr. 10, 1852, aged 57, m. Mar. 6, 1817, by Rev. John Osborne, Anna Dame, dau. of Joseph, both of Durham.
BURNHAM, Frederick, m. Oct. 16, 1825, in Wolfeboro, Lydia Brown, both of Dover.
BURNHAM, Thomas, m. Dec. 11, 1829, by Rev. Nathaniel Berry, Eliza Ham, d. July 8, 1888, aged 84, both of New Durham.
6) BURNHAM, Col. Joseph S., son of Robert, b. Mar. 1, 1811, d. Feb. 25, 1890, m. Jan. 1, 1845, by Rev. Henry Drew, Mary Ann Langley, of New Durham, b. Mar. 1, 1817, d. Apr. 20, 1894, dau. of James.
BURNHAM, Joseph, son of Joseph P., b. Dec. 27, 1830, d. Sept. 11, 1872, m. July 22, 1849, by Rev. Charles N. Smith, Harriet N. Boutwell, both of Exeter.
BURNHAM, John Langdon, son of Joseph, b. Feb. 6, 1819, m. Dec. 22, 1850, Louisa G. Whitehouse, b. Aug. 30, 1824.

BURNHAM, Joseph W., m. Mar. 12, 1865, in Dover, Frances E. Willey.
BURNHAM, Royal R., m. Apr. 3, 1865, in Dover, Emily A. Foss.
BURNHAM, John M., m. Oct. 29, 1870, by Rev. Elmer Hewitt, Abby J. Moulton.
7) BURNHAM, James W., son of Joseph, b. Jan. 22, 1856, d. May 1, 1908, m. Dec. 20, 1877, Lydia Buzzell, dau. of John E.
BURNS, Thomas, m. Feb. 19, 1795, by Rev. Isaac Smith, Nancy Greeley, both of Gilmanton.
BURNS, James, m. Sept. 18, 1798, by Rev. Isaac Smith, Betsy Greeley, both of Gilmanton.
BURPEE, Henry W., m. Aug. 6, 1864, in Dover, Georgianna Tuttle.
BURR, William, m. July 27, 1868, in Dover, Rosalie A. Ham.
BURROWS (BURROUGHS), Daniel, m. Mar. 22, 1864, in Dover, Mary Ann Webber.
BURROWS (BURROUGHS), Charles L., m. Apr. 6, 1870, in Dover, Lucretta Pinkham.
BUSBY, Nahum J., m. Aug. 5, 1873, in E. Boston, Mass., Lizzie Kidder, dau. of James.
BUTLER, Gen. Henry, m. Mar. 22, 1810, by Rev. Isaac Smith, Mrs. Ruth Parsons.
BUTLER, Francis, d. Apr. 30, 1831, aged 38, m. July 14, 1816, Hannah Chesley, b. Jan. 1, 1799, d. Feb. 26, 1881, dau. of Benjamin.
BUTLER, Thomas, Jr., d. Aug. 11, 1854, aged 44, m. Aug. 21, 1831, Hannah Lord, b. 1808, d. 1851.
BUTLER, James, m. July 9, 1840, in Berwick, Me., Betsey Hall.
BUTLER, John S., m. Aug. 8, 1844, by Rev. Ransom Dunn, Lucinda J. Farnham, d. Nov. 15, 1896, aged 73, dau. of David.
BUTLER, James, son of Francis, b. Aug. 20, 1823, m. Nov. 1851, Emily Woodman, dau. of Moses.
BUTLER, Francis, m. Aug. 31, 1861, in Lebanon, Me., Martha A. Jones, b. May 2, 1845, dau. of James.
BUTLER, Frederick, m. Apr. 25, 1865, in Dover, Sarah J. Card.
BUTMAN, Charles W., of Lee, b. 1840, m. Apr. 28, 1877, in Lee, Annie Bell Pike, of Epping, b. 1856.
BUTTERFIELD, Charles H., m. Feb. 6, 1868, in Dover, Mary E. Clancy.
BUTTERFIELD, Ira A., m. Dec. 23, 1868, in Dover, Eliza J. Granville.
4) **BUZZELL**, Henry, son of John, m. (1) near 1739, Abigail Daniels, m. (2) Sept. 12, 1745, Judith Horn, of Dover.
5) BUZZELL, Joseph, son of John, b. Aug. 12, 1733, m. Mar. 17, 1755, by Rev. John Adams, Sarah Evans, dau. of Robert.

BUZZELL, Solomon, d. Sept. 4, 1813, aged 52, m. (1) May 25, 1786, Elizabeth (Burnham) Burnham, wid. of John, b. June 28, 1759, d. Aug. 3, 1797, aged 38, dau. of Jeremiah, m. (2) Susannah (Libbey) Clark, wid. of William, Jr.

BUZZELL, Lemuel H., son of Samuel, d. May 30, 1840, aged 68, m. Avis Emerson, b. May 27, 1778, d. Nov. 17, 1845, dau. of Capt. Smith.

BUZZELL, Ithamax, m. Mar. 18, 1791, by Rev. Isaac Smith, Hannah Buzzell, both of New Durham Gore.

BUZZELL, Eben, dead in 1804, son of William, m. near 1800 (?), Rebecca Ham.

BUZZELL, Nicholas, m. May 8, 1800, by Rev. Isaac Smith, Hannah French.

BUZZELL, Ichabod, m. Feb. 12, 1805, by Rev. Isaac Smith, Dolly Burleigh, both of Gilmanton.

BUZZELL, Miles, of Barrington, d. May 7, 1856, aged 68, m. 1811, by Rev. John Osborne, Deliverance Snell, of Lee, d. Sept. 27, 1841, dau. of John.

BUZZELL, John Burnham, d. Jan. 6, 1824, aged 32, m. Jan. 20, 1820, by Rev. Joseph Haven, Susanna Odiorne, b. Sept. 15, 1789, d. 1832, dau. of John, both of Rochester.

BUZZELL, James, d. May 12, 1868, aged 66, m. Sept. 10, 1825, Susan Thompson, b. June 20, 1800, d. Feb. 3, 1873, dau. of Job, both of Lee.

BUZZELL, Samuel T., of Lee, m. int. Oct. 7, 1841, in Lee, Susan J. Pierce, of Barrington.

BUZZELL, Capt. John S., son of Samuel F., d. Feb. 8, 1898, aged 75, m. (pub. Aug. 22, 1848, in Barrington), Olive J. Young, d. Dec. 4, 1895, aged 66, dau. of Eben.

BUZZELL, Elder Hezekiah D., d. Sept. 6, 1858, aged 80, m. Jan. 9, 1849, in Tuftonboro, Mrs. Charlotte (Clark) Tibbetts, wid. of Levi, d. July 1, 1850, aged 66.

BUZZELL, Lemuel R., of Lee, b. 1811, m. Dec. 25, 1856, by Rev. Alvin Tobey, Emily F. Gear, of Madbury, b. 1832.

BUZZELL, Samuel H., m. Dec. 15, 1862, in Dover, Josie M. Fernald.

BUZZELL, James W., m. Sept. 22, 1866, by Rev. James Rand, Mrs. Nellie O. Fields.

BUZZELL, John H., m. Nov. 14, 1866, in Dover, Annie E. Emerson.

BUZZELL, James, of Lee, b. 1842, m. May 15, 1877, in Lee, Martha Ella Tuttle, of Barrington, b. 1852.

CALDWELL, John, of Barrington, m. int. Dec. 18, 1830, in Lee, Sally Langley, of Lee.

CALDWELL, Daniel T., son of William, d. Mar. 15, 1904, aged 70, m. (pub. Nov. 22, 1855, in Barrington), Mary S. Swain, d. Mar. 17, 1909, aged 75, dau. of Israel.

CAMPBELL, John F., m. Nov. 23, 1864, by Rev. Asa Piper, Hannah -----.

6) **CANNEY**, Daniel, son of Isaac, b. Feb. 1768, d. Feb. 1846, m. before 1791, Jane -----, d. Sept. 14, 1801, aged 29, m. (2) Elizabeth Berry, m. (3) Nov. 12, 1812, Sarah Nelson.

8) CANNEY, John, son of Isaac, b. Dec. 16, 1845, d. Jan. 24, 1923, m. Mar. 13, 1869, in Dover, Cynthia A. Huntoon, b. Nov. 1, 1850, d. Mar. 1, 1922, dau. of George W.

CARD, John E., son of John, d. July 5, 1916, aged 85, m. Dec. 18, 1858, in Alton, Ellen F. Emerson.

CARLETON, Parker, m. May 21, 1865, by Rev. James Rand, Isabelle Raitt.

CARLETON, James, m. Apr. 8, 1869, in Dover, Annie M. Parcher.

CARR, Moses, Jr., of Somersworth, son of Moses, b. May 28, 1746, m. Nov. 13, 1782, by Rev. Matthew Merriam, Hannah Hamilton, of Berwick, Me., d. 1843, aged 82.

CARR, Samuel Wentworth, of Dover, son of Col. James, b. Oct. 6, 1794, d. Nov. 25, 1853, m. Dec. 15, 1825, Rebecca H. Odiorne, of Rochester, b. June 24, 1804, d. Oct. 25, 1851, dau. of John.

CARTER, Benjamin, of Dover, d. July 5, 1826, aged 63, m. (1) Feb. 23, 1792, Hannah Runnels, b. Mar. 16, 1776, d. Apr. 10, 1809, dau. of Col. Daniel, of Londonderry, m. (2) Mar. 24, 1810, by Rev. Caleb Sherman, Mehitable Lapish, of Durham, d. Nov. 1820, dau. of Robert.

CARTER, Benjamin, of Dover, m. (pub. May 26, 1810, in Durham), Mehitable Lapish, of Durham, dau. of Robert.

CARTER, Sanborn B., of Ossipee, m. Aug. 29, 1868, by Rev. Asa Piper, Mrs. Mary Sweat, of Wakefield.

CARTLAND, Tobias, m. int. Sept. 14, 1831, in Lee, Mary Peasley, both of Lee.

CARTLAND, Daniel, m. int. Oct. 5, 1832, in Lee, Elizabeth Ann Garland, both of Lee.

4) CARTLAND, Moses A., son of Jonathan, b. Nov. 17, 1805, d. July 5, 1863, m. Apr. 26, 1846, Mary Page Gove, d. July 21, 1860, aged 36.

4) CARTLAND, Samuel, son of Jonathan, d. Apr. 10, 1888, aged 66, m. June 1, 1854, in Lee, Caroline M. Ryan, both of Lee.

4) CARTLAND, Jonathan, son of Jonathan, b. June 4, 1815, d. Sept. 11, 1885, m. (1) Mar. 8, 1855, in Lee, Mary Jane Smith, d. Apr. 15, 1858, aged 33, both of Lee, m. (2) Anna -----, d. Feb. 18, 1890, aged 82.

CASWELL, Joseph, m. Mar. 13, 1779, by Rev. Isaac Smith, Lydia Evans.
CASWELL, Thomas, d. Sept. 21, 1875, aged 74, m. Dec. 23, 1824, by Elder Enoch Place, Sally Evans, d. Jan. 11, 1864, aged 62, both of Strafford.
CASWELL, John J., m. Jan. 2, 1844, by Rev. John Winkley, Mary Tasker, both of Strafford.
CASWELL, James M., of Strafford, b. Jan. 27, 1828, d. Jan. 12, 1902, m. (1) Sarah A. -----, d. Jan. 18, 1853, aged 28, m. (2) Mar. 17, 1856, by Elder Enoch Place, Abby J. Drew, of Barrington, b. Jan. 11, 1835, d. Apr. 30, 1925.
CASWELL, Joseph O., of Strafford, b. 1830, d. 1912, m. May 30, 1856, by Elder Enoch Place, Martha S. Libbey, of Dover, b. 1823, d. 1912.
CASWELL, Charles C., son of Thomas, d. Aug. 15, 1919, aged 83, m. (1) Apr. 1, 1860, by Elder Enoch Place, Betsey M. Foss, b. Jan. 13, 1821, d. Oct. 20, 1878, both of Strafford, m. (2) Martha H. (Twombly) Felker, wid. of Levi W., b. Apr. 24, 1841, d. Dec. 31, 1910.
CASWELL, James M., m. July 30, 1862, in Dover, Amanda M. Hussey.
CASWELL, Newell F., m. Sept. 24, 1868, in Dover, Mary G. Tanner.
CATE, William, of Barrington, d. May 1806, m. early as 1734, ----- ---.
CATE, Frederick, m. Nov. 14, 1797, by Rev. Joseph Haven, Lydia Scates, b. June 15, 1777, dau. of Benjamin, both of Rochester.
CATE, James, son of Joseph, b. Jan. 17, 1803, m. Apr. 26, 1827, in Tamworth, Ruth James, d. Jan. 1892, aged 83, both of Tamworth.
CATE, Eleazer R., son of Joseph, d. Dec. 29, 1901, aged 87, m. Aug. 7, 1836, by Rev. Joseph Boodey, Elizabeth D. Evans, d. Mar. 12, 1901, aged 88, dau. of Samuel, both of Somersworth.
CATE, William, m. Sept. 15, 1839, by Rev. John Winkley, Nancy Scruton, both of Newmarket.
CATE, Joseph H., son of Eben, b. July 27, 1830, d. Dec. 16, 1913, m. Dec. 13, 1851, by Rev. Arthur Caverno, Susan M. Henderson, b. Dec. 27, 1832, d. Mar. 31, 1900.
CATE, George V., of Strafford, b. 1840, m. int. Nov. 28, 1861, in Lee, Henrietta C. Lane, of Lee, b. 1839.
CATER, Horace G., son of John, Jr., d. Apr. 13, 1903, aged 78, m. Apr. 30, 1848, in Barrington, Elizabeth Lucy Hayes, d. May 20, 1905, aged 78, dau. of Jacob, both of Barrington.

NEW HAMPSHIRE MARRIAGES SUPPLEMENT

CATER, Alonzo H., of Farmington, b. July 13, 1833, d. Oct. 16, 1924, m. Feb. 4, 1855, by Rev. Joseph Boodey, Hannah S. Whitehouse, of Strafford, b. Oct. 8, 1836, d. Jan. 10, 1921.

CATER, Joel, Jr., of Barrington, m. Aug. 8, 1858, in Barrington, Mrs. Mahala W. (Hayes) Cater, of Dover, wid. of Richard.

CATER, Charles G., m. Aug. 17, 1867, by Rev. James Rand, Lydia R. Hayes.

CAVERLY, Deac. Ira, b. 1804, d. 1877, m. (1) Apr. 24, 1825, by Rev. Enoch Place, Lydia Libbey, d. Aug. 24, 1839, aged 35, both of Strafford, m. (2) Sarah H. Colcord, b. 1806, d. 1886.

CAVERLY, Capt. Azariah, d. Dec. 14, 1843, aged 51, m. (1) Sally Adams, d. May 28, 1830, aged 38, m. (2) Sept. 23, 1832, by Elder Enoch Place, Eliza Tasker, b. 1813, d. 1870, both of Strafford.

CAVERLY, Maj. Joseph, of Strafford, son of Lt. John, d. Jan. 23, 1853, aged 57, m. Feb. 27, 1833, by Rev. Joseph Boodey, Lavina French, of New Durham, d. July 19, 1889, aged 88.

CAVERLY, Joel, of Strafford, d. Jan. 12, 1892, aged 80, m. Oct. 30, 1836, by Elder Samuel Sherburne, Mary S. Caverly, of Barrington, d. Oct. 15, 1904, aged 86.

CAVERLY, Ebenezer, son of Moses, b. Mar. 21, 1808, d. Jan. 2, 1880, aged 71, m. June 29, 1852, by Elder Elias Hutchins, Abba A. Caverly, d. Dec. 8, 1902, aged 73, dau. of Solomon, both of Barrington.

CAVERLY, George A., b. 1833, d. 1916, m. May 16, 1854, in Strafford, Martha Boodey, b. 1834, d. 1923.

CAVERLY, Seth William, m. June 30, 1855, in Barrington, Asenath Abigail Boodey, b. Feb. 17, 1838, d. Nov. 13, 1917, both of Strafford.

CAVERLY, Asa, d. Dec. 2, 1886, aged 85, m. Apr. 11, 1859, by Elder Enoch Place, Betsey Y. Sanders, d. Jan. 4, 1890, aged 66.

CAVERLY, George W., of Strafford, m. Sept. 11, 1859, in Strafford, Mary E. Lucy, of Nottingham, d. Dec. 20, 1859, aged 22, m. (2) Oct. 17, 1870, in Dover, Lizzie A. Seward.

CAVERNO, Jeremiah, of Strafford, m. (pub. Apr. 17, 1829, in Barrington), Dolla K. Balch, of Barrington.

CAVERNO, George S., d. Oct. 21, 1916, aged 74, m. Jan. 30, 1867, in Dover, Ida S. Hanson, d. Oct. 21, 1918, aged 78.

CAVERNO, Arthur J., m. July 6, 1868, by Rev. James Drummond, Mary A. Sinnott.

CAVERNO, Horace F., of Lee, m. Feb. 25, 1873, in Lee, Rebecca Daniels, of Barrington.

CHADBOURNE, Col. Benjamin, of Berwick, Me., d. Mar. 1799, m. (1) near 1743, Mary Heard, m. (2) Oct. 10, 1751, Mary Chesley, of Durham, dau. of Capt. Jonathan.

CHADBOURNE, Lt. Joseph, m. Nov. 19, 1762, by Rev. Jacob Foster, Mary Hamilton.
CHADBOURNE, Sgt. Simeon, son of Humphrey, b. May 16, 1750, d. Oct. 29, 1846, m. (1) Jan. 13, 1778, by Rev. Matthew Merriam, Katharine Hanscom, both of Berwick, Me., m. (2) Apr. 18, 1780, by Rev. Matthew Merriam, Elizabeth Yeaton, both of Berwick, Me.
CHADBOURNE, Andrew A., m. Feb. 6, 1867, in Dover, Rachael A. Libbey.
CHADWICK, Jacob, of Somersworth, son of William, b. Oct. 1756, m. May 14, 1778, by Dr. Belknap, Sarah Cromwell, of Dover.
CHADWICK, James, m. (pub. May 26, 1804, in Berwick, Me.), Lankis Ricker.
CHADWICK, George H., m. July 7, 1873, in Dover, Mary A. Osborne.
4) **CHAMBERLAIN**, Col. Jacob, son of William, b. 1738, d. 1816, m. early as 1763, Alice -----.
CHAMBERLAIN, Moses, b. 1760, d. 1832, m. May 23, 1784, by Rev. Joseph Haven, Mary Nason, b. 1758, d. 1836, both of Rochester.
CHAMBERLAIN, George, son of Ephraim, d. 1822, m. 1788, Dorothy Buzzell, b. 1765, d. 1854.
CHAMBERLAIN, Amos, of Lebanon, Me., m. Jan. 1, 1788, by Rev. Isaac Smith, Sally Rogers, of New Durham Gore.
CHAMBERLAIN, Samuel Nason, son of Moses, b. Jan. 20, 1787, d. 1846, m. Mar. 8, 1812, Mary Moody, b. 1789, d. 1874, dau. of Deac. John.
CHAMBERLAIN, Samuel, m. (pub. Feb. 14, 1826, in Rochester), Susan Tebbetts.
CHAMBERLAIN, Joshua P., of Alton, son of Jacob, d. Sept. 8, 1891, aged 76, m. Sept. 29, 1839, by Elder Enoch Place, Sally Sloper, of Strafford.
CHAMBERLAIN, Daniel G., m. Mar. 12, 1846, by Rev. Joseph Boodey, Lucy C. Huckins, d. Jan. 27, 1903, aged 86, dau. of John, both of Alton.
CHAMBERLAIN, Samuel Gardner, of Milton, son of Samuel, d. Jan. 2, 1911, aged 83, m. Aug. 28, 1850, Mary E. Fall, of Lebanon, Me., d. Nov. 4, 1890, dau. of Daniel.
CHAMBERLAIN, Charles Burnham, of Lebanon, Me., son of Amos, b. Mar. 19, 1830, m. (pub. Oct. 19, 1852, in Somersworth), Sarah Smith Cooper, of Wakefield.
CHAMBERLAIN, John F., m. Mar. 25, 1861, in Rochester, Harriet N. Corson, both of Lebanon, Me.
CHAMBERLAIN, John F., m. Nov. 30, 1863, by Rev. James Rand, Josephine A. Horn.
CHAMBERLAIN, Edward B., m. May 19, 1867, by Rev. George T. Day, Hannah P. Smith.

CHAMBERLAIN, George W., m. Nov. 21, 1870, in Dover, Mary E. Mancer.
CHAMPION, Marden, of Effingham, m. (pub. Mar. 6, 1827, in Somersworth), Sabra Brown.
CHAMPION, Charles W., m. Mar. 20, 1865, in Dover, Carrie Berry.
CHANDLER, Jeremiah, m. Dec. 14, 1791, by Rev. Isaac Smith, Dolly Rundlet, both of Gilmanton.
CHANDLER, Josiah, of Dedham, Mass., d. Jan. 12, 1855, aged 40, m. May 3, 1846, in Moultonboro, Caroline Copp, of Moultonboro, d. Oct. 22, 1884, aged 60, dau. of Jonathan.
CHANDLER, Elisha M., m. Mar. 10, 1868, in Dover, Mary E. Poole.
CHAPMAN, Edmund, b. July 15, 1778, m. Oct. 15, 1804, in Newmarket, Susan Lord, b. Dec. 22, 1774.
CHAPMAN, John, d. July 27, 1846, aged 48, m. July 13, 1820, by Rev. Joseph Haven, Louisa Ann Barker, d. July 28, 1837, aged 49, dau. of David, both of Rochester.
CHAPMAN, Hail, m. int. Apr. 22, 1827, in Lee, Mary Woodman, both of Lee.
CHAPMAN, George W., of Lee, m. int. June 9, 1827, in Lee, Sally Burnham, of Newmarket.
CHAPMAN, Thomas J., m. Nov. 28, 1833, Dolly Durgin, b. Feb. 22, 1813, d. Dec. 31, 1864, dau. of Nicholas.
CHAPMAN, Daniel C., of Durham, m. Jan. 11, 1851, in Newmarket, Susan Daniels, of Newmarket.
CHAPMAN, Hiram T., m. Aug. 12, 1854, by Elder Israel Chesley, Sarah F. Foss, both of Newmarket.
CHAPMAN, Edward T., m. Feb. 20, 1867, by Rev. Charles Tenny, Abby E. Vickery.
CHASE, John, m. Oct. 28, 1778, by Rev. Isaac Smith, Lydia Norris.
CHASE, John, m. int. Dec. 13, 1806, in Lebanon, Me., Margaret Brock.
CHASE, William, m. Apr. 10, 1814, in Somersworth, Abigail Varney.
3) CHASE, John G., d. Sept. 10, 1863, aged 66, m. (1) Oct. 15, 1823, by Rev. J. W. Clary, Lydia Roberts, of Somersworth, d. Aug. 22, 1829, aged 27, m. (2) (pub. Mar. 1, 1831, in Somersworth), Caroline Corson.
CHASE, Levi B., of Tuftonboro, d. Mar. 21, 1867, aged 70, m. Nov. 24, 1830, in Wolfeboro, Sarah Nute, of Wolfeboro.
CHASE, Luther, of Berwick, Me., m. int. July 26, 1834, in Lebanon, Me., Judith Nisbett.
CHASE, Enoch Wingate, son of Simon, b. Apr. 20, 1817, m. July 31, 1839, by Rev. Francis V. Pike, Martha Jane Roberts, of Rochester.
CHASE, Joseph T., m. Oct. 22, 1866, in Dover, Ellen J. Corson.

CHASE, Charles F., m. Aug. 21, 1869, in Dover, Susan Marden.
CHASE, George F., m. Feb. 17, 1870, in Dover, Ida F. Bolter.
CHASE, William H., m. Jan. 5, 1871, in Dover, Lucy A. Hutchins.

3) **CHESLEY**, Lt. Philip, son of Philip, grandson of Philip[1], b. 1676, living in 1715, m. (1) July 8, 1706, Hannah Sawyer, b. Apr. 9, 1685, dau. of William, m. (2) after 1708, Elizabeth (Leighton) Cromwell, wid. of Philip, dau. of Thomas.

3) CHESLEY, Joseph, son of Capt. Thomas, will Apr. 13, 1730, proved June 7, 1731, of Oyster River, m. (1) near 1710, Hannah Buss, dau. of Rev. John, m. (2) Dec. 18, 1717, by Rev. Nathaniel Rogers, in Portsmouth, Sarah Cutt, of Portsmouth, dau. of John.

3) CHESLEY, Samuel, son of Capt. Thomas, b. 1691, m. near 1723, Ann Daniel, b. 1705, dau. of Joseph,

CHESLEY, Capt. Thomas, son of Joseph, d. 1778, m. near 1739, Mary Hill, d. 1810, dau. of Samuel.

5) CHESLEY, Lemuel, of Durham, son of Lemuel, d. Nov. 20, 1789, d. Apr. 17, 1821, m. Mar. 29, 1769, in Dover, Hannah Randall, of Lee, dau. of Simon.

4) CHESLEY, Joseph, son of Joseph, b. about 1711, m. Apr. 25, 1771, Comfort Smith, age 16, dau. of Deac. Ebenezer. (Was this a second marriage?)

6) CHESLEY, Aaron, son of George, b. May 28, 1764, d. Mar. 1823, m. Nov. 29, 1781, Ruth Bennett, b. 1753, dau. of Benjamin.

6) CHESLEY, Lemuel, son of Lemuel, d. Mar. 27, 1855, aged 90, m. Oct. 9, 1793, by Rev. William Hooper, Love Hull, of Northwood, d. 1872, aged 102.

CHESLEY, John, m. Feb. 23, 1797, in Dover, Elizabeth Blake.

6) CHESLEY, Paul, of Durham, son of Philip, m. (1) July 17, 1803, by Rev. William Hooper, Sally Hooper, dau. of Rev. William, m. (2) Apr. 3, 1816, Polly Demeritt, dau. of Andrew.

6) CHESLEY, Daniel, of Durham, son of Philip, d. Nov. 21, 1844, aged 63, m. (1) May 23, 1804, by Rev. William Hooper, Hannah Demeritt, of Madbury, d. Mar. 13, 1821, aged 38, dau. of Paul, m. (2) Rosamond Knight, d. Sept. 9, 1864, aged 78.

6) CHESLEY, Richard Furber, son of James, b. Oct. 28, 1781, d. Sept. 7, 1827, aged 46, m. Jan. 29, 1806, by Rev. Joseph Haven, Nancy Twombly, d. Jan. 3, 1867, aged 80, both of Dover.

6) CHESLEY, Rev. Israel, son of Benjamin, b. Nov. 24, 1788, d. Sept. 29, 1866, m. Oct. 25, 1812, by Rev. John Osborne, Elizabeth Folsom, of Newmarket, b. Sept. 10, 1790, d. May 23, 1866, dau. of Col. John.

6) CHESLEY, Jonathan, son of Capt. Jonathan, m. Feb. 12, 1815, by Rev. John Osborne, Mrs. Sarah Frost, of Lee.

CHESLEY, Thomas, b. Mar 13, 1792, m. Feb. 10, 1816, by Rev. John Osborne, Joanna Folsom, of Newmarket, b. Sept. 29, 1791, d. Aug. 7, 1879, aged 88.

7) CHESLEY, Capt. Stephen P., son of Samuel and Nancy, b. Mar. 19, 1804, d. Nov. 19, 1869, m. (1) Mar. 12, 1826, by Rev. J. W. Clary, Hannah C. Pendexter, b. Oct. 28, 1803, d. June 3, 1834, dau. of Edward, m. (2) Jan. 26, 1835, by Rev. Alvin Tobey, Elizabeth P. Woodman, b. Oct. 3, 1804, d. Aug. 19, 1847, m. (3) June 3, 1848, Mrs. Abigail York, b. Feb. 26, 1807, d. Dec. 7, 1852.

7) CHESLEY, William P., son of Paul, m. Nov. 11, 1827, Louisa J. Chesley, b. Aug. 31, 1809, d. June 27, 1889, dau. of Lt. James.

7) CHESLEY, Benjamin, son of Miles, b. July 27, 1802, m. May 1, 1828, Sally McDuffee.

7) CHESLEY, John M. of Barrington, son of Lemuel, b. Oct. 21, 1803,. m. (pub. Nov. 5, 1833, in Lee), Sarah Jane Jenkins, of Lee, d. Dec. 19, 1874, aged 66, dau. of John.

7) CHESLEY, John, Jr., son of John, d. Aug. 6, 1888, aged 83, of Epsom, m. Aug. 21, 1834, by Elder Samuel Sherburne, Joanna Tibbetts, of Madbury, b. Oct. 12, 1816, d. June 8, 1906, dau. of Israel.

7) CHESLEY, Plummer, son of Paul, m. Oct. 9, 1834, Elmira Hart, dau. of John.

7) CHESLEY, Samuel P., of Durham, son of Capt. Joseph, b. 1815, d. Jan. 16, 1858, m. (1) int. Jan. 3, 1836, in Dover, Elizabeth Burley, of Sanbornton, b. June 19, 1806, d. Jan. 8, 1857, dau. of Robert, m. (2) (pub. Dec. 10, 1857, in Great Falls), Lydia J. Lewis, of Brunswick, Me.

7) CHESLEY, Alfred, of Durham, son of Thomas, b. July 28, 1809, d. Apr. 25, 1885, m. (1) Octavia Adams Shaw, b. May 22, 1808, d. Apr. 28, 1859, aged 51, m. (2) (pub. May 2, 1861, in Great Falls), Julia M. Hooper, of Berwick, Me.

7) CHESLEY, James, son of Miles, b. June 15, 1813, m. Feb. 5, 1837, Eliza F. Chapman.

CHESLEY, Philip, son of Thomas, d. Jan. 18, 1887, aged 73, m. (pub. Apr. 11, 1837, in Madbury), Mary Jane Meserve, dau. of Samuel, d. Aug. 6, 1887, aged 68, both of Madbury.

CHESLEY, John, m. int. Aug. 25, 1839, in Lee, Mercy J. Hoitt.

7) CHESLEY, Sylvester M., of Durham, son of Capt. Joseph, d. June 16, 1847, aged 25, m. Dec. 21, 1842, in Durham, Maria Roberts, of Dover, dau. of Thomas A.

7) CHESLEY, Jonathan Furber, of New Durham, son of Miles, b. May 30, 1811, d. Apr. 1886, m. May 30, 1843, by Rev. Nathaniel

Berry, Abigail E. Stevens, d. Sept. 30, 1906, aged 86, of Alton, dau. of John H.

7) CHESLEY, Moses Horne, son of Miles, b. Dec. 6, 1817, d. May 4, 1897, m. (1) July 11, 1843, by Rev. Nathaniel Berry, Abigail Ann Berry, d. Apr. 1, 1854, aged 36, both of New Durham, m. (2) Oct. 25, 1860, in Wolfeboro, Sarah E. Chesley, of Wolfeboro, b. Jan. 7, 1841, d. Mar. 11, 1875.

CHESLEY, Cyrus, son of Moses, b. May 29, 1817, d. 1873, m. Dec. 26, 1843, Maria A. Hanson, dau. of John.

7) CHESLEY, George H., son of Lemuel, b. Dec. 15, 1822, d. Mar. 27, 1909, m. (1) in 1845, Irene F. Hanson, m. (2) Elizabeth J. Snell.

7) CHESLEY, Israel B., of Lee, son of Rev. Israel, b. Sept. 6, 1815, d. Apr. 6, 1862, m. (1) (pub. Nov. 2, 1847, in Nottingham), Elizabeth Glass, of Nottingham, b. Feb. 9, 1820, d. Mar. 11, 1850, m. (2) (pub. Apr. 15, 1858, in Portsmouth), Ruth A. Boardman, of Newburyport, Mass.

CHESLEY, Joshua R., son of Joseph R., d. May 16, 1902, aged 73, m. Dec. 23, 1849, by Elder Samuel Sherburne, Mary E. Swain, d. July 29, 1898, aged 66, dau. of Daniel.

7) CHESLEY, John F., of Lee, son of Rev. Israel, b. June 25, 1820, m. (pub. Sept. 6, 1853, in Newburyport, Mass.), Abby S. George, of Newburyport, Mass.

8) CHESLEY, Joseph Plummer, son of Samuel P., b. May 8, 1836, m. (pub. Feb. 12, 1857, in S. Berwick, Me.), Sarah Ann Whitehouse, d. May 23, 1894, aged 57, dau. of Jacob, both of Great Falls.

CHESLEY, Andrew C., d. Dec. 27, 1872, aged 43, m. Oct. 1, 1861, in Dover, Sarah F. Furbish, d. Mar. 21, 1888, aged 48, dau. of R. Furbish.

CHESLEY, John S., son of Stephen P., b. 1839, d. 1896, m. Oct. 22, 1861, by Rev. Alvin Tobey, Addie Nancy Sanborn, of Loudon, b. 1839, d. 1917.

CHESWELL, Wentworth, of Newmarket, m. Sept. 13, 1767, Mary Davis, of Durham, b. Feb. 19, 1750, dau. of David.

CHESWELL, Thomas E., d. Mar. 23, 1923, aged 79, m. Dec. 22, 1862, in Dover, Mary F. Wentworth.

CHICK, Richard, son of Thomas, d. 1737, m. July 11, 1702, by Rev. John Pike, Martha Lord, b. Oct. 14, 1679, dau. of Nathan, Jr.

CHICK, Richard, son of Richard, m. Jan. 19, 1728, in Berwick, Me., Bethiah Gould.

CHICK, Nathan, son of Richard, m. Jan. 8, 1742, in Berwick, Me., Mary Small.

CHICK, Richard, m. Oct. 30, 1760, in S. Berwick, Me., Hannah Lord.

CHICK, Thomas, d. May 3, 1826, aged 34, m. May 27, 1813, in Barrington, Mary Holmes, d. May 12, 1860, aged 67.
CHICK, John, of Somersworth, m. Feb. 23, 1861, in Lebanon, Me., Elizabeth Lord.
CHURCHILL, James C., of Nottingham, m. Jan. 8, 1808, by Rev. John Osborne, Eliza Osborne, of Lee, dau. of Rev. John.
CHURCHILL, Albert, m. June 28, 1863, in Dover, Belinda E. Colbath.
CILLEY, Bradbury L., m. Aug. 3, 1864, in Dover, Amanda C. Morris.
2) **CLARK**, James, d. 1767, m. Jan. 16, 1717/18, Sarah Leighton, d. 1770, dau. of John.
CLARKE, John, m. Nov. 26, 1747, by Rev. Jos. Adams, Abigail Peverly, b. Mar. 14, 1727, dau. of Nathaniel, both of Portsmouth.
CLARK, Joseph, of Wells, Me., m. Dec. 12, 1751, Sarah Hill, dau. of Samuel.
CLARKE, Annaniah, m. Feb. 2, 1755, by Rev. Amos Main, Mary Hanson, of Somersworth.
CLARK, Abraham, of Madbury, m. (pub. May 7, 1757, in Wells, Me.), Elizabeth Gooch.
CLARK, Moses, son of Samuel, b. Oct. 24, 1737, d. 1819, m. Nov. 24, 1763, Mehitable French, b. July 23, 1741, dau. of Thomas.
CLARKE, Lt. Jacob, b. Apr. 15, 1749, d. July 3, 1823, m. Aug. 24, 1775, by Dr. Belknap, Mary Ricker, d. Nov. 30, 1830, aged 76.
CLARK, Josiah, b. 1742, d. 1834, m. Feb. 13, 1776, by Rev. Matthew Merriam, Patience Hanson, dau. of Ebenezer and Martha, both of Berwick, Me.
CLARK, Hanson, b. 1756, m. Oct. 27, 1778, by Rev. Matthew Merriam, Sarah Lord.
CLARK, John, of Sanbornton, m. Nov. 9, 1784, by Rev. Isaac Smith, Jean Sanborn, of Northfield.
CLARK, John, of Campton, m. Dec. 22, 1785, by Rev. Isaac Smith, Lydia Leavitt, of Northfield.
CLARK, Charles Goodwin, son of William, m. Sept. 24, 1789, by Rev. Matthew Merriam, Sarah Holmes, d. July 29, 1843, aged 86.
CLARK, Joseph, b. Mar. 9, 1759, d. Dec. 21, 1838, m. near 1790, Anna Hilton Burleigh.
CLARK, Benjamin, m. Nov. 24, 1791, by Rev. Isaac Smith, Abigail Clark, both of Gilmanton.
CLARK, Peter, m. Feb. 26, 1792, by Rev. Jonathan Tompson, Betsey Hamilton, d. Mar. 1793, dau. of Col. Hamilton.
CLARK, Eli, m. Sept. 20, 1793, by Rev. Isaac Smith, Statira Colbath, both of Barnstead.
CLARK, Joseph Jr., m. Sept. 21, 1795, by Rev. Isaac Smith, Anna Smith, both of Gilmanton.

CLARK, Abijah, of Rochester, b. 1766, d. Sept. 12, 1814, m. Hannah
-----, b. 1774, d. 1861.
CLARK, James, m. July 3, 1800, by Rev. Isaac Hasey, Lydia Brock.
CLARK, Daniel, of Exeter, d. 1829, aged 50, m. Jan. 28, 1802, by
Rev. Joseph Haven, Rachel Wiggin, of Rochester.
CLARK, Joseph, d. Dec. 17, 1840, aged 59, m. Nov. 25, 1802, by
Rev. John Osborne, Anna (Kelly) Demeritt, of Lee, wid. of Samuel,
b. Dec. 5, 1770, d. 1860, dau. of Samuel.
CLARK, Remembrance, of Madbury, son of Remembrance, b. Jan. 3,
1782, d. Nov. 1810, m. 1806, by Rev. John Osborne, Mary
Rollins, of Lee.
CLARK, David, b. May 22, 1782, m. Mar. 9, 1806, Mary Burnham, b.
July 11, 1781, dau. of John.
CLARK, John N., d. Mar. 3, 1829, aged 36, m. near 1813, Elizabeth
Canney, b. Apr. 6, 1794, d. Apr. 15, 1867, dau. of Daniel and
Jane, of Farmington.
CLARK, Johnson, of Wakefield, d. 1823, m. Nov. 8, 1821, in
Wakefield, Hannah Stanton, of Brookfield, d. 1827.
CLARK, Jonathan, m. Mar. 4, 1822, in Sanford, Me., Harriet Allen,
dau. of Elisha.
CLARK, Benjamin, m. Dec. 19, 1822, by Rev. Joseph Haven, Abigail
P. Richardson, d. Dec. 12, 1862, aged 61, both of Rochester.
CLARKE, Enoch, m. Dec. 29, 1822, by Rev. J. W. Clary, Harriet
Horne, d. Feb. 16, 1839, aged 44, both of Dover.
CLARK, Deac. James, of Exeter, m. (pub. Feb. 10, 1824, in
Rochester), Mary Richards.
CLARKE, George W., of Berwick, Me., d. Nov. 30, 1868, aged 68, m.
Dec. 20, 1824, by Rev. J. W. Clary, Abigail Ricker, of Dover, d.
Jan. 6, 1867, aged 63.
CLARK, David, of Windham, m. int. Aug. 30, 1832, in Lee, Sally
Clay, of Lee.
CLARK, George W., d. Dec. 9, 1847, m. int. Aug. 10, 1834, in Dover,
Ann Mathes.
CLARK, James V., of Strafford, d. July 14, 1880, aged 71, m. Apr.
15, 1835, by Rev. Jared Perkins, Elizabeth Nute, of Dover, b. Jan.
23, 1809, d. Feb. 16, 1892.
CLARK, William H., of Stratham, m. Nov. 29, 1836, by Rev. William
Demeritt, Mary E. Hoitt, of Lee.
CLARK, Joseph T., b. 1813, d. Oct. 3, 1840, aged 27, m. int. Apr. 18,
1838, in Dover, Elizabeth Caverly, b. 1814, d. 1849.
CLARK, Timothy L., m. June 27, 1844, by Rev. John Winkley,
Patience M. Leighton, both of Strafford.
CLARK, Thomas C., m. Jan. 1, 1845, Elizabeth (Mathes) Kent, wid.
of John C., b. May 20, 1817, d. Dec. 17, 1902, dau. of Abraham.

CLARK, Albert G., m. May 27, 1846, in Wakefield, Mary A. Cook, b. 1821, d. 1864, dau. of John.

CLARK, David C., of Dover, son of Joseph, d. Dec. 30, 1908, aged 81, m. Apr. 4, 1858, in Nottingham, Eliza J. Daniels, of Barrington, d. June 8, 1922, aged 85, dau. of Joseph.

CLARK, Wilson R., m. Oct. 5, 1863, in Dover, Sarah E. Swain.

CLARK, John A., of Strafford, m. Nov. 24, 1864, by Rev. John Winkley, Lucy A. Thompson, of Barrington.

CLARK, John, m. June 14, 1865, in Dover, Nellie E. Stanton.

CLARKE, Linus E., m. Jan. 6, 1867, in Dover, Mary Ellen Hill.

CLARK, Horace W., m. Mar. 15, 1867, in Dover, Julia A. Mix.

CLARK, William P., m. Nov. 24, 1868, in Dover, Elizabeth S. Davis.

CLARK, George E., m. Mar. 3, 1869, in Dover, Elizabeth Gilman.

CLARK, George W., d. May 24, 1912, aged 77, m. Aug. 3, 1869, in Dover, Nellie Brooks.

CLARK, Benjamin F., m. Aug. 30, 1869, in Dover, Electra J. Long.

CLARKE, Joseph A., of Strafford, m. Oct. 21, 1869, in Lee, Georgia M. Sewell, of Lee.

CLARK, Charles H., son of John S., d. Sept. 30, 1918, aged 67, m. Feb. 21, 1870, in Dover, Georgia A. Dolliver.

CLARK, George G., m. June 20, 1870, in Dover, Mary F. E. Lock.

CLARK, Charles H., of Dover, m. July 3, 1873, in Dover, Mary J. Smith, of S. Berwick, Me.

CLAY, Alphonzo (Alpheus?), d. Jan. 30, 1874, aged 73, m. Aug. 16, 1826, by Rev. John Osborne, Esther Lamos, b. May 18, 1808, d. Jan. 7, 1894, both of Lee.

CLAY, Asa, m. Nov. 24, 1830, by Rev. William Demeritt, Polly Lamos, both of Lee.

CLAY, Mark, m. int. Jan. 26, 1833, in Lee, Lucinda Glover, both of Lee.

CLEMENTS, Joshua, m. Sept. 26, 1790, by Rev. Isaac Smith, Nabby Head, both of Pembroke.

CLEMENTS, Edward S., of Rollinsford, son of James, b. 1815, m. (1) (pub. Jan. 2, 1838, in Great Falls), Ann Springer, both of Somersworth, m. (2) Dec. 4, 1860, in Rollinsford, Betty French, of Rollinsford.

CLEMENTS, Leander, son of Samuel, d. June 14, 1914, aged 83, m. (pub. July 15, 1858, in Great Falls), Susan A. Clough, d. Mar. 16, 1906, aged 75, both of Milton.

CLIFFORD, Ithiel, m. Feb. 8, 1785, by Rev. Isaac Smith, Molly Smith, both of Pittsfield.

CLIFFORD, David, m. Dec. 25, 1798, by Rev. Isaac Smith, Mary Mudgett, both of Gilmanton.

CLIFFORD, Gilman, m. Dec. 22, 1813, by Rev. Isaac Smith, Deborah Sanborn, both of Gilmanton.

CLIFFORD, Isaac N. of Biddeford, Me., m. Dec. 31, 1859, in Dover, Annette Elizabeth Chesley, of Durham, b. Apr. 13, 1839, dau. of Rev. Alfred.

CLIFFORD, Simon J., m. Jan. 13, 1865, in Dover, Paulina Goodwin.

3) **CLOUGH**, Benoni, son of John, b. May 23, 1675, m. Hannah -----.

4) CLOUGH, Ichabod, son of Benoni, b. June 29, 1697, d. 1745, m. Dec. 20, 1722, Rebecca Clough.

5) CLOUGH, Zaccheus, son of Ichabod, b. 1725, d. 1810, m. Love Meader, b. 1734, dau. of Nathaniel.

CLOUGH, Isaiah, m. Oct. 5, 1775, by Rev. Isaac Smith, Mary Chapman.

CLOUGH, Daniel, m. Mar. 18, 1776, by Rev. Isaac Smith, Deborah Mason.

CLOUGH, Simon Jr., m. May 4, 1780, by Rev. Isaac Smith, Mary Avery.

CLOUGH, Josiah, of Northwood, m. Apr. 19, 1785, by Rev. Isaac Smith, Mary Young, of Gilmanton.

CLOUGH, Jonathan, m. Nov. 23, 1791, by Rev. Isaac Smith, Mary Page, both of Gilmanton.

CLOUGH, Perley, b. July 5, 1770, d. Mar. 18, 1856, m. Dec. 30, 1792, by Rev. Isaac Smith, Sally Smith, of New Durham Gore., b. July 1, 1773.

6) CLOUGH, William, son of Zaccheus, b. Dec. 5, 1768, d. Dec. 31, 1853, m. Feb. 14, 1793, Susanna Runnels, b. July 4, 1773, d. Nov. 25, 1865, dau. of Job, both of Lee.

CLOUGH, Benjamin, of Northwood, m. Nov. 25, 1802, by Rev. Isaac Smith, Betsy Thompson, of Gilmanton.

CLOUGH, Joseph Jr., m. Mar. 29, 1804, by Rev. Isaac Smith, Hannah Willey.

CLOUGH, Aaron, m. June 26, 1806, by Rev. Isaac Smith, Hannah Gale.

CLOUGH, Nehemiah, m. June 11, 1815, by Rev. Isaac Smith, Sally Rowe, both of Gilmanton.

CLOUGH, Daniel, son of Jonathan, b. May 9, 1804, d. Sept. 22, 1891, m. Mar. 17, 1834, Sally H. Caverly, b. Oct. 16, 1811.

CLOUGH, Frank B., m. Dec. 23, 1868, in Dover, Julia A. Nute.

CLOUTMAN, Thomas, b. 1745, d. 1833, m. Apr. 11, 1771, by Dr. Belknap, Sarah Gilman, of Exeter, d. Apr. 5, 1826, aged 75.

CLOUTMAN, Hezekiah, m. June 26, 1791, by Rev. Joseph Haven, Abigail Card, d. Dec. 20, 1845, aged 74, both of Rochester.

CLOUTMAN, John F., son of John F., b. Dec. 27, 1831, m. (1) Mar. 4, 1854, in Rochester, Amanda M. Davis, d. 1868, both of Farmington, m. (2) Ella E. Kimball.

COBURN, Edward, of Weston, Mass., b. 1824, m. (1) Oct. 18, 1849, in Northwood, Dolly Bennett, of Northwood, dau. of John, m. (2) Dec. 29, 1854, in Lee, Hannah C. Bennett, b. 1830.

COBURN, Frank F., m. Aug. 26, 1867, by Rev. Robert S. Stubbs, Carrie N. Cleaves.

COCKING, Charles R., d. Mar. 11, 1902, m. Sept. 16, 1864, Marianna Davis, b. Apr. 28, 1847, dau. of Samuel.

COCKING, Edward H., m. Dec. 31, 1868, in Dover, Sarah M. Foss.

COE, John, son of Rev. Curtis, b. Feb. 13, 1797, d. Dec. 2, 1861, m. Sept. 28, 1823, Lavinia T. Senter, b. Nov. 7, 1800, d. Oct. 12, 1883, dau. of Samuel M.

3) COFFIN, Capt. Tristram, b. 1691, d. June 21, 1751, m. (1) Nov. 15, 1719, in Kittery, Me., Jane Heard, b. June 18, 1699, dau. of John and Phebe, m. (2) Nov. 24, 1726, by Rev. Hugh Adams, Hannah Smith, of Durham, b. Sept. 20, 1703, d. Sept. 28, 1789, dau. of John.

COFFIN, Nathan, b. Aug. 28, 1749, m. (1) Martha Bowen, m. (2) June 20, 1776, by Rev. Jos. Adams, Dorcas Bartlett, both of Kittery, Me.

COFFIN, Benjamin, m. Jan. 2, 1800, by Rev. Isaac Smith, Eunice Kelley, dau. of Jacob.

COFFIN, Jonathan, of Tuftonboro, b. 1781, d. 1862, m. (1) int. Feb. 1803, in Tuftonboro, Sally Gilman, of Alton, dau. of Moses, m. (2) ----- -----.

COFFIN, Stephen, of Wolfeboro, d. Mar. 4, 1867, m. (1) Deborah Philbrook, d. Oct. 4, 1838, aged 38, m. (2) Apr. 3, 1839, by Elder Enoch Place, Caroline E. Foss, of Poughkeepsie, N.Y.

COFFIN, Edwin A., m. July 4, 1867, in Dover, Catherine Long.

COFFIN, Benjamin, m. Oct. 19, 1867, by Rev. Alden Sherwin, Henrietta Hodgkins.

COGSWELL, Moses, m. June 13, 1781, by Rev. Isaac Smith, Hannah Foster.

COGSWELL, Dr. William, of Atkinson, m. July 22, 1786, by Rev. Isaac Smith, Judith Badger, of Gilmanton.

COGSWELL, Parson, m. Apr. 9, 1811, by Rev. Isaac Smith, Mary S. Badger.

COGSWELL, John, of Landaff, m. Dec. 1, 1814, by Rev. Isaac Smith, Mrs. Ruth Butler.

COLBATH, Lional, of Farmington, m. (pub. June 25, 1857, in Alton), Mary B. Rines, of New Durham, d. Feb. 12, 1916, aged 81, dau. of Henry.

COLBATH, Joseph W., m. Feb. 12, 1862, in Dover, Martha F. Hussey.
COLBATH, Levi F., m. Dec. 31, 1866, in Dover, Annie Turner.
COLBATH, Lafayette, m. Aug. 21, 1867, by Rev. Silas Curtis, Sadie A. Langley.
COLBATH, Walter J., m. Sept. 23, 1869, by Rev. Asa Piper, Lauretta Allen, both of Wakefield.
COLBATH, John L., m. May 27, 1870, in Dover, Sarah L. Batson.
COLBY, Elder John J. G., of Ossipee, d. June 5, 1877, aged 81, m. Nov. 24, 1830, by Rev. Isaac Willey, Camela Horne, of Rochester, d. Aug. 4, 1886.
COLBY, Ira N., m. Sept. 26, 1866, by Rev. Francis E. Abbott, Amanda J. Conner.
COLCORD, Edison, m. Mar. 26, 1807, by Rev. Isaac Smith, Sarah Weeks, both of Gilmanton.
COLCORD, Bradbury, of Nottingham, m. int. Mar. 18, 1826, in Lee, Abigail Knowles, of Lee.
COLE, Robert, m. July 12, 1726, in Kittery, Me., Judith Tuttle.
COLE, Robert, m. Nov. 22, 1726, in Kittery, Me., Phebe Sheppard.
COLE, Abner, son of Thomas, of Kittery, Me., d. 1791, m. Oct. 13, 1731, in Kittery, Me., Patience Spinney, b. Dec. 3, 1713, d. 1791, dau. of Samuel.
COLE, Robert, m. Sept. 29, 1750, in Kittery, Me., Mary Pendexter.
COLE, John, of Kittery, Me., son of John, b. Nov. 23, 1735, d. 1798, m. (1) in 1759, Eunice Nichols, m. (2) Jan. 25, 1768, in Berwick, Me., Elizabeth Buffum, b. Aug. 26, 1743, dau. of Joshua, of Berwick, Me.
COLE, Capt. Amos, of Dover, m. Elizabeth Wallingford, b. near 1736, d. July 11, 1776, dau. of Col. Thomas.
COLE, Ichabod, son of Robert, m. Nov. 8, 1770, in Kittery, Me., Elizabeth Gowell, d. Oct. 1834, aged 85, dau. of Capt. John.
COLE, James C., son of Edward, b. in 1791, d. Dec. 11, 1867, m. Betsey D. Nutter, b. in 1789, d. Jan. 16, 1866.
COLE, Amos, m. Nov. 22, 1822, in S. Berwick, Me., Betsey -----.
COLE, Edmund, m. in 1826, in Berwick, Me., Theodate Ricker.
COLE, Abner, m. Dec. 21, 1828, in Eliot, Me., Esther D. Spinney.
COLE, Levi, m. June 27, 1831, in Eliot, Me., Elizabeth Hanson.
COLE, Ichabod, m. June 27, 1831, in Kittery, Me., Mary K. Tetherly.
COLE, Ichabod, son of Ichabod, b. July 12, 1818, m. Nov. 25, 1841, Mary E. Tetherly, d. Nov. 19, 1892, dau. of Charles.
COLE, Samuel, m. Oct. 30, 1842, in Eliot, Me., Sarah A. Tetherly, dau. of Charles.

COLE, John W., d. Jan. 15, 1878, aged 65, m. July 29, 1849, by Elder Elias Hutchins, Rachel A. Woodman, d. Apr. 26, 1894, aged 62.
COLE, Ephraim, m. Jan. 29, 1853, in Kittery, Me., Elizabeth Dutton.
COLE, John W., m. July 16, 1862, in Dover, Frances K. West.
COLE, Asa T., m. May 16, 1867, in Dover, Louisa Cushman.
COLE, John W., m. Dec. 30, 1867, in Dover, Sarah J. Scully.
COLE, Nathan H., m. July 4, 1869, in Dover, Emma Gilman.
COLEMAN, Sumner, m. Apr. 1828, by Rev. Mr. Sargent, Elizabeth Horne, d. Oct. 25, 1891, aged 82, dau. of Gershom, both of Somersworth.
COLEMAN, Oliver W., son of Oliver, b. 1838, d. Jan. 15, 1912, m. July 4, 1863, in Dover, Emma Davis, b. 1845, d. Feb. ????
COLEMAN, Charles, of Brookfield, m. July 19, 1865, by Rev. Asa Piper, Salome A. Cotton, of Wolfeboro.
COLEMAN, James H., m. Dec. 9, 1866, in Dover, Martha A. Clements.
COLEMAN, John, m. Mar. 11, 1869, by Rev. Robert S. Stubbs, Abby F. Card.
COLEMAN, Winthrop S., m. Dec. 24, 1870, in Dover, Jennie Leighton.
COLEMAN, Charles C., m. June 7, 1874, in Dover, Sarah Ellen Hayes.
COLWELL, William, of Lee, m. (pub. Dec. 16, 1823, in Nottingham), Abigail Tebbets, of Madbury.
COMBS, Isaac, m. Aug. 20, 1867, in Dover, Lydia Richardson.
COMMICHAW, W. H., m. July 19, 1870, in Dover, Anna Bates.
CONNOR, William, m. Sept. 19, 1796, by Rev. Joseph Haven, Elizabeth Rollins, of Rochester, b. in 1749, d. Aug. 1798.
CONNOR, Patrick, of Lee, b. 1830, m. int. Jan. 22, 1858, in Lee, Catharine Hask (?), of Newmarket, b. 1828.
COOK, Ebenezer, d. 1827, m. Sept. 25, 1783, by Dr. Belknap, Hannah Brown.
COOK, Jedediah, of Madbury, d. Nov. 1806, aged 48, m. Aug. 7, 1787, in Barrington, Katherine Tuttle, of Barrington, d. Oct. 11, 1842, aged 77.
COOK, Jeremiah, d. Dec. 5, 1851, aged 76, m. Mar. 22, 1798, by Rev. Joseph Haven, Hannah Wentworth, d. Nov. 29, 1845, aged 69, both of Rochester.
COOK, Richard, b. 1775, d. 1829, m. Oct. 30, 1803, in Milton, Polly Huggins, of Wakefield, d. Mar. 13, 1869, aged 87.
COOK, Jotham, m. (pub. June 23, 1804, in Portsmouth), Nancy Stocker.

COOK, Ebenezer, b. 1790, d. 1850, m. Apr. 4, 1810, by Rev. Jeremiah Shaw, Hannah Batchelder, b. 1792, d. 1868.

COOK, Timothy, of Tamworth, m. Apr. 3, 1815, by Rev. Isaac Smith, Mary Price, of Gilmanton.

COOK, John, b. Aug. 6, 1803, d. Mar. 14, 1851, m. (1) Nov. 22, 1827, by Rev. J. W. Clary, Dorothy S. Moulton, of Somersworth, b. Feb. 8, 1806, d. June 17, 1836, m. (2) Feb. 1837, by Rev. David Root, Esther F. Bickford, d. July 3, 1885, aged 76.

COOK, Parker, m. Apr. 12, 1830, in Middleton, Mary Jones, d. Jan. 26, 1890, aged 84, dau. of Samuel, both of Middleton.

COOK, Eli, son of William, d. Sept. 15, 1886, aged 78, m. Jan. 27, 1831, by Rev. John G. Dow, Sarah Horne, d. Jan. 4, 1875, aged 64, both of Somersworth.

COOK, William, son of Jeremiah, b. Oct. 17, 1798, d. July 7, 1874, m. (1) int. Aug. 24, 1834, in Dover, Clarissa Hayes, m. (2) Mary Yeaton, b. Dec. 1, 1802, d. Dec. 31, 1890, dau. of George.

COOK, Isaac, of Somersworth, d. Mar. 9, 1857, aged 52, m. Mar. 6, 1835, in Milton, Elizabeth Peavey, of Milton, b. Jan. 12, 1821, d. Aug. 5, 1899.

COOK, Daniel, d. Oct. 20, 1856, aged 38, m. June 3, 1841, by Rev. Aaron Ayer, Mary Roberts.

COOK, Joseph, son of Jeremiah, d. Aug. 12, 1892, aged 83, m. (1) Rebecca Ricker, b. 1816, d. 1843, m. (2) Dec. 28, 1843, in Milton, Lydia Blaisdell, d. Oct. 28, 1890, aged 83, dau. of Enoch, both of Milton.

COOK, John A., of Wakefield, son of John, b. 1819, d. 1870, m. May 28, 1846, in Wolfeboro, Sarah Young, of Wolfeboro, b. 1816, d. 1893.

COOK, Robert, d. Feb. 27, 1871, aged 60, m. int. Nov. 3, 1847, in Dover, Jane Murphy, b. 1817, d. 1893.

COOK, George W., of Dover, aged 17, d. Apr. 29, 1885, aged 49, m. Sept. 12, 1855, in Alton, Ann Willard, of Wakefield, aged 45.

COOK, Peter, m. June 12, 1861, by Rev. Francis E. Hicks, Sarah Jane Gage, b. 1840, d. 1916.

COOK, William H., m. May 18, 1862, in Dover, Nancy C. Ramsbottom.

COOK, Samuel G., m. Mar. 21, 1867, by Rev. Asa Piper, Rebecca H. Downs, both of Wakefield.

COOK, John H., son of Robert, d. Mar. 31, 1907, aged 62, m. Mar. 19, 1874, in Dover, Sena Foss, both of Dover.

COOK, John, of Rockport, Me., m. Apr. 3, 1874, by Rev. Asa Piper, Fannie Pugsley, of Shapleigh, Me.

COOLEY, Charles E., m. Mar. 18, 1865, in Dover, Carrie Wilkins.

COOPER, Levi C., son of Moses, b. in 1825, d. Jan. 15, 1907, m. (1) int. June 4, 1849, in Dover, Hannah F. Lucas, b. in 1823, d. July 23, 1870, m. (2) Jennie M. Wentworth, b. in 1847, d. Apr. 8, 1923, dau. of Josiah.

COOPER, Joseph W., of Newburyport, Mass., m. June 5, 1852, Mahala Jane Grover, b. Oct. 20, 1832, dau. of Henry.

COPP, Lt. Samuel, son of Jonathan, b. Apr. 18, 1742, d. Oct. 4, 1816, m. (1) Hannah Hayes, m. (2) Sarah (Scates) Knox Wentworth.

COPP, Amasa, b. Oct. 8, 1788, d. Jan. 7, 1871, m. (1) Dec. 31, 1813, in Portsmouth, Charlotte King Atkinson, d. Nov. 4, 1815, aged 25, dau. of William, m. (2) Eliza L. Remick, b. 1799, d. 1873, dau. of John.

COPP, Maj. Jonathan, of Wolfeboro, d. June 17, 1831, aged 56, m. June 19, 1814, by Rev. Joseph Haven, Mary Clark, of Tuftonboro, d. Mar. 2, 1826, aged 34.

COPP, Jonathan, d. Mar. 4, 1869, aged 76, m. Apr. 3, 1817, by Rev. Jeremiah Shaw, Abigail Batchelder, d. Jan. 22, 1880, aged 83.

COPP, Reuben H., of Farmington, son of Isaac, d. Apr. 20, 1899, aged 74, m. Oct. 31, 1853, by Elder Elias Hutchins, Hannah J. Burke, of Wolfeboro, d. Dec. 16, 1865, aged 33, dau. of Stephen.

COPP, Edwin H., m. June 19, 1870, by Rev. Asa Piper, Susan J. McDaniels, both of Wakefield.

COPP, Henry N., of Washington, D.C., m. July 26, 1870, by Rev. Asa Piper, Mary A. Hobbs, of Wakefield.

CORLISS, John C., d. Jan. 8, 1875, aged 63, m. (1) Apr. 6, 1833, in Wakefield, Louise Burrows, d. Apr. 13, 1857, aged 46, both of Wakefield, m. (2) Jan. 20, 1858, in Milton, Mrs. Eliza Twombly.

CORLISS, Joseph H., m. Oct. 6, 1866, in Dover, Helen M. Allen.

2) **CORSON**, Ichabod, son of Samuel, d. July 1801, aged 77, m. near 1749, Abigail Roberts.

CORSON, Daniel, d. May 28, 1813, m. Oct. 14, 1787, by Rev. Isaac Hasey, Shore Mills.

CORSON, John, d. Apr. 18, 1855, aged 82, m. Nov. 13, 1794, by Rev. Isaac Hasey, Tamsin Hodgdon, d. July 10, 1865, aged 91 yrs., 1 mo., 16 das., dau. of Thomas.

CORSON, Joseph, d. Mar. 22, 1852, aged 79, m. Oct. 11, 1795, by Rev. Joseph Haven, Abra Horne, d. Jan. 4, 1862, aged 87.

CORSON, David M., son of David, d. Feb. 14, 1860, aged 72, m. Oct. 14, 1808, in Wakefield, Alpha Remick, of Milton, b. Sept. 29, 1789, d. June 9, 1847, aged 57, dau. of John.

CORSON, Thomas, son of John, d. Mar. 13, 1875, aged 75, m. int. June 5, 1821, Eliza G. Jewett, of Milton, d. Nov. 2, 1877, aged 75.

NEW HAMPSHIRE MARRIAGES SUPPLEMENT

CORSON, Robert S., son of Robert, d. 1885, aged 68, m. (pub. Dec. 28, 1841, in Ossipee), Sarah Nay, b. 1817, d. 1908, dau. of Joseph.

CORSON, Ichabod, Jr., m. int. Oct. 12, 1846, in Dover, Mrs. Susan (Whitehouse) Burley, wid. of Hiram, both of Dover.

CORSON, William E., of Milton, son of David, d. Sept. 16, 1869, aged 52, m. Jan. 11, 1849, in Ossipee, Cordelia N. Ambrose, of Ossipee, b. Nov. 28, 1825, d. July 15, 1895, dau. of Deac. Jonathan.

CORSON, William, of Alton, b. Dec. 2, 1826, d. Nov. 27, 1902, m. Apr. 28, 1853, in Wolfeboro, Susan R. Hayes, of Wolfeboro, b. Feb. 4, 1838, d. July 25, 1902.

CORSON, John, m. Feb. 13, 1854, in Newmarket, Alice Ellen Burnam, both of Durham.

CORSON, Charles H., of Durham, aged 21, m. Jan. 7, 1857, in Newmarket, Sarah A. Ellison, of Newmarket, aged 18.

CORSON, Elbridge H., m. Dec. 25, 1866, by Rev. James Rand, Eliza A. Wiggin.

COSTELLO, William, son of John, b. 1780, m. Feb. 28, 1806, Elizabeth Teed.

COSTELLOE, John, a "Dublin Lad" Master Tate says will of 1795, d. Sept. 2, 1802, m. Dec. 20, 1774, by Dr. Belknap, Lydia (Wallingford), Lord of Berwick, Me., widow of Samuel, b. Apr. 25, 1742, d. 1819, dau. of Thomas.

COTTLE, Charles, of Brookfield, b. 1808, d. 1892, m. Feb. 25, 1834, in Wolfeboro, Mrs. Eliza (Cotton) Page, of Wolfeboro, wid. of David, b. 1799, d. 1865.

COTTLE, Joshua, Jr., of Brookfield, d. Mar. 15, 1865, aged 86, m. Apr. 29, 1846, by Elder William K. Lucas, Martha Weeks, of Wakefield, b. 1817, d. 1888, dau. of Phineas.

COTTON, Solomon, m. (1) May 14, 1702, Margaret Fernald, b. Mar. 27, 1681, d. Jan. 12, 1719/20, dau. of William, m. (2) Dec. 3, 1721, by Rev. Nathaniel Rogers, Judith Permat, d. Mar. 5, 1744.

COTTON, Joseph, m. Nov. 29, 1798, by Rev. Isaac Smith, Sally Libbey.

COTTON, Rev. George O., son of William, d. Nov. 29, 1839, aged 65, m. Feb. 7, 1799, in Wolfeboro, Sally Wiggin, b. May 21, 1776, d. July 25, 1864, dau. of Mark, both of Wolfeboro.

COTTON, Samuel, of Wolfeboro, son of George C., d. Feb. 8, 1852, aged 72, m. (1) Apr. 24, 1809, in Wolfeboro, Sally Fernald, of Brookfield, d. June 15, 1830, aged 40, m. (2) Mar. 7, 1831, in Wolfeboro, Abigail Hobbs, of Effingham, d. Feb. 22, 1864, aged 66.

COTTON, James M., of Wolfeboro, m. Sept. 30, 1865, by Rev. Asa Piper, Hannah P. Dearborn.
COURSER, William M., m. July 27, 1869, in Dover, Mary E. Wentworth.
COUSENS, Israel, m. Jan. 29, 1868, by Rev. Robert S. Stubbs, Mrs. Tryphina Kimball.
COWELL, Jesse, b. 1818, d. Nov. 1891, m. int. June 15, 1844, in Lebanon, Me., Mary Ann Fall, of Ossipee, d. Aug. 1888.
COWELL, Edmund E., son of Isaac, b. Oct. 25, 1825, d. Aug. 3, 1898, m. Feb. 1858, Elizabeth Jane (Chamberlain) Hussey, wid. of Alexander, b. Nov. 24, 1829, d. May 18, 1923, dau. of Samuel.
COWELL, Charles J., m. Aug. 21, 1863, in Dover, Martha A. Grant.
COX, John, m. May 22, 1694, by Rev. John Pike, Hannah (Roberts) Hill, wid. of William, dau. of William.
COX, Henry, m. Feb. 7, 1867, by Rev. James Drummond, Catherine Hughes.
CRAM, John, of Pittsfield, m. Nov. 9, 1802, by Rev. Isaac Smith, Mrs. Sarah Nelson, of Gilmanton.
CRANE, Elisha, of Portsmouth, m. (pub. Dec. 6, 1825, in York, Me.), Nancy Kingsbury, of York, Me.
CRAWFORD, Daniel, of Durham, b. Aug. 1752, d. Mar. 5, 1837, m. (1) near 1779, Mary Bennett, d. June 21, 1820, aged 72, dau. of Benjamin, m. (2) Dec. 23, 1821, Peggy Stockbridge, widow, of Barrington.
CRAWFORD, Erastus A., of Norfolk, N.Y., d. Oct. 21, 1898, aged 74, m. (1) (pub. Jan. 26, 1847, in Somersworth), Jane S. Porter, of Conway, d. Mar. 14, 1896, aged 76, m. (2) Mar. 28, 1898, in Fryeburg, Me., Alice M. Osgood.
CRAWFORD, Festus, b. Feb. 3, 1822, d. Dec. 17, 1895, m. Nov. 25, 1847, by Rev. Mr. Farwell, Mary Frances Tibbetts, b. May 22, 1827, d. Nov. 17, 1919.
CRESSEY, Caleb, of Mount Vernon, Me., m. int. Nov. 29, 1822, in Lee, Joanna Fletcher, of Lee.
CRITCHERSON, William H., of Lee, m. int. Dec. 23, 1841, in Lee, Eliza Burnham, of Durham.
CRITCHERSON, Charles M., b. 1843, m. int. Mar. 26, 1864, in Lee, Sarah F. Glover, b. 1843, both of Lee.
CRITCHET, Caleb, m. int. Sept. 1, 1810, in Lebanon, Me., Jane Brock.
CRICHET, Reuben, d. July 11, 1882, aged 86, m. July 1, 1821, by Elder Enoch Place, Betsey Dame, d. Feb. 20, 1875, aged 74, both of Strafford.

CROCKETT, John, son of Dr. Hezekiah, b. 1818, d. Nov. 30, 1915, m. May 22, 1845, Elizabeth Main, b. 1823, d. June 29, 1882, dau. of David.

3) **CROMMETT**, John, son of John, d. Jan. 24, 1758, m. Sobriety Thomas, d. 1780, dau. of James.

CROMMETT, James S., m. May 22, 1868, in Dover, Sarah M. Morrison.

CROMWELL, Samuel, Jr., of Durham, m. Nov. 1779, Rebecca Murray, of Madbury, d. Jan. 1804.

CROMWELL, Oliver, b. 1782, d. Feb. 6, 1853, m. (1) (pub. May 17, 1806, in Durham), Eleanor Holmes, of Portsmouth, d. 1821, m. (2) Mar. 17, 1822, in Raymond, Mary Cram, d. May 29, 1855, aged 70.

CROSBY, John M., d. Apr. 21, 1919, aged 77, m. Oct. 28, 1869, in Dover, Sarah Ida B. Mathes.

CROSBY, Charles W., m. Sept. 23, 1873, in Farmington, Addie E. Martin.

CROSS, Joseph, b. 1790, d. May 16, 1833, m. Apr. 8, 1813, by Rev. Joseph Haven, Elizabeth Garland, b. 1795, d. Sept. 1, 1879, both of Rochester.

CROSS, Lewis, son of Richard, b. June 7, 1807, d. Jan. 15, 1883, m. by Rev. Isaac Willey, Mary Clark, b. Apr. 28, 1810, d. Dec. 18, 1894, both of Rochester.

CROSSLAND, Joseph, m. July 18, 1870, in Dover, Minerva A. Tibbetts.

CUMMINGS, James, m. June 28, 1838, by Rev. John Winkley, Betsey Scruton, d. Jan. 8, 1887, aged 67, dau. of Thomas, both of Dover.

2) **CURRIER**, Jacob Morrill, b. Mar. 15, 1771, d. Mar. 31, 1837, m. (1) Sept. 13, 1796, Sarah Chase, b. Sept. 24, 1773, d. Nov. 30, 1803, m. (2) Oct. 28, 1804, Sophia Cogswell, b. July 20, 1786, d. Sept. 18, 1817, dau. of Col. Amos.

CURRIER, Ebenezer, m. Nov. 1798, in Dover, Elizabeth Evans.

CURRIER, Andrew, of Pittsburg, m. June 26, 1867, in Lee, Mrs. Mary Smith, of Lee.

CURTIS, Edmund, m. Oct. 23, 1803, in Dover, Lydia Gage.

CURTIS, Levi W., m. Nov. 15, 1866, in Dover, Annie E. Murray.

3) **CUSHING**, Peter, son of Peter, b. Feb. 22, 1757, d. May 1804, m. (1) Apr. 11, 1784, by Dr. Belknap, Hannah Hanson, b. July 11, 1766, d. 1800, dau. of John, m. (2) June 8, 1802, by Rev. Joseph Hilliard, Sally Hall, of Berwick, Me.

4) CUSHING, Thomas Hanson, son of Peter, b. Feb. 26, 1805, d. May 6, 1868, m. Jan. 10, 1847, by Rev. Homer Barrows, Caroline Torr, d. Jan. 4, 1911, aged 84, dau. of Benjamin, both of Dover.

CUTTING, Simon R., m. Oct. 21, 1869, in Dover, Alice N. Brawn.
CUTTS, Richard Foxwell, of Berwick, Me., b. 1757, d. 1830, m. Jan. 9, 1785, in Saco, Me., Elizabeth Cutts, of Saco, Me., b. 1766, d. 1810.
CUTTS, Capt. Edward, of Portsmouth, Mass., d. Sept. 1824, aged 61, m. Apr. 19, 1796, in Newburyport, Mass., Mary Carter, of Newburyport, Mass., d. Mar. 11, 1840, aged 73, dau. of Nathaniel.
CUTTS, Thomas J., son of Thomas J., b. July 6, 1839, d. Mar. 15, 1933, m. Sept. 23, 1862, Lydia M. Jewett, b. Sept. 22, 1842, d. May 19, 1922, dau. of Asa.
5) **DAME,** Jonathan, son of Richard, bpt. Apr 11, 1726, d. Jan. 3, 1802, m. Nov. 20, 1750, by Rev. Amos Main, Mercy Hanson Varney, b. Mar. 15, 1730, d. Mar. 29, 1810, dau. of Stephen.
5) DAME, John, son of Richard, b. 1738, d. May 13, 1814, m. Nov. 19, 1767, Elizabeth Furber, (Was this a second marriage?)
DAME, Richard, son of John, b. Sept. 21, 1772, m. Dec. 2, 1798, Hannah Bickford, dau. of Winthrop.
DAME, Caleb, b. 1772, d. May 29, 1864, m. (1) Abigail Guppey, d. Apr. 2, 1813, aged 41, m. (2) Tamson Twombly, d. Sept. 26, 1839, aged 60, dau. of James.
7) DAME, Deac. Benjamin, son of George, b. Sept. 25, 1779, d. Nov. 18, 1847, aged 68, m. Feb. 7, 1802, by Rev. William Hooper, Sally Crawford, b. Feb. 20, 1780, d. Sept. 26, 1864, aged 84, dau. of Daniel, both of Durham.
7) DAME, Israel, son of Hunking, b. Aug. 26, 1788, d. Apr. 3, 1872, m. in 1810, by Rev. John Osborne, Hannah Durgin, of Lee, b. May 3, 1794, d. Sept. 21, 1870, aged 76, dau. of Josiah.
7) DAME, Jabez, Jr., son of Jabez, b. 1782, d. Jan. 26, 1850, m. (1) Dec. 8, 1811, by Rev. Joseph Haven, Elizabeth Hanson Cushing, b. 1786, d. July 19, 1823, both of Rochester, m. (2) Dec. 12, 1824, by Rev. Thomas C. Upham, Hannah Goodwin, widow, both of Rochester.
DAME, Jason, son of Joseph, b. Mar. 9, 1793, m. Dec. 15, 1816, Mary Sias, b. Apr. 8, 1794.
7) DAME, Theophilus, of Rochester, son of Richard, b. Apr. 12, 1800, m. Oct. 28, 1824, by Rev. Joseph Boodey, Mary Ann Baker, of Somersworth, b. Aug. 15, 1804, dau. of Moses.
7) DAME, Joseph, son of Silas, b. Apr. 21, 1805, d. Sept. 12, 1884, m. Dec. 15, 1829, by Rev. Isaac Willey, Lydia McDuffee, Roberts, b. Oct. 14, 1807, d. Oct. 1, 1880, both of Rochester.
DAME, Asa, son of Joseph, b. Feb. 9, 1789, d. Nov. 25, 1861, m. Feb. 11, 1841, Lucia Bickford, b. Sept. 14, 1812, d. June 7, 1902, dau. of Robert.

7) DAME, Jabez, son of Caleb, b. 1799, d. June 6, 1863, m. (1) Elizabeth Bickford, b. 1808, d. Jan. 28, 1842, dau. of Col. Stephen, m. (2) Martha -----, b. 1816, d. Nov. 19, 1901.

DAME, Samuel Hiram, son of Samuel, d. Feb. 22, 1907, aged 84, m. (1) June 3, 1851, in Dover, Mary E. Henderson, dau. of Samuel H., m. (2) May 15, 1890, in Dover, Eliza S. Dame, dau. of William F.

DAME, Israel S., of Lee, b. 1831, m. Jan. 7, 1858, by Rev. Thomas J. Greenwood, Mary Hanson, of Dover, b. 1881.

DAME, Charles C., b. Aug. 23, 1839, d. Feb. 10, 1919, m. (pub. Sept. 26, 1861, in Strafford), Mary A. Berry, b. Sept. 24, 1840, d. Jan. 23, 1913.

DAME, William, son of Joseph, b. Sept. 7, 1827, d. July 27, 1887, m. May 24, 1862, in Dover, Drusilla Glidden, b. Feb. 1824, d. Sept. 23, 1895.

DAME, William H., of Rochester, m. Nov. 12, 1862, in Rochester, Nancy E. Witham, of Milton.

DAME, John W., m. Dec. 2, 1862, in Dover, Mary J. C. Hanson.

DAME, John W., m. Sept. 17, 1864, in Dover, Mary A. Glidden.

DAME, Albert W., m. Sept. 21, 1867, in Dover, Addie A. Roberts.

DANFORTH, William, m. May 30, 1866, in Dover, Mercie R. Perkins.

DANFORTH, John H., m. Sept. 28, 1867, by Rev. Robert S. Stubbs, Anna M. Lovering.

DANIELS, Hayes, m. July 9, 1826, in Lee, by Rev. John Osborne, Mehitable Daniels, both of Dover,

DANIELS, Nathaniel, m. int. Apr. 18, 1840, in Lee, Mary Ann Landley, both of Lee.

DANIELS, John D., m. Sept. 15, 1864, in Dover, Esther G. Tuttle.

2) **DAVIS**, "Sargent" Joseph, b. Jan 26, 1659, m. before 1693, Mary Stevens; he was called "Senior" in 1718.

3) DAVIS, James, son of Moses, b. 1687, m. (1) May 19, 1719, by Rev. Hugh Adams, Mary Stevenson, b. Sept. 21, 1681, dau. of Bartholomew, m. (2) Oct. 4, 1728, by Rev. Hugh Adams, Elizabeth Dunn, b. 1689, dau. of Nicholas.

3) DAVIS, Thomas, son of Col. James, b. Oct. 20, 1690, d. 1778, m. ----- -----.

3) DAVIS, Solomon, son of Moses, b. 1695, m. Feb. 4, 1724/25, by Rev. Jos. Adams, Elizabeth Davis, dau. of John.

DAVIS, David, son of David, m. near 1749, Elizabeth Crommett, dau. of Joshua.

DAVIS, Moses, son of Jeremiah, b. Dec. 20, 1737, m. near 1760, Anna Davis, b. Oct. 12, 1741, dau. of Nathaniel.

6) DAVIS, Aaron, of Madbury, son of Moses, d. Oct. 1791, m. Nov. 7, 1776, by Dr. Belknap, Susanna Otis, of Dover, dau. of Stephen.

DAVIS, Eleazer, son of Samuel, m. Jan. 1781, by Rev. William Hooper, Keziah Langley, wid. of Jonathan, both of Durham.

DAVIS, David, son of David, b. Aug. 25, 1760, d. Nov. 19, 1835, m. Jan. 4, 1792, Hannah Gerrish, b. Aug. 11, 1770, d. 1866.

6) DAVIS, Moses, son of Thomas, b. Oct. 10, 1773, d. Jan. 16, 1860, m. in 1793, Nancy Allen, b. 1773, d. July 10, 1854.

DAVIS, Isaac, of Alton, m. Jan. 7, 1802, by Rev. Isaac Smith, Mary Kelley, of Gilmanton, dau. of Jacob.

DAVIS, Benaiah, of Alton, m. Jan. 1, 1807, by Rev. Isaac Smith, Abigail Gilman, of Gilmanton.

DAVIS, Jacob, m. Nov. 15, 1810, by Rev. Isaac Smith, Lois Kelley.

DAVIS, Clement M., son of John, b. Sept. 1, 1795, m. July 12, 1817, by Rev. John Osborne, Sarah J. (Davis) Stevens, b. Mar. 5, 1798, both of Durham.

DAVIS, Stephen, son of John, b. Oct. 24, 1800, d. Jan. 9, 1827, m. Apr. 19, 1821, by Rev. Federal Burt, Clarissa Trickey.

DAVIS, Capt. Zebulon, of Lee, m. (1) int. Dec. 28, 1822, in Lee, Rebecca Page, of Rochester, m. (2) int. June 25, 1832, in Lee, Sally Huckins, d. Mar. 28, 1884, aged 73, both of Lee.

DAVIS, Jonathan, m. Mar. 1825, Elizabeth Emerson, dau. of Moses, both of Lee.

DAVIS, Jonathan, of Berwick, Me., m. int. May 1, 1825, in Lee, Alice Dame, of Lee.

DAVIS, Alva B., of Middleton, b. Feb. 20, 1803, d. Nov. 21, 1871, aged 88, m. Nov. 24, 1825, by Rev. Joseph Boodey, Sally B. Young, of New Durham, b. July 1, 1807.

DAVIS, David, son of David, b. Feb. 11, 1799, d. Apr. 25, 1882, m. Feb. 8, 1826, Eunice (Meserve) Demeritt, wid. of Isaac, b. Aug. 12, 1805, d. July 16, 1880, dau. of Col. Vincent.

8) DAVIS, Franklin, son of Nathaniel, b. Dec. 7, 1804, d. Apr. 8, 1868, m. Apr. 18, 1827, Emily Gilmore, dau. of Jeremiah.

(8) DAVIS, Stevens, son of Nathaniel, b. Sept. 21, 1801, m. Aug. 1827, Statira Crowell.

DAVIS, Moses Jr., of Lee, d. Oct. 28, 1833, aged 24, m. July 10, 1831, by Rev. John Osborne, Ruth M. Hill, of Epping, d. Dec. 15, 1868, aged 58.

DAVIS, David M., son of Nathaniel, d. Dec. 1, 1845, aged 30, m. Oct. 26, 1834, by Elder Jacob Davis, in Milton, Louisa F. Meserve, b. Feb. 14, 1818, d. Dec. 7, 1901.

DAVIS, Nathaniel Goodrich, son of David, of Lee, d. 1885, aged 72, m. June 10, 1836, Elizabeth E. Jones, of Durham, b. Feb. 20, 1812, d. Jan. 1869, dau. of Thomas.

DAVIS, Weare, of Lee, d. July 22, 1893, aged 77, m. Jan. 29, 1839, Sarah Dockham, of Durham, d. Apr. 10, 1890, aged 79.

NEW HAMPSHIRE MARRIAGES SUPPLEMENT

DAVIS, Timothy G., of Barnstead, m. int. Sept. 14, 1839, in Lee, Abigail G. Otis, of Lee.

DAVIS, Ephraim, of Lee, m. int. Oct. 5, 1839, in Lee, Lydia Currier, of Newtown.

DAVIS, David E., m. int. Oct. 30, 1841, in Lee, Mary York, both of Lee.

DAVIS, Cyrus K., son of Nathaniel, d. Sept. 26, 1845, aged 28, m. Sept. 28, 1843, by Rev. A. M. Swain, Sarah Twombly, d. July 6, 1851, aged 36, dau. of James.

DAVIS, Daniel N., son of Daniel, d. Oct. 26, 1893, aged 79 m. (pub. Dec. 23, 1845, in Great Falls, Precilla Nason.

7) DAVIS, Eleazer, Jr., of Alton, son of Eleazer, b. Apr. 18, 1815, d. Jan. 16, 1895, m. Apr. 12, 1846, by Rev. Jacob Stevens, Anna P. Waldron, of Dover, b. May 20, 1826, d. May 11, 1863, dau. of Wells.

DAVIS, Newell C., son of Israel, b. 1822, d. Aug. 12, 1902, m. May 4, 1846, by Rev. Jacob Stevens, Mary Ann Emerson, b. July 9, 1821, d. Dec. 14, 1881, dau. of Daniel.

DAVIS, John W., of Somersworth, b. 1826, d. 1901, m. Mar. 19, 1848, in Lebanon, Me., Mary L. Corson, of Lebanon, Me., b. Nov. 23, 1830, d. Apr. 6, 1914, aged 83, dau. of John.

6) DAVIS, Timothy Gerrish, son of David, b. Dec. 3, 1827, d. May 6, 1893, m. (pub. Dec. 5, 1848, in Newmarket), Mary D. Bartlett.

DAVIS, Obadiah, of Lee, m. Oct. 8, 1849, in Lee, Mrs. Elizabeth A. Dow, of Boston, Mass.

9) DAVIS, David O., son of Andrew, m. Mar. 1, 1853, Martha Abigail Demeritt, b. Jan. 14, 1836, dau. of Ebenezer.

8) DAVIS, Charles Franklin, son of Calvin, b. Dec. 21, 1831, d. July 24, 1878, m. (pub. Feb. 7, 1854, in Newmarket), Sarah Abigail Drew, b. Dec. 4, 1834, dau. of Lemuel.

DAVIS, George W., son of Solomon, b. Mar. 2, 1822, d. Feb. 14, 1910, m. May 17, 1855, by Elder Elias Hutchins, Mary Elizabeth Davis, b. Mar. 4, 1825, dau. of Jacob, both of Nottingham.

DAVIS, Almon M., b. 1835, m. int. May 23, 1858, in Lee, Harriet A. Kenison, b. 1840, both of Lee.

DAVIS, Erastus E., m. June 6, 1858, by Rev. Samuel Sherburne, Sarah A. Philbrick, b. May 12, 1839, d. Feb. 8, 1907, dau. of Lemuel, both of Lee.

DAVIS, Albert W., of Lee, b. 1832, m. int. Dec. 21, 1858, in Lee, Isabel A. Tilton, of Deerfield, b. 1835.

6) DAVIS, George Washington, of Great Falls, son of David, b. June 29, 1833, d. Mar. 15, 1901, m. (pub. July 12, 1860, in Newmarket), Hannah Frank Harvey, of Newmarket, b. Nov. 7, 1841, dau. of Nathan.

DAVIS, George H., m. Oct. 12, 1864, in Dover, S. A. Jameson.
DAVIS, Wells P., m. Jan. 21, 1866, by Rev. Ezra Haskell, Susan P. Stiles.
DAVIS, Augustus A., m. May 28, 1868, in Dover, Jennie Woodus, d. May 1, 1929, aged 84.
DAVIS, Samuel Caverno, son of Samuel, b. Mar. 15, 1842, m. Sept. 30, 1868, Frances Tuttle, d. Nov. 20, 1887, dau. of Thomas.
DAVIS, Samuel, Jr., m. Sept. 27, 1869, in Dover, Eliza A. Witham.
DAVIS, Miles, m. Jan. 30, 1870, in Dover, Hannah E. Morrison, d. Feb. 12, 1908, aged 63.
DAVIS, Wilbur F., m. Dec. 25, 1871, by Rev. Asa Piper, Hattie E. York, both of N. Shapleigh, Me.
DAVIS, John B., m. Sept. 10, 1873, in Farmington, Mrs. Patience Rollins.
DAVIS, Eugene A., m. Nov. 3, 1873, in Dover, Fannie Scriggins, both of Dover.
DAY, Warren, of Northwood, m. May 22, 1845, by Rev. John Winkley, Irene Roberts, of Strafford.
DAY, John, m. Feb. 17, 1866, in Dover, Octavie Wallace.
DAY, George W., of Newfield, Me., m. Nov. 24, 1869, by Rev. Asa Piper, Etta M. Butler, of Acton, Me.
DAY, John L., m. Aug. 7, 1870, by Rev. Asa Piper, Susan A. Patch, both of Newfield, Me.
DEAN, Thomas, m. Feb. 25, 1790, by Rev. Isaac Smith, Lucy Price.
DEAN, Frank, m. Nov. 5, 1865, in Dover, Helen L. Nichols.
DEARBORN, William, of Milton, son of Nathaniel, m. Aug. 30, 1822, by Rev. Joseph Hilliard, Evelina B. Drew, of Somersworth, d. Aug. 29, 1871, aged 72.
DEARBORN, Lewis, m. Nov. 17, 1823, in Wakefield, Sarah Little Piper, of Wakefield, b. Oct. 13, 1794, d. Oct. 1831, aged 40, dau. of Rev. Asa.
DEARBORN, Josiah, of Effingham, m. (pub. May 29, 1827, in Ossipee), Belinda K. Quarles, d. Oct. 6, 1853, aged 42, dau. of Samuel.
DEARBORN, John C., of Milton, son of Joseph, d. Jan. 10, 1860, aged 26, m. Feb. 28, 1854, in Nashua, Harriet E. Leland, of Nashua.
DEARBORN, William B., m. Sept. 11, 1865, in Dover, Laura A. Roberts.
DEARBORN, John E., m. Feb. 7, 1867, by Rev. James Rand, Elvira A. Johnson, d. Apr. 21, 1927, aged 77, dau. of Dennis.
DECATER, Lorenzo E., m. Aug. 17, 1851, in Berwick, Me., Nancy J. Varney.
DECATER, Samuel H., m. Nov. 10, 1870, in Dover, Emma V. Thayer.

DEERING, George H., m. June 18, 1868, in Dover, Annie E. Swain.
DELAND, Ambrose, of Wolfeboro, m. (1) Aug. 13, 1849, in Wolfeboro, Hannah Evans, of Alton, m. (2) in 1858, in Wolfeboro, Rosannah Wiggin.
DELAND, Samuel J., m. Apr. 24, 1851, by Elder Joseph Spinney, Maria Cowell, d. Mar. 19, 1900, aged 80, both of Brookfield.
DELAND, George W., m. Dec. 25, 1869, in Dover, Belle Coleman.
DELOID, Charles H., m. Dec. 25, 1866, in Dover, Elizabeth C. Mack.
4) **DEMERITT**, Israel, son of Samuel, b. Mar. 6, 1754, d. Nov. 7, 1827, m. near 1775, Lois Demeritt, b. Aug. 16, 1758, d. Oct. 9, 1838, dau. of John.
4) DEMERITT, Jonathan, son of Ebenezer, b. Aug. 30, 1753, d. Aug. 31, 1833, m. near 1775, Deborah Demeritt, b. Nov. 26, 1758, d. Apr. 29, 1846, dau. of Samuel.
4) DEMERITT, Capt. Daniel, son of Ebenezer, b. 1760, d. Apr. 3, 1822, m. Dec. 1781, Sarah Hayes, d. Sept. 24, 1855, aged 91, both of Madbury.
4) DEMERITT, Samuel, son of Samuel, b. June 17, 1756, d. Nov. 1, 1801, m. (1) Sally Tibbetts, m. (2) June 7, 1796, by Rev. William Hooper, Anne Kelley, b. Dec. 5, 1770, d. 1860, dau. of Samuel.
4) DEMERITT, Lt. Nathaniel, son of Capt. Samuel, b. Oct. 26, 1751, d. Jan. 18, 1827, m. June 19, 1783, Mary McCrillis, b. Apr. 9, 1756, d. Sept. 3, 1847, dau. of William.
4) DEMERITT, Paul, son of Joseph, b. 1774, m. near 1798, Martha Woodman.
DEMERITT, John, m. Sept. 19, 1799, by Rev. William Hooper, Abigail Leathers, dau. of Robert, both of Durham.
5) DEMERITT, Davis, son of Maj. John, b. Oct. 20, 1786, d. 1860, m. June 23, 1805, by Rev. William Hooper, Nabby Emerson, dau. of Samuel, both of Madbury. (they moved to Montpelier, Vt.)
5) DEMERITT, Gen. Samuel, of Madbury, son of Israel, d. July 23, 1840, aged 58, m. in 1807, by Rev. John Osborne, Sarah Torr, of Dover, d. Jan. 1, 1860, aged 70, dau. of Lt. Andrew.
5) DEMERITT, Samuel, son of Jonathan, b. Sept. 30, 1787, d. 1856, m. near 1820, Alice Locke, d. Apr. 19, 1866, aged 79.
5) DEMERITT, Moses Odell, of Newmarket, son of Moses, b. Nov. 8, 1793, d. Feb. 28, 1856, m. Apr. 10, 1821, by Rev. Joseph A. Merrill, Sarah Ann Meserve, b. May 30, 1802.
5) DEMERITT, Ebenezer Thompson, son of Jonathan, b. Apr. 7, 1792, d. Sept. 26, 1863, m. (1) Oct. 28, 1821, by Rev. J. W. Clary, Hannah Y. Demeritt, d. Mar. 14, 1830, aged 43 yrs., 1 mo., 9 das., dau. of Ebenezer, m. (2) Dec. 24, 1831, Sophia Young, d. Jan. 8, 1870, aged 75 yrs., 11 mos., 4 das.

NEW HAMPSHIRE MARRIAGES SUPPLEMENT

5) DEMERITT, Timothy, son of John, b. May 23, 1808, m. (1) Aug. 20, 1830, Deborah Emerson, m. (2) Hannah (Clay) Pinkham, wid. of Richard.

DEMERITT, Samuel, Jr., of Lee, m. int. Aug. 22, 1830, in Lee, Olive W. Peirce, of Barrington.

5) DEMERITT, Timothy H., of Nottingham, son of Eli, b. May 7, 1805, m. (1) Aug. 22, 1830, Deborah Emerson, of Lee, dau. of Moses, m. (2) July 24, 1836, Clarissa Lee, b. July 2, 1802, d. Dec. 25, 1882.

5) DEMERITT, Thomas, 2nd, of Northwood, son of Moses, m. Feb. 23, 1832, by Rev. Enoch Place, Mary Clark, of Barnstead.

5) DEMERITT, Capt. Andrew E., son of Andrew, d. Jan. 16, 1862, aged 57, m. int. July 30, 1837, in Lee, Hannah Cartland, d. Oct. 8, 1878, both of Lee.

5) DEMERITT, Stephen, son of Israel, b. Dec. 16, 1806, d. Jan. 27, 1867, m. May 11, 1840, Nancy P. Chesley, b. Oct. 31, 1810, d. Aug. 23, 1894, dau. of Samuel.

DEMERITT, Capt. Isaac, m. June 21, 1840, by S. P. Montgomery, Esq., Tamson H. Montgomery, d. Jan. 24, 1898, aged 88.

5) DEMERITT, Daniel, son of John, b. July 2, 1812, d. Aug. 24, 1849, aged 29, m. July 3, 1842, by Elder A. Tuttle, Lorinda P. Batchelder, d. Feb. 20, 1882, aged 63.

DEMERITT, Col. Thomas J., m. int. July 16, 1842, in Lee, Avis Buzzell, d. July 21, 1850, aged 42, both of Lee.

6) DEMERITT, Brackett Johnson, son of Moses, b. Nov. 12, 1821, m. Apr. 19, 1843, by Rev. Samuel Sherburne, Finette Welch, both of Nottingham.

DEMERITT, Israel, b. 1825, m. Nov. 19, 1855, in Dover, Frances W. Demeritt, d. Mar. 8, 1901, aged 69, both of Lee.

DEMERITT, Orlando, m. June 21, 1865, in Dover, Jennie B. Hartford.

DEMERITT, Seorim, son of Jacob J., d. Apr. 10, 1908, aged 70, m. Apr. 4, 1867, in Dover, Fanny A. Joy.

DEMERITT, Albert W., m. Apr. 4, 1867, in Dover, Maria Varney.

DEMERITT, Andrew W., m. July 6, 1869, in Dover, Carrie A. Dorman.

DEMERITT, A. M., m. Nov. 26, 1869, in Dover, Martha L. Maxwell.

DEMERITT, James Young, son of James, d. June 28, 1913, aged 67, m. Sept. 14, 1870, in Dover, Martha C. Ward, d. June 17, 1927, aged 80.

DEMERITT, George P., m. Dec. 21, 1873, in Dover, Fannie Jasper.

DENBOW, Salathiel, m. (1) Dec. 19, 1720, by Rev. J. Adams, Rachel Peavey, m. (2) Sept. 10, 1740, Mary Hill, dau. of Benjamin.

DENNETT, Jeremiah, of Portsmouth, son of Ephraim, b. Dec. 25, 1752, d. July 18, 1818, m. Jan. 21, 1772, in Greenland, Susanna Peverly, d. Nov. 9, 1821.

DENNETT, George, m. Jan. 4, 1776, by Rev. Isaac Smith, Olive Bean.

DENNETT, George, of Portsmouth, son of Jeremiah, b. Feb. 27, 1777, d. Jan. 31, 1834, m. (1) Nov. 13, 1800, Elizabeth Shackford, of Newington, d. Feb. 21, 1803, dau. of John, m. (2) Sept. 18, 1803, Margaret Staples.

DENNETT, Mark, of Portsmouth, son of Jeremiah, b. Mar. 30, 1783, d. Aug. 19, 1858, m. (1) Mar. 1, 1810, Olive Fabyan, of Newington, b. 1790, d. May 8, 1834, dau. of Samuel, m. (2) Sept. 6, 1835, Susanna Thompson Huntress, of Newington, b. Dec. 23, 1796, d. Sept. 9, 1890, dau. of John H.

DENNETT, Charles, b. Sept. 28, 1788, d. Mar. 4, 1867, m. Nov. 11, 1813, by Rev. Joseph Haven, Nabby Ham, b. Jan. 8, 1792, d. Sept. 21, 1876, dau. of Israel.

DENNETT, Jeremiah, of Portsmouth, son of Jeremiah, b. Oct. 19, 1790, d. 1874, m. Oct. 7, 1845, Hannah Cate, b. 1793, d. Oct. 7, 1848.

DENNIS, William B., m. May 7, 1867, in Dover, Leah Helen Goodwin, d. June 1, 1917, aged 68.

DENSMOOR, Samuel, of Conway, m. int. Nov. 20, 1822, in Lee, Eliza F. Rundlett, of Lee.

DIAMOND, Reuben, m. Sept. 9, 1782, by Rev. Isaac Smith, Elizabeth Swasey.

DIAMOND, Daniel H., m. Sept. 26, 1867, by Rev. Robert S. Stubbs, Margaret White.

DICKEY, Stephen G., of Alton, son of George, d. June 9, 1890, aged 79, m. Oct. 16, 1838, by Rev. Nathaniel Berry, Elmira Whitehouse, of Farmington.

DILLINGHAM, Latimer Charles, m. (1) Apr. 17, 1856, in Somersworth, Sarah Ellen Gilpatrick, m. (2) Mary Fowler, of Biddeford, Me.

DIXON, Thomas, son of Thomas, d. Feb. 14, 1820, aged 55, m. May 7, 1787, Sarah Remick, d. Nov. 24, 1846, aged 87, dau. of Ichabod.

DIXON, Stephen, son of Ichabod, b. July 12, 1783, d. Dec. 31, 1863, m. (1) Dec. 6, 1810, by Rev. Isaac Hasey, Mary Stevens, d. Nov. 3, 1853, aged 65, m. (2) Mar. 19, 1855, Mary Jones, d. May 1890.

DIXON, Benjamin, son of Stephen, b. July 9, 1816, d. May 11, 1893, m. July 9, 1837, in Lebanon, Me., by Elder Theodore Stevens, Hannah Jones, b. Mar. 5, 1815, d. Apr. 25, 1893, dau. of Thomas.

DIXON, Stephen, son of Stephen, b. Dec. 5, 1827, d. Feb. 9, 1895, m. (1) Feb. 3, 1849, Sarah J. Jones, b. June 9, 1828, d. Feb. 9, 1856, m. (2) Oct. 9, 1858, Hannah J. Corson, b. Nov. 2, 1840, d. May 20, 1868, dau. of Samuel, m. (3) Mar. 17, 1869, Alma L. Hurd, b. July 7, 1844, d. Dec. 31, 1926, dau. of Benjamin C.

DIXON, Ichabod W., son of Stephen, b. June 27, 1824, d. May 6, 1866, m. Oct. 20, 1849, in Lebanon, Me., Nancy J. Harmon, b. Apr. 26, 1827, d. Mar. 11, 1898, dau. of Simon.

DIXON, Thomas, son of Stephen, b. June 27, 1824, d. May 17, 1861, m. Aug. 15, 1850, Mary E. Varney.

DOCKHAM, David S., m. Apr. 14, 1874, in Farmington, Mary E. Herring, both of Farmington.

DODGE, Charles E., m. Mar. 8, 1866, in Dover, Hannah A. Durgin.

4) **DOE**, Gideon, son of Nicholas, b. 1740, d. Apr. 8, 1820, m. (1) in 1765, Elizabeth Conner, m. (2) 1798, Eunice Hill, m. (3) Sarah Gilman.

5) DOE, Simeon, son of Nathaniel, b. Aug. 31, 1758, m. Mar. 23, 1786, in Rochester, Mary Weymouth.

DOE, Francis, m. (1) Dec. 24, 1797, by Rev. Nathaniel Ewer, Deborah Smith, m. (2) Molly (Ellison) Gleason, wid. of John.

DOE, Ebenezer, m. Jan. 18, 1810, Susanna Joy, b. Sept. 5, 1774, d. Jan. 26, 1845, dau. of Samuel.

DOE, Francis, of Lee, m. July 14, 1814, by Rev. John Osborne, Mrs. Mary Gleason, of Barrington. (Was this a second marriage?).

DOE, Samuel, son of Francis, m. Mar. 21, 1822, Nancy Ellison, both of Lee.

DOE, Nicholas, of Newmarket, m. int. May 14, 1825, in Lee, Abigail Noble, of Lee.

DOE, Gideon, of Newfield, Me., d. Mar. 2, 1885, aged 79, m. (1) Matilda -----, m. (2) (pub. Mar. 2, 1841, in Durham), Lydia Ann Dockham, of Durham, d. May 22, 1888, aged 82.

DOE, John, of Newmarket, m. Mar. 11, 1849, by Rev. Oliver Ayer, Mary Kent, of Durham, dau. of Richard.

DOE, Joseph D., b. 1837, d. 1914, m. int. Oct. 6, 1857, in Rollinsford, Sarah C. Morgan, b. 1837, d. 1904, both of S. Berwick, Me.

DOLLOFF, Stephen, of Exeter, m. int. Apr. 29, 1827, in Lee, Judith Ann Rowell, of Lee.

DONALDSON, George W., m. Dec. 13, 1864, in Dover, Abbie A. Drew.

DORE, Richard, m. Feb. 8, 1757, by Rev. Amos Main, Patience Tebbetts, of Lebanon, Me.

4) DORE, James, son of Philip, bpt. Aug. 20, 1749, m. Aug. 3, 1769, by Rev. Isaac Hasey, Hannah Hussey.

4) DORE, Henry, son of Henry, bpt. Aug. 20, 1749, m. May 27, 1773, by Rev. Isaac Hasey, Frances Stevens.

4) DORE, Daniel, son of John, d. Jan. 31, 1831, aged 77, m. Nov. 22, 1781, Dorcas Garland, d. May 4, 1836, aged 76, dau. of Dodivah.

4) DORE, Benaiah, of Lebanon, Me., son of John, b. Mar. 15, 1764, d. Feb. 2, 1854, m. (1) Oct. 1, 1786, by Rev. Matthew Merriam, Experience Andrews, of Berwick, Me., dau. of Elijah, m. (2) int. July 5, 1807, in Milton, Mary (Pray) Allen, wid. of Elisha, d. Nov. 17, 1863, aged 82.

4) DORE, Wentworth, son of John, d. Aug. 24, 1845, aged 74, m. May 7, 1797, by Rev. Benjamin Randall, Lydia Kimball, d. Dec. 5, 1850, aged 89, both of Rochester.

4) DORE, Andrew, son of John, of Lebanon, Me., m. (1) June 3, 1798, by Rev. Joseph Haven, Margaret Sargent, m. (2) Mary (Ricker) Downs, wid. of Gershom, d. Feb. 8, 1845, aged 72, dau. of Aaron.

DORE, Isaac, son of Benniah, d. July 1, 1891, aged 70, m. Feb. 6, 1848, in Newfield, Me., Abby Howe, d. Apr. 22, 1895, aged 73, dau. of Phineas, both of Milton.

DORE, (DORR), William T., of Ossipee, b. Oct. 2, 1830, d. Dec. 14, 1896, m. (pub. May 11, 1852, in Wolfeboro), Nancy H. Fernald, of Wolfeboro, b. May 3, 1832, d. Jan. 19, 1868.

DORE, Simon C., son of George W., d. Oct. 2, 1913, aged 74, m. May 5, 1861, Hannah W. Hill, d. Apr. 6, 1911, aged 72, dau. of Daniel.

DORE, Charles H., m. Mar. 12, 1866, by Rev. James Rand, Orris E. Adams.

DORE, Charles A., son of Oliver, d. Mar. 26, 1910, aged 70, m. Mar. 26, 1866, in Dover, J. Abbie Leavitt.

DORE, Daniel C., m. Apr. 3, 1869, in Dover, Emma A. Town.

DOW, Samuel, of Bow, m. Jan. 22, 1784, by Rev. Isaac Smith, Betty Maxfield, of Chichester.

DOW, Benjamin, m. May 16, 1784, by Rev. Isaac Smith, Dorothy Conner.

DOW, Jeremiah, son of Jeremiah, b. 1764, d. Jan. 9, 1852, m. Jan. 15, 1786, by Rev. Joseph Haven, Elizabeth Perkins, of Rochester, b. 1766, d. Apr. 6, 1855, dau. of Solomon.

DOW, Jacob, of Pittsfield, m. (pub. Sept. 4, 1827, in Gilmanton), Sally Swain, of Gilmanton.

DOW, James, m. Sept. 16, 1827, Mehitable Ellison.

DOW, Stephen, of Lee, m. (pub. Mar. 3, 1829, in Epping), Mary R. Chase, of Epping.

DOW, Daniel, m. Nov. 5, 1847, by Rev. John Winkley, Diana Kelley, both of Pittsfield.

DOW, George Prince, m. Dec. 13, 1866, by Rev. Daniel Tappan, Adah B. Tappan, of Salem, Mass.

DOWNING, David R, m. Dec. 6, 1849, in Milton, Nancy Peavey, d. Apr. 19, 1875, aged 71, dau. of David.

DOWNING, Stephen, son of Royal B., d. Apr. 5, 1880, aged 65, m. Aug. 14, 1853, in Milton, Clarissa P. Cook

DOWNING, John, m. June 1, 1864, in Dover, Caroline Ford.

DOWNING, William J., m. Nov. 6, 1868, in Dover, Jane C. French.

5) **DOWNS**, Moses, son of William, d. 1810, m. Mar. 2, 1797, in Berwick, Me., Abigail Nock, dau. of Nathaniel.

DOWNS, Aaron, of Rochester, b. June 22, 1780, d. July 14, 1850, m. (1) Sept. 4, 1805, by Rev. Joseph Haven, Rebecca Lord, of Milton, b. Oct. 16, 1786, d. 1812, m. (2) May 29, 1816, by Rev. Joseph Boodey, Martha P. Nutter, b. Oct. 26, 1788, d. Aug. 20, 1870.

DOWNS, James, son of Moses, b. May 16, 1793, d. Oct. 3, 1882, aged 89, m. Nov. 11, 1813, by Rev. Joseph Boodey, Judith Wentworth, both of Milton.

DOWNS, James B., of Farmington, son of John, b. 1806, d. Feb. 26, 1886, m. Nov. 22, 1827, Rhoda Goodwin, b. 1806, d. 1904, dau. of Thomas.

DOWNS, Stephen, son of Stephen, b. Sept. 6, 1808, d. 1862, m. int. Feb. 13, 1831, Lydia Gove Hill, b. 1799, d. Sept. 11, 1874, dau. of Jeremiah.

DOWNS, Frederick G., son of Stephen, b. May 28, 1806, d. Feb. 15, 1891, m. Feb. 22, 1832, by Rev. Isaac Willey, Ruth T. Roberts, of Rochester b. Apr. 15, 1812, d. Jan. 15, 1896.

DOWNS, Aaron, m. (pub. Feb. 6, 1838, in Lebanon, Me.), Maria Tuttle, d. Dec. 27, 1846, aged 36.

DOWNS, Henry, son of James, b. Nov. 11, 1819, d. 1905, m. int. Apr. 28, 1844, in Dover, Elizabeth L. Drew, b. 1827, d. 1902.

DOWNS, J. Hanson, son of Moses, d. Dec. 14, 1898, aged 72, m. Dec. 8, 1847, in Milton, Emily P. Duntley, d. Dec. 5, 1897, aged 68, dau. of Hazen, both of Milton.

DOWNS, John T., son of James, b. Feb. 12, 1830, d. May 2, 1900, m. June 27, 1850, in Milton, Olive A. Wentworth, b. June 28, 1829, d. Aug. 16, 1905, dau. of Jacob, both of Milton.

DOWNS, John, son of Moses, d. Mar. 22, 1898, aged 68, m. Apr. 15, 1854, in Milton, Mrs. Sophia (Savory) Shattuck, d. May 21, 1897, aged 70, dau. of Richard.

DOWNS, Simon F., son of James B., b. 1835, d. 1893, m. Apr. 27, 1854, in Milton, Clara A. Rankins, b. 1837, d. 1860.

DOWNS, Frederick A., of S. Berwick, Me., d. Nov. 13, 1874, aged 41, m. (pub. Dec. 9, 1858, in Rochester), Emma F. Hanson, of Berwick, Me., d. Aug. 23, 1887, aged 50.

DOWNS, Jacob, of Westford, Mass., b. near 1801, m. Dec. 23, 1868, in Lee, Mrs. Mindwell A. Hall, of Lee, wid. of Thomas, b. near 1801.

DRAKE, Abraham, of Effingham, d. May 3, 1813, aged 39, m. Jan. 30, 1799, in Tamworth, Susanna Leighton, of Ossipee.

DRAKE, Meshach W., m. June 20, 1822, in Effingham, Lydia S. Taylor.

DRAKE, Guy, m. Mar. 13, 1825, by Rev. J. W. Clary, Susan Blanchard, both of Dover.

5) **DREW**, Elijah, son of Joseph, b. 1740, d. Mar. 11, 1811, m. Nov. 25, 1760, in Portsmouth, Abigail Thomas, dau. of John.

5) DREW, Joseph, son of Joseph, b. Oct. 26, 1738, d. Mar. 18, 1776, m. 1769, Elizabeth (Davis) Crommett, wid. of Ebenezer, dau. of David.

DREW, Samuel, m. Aug. 13, 1795, Polly Edgerly, b. 1773, d. Nov. 7, 1824, aged 51, dau. of Moses.

DREW, John, m. June 23, 1801, by Rev. Isaac Smith, Sally Allard, both of Barnstead.

DREW, John, d. Apr. 18, 1846, aged 83, m. Nov. 23, 1812, Mary Brown, b. Mar. 12, 1784, d. Dec. 25, 1853, dau. of Nicholas.

6) DREW, Dr. Stephen, of Brookfield, Me., son of Elijah, b. Apr. 7, 1791, d. Feb. 25, 1872, m. Oct. 26, 1817, Harriet Watson, of Milton, b. Apr. 9, 1795, d. May 7, 1876, aged 81.

7) DREW, William Pickering, son of William, b. Nov. 13, 1796, d. June 29, 1848, m. (1) Mar. 28, 1824, by Rev. J. W. Clary, Lois G. Meserve, d. Dec. 31, 1826, aged 27, dau. of Israel, m. (2), June 28, 1829, by Rev. Hubbard Winslow, Eliza H. Demeritt, d. Aug. 7, 1876, aged 70, dau. of Jonathan.

DREW, Tobias R., d. Nov. 29, 1828, aged 27, m. Apr. 22, 1824, by Rev. Enoch Place, Eliza B. Lougee, d. Oct. 10, 1885, aged 83, both of Barrington.

DREW, Jeremiah O., m. int. Aug. 28, 1825, in Dover, Tamson Whitehouse, b. May 24, 1808, d. Jan. 20, 1895, aged 86, dau. of Reuben.

DREW, Charles, b. Aug. 30, 1800, d. Mar. 15, 1832, m. Feb. 20, 1827, in Portsmouth, Delaime Canney, b. Feb. 15, 1805, d. Mar. 30, 1852, both of Dover.

DREW, John P., d. Mar. 9, 1896, aged 85, m. Nov. 24, 1831, by Elder Enoch Place, Mary Willey, d. Mar. 3, 1892, aged 80, both of Strafford.

DREW, Jacob, Jr., d. June 29, 1876, aged 65, m. Feb. 28, 1833, by Elder Enoch Place, Susan Jane Mills, d. Apr. 5, 1898, aged 85, both of Strafford.

7) DREW, Nathaniel, son of Daniel, d. July 18, 1855, aged 50, m. int. Mar. 17, 1833, in Dover, Sabrina Spurling, d. Sept. 14, 1877, aged 67, dau. of Robert.

DREW, John T., m. May 14, 1833, by Rev. John Winkley, Alice Waterhouse, both of Barrington.

DREW, Isaac, b. 1813, d. Nov. 6, 1869, m. May 7, 1837, in Somersworth, Elizabeth Tuttle, d. Aug. 13, 1894, aged 82.

DREW, Dr. Stephen Watson, of Haverhill, Mass., son of Stephen, b. Aug. 15, 1818, d. Feb. 18, 1875, aged 56, m. June 20, 1843, by Rev. Isaac Willey, Mary Yeaton Chase, of Rochester, dau. of Simon.

7) DREW, Paul, son of William, d. Mar. 11, 1852, aged 36, m. Nov. 26, 1844, by Rev. Eben Francis, Clarinda Drew, d. Mar. 7, 1902, aged 81 yrs., 3 mos., 22 das.

6) DREW, John, son of Joseph, b. Dec. 30, 1823, d. Apr. 10, 1886, m. Mar. 2, 1848, by Rev. E. G. Page, Martha Ann Mathes, b. June 28, 1826, d. Jan. 12, 1907, dau. of Abraham, both of Durham.

DREW, Mesheck, of Barrington, m. Apr. 21, 1848, in Newmarket, Elizabeth Woodbury, of Newmarket.

DREW, Stephen F., of Trobridge, Vt., m. Mar. 10, 1850, in Newmarket, Mary A. Hanson, of Newmarket.

DREW, Greenleaf S., m. Sept. 26, 1852, by Elder Samuel Sherburne, Mary Elizabeth Chesley, d. June 12, 1899, aged 64, dau. of Samuel.

DREW, Reuben W., of Dover, m. Sept. 29, 1852, Susan M. Ham, of Rollinsford.

DREW, Henry A., of Durham, d. June 10, 1916, aged 90, m. (1) Feb. 1, 1853, by Rev. Alvin Tobey, Sarah Tuttle, of Strafford, b. July 15, 1825, d. June 9, 1865, aged 40, dau. of William, m. (2) Abbie -----, b. Feb. 10, 1829, d. Dec. 16, 1887.

DREW, Asa B., b. May 23, 1830, d. June 23, 1866, m. int. Oct. 5, 1853, in Lebanon, Me., Hannah M. Pinkham, b. June 24, 1832, d. Sept. 28, 1914, dau. of James.

DREW, Abednego, son of Swain, d. Nov. 9, 1900, aged 61, m. Aug. 2, 1859, by Elder Samuel Sherburne, Mary E. Swain, d. Nov. 20, 1903, aged 68, dau. of Richard, both of Barrington.

DREW, Jacob J., m. (1) July 12, 1862, in Dover, Mary E. Downs, m. (2) June 18, 1873, in Dover, Mary A. Wadleigh, of Bath, Me.

DREW, Charles H., m. Aug. 22, 1863, by Rev. James Rand, Emma Fife.

DREW, Henry L., son of Benjamin, d. Feb. 1, 1912, aged 75, m. Nov. 26, 1864, in Dover, Mary L. Joice.
DREW, George A., m. Dec. 31, 1867, in Dover, Eleanor A. Ham.
DREW, Henry, m. Jan. 3, 1869, by Rev. Asa Piper, Emeline Dyer, both of Brookfield.
DREW, John S., m. Nov. 13, 1869, in Dover, Abby D. Chamberlain.
DREW, Manning A., m. Sept. 1, 1870, in Dover, Isabel A. Flanders.
DREW, Albert R., m. July 3, 1873, in Strafford, Abbie I. Tilton.
DREW, Samuel T., of Dover, m. (pub. Feb. 20, 1874, in Haverhill, Mass.), Emma C. Fairbanks, of Cambridgeport, Mass.
DROWN, Samuel, son of Samuel, b. 1728, d. 1795, m. Feb. 21, 1754, by Rev. Amos Main, Mary Seavey, d. Sept. 1784, aged 61, dau. of Ithamar.
DUDA, Joseph, of Northwood, m. Oct. 6, 1793, by Rev. Isaac Smith, Olive Garmon, of Gilmanton.
DUDLEY, Stephen Jr., m. Jan. 10, 1782, by Rev. Isaac Smith, Molly Gilman.
DUDLEY, John, of Barnstead, m. Nov. 10, 1801, by Rev. Isaac Smith, Hannah Young, of Gilmanton.
DUDLEY, Nathaniel, m. Nov. 22, 1803, by Rev. Isaac Smith, Mary Smith.
DUESBURY, Frederic W., m. Jan. 28, 1869, in Dover, Susan A. Hope.
DUNN, Enoch, of Dover, d. Apr. 7, 1848, aged 51, m. Oct. 9, 1820, in Wolfeboro, Elizabeth Fullerton, of Wolfeboro, b. 1800, d. 1885.
DUNNELLS, Calvin, of Newfield, Me., m. Nov. 6, 1875, by Rev. Asa Piper, Cora E. Merrill, of Parsonfield, Me.
DUNTLEY, Ariel, d. May 29, 1848, aged 36, m. Dec. 26, 1844, in Milton, Mary Ricker, both of Milton.
DUNTLEY, Amos G., of Milton, m. Nov. 31, 1867, by Rev. Asa Piper, Mary P. Sawyer, of Wakefield.
DUNTLY, Hazon, of Sandwich, son of Stephen, d. Nov. 15, 1884, aged 79, m. Oct. 18, 1829, by Rev. Nathaniel Berry, Phebe Leighton, of Farmington, d. Nov. 26, 1871, aged 59, dau. of Jedediah.
2) **DURGIN**, James, m. in 1696, Susanna Davis, wid. of David.
2) DURGIN, William, m. early as 1710, Elizabeth Pinder, d. Oct. 24, 1721, dau. of John.
3) DURGIN, William, son of James, b. 1705, d. Apr. 16, 1781, m. near 1735 Margaret Crommett, b. Apr. 6, 1715, dau. of John.
3) DURGIN, William, son of Francis, b. 1717, d. 1789, m. Hannah Elliot.
3) DURGIN, Josiah, son of William, m. June 21, 1749, Lydia Coffin, d. Sept. 4, 1783.

4) DURGIN, John, son of John, b. Apr. 1729, m. Nov. 7, 1751, Susanna Pitman, b. May 7, 1734, dau. of John.

DURGIN, Josiah, son of Josiah, b. 1751, d. July 14, 1833, m. Dec. 3, 1781, Hannah Stevens, d. Jan. 5, 1849, aged 85.

5) DURGIN, James, son of Lt. James, d. July 2, 1808, m. Dec. 6, 1807, by Rev. William Hooper, Elizabeth Yeaton, d. July 2, 1808, both of Durham.

DURGIN, Trueworthy, son of Stephen, m. Jan. 24, 1811, Sally Cilley, of Epping.

DURGIN, Trueworthy, d. Sept. 19, 1865, aged 71, m. int. (1) Aug. 1812, in Tuftonboro, Sally Hall, both of Tuftonboro, m. int. (2) Apr. 26, 1821, in Tuftonboro, by Rev. Jeremiah Shaw, Abigail Haines, of Moultonboro, d. 1872, aged 76.

5) DURGIN, Steven, son of Josiah, b. Sept. 4, 1798, d. 1851, m. (1) Aug. 27, 1824, by Rev. John Osborne, Sarah York, of Lee, d. 1830, aged 23, dau. of Eliphalet, m. (2) Nov. 24, 1831, by Rev. John Osborne, Hannah Kenniston, b. July 4, 1802, d. 1875, both of Lee.

DURGIN, Walter, of Lee, b. Jan. 30, 1801, d. Sept. 17, 1881, m. May 19, 1830, Hannah Woodman, of Barrington, d. Nov. 25, 1875, aged 73.

DURGIN, James, son of Nicholas, b. Nov. 4, 1808, m. Jan. 20, 1831, Martha Heath, of Hampstead.

DURGIN, Stephen, m. int. Oct. 23, 1831, in Lee, Hannah Kenniston, both of Lee.

DURGIN, Samuel, son of Nicholas, b. Jan. 1811, m. May 1, 1834, Lydia Ann Emery.

DURGIN, James, of Quincy, Mass., m. (pub. Feb. 9, 1841), Hannah M. Varney, of Dover, d. Oct. 15, 1903, aged 82, dau. of James.

DURGIN, Charles C., of Gilmanton, son of Walter, m. Mar. 26, 1854, in Milton, Christine H. Hanson, of Lebanon, Me., b. Jan. 27, 1827, dau. of Daniel.

DURGIN, Simeon, son of Silas, d. Jan. 20, 1902, aged 73, m. (pub. Nov. 7, 1854, in Newburyport, Mass.), Mary Jane Mooney, both of Alton.

DURGIN, Horace J., m. Apr. 16, 1862, in Dover, Sarah F. Bradeen.

DURGIN, George W., d. Feb. 19, 1907, aged 72, m. Feb. 23, 1864, in Dover, Sarah E. D. Gray.

DURGIN, Benjamin F., of Newfield, Me., m. June 28, 1865, by Rev. Asa Piper, Amelia Edgecomb.

DURGIN, James W., m. Jan. 27, 1866, in Dover, Hannah M. Varney.

DURGIN, Albert F., m. Aug. 20, 1868, by Rev. Robert S. Stubbs, Almira P. Wentworth, d. July 4, 1887, aged 48, dau. of Jonathan.

DURGIN, George H., of Newfield, Me., m. Oct. 9, 1874, by Rev. Asa Piper, Mrs. Elizabeth Sprague, of Shapleigh, Me.

4) **DURRELL**, Lt. Eliphalet, son of Joseph, b. 1748, d. Nov. 12, 1825, m. (1) Dolly Bennett, b. 1759, dau. of Caleb, m. (2) Nov. 20, 1801, Hannah (Batchelder) Tilton, d. Nov. 29, 1842, aged 78.

4) DURRELL, John Samuel, son of Nicholas, b. Dec. 17, 1774, d. May 10, 1845, m. Dec. 1797, in Dover, (1) Elizabeth Hayes, b. Jan. 12, 1775, m. (2) in 1805, Abra (Wallingford) Moulton, wid. of William, b. Apr. 14, 1769, d. July 27, 1846, aged 78, dau. of Col. John.

DURRELL, Newman, of Newmarket, m. int. Aug. 27, 1821, in Lee, Sally Osborne, of Lee.

DURRELL, George, m. Oct. 10, 1868, by Rev. Asa Piper, Elizabeth Rogers, both of Wakefield.

DUSTIN, Adrian C., m. Sept. 22, 1868, in Dover, Mary F. Berry.

DUSTIN, Albert B., m. Dec. 24, 1868, by Rev. Robert S. Stubbs, Abbie L. Card.

DWINELL, Otis S., m. June 3, 1866, in Dover, Flavia Chase.

DYER, Albert P., m. Dec. 25, 1869, in Dover, Mary Ann Davis.

EADIE, William, m. Apr. 6, 1871, in Dover, Isabelle A. Mack.

EARL, Edmund, b. 1787, d. 1868, m. (pub. Oct. 29, 1850, in S. Berwick, Me.), Mary I. Doick, b. 1797, d. 1862.

EASTMAN, William, m. May 5, 1777, by Rev. Isaac Smith, Sarah Caton.

EASTMAN, William, of Tamworth, m. Feb. 28, 1790, Sally Edgerly, d. 1826, aged 60, dau. of Samuel.

EASTMAN, Stephen, m. Aug. 21, 1801, in Gilmanton, Hannah Page.

EASTMAN, Ebenezer, m. Mar. 17, 1803, by Rev. Isaac Smith, Deborah Greeley.

EASTMAN, Stephen, m. Aug. 21, 1808, by Rev. Isaac Smith, Hannah Page, both of Gilmanton.

EASTMAN, Samuel, m. Mar. 3, 1811, by Rev. Isaac Smith, Dorothy Kimball, both of Gilmanton.

EASTMAN, George A., b. Feb. 14, 1829, d. Mar. 6, 1910, m. (pub. Jan. 22, 1850, in Somersworth), Joanna Estes, b. Apr. 16, 1832, d. Dec. 22, 1885.

EATON, John S., of Dodge Co., Neb., m. Aug. 1868, in Lee, Francena J. Sawyer, of Lee.

3) **EDGERLY**, Samuel, son of Thomas, b. 1700, d. 1769, m. ----- ----.

3) EDGERLY, Joseph, son of Thomas, b. 1702, m. (1) Sarah Rollins, b. Mar. 29, 1709, dau. of Moses, m. (2) -----Sanborn, widow, m. (3) Judith Currier, wid. of William, d. 1816.

3) EDGERLY, John, Jr., son of John, b. 1703, m. <u>1737</u> Hannah Ambler, b. Jan. 24, 1718/19, dau. of John.
4) EDGERLY, John, son of Zechariah, <u>b. 1735, d. 1796</u>, m. Sarah Chesley, dau. of Paul.
5) EDGERLY, John, <u>of</u> Meredith, son of Jonathan and Elizabeth, b. July 15, 1762, m. <u>Apr. 7, 1785, by Rev. Isaac Smith</u>, Bridget Avery, <u>of Gilmanton</u>.
EDGERLY, Nathaniel, m. Nov. 9, 1826, Hannah Tuttle.
EDGERLY, Dr. Isaiah, of Gilmanton, b. Aug. 17, 1800, <u>d. May 20, 1870</u>, m. Mar. 26, 1828, Matilda T. Bourne, <u>b. Aug. 5, 1794</u>.
6) EDGERLY, Daniel, son of Nathaniel, d. Aug. 19, 1886, aged 76, m. Dec. 26, 1833, Mary Kent, d. Oct. 12, 1883, aged 70, dau. of Ebenezer.
6) EDGERLY, Rev. David S., <u>of</u> New Durham, son of Jeremiah, b. 1818, m. (1) <u>Nov. 17, 1836, by Rev. Nathaniel Berry</u>, Olive W. Place, <u>of</u> Alton, m. (2) July 22, 1851, by Elder Elias Hutchins, Almira B. Chamberlain, dau. of Samuel F.
EDGERLY, Matthais D., of Durham, m. (pub. Aug. 27, 1837), Sarah Clark, of Lee.
6) EDGERLY, Elias S., son of Thomas C., b. 1820, d. <u>Dec. 2, 1850</u>, m. Mary M. Leighton, d. Dec. 19, 1898, aged 87, dau. of Jedediah.
7) EDGERLY, Judge James H., son of Thomas T., <u>b. June 28, 1814</u>, d. Dec. 3, 1892, aged 78, m. Sept. 29, 1841, by Rev. Francis V. Pike, Emeline Roberts, b. 1816, d. 1884, dau. of John.
6) EDGERLY, Albert L., son of John and Anna, <u>d. Jan. 29, 1903, aged 77</u>, m. Oct. 12, 1848, in Tuftonboro, Nancy M. Hersey, of Tuftonboro, <u>d. May 26, 1891, aged 69</u>, dau. of James.
6) EDGERLY, Hiram V. R., son of Thomas C., b. <u>1821</u>, d. June 22, 1909, m. Jan. 24, 1850, in Farmington, Lydia A. Knox, <u>d. Feb. 20, 1906, aged 77</u>, dau. of Jesse, both of Milton.
EDGERLY, James B., m. (pub. Feb. 5, 1850, in Durham), Sophronia D. Durgin, d. Nov. 1886, aged 68, <u>both of Durham</u>.
EDGERLY, Charles R., son of John, d. Feb. 16, 1907, aged 81, m. Apr. 18, 1863, by Rev. James Rand, Mary J. Kelley.
EDGERLY, Eli, son of Daniel, b. Sept. 16, 1839, m. Nov. 24, 1867, Emily Long, b. Feb. 6, 1844, dau. of Henry.
EDGERLY, Henry I., m. Dec. 25, 1870, in Dover, Sarah A. Whitten.
EDGERLY, James A., son of James, d. Feb. 8, 1908, aged 61, m. Nov. 19, 1874, in Rochester, Annie A. Wood.

EDWARDS, David, m. May 15, 1792, by Rev. Isaac Smith, Betty Gilman, both of Gilmanton.
EDWARDS, Jonathan, m. Apr. 11, 1793, by Rev. Isaac Smith, Polly Copp.

EDWARDS, Timothy, m. Dec. 21, 1794, by Rev. Isaac Smith, Anna Gilman, both of Gilmanton.
EDWARDS, Jonathan, m. Aug. 3, 1800, by Rev. Isaac Smith, Sally Copp, both of Gilmanton.
ELKINS, James, m. Apr. 20, 1784, by Rev. Isaac Smith, Elizabeth Florence, both of Gilmanton Gore.
ELKINS, James, m. Sept. 17, 1788, by Rev. Isaac Smith, Hannah Haines, both of Gilmanton.
ELKINS, John E., m. July 28, 1873, in Rochester, Ella J. Horne, both of Farmington.
ELLIOT, Arthur F. R., of Pittsfield, son of Joseph, d. Jan. 31, 1890, aged 63, m. May 13, 1846, by Rev. John Dow, Ann Twombly, of Dover, b. July 31, 1826, d. Dec. 22, 1888, aged 62, dau. of Isaac.
ELLIOT, Nathaniel, m. July 11, 1869, in Dover, Rachael Morris.
ELLIS, John, m. Dec. 20, 1753, by Rev. Amos Main, Judith Ash, of Lebanon, Me., dau. of Thomas, Jr.
ELLIS, Jonathan, m. Dec. 1, 1755, by Rev. Amos Main, Abigail Richards.
ELLIS, Reuben, m. June 12, 1803, by Rev. Benjamin Randall, Esther N. Buzzell.
ELLIS, Jacob, m. (pub. Feb. 14, 1826, in Rochester), Lois Richards.
ELLIS, Alvah, of Alton, son of Jacob, d. Oct. 19, 1899, aged 79, m. Feb. 4, 1844, by Rev. Nathaniel Berry, Lydia Glidden, of Gilford, d. Nov. 5, 1874, aged 50.
ELLIS, Daniel, m. Dec. 24, 1851, in Alton, Mariah Ellis, d. Dec. 19, 1900, aged 83, dau. of John W., both of Alton.
ELLIS, Moses A., son of Moses, d. July 19, 1810, aged 73, m. (pub. July 8, 1858, in Barnstead), Mrs. Sarah M. Lougee, both of Alton.
ELLIS, Daniel L., m. Nov. 1, 1869, in Dover, Phoebe F. Ricker.
ELLISON, Joseph, of Barrington, m. Oct. 21, 1817, Elizabeth Doe, dau. of Francis.
ELLISON, Joseph, of Nottingham, m. Dec. 24, 1867, in Lee, Elizabeth A. Williams, of Barrington.
ELVILACHER, Edmund T., m. Sept. 21, 1868, by Rev. Robert S. Stubbs, Julia E. Kenney.
ELWELL, Josiah, m. Mar. 22, 1863, in Dover, Abbie Hobbs.
ELWELL, John F., m. July 22, 1866, in Dover, Hattie H. T. Holbrook.
ELWELL, George E., m. Dec. 24, 1869, in Dover, Elizabeth Morton.
4) **EMERSON**, Samuel, son of Micah, b. Sept. 1, 1726, d. Oct. 7, 1785, m. Nov. 14, 1748, in Rochester, Dorothy Chamberlain, b. Mar. 7, 1731, d. Feb. 18, 1825, dau. of William.

4) EMERSON, Capt. Smith, son of Timothy, b. Dec. 26, 1745, d. July 26, 1814, m. near 1767, Hannah R. Thompson, b. July 29, 1749, d. Dec. 25, 1841, dau. of Samuel.

4) EMERSON, Joseph, son of Solomon, d. 1826, aged 90, m. near 1775, Temperance Dame.

EMERSON, Edward Winslow, son of Moses, b. Aug. 25, 1755, d. Nov. 10, 1805, m. 1785, Mary Willey, b. Oct. 26, 1758, d. Feb. 22, 1838, dau. of Joshua.

EMERSON, Eliphalet, Jr., m. (pub. Apr. 2, 1814, in Barnstead), Prudence Bunker.

EMERSON, John Taylor, son of Edward, b. Dec. 17, 1788, m. Oct. 24, 1815, by Rev. John Osborne, Mary Hanson, b. Aug. 17, 1795, d. July 27, 1860, both of Madbury.

EMERSON, Daniel, son of Samuel, b. Dec. 1792, m. in 1819, Kezia Elkins, b. Feb. 24, 1799, dau. of Joseph.

EMERSON, John, of Lee, m. int. June 10, 1821, in Lee, Mary French, of Epping.

EMERSON, Richard Fitts, son of Samuel, b. Sept. 15, 1789, d. Nov. 12, 1860, m. June 22, 1823, Delia H. Goss.

6) EMERSON, Timothy, son of Andrew, b. July 23, 1803, d. Dec. 15, 1877, m. Sept. 23, 1823, Sophia Place, b. Sept. 24, 1803, d. Feb. 26, 1871, dau. of John.

5) EMERSON, Daniel, of Lee, son of Joseph, d. Apr. 17, 1880, aged 88, m. Nov. 21, 1826, by Rev. John Brodhead, Sukey C. Dow, of Epping, d. Feb. 27, 1870, aged 76, dau. of Zebulon.

EMERSON, Daniel Emery, son of Daniel, b. May 7, 1826, d. May 11, 1893, m. Nov. 18, 1846, by Rev. Samuel Kelley, Elizabeth R. Roberts, b. 1827.

EMERSON, Seth R., of Alton, son of William, d. Feb. 10, 1891, aged 64, m. (1) Emily Ann Rollins, b. June 25, 1830, d. Aug. 3, 1855, aged 25, dau. of Ichabod, m. (2) Nov. 25, 1858, in Gilford, Emily O. Grant, of Gilford.

7) EMERSON, Smith, of Durham, son of Joshua F., b. Nov. 16, 1820, m. May 31, 1852, in Newburyport, Mass., Abby Mary Snell, of Lee, b. Aug. 2, 1828.

7) EMERSON, John Place, son of Timothy, b. July 28, 1832, m. Aug. 26, 1860, Mary M. Bunker.

6) EMERSON, John O., son of Moses, b. Nov. 9, 1835, m. (1) Sarah Langley, m. (2) Oct. 26, 1869, in Dover, Clara L. Wentworth.

EMERSON, George H., m. Nov. 27, 1864, by Rev. James Rand, Mary E. Pickering.

EMERSON, Charles W., m. May 27, 1865, by Rev. Ezra Haskell, Mary A. Randlett.

EMERSON, Daniel H., of Wakefield, m. Nov. 2, 1866, by Rev. Asa Piper, Adelia F. Sceggel, of Wolfeboro.
EMERSON, Daniel, of Madbury, m. Dec. 8, 1873, in Barrington, Mrs. Sarah A. Pierce, of Barrington.
5) **EMERY**, Job, son of Joseph, b. Jan. 29, 1745, d. May 17, 1828, m. Sept. 10, 1770, by Rev. Jacob Foster, Mary Hubbard, b. Jan. 12, 1745, d. Feb. 24, 1812, dau. of Joseph.
EMERY, Daniel, of Cox-Hall, b. 1759, d. 1830, m. Sept. 12, 1779, by Rev. Matthew Merriam, Elizabeth Brackett, of Berwick, Me.
EMERY, Oliver H., m. Oct. 25, 1829, by Rev. Jacob Foster, Hannah Porter, both of Dover.
EMERY, Daniel C., of Milton, son of Timothy, d. Feb. 4, 1898, aged 74, m. Jan. 28, 1846, in Middleton, Abigail Whitehouse, of Middleton, d. Mar. 26, 1894, aged 68, dau. of Amos.
EMERY, Timothy K., m. Nov. 18, 1849, in Milton, Hannah Pinkham, d. Sept. 5, 1851, aged 22.
EMERY, Rufus, Jr., son of Rufus M., m. (pub. Jan. 12, 1860, in Portsmouth), Lizzie M. Mugridge.
EMERY, John W., m. Mar. 28, 1864, in Dover, Evelyn F. Pinkham.
ENGLAND, Thomas, m. Jan. 3, 1870, in Dover, Ellen F. Hartford.
EVANS, Daniel, m. June 11, 1753, Eleanor Bamford, both of Barrington.
EVANS, Daniel, m. Dec. 21, 1775, by Rev. Isaac Smith, Hannah Quimby.
EVANS, Miles, son of Daniel, d. Jan. 1, 1816, aged 70, m. (1) ----- ----, of Mania, d. Feb. 10, 1798, aged 50, m. (2) Aug. 1801, Dorcas Heard, b. 1768, d. Apr. 1806, m. (3) Nov. 3, 1814, by Rev. J. W. Clary, Eunice (Smith) Church, wid. of Benjamin, dau. of Dr. Chaney Smith.
5) EVANS, Aaron, son of Solomon, b. July 17, 1781, d. Aug. 17, 1863, m. near 1809, Phebe -----, d. May 5, 1849, aged 67.
EVANS, William, m. Apr. 19, 1827, by Rev. John Winkley, Sarah Twombley, both of Strafford.
EVANS, Joseph G., son of David, b. 1805, d. 1881, m. Dec. 30, 1827, in Wakefield, Abigail Pickering, of Wakefield, d. Mar. 8, 1855, aged 53.
EVANS, Reuben, m. Dec. 10, 1829, by Rev. John Winkley, Martha Brown, both of Strafford.
EVANS, Albert, of Strafford, son of Lemuel, d. Dec. 2, 1905, aged 81, m. Jan. 9, 1850, by Elder Samuel Sherburne, Elizabeth A. Swain, of Barrington, d. Nov. 11, 1910, aged 90, dau. of Israel.
EVANS, John, of Barrington, son of Deac. William, b. 1813, d. 1885, m. (pub. Jan. 18, 1853, in Somersworth), Rhoda Twombly, of Berwick, Me., b. 1817, d. Mar. 13, 1902, dau. of Peter.

EVANS, George H., m. Dec. 26, 1861, by Rev. John Winkley, Lydia A. Brock, both of Strafford.

EVANS, Charles E., of Strafford, m. Apr. 24, 1869, by Rev. John Winkley, Lavina Thompson, of Barrington.

EVANS, James T., m. July 24, 1873, in Great Falls, Sarah A. Moulton.

FABYAN, John, of Newington, son of Samuel, b. Sept. 2, 1787, d. Jan. 27, 1871, m. Dec. 8, 1811, Catherine Dennett, b. June 25, 1788, d. May 3, 1872, dau. of Jeremiah.

FALL, John, of Berwick, Me., son of Philip, m. Oct. 26, 1710, in Berwick, Me., Judith Heard, dau. of Samuel.

FALL, Tristram, d. Mar. 23, 1854, aged 78, m. Aug. 8, 1796, by Rev. Matthew Merriam, Anna Lord, b. 1778, d. 1853, dau. of Humphrey.

FALL, Daniel, of Lee, m. int. May 19, 1833, in Lee, Eleanor Ham, of Newmarket.

FALL, Ivory, Jr., m. (pub. Oct. 13, 1845, in Lebanon, Me.), Abby Fernald, d. Nov. 24, 1894, aged 75, dau. of James.

FALL, John J., m. July 6, 1865, in Dover, Sarah Carlton.

FALL, Frank, d. June 30, 1873, aged 25, m. Sept. 10, 1868, in Dover, Emma Ricker.

FARNHAM, Paul, m. June 10, 1753, by Rev. Amos Main, Elizabeth Door.

FARNHAM, Ira, of Shapleigh, Me., b. Mar. 26, 1806, d. May 5, 1882, m. Apr. 2, 1827, in Wakefield, Sally Rogers, of Wakefield, b. Dec. 9, 1805, d. Jan. 18, 1883.

FARNHAM, Samuel W., m. Dec. 8, 1847, by Rev. Charles Chamberlain, Mary Jane C. Bunker, dau. of James.

FARNHAM, Ezra, son of John, b. Oct. 10, 1831, d. July 26, 1884, m. June 3, 1855, in Acton, Me., Harriet A. Hubbard, b. Jan. 18, 1837, d. Mar. 10, 1829, both of Acton, Me.

FARNHAM, John, m. Sept. 19, 1867, by Rev. James Drummond, Jane Farrell.

FARNHAM, Henry C., m. Feb. 20, 1869, in Dover, Lizzie S. Merrill.

FARNSWORTH, N. H., m. Nov. 30, 1864, in Dover, Hannah L. Kimball.

FARR, John, m. Dec. 1, 1869, in Dover, Clara J. Peaslee.

FARRAR, Jonathan, m. June 5, 1792, by Rev. Isaac Smith, Molly Folsom.

FARRINGTON, Dr. James, of Conway, son of Jeremiah, b. Oct. 1791, d. Oct. 29, 1859, m. Mar. 8, 1827, by Rev. Isaac Willey, Mary Dame Hanson, b. Apr. 23, 1800, d. Apr. 25, 1853, dau. of Joseph.

FARRINGTON, Dr. James, Jr., son of Elijah, m. Feb. 25, 1851, in Rochester, Harriet Louise Chase, dau. of Simon.
FARRINGTON, James C., of Fryeburg, Me., b. 1834, m. int. Jan. 31, 1856, Julia York, of Lee, b. 1838.
FAXON, Charles A., son of Ebenezer, d. Nov. 7, 1910, aged 70, m. July 8, 1866, in Dover, Ellen A. Ham.
FAXON, Eben F., m. Apr. 16, 1871, in Dover, Annie Young.
FELKER, Andrew Jackson, son of Levi, b. May 21, 1830, d. Mar. 2, 1920, aged 89, m. (pub. Nov. 7, 1854, in Barrington), Lydia Ann Seavey, b. Oct. 26, 1835, d. July 12, 1902, dau. of William H., both of Barrington.
FELKER, Levi W., son of Levi, b. Sept. 30, 1839, d. Aug. 18, 1869, m. Sept. 13, 1859, Martha H. Twombly, b. Apr. 24, 1841, d. Dec. 31, 1910, both of Barrington.
FELKER, S. Francis, m. June 29, 1867, by Rev. Robert S. Stubbs, Jennie L. Tibbetts.
FELLOWS, Joseph, of Vasselboro, Me., m. Sept. 18, 1788, by Rev. Isaac Smith, Molly Clark, of Gilmanton.
FELLOWS, Michael, m. Mar. 12, 1837, Mary Underwood Hill, b. Oct. 28, 1805, d. May 25, 1893, dau. of David.
FELLOWS, Edward H., m. Jan. 6, 1866, in Dover, Mary Shearden.
FELLOWS, William, m. Dec. 3, 1868, in Dover, Fannie M. C. Perkins.
FELLOWS, James, m. June 12, 1874, by Rev. Asa Piper, Mary A. Pike, both of Wakefield.
FENDERSON, Nathaniel H., m. Jan. 30, 1865, in Dover, Louise D. Harmon.
FENNER, Benjamin W., m. May 20, 1869, in Dover, Azella A. Vickery.
FERGUSON, Charles P., m. Feb. 8, 1864, in Dover, Mary A. Chase.
FERNALD, Amos, m. int. Sept. 23, 1829, in Lee, Deborah Allen, both of Lee.
FERNALD, John H., m. June 6, 1830, in Eliot, Me., Polly Cole.
FERNALD, John E., of Nottingham, b. Dec. 23, 1823, d. May 1, 1895, m. (pub. Apr. 7, 1859, in Nottingham), of Lee, Sarah A. F. Thompson, of Lee, b. Dec. 12, 1833, d. Dec. 14, 1917.
FERNALD, Isaac, b. 1809, m. int. June 25, 1864, in Lee, Mrs. Nancy Drew, b. 1841, both of Lee.
FERNALD, William H. H., son of William H. K., b. Mar. 1842, d. June 4, 1885, m. Aug. 11, 1864, by Rev. James Rank, Laura Isabelle Canney, b. Mar. 29, 1843, d. Nov. 24, 1935, dau. of George.
FERNALD, John W., m. Jan. 1, 1869, by Rev. Robert S. Stubbs, Viola Jackson.

FERNALD, Edwin L., m. Mar. 24, 1869, in Dover, Ella Adelia Jones, d. Aug. 21, 1913, aged 62, dau. of Ephraim M.
FIFIELD, Charles N., m. int. Sept. 23, 1838, in Dover, Betsey N. Nutter, d. Feb. 8, 1911, aged 93, dau. of John H.
FINNEGAN, James, m. Oct. 27, 1865, by Rev. James Drummond, Bridget (Canavan) Nute, wid. of Lemuel F., b. Apr. 1837, d. June 2, 1891, dau. of Matthew.
FISH, Ira, son of John, m. Nov. 11, 1813, by Rev. Joseph Boodey, Louisa Twombley, b. Dec. 6, 1792, d. Dec. 1816, both of Milton.
FISH, Jacob, son of John, b. Apr. 20, 1805, d. Mar. 1, 1850, aged 47, m. Nov. 12, 1826, Sally Canney, b. May 30, 1806, dau. of Joseph.
FISHER, Col. Janvrin, d. Sept. 27, 1798, of Yellow Fever, m. May 25, 1786, at Rochester, Sarah Gage, b. 1764, d. July 6, 1795, dau. of Capt. John.
FISHER, Samuel C., of Francistown, son of Matthew, b. Nov. 29, 1822, d. July 10, 1909, m. (1) Nov. 11, 1847, by Rev. William P. Tilden, Mary Elizabeth Barnes, b. Sept. 16, 1826, d. Nov. 29, 1852, dau. of Benjamin, m. (2) Sarah J. Christie, b. Mar. 27, 1830, d. Feb. 2, 1898, dau. of Daniel M., m. (3) Apr. 15, 1899, in Dover, Emily Bacon.
FISHER, Erastus E., m. Dec. 13, 1865, in Dover, Sarah E. Place.
FISHLEY, George, Jr., of Portsmouth, m. (pub. Sept. 18, 1829, in Somersworth), Keziah Nason, of S. Berwick, Me.
FISKE, Jonathan, of Dover, m. Sept. 1824, in Newbury, Mass., Eliza Morse, of Newburyport, Mass.
FITZGERALD, Daniel, of Limerick, Me., m. June 17, 1790, by Rev. Isaac Smith, Nancy Clark, of Gilmanton.
FLAGG, Jonathan, b. 1772, d. Mar. 3, 1849, m. Jan. 25, 1791, by Rev. Joseph Haven, Mary Ham, b. 1772, d. Jan. 7, 1849, dau. of Aaron, both of Rochester.
FLAGG, Levi, of Alton, m. Oct. 9, 1801, by Rev. Isaac Smith, Sarah Odlin, of Gilmanton.
FLAGG, William, m. Jan. 16, 1862, in Dover, Eveline Bickford.
FLAGG, Joshua G., son of William, d. Apr. 3, 1907, aged 72, m. Dec. 18, 1862, in Dover, Emily C. Hussey, d. Aug. 21, 1909, aged 72, dau. of Moses.
FLANDERS, Thomas, m. Jan. 17, 1776, by Rev. Isaac Smith, Eunice Eastman.
FLANDERS, Thomas Jr., m. July 3, 1777, by Rev. Isaac Smith, Katharine Philbrick.
FLANDERS, Joseph, m. Mar. 6, 1781, by Rev. Isaac Smith, Hannah Hutchinson.

FLANDERS, Richard, of New Durham Gore, m. Feb. 10, 1791, in Gilmanton, by Rev. Isaac Smith, Eleanor Page, of Gilmanton.
FLANDERS, Joseph, m. Sept. 24, 1815, by Rev. Isaac Smith, Sophia Hall, both of Gilmanton.
FLANDERS, Dr. Thomas, of Lee, m. int. May 10, 1823, in Lee, Anna Hilliard, of Cambridge, Mass.
FLANDERS, Rev. John, m. in 1825, by Rev. William Demeritt, Mary McNeal.
FLANDERS, Stephen B., son of Ezekiel, d. July 29, 1902, aged 76, m. (pub. Aug. 3, 1847, in Gilmanton), Lydia A. Dickey.
FLANDERS, Ira M., m. Nov. 10, 1850, in Gilmanton, Sarah H. Plummer.
FLETCHER, Wesley H., m. Sept. 10, 1870, in Dover, Nellie M. Peck.
FLOWERS, Frederick, m. May 22, 1869, in Dover, Mary Simmons.
FLYNN, Michael, m. Nov. 28, 1867, by Rev. Robert S. Stubbs, Mary Fife.
4) **FOGG**, James, b. June 23, 1721, d. 1805, m. (1) Sept. 23, 1756, in Kittery, Me., Anne Remick, b. July 17, 1738, d. Apr. 1783, dau. of Isaac, m. (2) July 18, 1793, in Berwick, Me., Mercy (Horne) Twombly, wid. of Ezekiel, b. Aug. 17, 1748, d. Mar. 5, 1837, aged 88, dau. of John.
FOGG, James, b. 1732, d. 1805, m. int. May 14, 1793, in N. Berwick, Me., Mercy (Horne) Twombley, wid. of Ezekiel, b. Aug. 17, 1848, d. May 27, 1804, dau. of John.
FOGG, Jonathan, of Lee, m. int. Oct. 11, 1823, in Lee, Eunice Batchelder, of Kensington.
FOGG, John, of Newfields, m. (pub. May 29, 1838, in Durham), Betsey Clough, b. Dec. 23, 1810, d. Mar. 4, 1860, dau. of William.
FOGG, George, m. Nov. 18, 1854, by Elder Israel Chesley, Lydia A. Bennett, both of Nottingham.
FOGG, John W., m. Dec. 9, 1865, in Dover, Eliza J. Brown.
FOLLET, Samuel, of Lee, m. Aug. 19, 1804, Peggy Bickford, of Durham, b. Nov. 11, 1785, dau. of Samuel.
FOLLET, Richard, of Durham, son of John, b. May 6, 1815, m. June 20, 1850, by Elder Samuel Sherburne, Martha J. Hoitt, of Dover.
FOLSOM, Thomas, b. May 11, 1769, m. Aug. 1797, Edner Ela.
FOLSOM, Gilman, d. Oct. 23, 1860, aged 73, m. Feb. 15, 1815, in Wolfeboro, Mary Rust, d. Mar. 27, 1854, aged 64, both of Wolfeboro.
FOLSOM, Deac. John, b. Apr. 30, 1797, d. Apr. 6, 1883, m. Dec. 27, 1820, in Wolfeboro, Hannah Blake, b. Oct. 14, 1797, d. May 2, 1895, both of Wolfeboro.

FOLSOM, Jeremiah, m. Oct. 8, 1834, in Gilford, Eliza Pike, b. June 16, 1810.
FOLSOM, Charles, of Wolfeboro, d. Feb. 3, 1866, aged 53, m. Apr. 12, 1839, in Wolfeboro, Sarah Richards, of Rochester, d. Apr. 2, 1880, aged 67.
FOLSOM, George L., d. June 9, 1915, aged 72, m. Mar. 13, 1867, by Rev. Francis E. Abbott, Nellie E. Otis.
FOOT, George E., m. June 3, 1866, in Dover, Sarah A. Rollins.
5) **FOOTMAN**, Francis, son of Thomas, b. Feb. 15, 1780, d. Apr. 17, 1806, m. July 1802, in Dover, Hannah Varney, d. Jan. 22, 1874, aged 93, dau. of Aaron.
FOOTMAN, Francis, m. (pub. Apr. 7, 1804), Martha Leathers.
5) FOOTMAN, Jonathan Gage, son of Thomas, b. Dec. 29, 1782, died at sea, m. July 9, 1805, at Rochester, Sarah Hodgdon, b. near 1776, d. Mar. 11, 1817, dau. of Caleb.
FORD, Steven S., m. Aug. 22, 1868, in Dover, Abbie Perkins.
FORD, Nathaniel, m. Mar. 17, 1869, by Rev. Robert S. Stubbs, Roxanna A. Hill.
FORD, Daniel, m. Sept. 13, 1869, in Dover, Jane Drew.
FOREMEN, John W., m. Apr. 23, 1870, in Dover, Melissa A. Day.
FORREST, James, m. Oct. 16, 1785, by Rev. Isaac Smith, Anna Ellison, both of Northfield.
FOSS, Jeremiah, b. Aug. 8, 1751, d. Jan. 11, 1835, m. Dec. 8, 1778, by Dr. Belknap, Abra Hayes, both of Barrington.
FOSS, Joshua, of Barrington, d. June 30, 1831, aged 69, m. Mar. 15, 1780, in Strafford, Hannah Blake, d. Oct. 23, 1848, aged 80, of Madbury.
FOSS, Richard, son of George, b. May 15, 1760, d. Mar. 15, 1802, m. Nov. 28, 1782, by Rev. Joseph Haven, Marcy Berry, b. Apr. 10, 1755, d. Oct. 30, 1827.
FOSS, William, son of George, b. May 15, 1760, d. Feb. 3, 1830, m. (1) Apr. 21, 1785, Elizabeth Hayes, b. Aug. 12, 1767, d. Aug. 20, 1806, m. (2) Margaret Babb, d. Oct. 6, 1836, aged 62.
FOSS, Edward, m. Nov. 29, 1785, by Rev. Isaac Smith, Olive Chapman.
FOSS, Samuel, d. Jan. 19, 1826, aged 59, m. Nov. 25, 1789, in Barrington, Betsey Babb, d. Feb. 12, 1871, aged 99, dau. of William.
FOSS, Nathan, d. June 30, 1843, aged 75, m. Mar. 7, 1790, in Barrington, Alice Babb, d. May 20, 1859, aged 90.
FOSS, Daniel, m. May 6, 1802, by Rev. Isaac Smith, Merriam Hewitt.
FOSS, John, of Barrington, m. (pub. Nov. 26, 1803, in Dover), Eliza Titcomb, of Dover.

FOSS, Samuel, d. Sept. 25, 1824, aged 57, m. Judith Hill, b. Nov. 15, 1784, dau. of Andrew.

FOSS, Samuel, 3rd, d. Aug. 1, 1857, aged 76, m. Jan. 3, 1811, Elizabeth Hayes, d. Apr. 2, 1851, aged 60.

FOSS, Benjamin, d. Dec. 30, 1849, aged 58, m. Nov. 3, 1811, by Rev. Moses Cheney, Patience Horn, d. Nov. 2, 1836, aged 43, both of Farmington.

FOSS, John, of Milton, son of Joshua, b. July 25, 1789, d. Jan. 17, 1869, m. Dec. 7, 1815, by Rev. Joseph Haven, Lydia Wingate, of Farmington, b. July 30, 1786, d. Oct. 30, 1862.

FOSS, Nathan, m. in 1818, in Strafford, Abigail Berry, d. Dec. 24, 1836, aged 45.

FOSS, Col. Oliver S., d. Oct. 4, 1841, aged 41, m. (pub. Sept. 26, 1820, in Dover), Sarah Ann Sawyer, b. Oct. 17, 1802, d. Nov. 4, 1830, dau. of Jacob.

FOSS, Taylor, of Strafford, m. int. June 2, 1821, in Lee, Betsey Bodge, of Lee.

FOSS, Israel, Jr., of Strafford, d. Mar. 31, 1879, aged 79, m. Feb. 17, 1824, by Elder Enoch Place, Hannah Thompson, of Barrington, d. Jan. 9, 1827, aged 25.

FOSS, James Babb, son of Nathan, b. Oct. 6, 1795, d. Dec. 1, 1882, m. Apr. 8, 1824, by Elder Enoch Place, Sarah Waldron, b. in 1802, d. Sept. 1, 1884, dau. of Aaron, both of Strafford.

FOSS, John B., b. 1800, d. 1880, m. Aug. 15, 1824, by Elder Enoch Place, Catharine Hill, b. 1800, d. 1880, both of Strafford.

FOSS, Chadbourn, m. Dec. 23, 1824, in Lebanon, Me., Patience Varney.

FOSS, Benjamin T., d. Sept. 11, 1882, aged 79, m. July 12, 1827, by Elder Enoch Place, Sophia G. Jones, b. Nov. 19, 1889, aged 80, dau. of William, both of Strafford.

FOSS, Enos, m. Dec. 30, 1827, by Rev. John Winkley, Sally Berry, d. Mar. 10, 1830, aged 22, both of Strafford.

FOSS, Mark, m. Jan. 3, 1828, by Rev. John Winkley, Samson Foss, b. Oct. 3, 1810, both of Strafford.

FOSS, Lemuel, son of Richard, b. June 28, 1795, d. Jan. 23, 1867, aged 72, m. Dec. 4, 1828, by Elder Enoch Place, Sarah Foss, b. Aug. 9, 1805, d. June 1, 1862, aged 55, both of Strafford.

FOSS, Woodbury M., d. May 7, 1869, aged 65, m. Apr. 5, 1829, by Rev. John Winkley, Eliza Foss, d. June 26, 1887, aged 76, both of Strafford.

FOSS, Solomon, b. 1806, d. 1884, m. Apr. 20, 1829, by Rev. John Winkley, Mary Waterhouse, b. 1807, d. 1885, both of Strafford.

FOSS, Robert W., b. Oct. 27, 1808, d. Sept. 12, 1886, aged 77, m. Jan. 6, 1830, by Elder Enoch Place, Eliza W. Jones, b. May 18, 1810, d. Jan. 11, 1891, dau. of William, both of Strafford.

FOSS, John P., d. Oct. 4, 1890, aged 88, m. Mar. 10, 1831, by Elder Enoch Place, Mahala Welch, d. Dec. 6, 1886, aged 80, both of Dover.

FOSS, Enos Hoag, d. Nov. 25, 1878, m. Mar. 17, 1831, by Elder Enoch Place, Sarah Pearl, d. May 11, 1876, aged 72, both of Strafford.

FOSS, John B., m. Nov. 24, 1832, by Rev. John Winkley, Alice Parshley, both of Strafford.

FOSS, Nathaniel, of Strafford, m. May 2, 1833, by Rev. John Winkley, Esther Tuttle, of Barrington.

FOSS, Richard, m. May 7, 1833, by Rev. John Winkley, Mary Ann Clark, both of Strafford.

FOSS, Elisha, m. May 2, 1834, by Rev. John Winkley, Lydia Foss, d. July 28, 1855, aged 42, both of Strafford.

FOSS, Cotton H., d. Dec. 14, 1896, aged 80, m. Aug. 18, 1836, by Elder Enoch Place, Harriet Foss, d. Mar. 30, 1900, aged 87, dau. of Nathan, both of Strafford.

FOSS, Jacob D., m. Sept. 18, 1837, by Rev. John Winkley, Hannah Foss, both of Boston, Mass.

FOSS, Dennis, d. Aug. 29, 1893, aged 81, m. Dec. 3, 1837, by Elder Enoch Place, Patience Scruton, b. Oct. 1, 1813, d. June 21, 1891, aged 77, dau. of Michael, both of Strafford.

FOSS, Jeremiah J., m. Dec. 20, 1838, by Elder Enoch Place, Martha Hayes, b. June 18, 1801, d. Nov. 21, 1858, both of Strafford.

FOSS, Sylvanus C., d. July 19, 1804, aged 83, m. June 6, 1839, by Elder Enoch Place, Lydia D. Foss, d. Nov. 11, 1887, aged 67, both of Strafford.

FOSS, Warren, d. Jan. 6, 1893, aged 77, m. (pub. Feb. 9, 1841, in Strafford), Deborah Jane Sloper, d. July 5, 1898, aged 79, dau. of William, both of Strafford.

FOSS, Nehemiah, b. July 11, 1818, d. Dec. 19, 1903, aged 85, m. Oct. 3, 1841, by Elder Enoch Place, Sarah Jane Leighton, b. July 24, 1824, d. May 26, 1880, both of Strafford.

FOSS, Leonard B., m. Apr. 20, 1843, Mary Ann Bunker, dau. of John.

FOSS, Thomas C., m. int. Aug. 4, 1844, in Dover, Margaret Ann Sayward, both of Dover.

FOSS, Daniel, m. (1), int. Mar. 2, 1846, in Dover, Sophronia A. Randall, d. Feb. 5, 1856, aged 34, m. (2) Oct. 17, 1856, in Dover, Mary Jane Otis.

FOSS, James J., of Strafford, m. Mar. 23, 1846, by Rev. John -----, Lucinda Smith, of Barrington.

FOSS, Erastus D., d. May 15, 1853, aged 28, m. July 11, 1847, by Elder Enoch Place, Frances Marion Merrill, d. Jan. 15, 1850, aged 22, both of Strafford.

FOSS, Azariah, d. Sept. 20, 1899, aged 78, m. June 18, 1848, in Middleton, Sarah A. Foss, d. June 9, 1909, aged 84, both of Strafford.

FOSS, Benjamin Wingate, son of John, b. Nov. 26, 1820, d. Sept. 13, 1913, aged 92, m. Oct. 23, 1848, by Rev. Homer Barrows, Lavinia Downs, b. Apr. 28, 1827, d. July 30, 1897, dau. of Moses, both of Milton.

FOSS, Aaron Waldron, son of James B., b. 1824, d. Nov. 25, 1910, m. in 1849, Elizabeth O. Caverly, d. Oct. 15, 1906, aged 73, dau. of Rev. John.

FOSS, Samuel M., m. June 1, 1849, in Rochester, Abigail Berry, both of Strafford.

FOSS, William S., son of Samuel, d. Aug. 30, 1922, aged 96, m. Dec. 15, 1849, by Rev. Homer Barrows, Judith Marden, both of Barrington.

FOSS, Joseph O., son of Isaac, d. Jan. 16, 1887, aged 65, m. near 1850, Ariana E. Boodey, d. Aug. 9, 1885, aged 56.

FOSS, James, of Madbury, m. May 17, 1851, by Rev. John Winkley, Eleanor M. Young, of Barnstead.

FOSS, Lorenzo D., b. Dec. 4, 1829, d. June 6, 1910, m. Nov. 27, 1851, by Rev. John Winkley, Emeline Binger, b. Apr. 14, 1826, d. July 15, 1893, both of Somersworth.

FOSS, Richard Waldron, son of James B., d. Oct. 6, 1901, aged 74, m. Nov. 27, 1851, by Elder Enoch Place, Emily Y. Place, d. Sept. 21, 1883, aged 51.

FOSS, Darius, m. (1) Dec. 14, 1851, by Rev. Homer Barrows, Almira N. Goodall, m. (2) Apr. 5, 1894, in Dover, Elmira Perry.

FOSS, John A., m. Feb. 17, 1853, by Elder Elias Hutchins, Hannah J. Bunker, b. July 12, 1834, d. Feb. 9, 1854, aged 19, dau. of William, both of Dover.

FOSS, Ansell, of Strafford, d. June 3, 1868, aged 49, m. (pub. Aug. 9, 1853, in Barrington), Elizabeth Rowe, of Holderness, dau. of John.

FOSS, Drew, b. Sept. 8, 1830, d. Nov. 29, 1919, aged 89, m. (pub. July 11, 1854, in S. Berwick, Me.), Betsey B. Hawkins, b. Sept. 5, 1836, d. Nov. 23, 1909, aged 73, dau. of Andrew, both of Dover.

FOSS, John H., son of Robinson, b. Dec. 9, 1831, m. (1) Sept. 10, 1856, Elizabeth Hannah Felker, b. June 25, 1877, d. Dec. 18,

1862, dau. of John, m. (2) Jan. 21, 1864, Augusta Ann Felker, b. Mar. 7, 1844, d. July 4, 1916, dau. of John.

FOSS, Eliphalet, m. Aug. 12, 1863, by Rev. James Rand, Cynthia D. Rand.

FOSS, Moses W., m. Aug. 7, 1865, in Dover, Ann Prescott.

FOSS, Marshall B., m. June 2, 1868, by Rev. Alden Sherwin, Julia M. Banks.

FOSS, Nathaniel, of Milton, m. Sept. 18, 1868, by Rev. Asa Piper, Mary Ellen Drew, of Brookfield.

FOSS, Edger M., m. Dec. 26, 1868, in Dover, Arabell Whitehouse.

FOSS, Alvah H., m. July 5, 1869, by Rev. Ezra Haskell, Philena Wentworth.

FOSS, Enos George, m. June 16, 1870, in Dover, Sarah J. Wood.

FOSS, Horace N., m. Jan. 2, 1871, in Dover, Nellie N. Faxon.

FOSS, John N., m. Feb. 20, 1871, in Dover, Sarah E. Davis.

FOSS, James H., of Barrington, m. Apr. 17, 1874, in Dover, Mrs. Lucretia W. Dill, of Rochester.

FOSS, Sampson B., m. Oct. 2, 1875, in Rochester, Martha J. England.

FOSTER, David C., d. Oct. 20, 1823, aged 31, m. (pub. Sept. 9, 1815, in Portsmouth), Lucy Maria French.

FOSTER, Rev. J. C., m. May 1, 1866, in Dover, Julia A. Gould.

FOSTER, Caleb C., son of Moses B., d. July 4, 1914, aged 77, m. July 14, 1869, in Dover, Mary Anna Flanders.

FOSTER, Albert S., m. Dec. 17, 1870, in Dover, Jane W. Perkins.

FOWLER, Jeremiah, son of John, b. Sept. 5, 1822, d. Jan. 24, 1889, m. near 1849, Lucy Brown.

FOWLER, John F., m. Nov. 19, 1863, in Dover, Dorcas A. Winn.

FOX, George, d. Apr. 22, 1882, aged 75, m. Nov. 9, 1834, in Wolfeboro, Drusilla C. Hersey, d. Nov. 29, 1893, aged 82, dau. of Elijah, both of Wolfeboro.

FOX, Elbridge Wood, son of Asa, d. Apr. 6, 1912, aged 77, m. Nov. 5, 1855, in Milton, Sarah E. Buck, d. May 21, 1914, aged 89, dau. of Reuben.

FOYE, William A., m. June 18, 1868, in Dover, Emily A. Smith.

FOYE, Charles E., m. Dec. 23, 1871, in Rochester, Mary E. Varney.

FREEMAN, Edmund J., m. Aug. 17, 1864, by Rev. Ezra Haskell, Fanny H. Horne.

FREEMAN, Eben C., m. Mar. 13, 1867, by Rev. Ezra Haskell, Adaline Sawyer.

FREEMAN, Charles F., m. Jan. 29, 1869, by Rev. Robert S. Stubbs, Carrie A. Frost.

FREEMAN, Franklin, m. Feb. 17, 1870, in Dover, Jennie Palmer, d. Sept. 16, 1911, aged 77, dau. of Thomas J.

FRENCH, L̲t̲. Thomas, b. May 10, 1738, m. near 1767, Mary Glidden, b. Mar. 23, 1736.

FRENCH, Edward, m. Feb. 10, 1791, by Rev. Isaac Smith, Rebecca Avery, both of Gilmanton.

FRENCH, Ebenezer, b. 1774, d. Nov. 26, 1824, m. Nov. 13, 1796, by Rev. Joseph Haven, Abigail Walker, b̲. 1772, d̲. Sept. 10, 1842, dau. of Richard, both of Rochester.

FRENCH, John, m. Jan. 18, 1816, by Rev. Isaac Smith, Lucy Prescott.

FRENCH, Samuel, m. int. Apr. 29, 1833, in Lee, Eliza Glover, both of Lee.

FRENCH, George W., Jr., m. July 9, 1865, in Dover, Lizzie J. French.

FRENCH, Charles, of Newfield, Me., m. Nov. 28, 1866, by Rev. Asa Piper, Sarah A. Wood.

FRENCH, Samuel D., m. Nov. 23, 1869, in Dover, Carrie G. Stilson.

FRIAS, Alfred, b. Aug. 29, 1844, d. June 16, 1892, m. June 10, 1868, by Rev. Robert S. Stubbs, Louisa Bunce, b. Oct. 23, 1849, d. July 23, 1912, dau. of Charles.

FROST, Mark, b̲. Oct. 1749, d̲. Oct. 5, 1835, m. Sept. 25, 1770, by Rev. Matthew Merriam, Hannah Horsum.

FROST, Eliot, b̲. Dec. 25, 1760, d̲. Jan. 15, 1849, m. July 20, 1786, by Rev. Matthew Merriam, Jane Clark, both of Kittery, Me.

FROST, Reuben, m. May 12, 1833, in Eliot, Me., Eliza Ann Cole.

FROST, Joseph A., m. Feb. 26, 1862, in Dover, Della P. Alvord.

FROST, Marcellus, m. Nov. 25, 1863, in Dover, Susan M. Tuttle.

FROST, Samuel B., m. May 24, 1864, in Dover, Annie L. Chase.

FROST, Leonard F., m. Jan. 20, 1868, in Dover, Esther Grant.

FROST, George S., d. May 7, 1931, aged 86, m. Dec. 6, 1870, in Dover, Martha Hale Lowe, d. Sept. 20, 1925, aged 84, dau. of Nathaniel.

FROST, Edgar A., m. (pub. Dec. 18, 1873, in Dover), Ellen G. Hayes, both of Dover.

FRYE, Sylvester, of Eliot, Me., son of Tobias, d. Feb. 19, 1895, aged 64, m. (pub. July 10, 1856, in Somersworth), Sarah Elizabeth Wakefield, d̲. Apr. 27, 1896, aged 59, dau. of Archibald.

FRYE, Russell E., m. Oct. 10, 1867, by Rev. Robert S. Stubbs, Mary S. Gilmore.

FRYE, Joseph W., m. Dec. 2, 1869, in Dover, Carrie J. Locke.

FULLERTON, John, d̲. Feb. 26, 1803, aged 53, m. Dec. 3, 1781, by Rev. Jeremiah Shaw, Anna H. Gould, d̲. Feb. 10, 1835, both of Wolfeboro.

FULLERTON, Andrew J., d. Oct. 1856, aged 37, m. Jan. 31, 1850, in Wolfeboro, Mary Getchell, b̲. 1818, d̲. 1902.

FURBER, Deac. Benjamin, d. Apr. 8, 1822, aged 70, m. Dec. 18, 1777, by Rev. Joseph Haven, Deborah Tibbetts, b. May 12, 1751, dau. of Edward.

FURBER, Theodore, d. May 5, 1859, aged 80, m. Feb. 16, 1809, by Rev. Joseph Haven, Abigail Walker, d. Dec. 1, 1860, aged 87, both of Farmington.

FURBER, John, d. May 21, 1844, aged 73, m. Mar. 13, 1816, by Rev. John Osborne, Comfort Tuttle, d. Oct. 24, 1830, aged 43.

FURBER, John F., m. (pub. Feb. 14, 1826, in Farmington), Mercy Varney.

FURBER, Daniel, d. July 11, 1893, aged 77, m. int. June 12, 1836, in Lee, Elizabeth J. Burley, b. May 27, 1816, d. May 3, 1903, both of Lee.

FURBER, Benjamin F., of Alton, son of Edward, d. Sept. 8, 1904, aged 82, m. June 4, 1853, in Dover, Sarah J. Babb, of Dover, dau. of Benjamin F.

FURBISH, Abraham, m. Dec. 4, 1766, in S. Berwick, Me., Anne Chick.

FURBUSH, Samuel, m. Jan. 5, 1764, in S. Berwick, Me., Sarah Guptill.

FURNESS, Edward, son of Edward, b. Sept. 16, 1819, m. (pub. Dec. 9, 1845, in Lee), Lucinda Stevens, both of Durham.

FURNESS, William P., of Durham, son of Edward, b. May 24, 1817, m. (pub. Dec. 23, 1845, in Haverhill, Mass.), Abby C. Choate.

2) **GAGE**, William, m. Oct. 6, 1748, by Rev. Amos Main, Mary Conner, both of Dover.

2) GAGE, Jonathan, b. 1734, d. Oct. 14, 1800, m. Mar. 29, 1759, by Rev. Jona. Cushing, Rebecca Hanson, b. Dec. 28, 1739, d. Mar. 30, 1806, dau. of Joseph.

3) GAGE, Joseph, son of Moses, d. Apr. 7, 1802, aged 37, m. (1) Oct. 1798, in Dover, Polly Wingate, d. May 26, 1799, aged 31, dau. of Joshua, m. (2) Esther Copp, dau. of David.

GAGE, Moses N., m. Oct. 15, 1870, in Dover, Sarah J. Lucas.

GALE, Jacob, m. Apr. 5, 1787, by Rev. Isaac Smith, Molly Rowell, both of Gilmanton.

GALE, Joseph, m. Apr. 16, 1789, by Rev. Isaac Smith, Sarah Smith, both of Gilmanton.

GALE, Daniel Jr., m. Aug. 5, 1790, by Rev. Isaac Smith, Dolly Smith, both of Gilmanton.

GALE, William, m. Apr. 29, 1865, in Dover, Emma T. Salmon.

GALE, Fernando, m. Nov. 7, 1865, in Dover, Lydia R. Wallingford.

GALLIGAN, James, m. Mar. 1, 1869, by Rev. Robert S. Stubbs, Isadore V. Nute.

GARDNER, John, 2nd, m. Apr. 29, 1849, in Rye, Emeline Locke, d. Mar. 22, 1897, aged 69, dau. of John, both of Portsmouth.

GARDNER, Charles B., m. Jan. 16, 1868, in Dover, Mary N. Tucker.

GARDNER, James A., m. Jan. 13, 1869, by Rev. Francis E. Abbott, Alta A. Moulton.

3) **GARLAND**, John, of Barrington, d. Oct. 1801, aged 83, m. Elizabeth Downs, b. July 25, 1714, dau. of Thomas[3].

GARLAND, James, son of Gideon, b. Aug. 21, 1772, d. Dec. 27, 1881, m. in 1805, by Rev. John Osborne, Polly Mills, of Durham, d. Jan. 31, 1872, aged 86.

GARLAND, Daniel H., of Durham, m. (pub. Nov. 20, 1849, in Newmarket), Eliza Tufts, of Newmarket.

GARLAND, Hiram, d. Nov. 18, 1880, aged 84, m. (pub. Feb. 19, 1850, in Somersworth), Sarah Knox. (Was this a second marriage?)

GARLAND, Jacob D., son of Alfred, d. Sept. 22, 1897, aged 66, m. (1) (pub. Apr. 20, 1852, in Farmington), Caroline W. Hamlin, of Somersworth, m. (2) Jan. 10, 1855, in Rochester, Anne A. Pinkham, of Farmington.

GARLAND, John W., m. Apr. 4, 1867, by Rev. James Rand, Olive J. Leighton.

GARMON, Joseph Jr., m. Nov. 23, 1794, by Rev. Isaac Smith, Sarah Hook, both of Gilmanton.

GARMON, Porter, m. Apr. 14, 1814, by Rev. Isaac Smith, Harriet Conner.

GASKILL, Thomas, of Newburyport, Mass., m. May 8, 1857, Martha Murray Grover, b. May 29, 1829, d. Dec. 17, 1872, dau. of Henry.

GEAR, Samuel, d. before 1733, m. Jan. 7, 1724/25, Abigail Hodgdon.

GEAR, Benjamin, m. Dec. 29, 1831, by Rev. Samuel Sherburne, Deborah Doe, dau. of Francis, both of Dover.

GEAR, Samuel, son of George, b. 1816, d. Oct. 22, 1896, m. June 1839, by Rev. Samuel Sherburne, Sally Brown, d. Apr. 6, 1883, aged 68, both of Barrington.

GEAR, James, of Lee, m. int. Mar. 31, 1843, in Lee, Abigail Watson, of Barrington.

GENSALOR, Manuel J., m. Sept. 23, 1865, in Dover, Abbie M. Palmer.

GERRISH, Timothy, m. Jan. 27, 1791, by Rev. Joseph Haven, Elizabeth Spencer, d. Oct. 15, 1850, aged 89, both of Rochester.

GERRISH, Paul, of Nottingham, d. Aug. 21, 1829, aged 59, m. Dec. 25, 1803, by Rev. John Osborne, Mary Drew, of Madbury.

GERRISH, John, of Northwood, m. (pub. Nov. 22, 1825, by Rev. John Osborne), Sally Lucy, of Nottingham.

GERRISH, George, d. Dec. 9, 1878, aged 78, m. (1) near 1829, in Mass., Ann Damon, b. Feb. 4, 1804, d. July 8, 1849, m. (2) July 5, 1851, Adah Knox, b. 1810, d. July 19, 1886, dau. of Samuel.

GERRISH, Josiah W., son of Nathaniel, d. June 13, 1903, aged 78, m. May 7, 1848, in Acton, Me., Susan R. Sanborn, d. Sept. 2, 1891, aged 70, dau. of Elisha.

GERRISH, Enoch, of Boscawen, m. int. Mar. 21, 1854, in Lee, Miranda O. Merrill, of Lee.

GERRISH, Daniel W., of Nottingham, d. Apr. 22, 1882, aged 60, m. (pub. Dec. 23, 1858, in Lee), Louisa W. Demeritt, of Lee.

GERRISH, Aurin J., m. Nov. 8, 1867, by Rev. Alden Sherwin, Josephine S. Jenness.

GERRY, Morgan L., of Alfred, Me., son of Gen. Ebenezer, m. Mar. 16, 1826, in Middleton, Rebecca F. Knight, of Meredith.

GIBBS, John F., of Dover, b. Jan. 22, 1830, d. Aug. 4, 1907, m. (1) int. July 14, 1852, in Dover, Temperance Thurlin, m. (2) June 7, 1862, in Dover, Nancy C. Knight, b. Jan. 11, 1838, d. Aug. 13, 1913.

GILE, Joseph A., m. Dec. 10, 1848, in Lee, Harriet B. Chandler, both of Andover, Mass.

GILES, Joseph, m. June 5, 1793, by Rev. Isaac Smith, Deliverance Clark, both of Gilmanton.

GILES, Paul, Jr., b. Nov. 29, 1812, d. Jan. 16, 1855, aged 63, m. in 1842, by Rev. John Osborne, Sarah Randall, of Lee, b. Mar. 27, 1818, d. 1879, aged 89, dau. of Job.

GILES, John, d. Sept. 1857, aged 41, m. Nov. 7, 1844, Hannah Emerson, b. Aug. 20, 1823, d. Sept. 5, 1868.

GILMAN, Nicholas, m. Mar. 12, 1760, in Gilmanton, Judith Piper.

GILMAN, Samuel, m. Dec. 28, 1775, by Rev. Isaac Smith, Alice Gilman.

GILMAN, Jonathan Jr., m. July 22, 1776, by Rev. Isaac Smith, Kezia Spokefield.

GILMAN, Jonathan, m. Aug. 28, 1777, by Rev. Isaac Smith, Elizabeth Colbey.

GILMAN, Col. David, of Newmarket, b. June 9, 1735, d. May 9, 1827, m. (1) Betsey -----, m. (2) July 21, 1778, by Rev. Nathaniel Ewer, Sarah (Smith) Hilton, wid. of Lt. Winthrop, dau. of Col. Joseph, m. (3) Betsey Ayer, widow.

GILMAN, John Jr., m. Mar. 20, 1780, by Rev. Isaac Smith, Hannah Weeks.

GILMAN, Ezekiel, m. July 15, 1784, by Rev. Isaac Smith, Betty Tilton, both of Gilmanton.

GILMAN, Zebulon, m. Sept. 15, 1785, by Rev. Isaac Smith, Betty Philbrick, both of Gilmanton.

GILMAN, Andrew, m. Nov. 20, 1785, by Rev. Isaac Smith, Elaine Folsom.
GILMAN, Daniel Jr., m. June 16, 1788, by Rev. Isaac Smith, Sarah Richardson, both of Gilmanton.
GILMAN, John 3rd, m. May 13, 1790, by Rev. Isaac Smith, Betty Smith, both of Gilmanton.
GILMAN, Josiah, m. Nov. 8, 1796, by Rev. Isaac Smith, Mary Page, both of Gilmanton.
GILMAN, Cotton, m. Dec. 4, 1798, by Rev. Isaac Smith, Deborah Ross, both of Gilmanton.
GILMAN, Samuel 3rd, m. July 7, 1799, by Rev. Isaac Smith, Lois Shepard, both of Gilmanton.
GILMAN, Israel, b. June 16, 1775, d. May 14, 1836, m. (1) June 9, 1800, in Tamworth, Susan Gilman, both of Tamworth, m. (2) June 1803, by Rev. Jeremiah Shaw, Betsey Morse, of Moultonboro.
GILMAN, Samuel 4th, m. Jan. 19, 1802, by Rev. Isaac Smith, Sally Jones, both of Gilmanton.
GILMAN, Nathaniel, m. Oct. 15, 1807, by Rev. Isaac Smith, Mary Mootrey (?), both of Gilmanton.
GILMAN, Ebenezer, m. Feb. 16, 1809, by Rev. Isaac Smith, Betsy Gilman, both of Gilmanton.
GILMAN, Samuel 5th, m. Mar. 16, 1809, by Rev. Isaac Smith, Betsy Thing, both of Gilmanton.
GILMAN, Theodore, of Wakefield, son of John, d. Nov. 27, 1857, aged 73, m. Jan. 15, 1810, by Rev. Joseph Haven, Mehitable Richards, of Rochester, b. 1784, d. 1868.
GILMAN, Stephen, of Alton, m. Sept. 30, 1811, by Rev. Isaac Smith, Mary S. Gale, of Gilmanton.
GILMAN, John, m. Dec. 24, 1812, by Rev. Isaac Smith, Mary Kelley.
GILMAN, Nicholas Jr., m. Nov. 1, 1813, by Rev. Isaac Smith, Polly Gilman.
GILMAN, James B., d. May 2, 1875, aged 77, m. int. Jan. 1823, in Tuftonboro, Clarissa H. Hersey, d. Mar. 28, 1852, aged 47, dau. of Samuel, both of Tuftonboro.
GILMAN, Andrew J., b. 1799, d. 1847, m. July 19, 1826, in Wakefield, Dolly Pike, of Wakefield, b. Apr. 5, 1802, d. 1886, dau. of Joseph.
GILMAN, Samuel E. P., son of Andrew P., d. June 6, 1916, aged 83, m. (pub. Dec. 18, 1856, in Alton), Nancy J. Cooper, d. Mar. 3, 1890, aged 53, dau. of Moses.
GILMAN, James A., m. May 14, 1867, by Rev. James Rand, Abby H. Hodgdon.
GILMAN, Joseph W., m. Nov. 8, 1869, in Dover, Martha A. Gale.

GILPATRICK, John, b. 1805, d. Mar. 13, 1890, m. Sept. 9, 1835, in Dover, by Rev. Daniel P. Cill, Abigail Young, d. May 1847, aged 33, dau. of John.

GILPATRICK, Otis F., of Limerick, Me., m. Nov. 14, 1874, by Rev. Asa Piper, Rosebell Perkins, of Great Falls.

GLIDDEN, Robert, m. Apr. 19, 1775, by Rev. Isaac Smith, Phebe Hinkson.

GLIDDEN, Phineas, of Gilmanton Gore, m. Dec. 17, 1782, by Rev. Isaac Smith, in Gilmanton, Elizabeth Page, of Gilmanton.

GLIDDEN, Caleb, m. Nov. 16, 1798, by Rev. Isaac Smith, Dolly Gilman, both of Gilmanton.

GLIDDEN, Deac. Guy, of Lee, b. 1800, d. 1880, m. int. Jan. 5, 1833, in Lee, Rebecca Sanborn, of Kingston, b. 1804, d. 1885.

GLIDDEN, John, of Alton, b. Nov. 1, 1817, m. Oct. 9, 1839, Mehitable Bunker, b. Feb. 12, 1812, dau. of Zechariah.

GLIDDEN, Joseph Francis, m. Jan. 15, 1840, Mary Jane Fields, b. Oct. 17, 1819, d. Jan. 30, 1876, dau. of John.

GLIDDEN, David S., of Lee, m. int. Jan. 18, 1845, in Lee, Charlotte M. Dearborn, of Lowell, Mass.

GLIDDEN, Levi, m. (pub. July 14, 1846, in Wolfeboro), Livona Dore, d. June 8, 1912, dau. of Henry, both of Alton.

GLIDDEN, Levi, son of Benjamin, d. Apr. 9, 1902, aged 79, m. (pub. Oct. 26, 1847, in Alton), Emily Coleman.

GLIDDEN, Noah, of Gilford, son of Noah, d. Mar. 30, 1913, aged 83, m. (pub. Apr. 18, 1848, in Alton), Mrs. Susanna Glidden, of Alton.

GLIDDEN, John H., d. Aug. 1884, aged 60, m. (1) (pub. Jan. 27, 1852, in Great Falls), Sarah Grant, d. Apr. 7, 1856, aged 30, m. (2) Nov. 14, 1857, in Milton, Sophronia W. Wing, both of Somersworth.

GLIDDEN, Isaac, son of Elijah, b. Feb. 4, 1830, d. Apr. 12, 1887, m. (pub. Feb. 15, 1853, in Somersworth), Experience D. Brackett, b. Apr. 27, 1832, d. Aug. 25, 1883, both of Berwick, Me.

GLIDDEN, James Jr., b. July 23, 1825, d. July 13, 1882, m. July 26, 1856, by Elder Elias Hutchins, Elizabeth J. Durgin, b. Dec. 29, 1837, d. July 6, 1899, both of Lee.

GLIDDEN, Howard M., of Lee, b. 1842, m. int. Dec. 1865, in Lee, Mabelle F. Wiggin, of Durham, b. 1845.

GLIDDEN, Henry S., m. Apr. 4, 1866, in Dover, Ella Walker.

GLIDDEN, David, of Gilmanton, m. Mar. 27, 1869, by Rev. Asa Piper, Mary T. Gilman, of Acton, Me.

GLIDDEN, Charles R., m. Feb. 26, 1870, in Dover, Mary A. Knights.

GLINES, Nathaniel S., d. May 2, 1872, aged 83, m. (1) Nov. 18, 1810, by Rev. Jeremiah Shaw, Elizabeth Richardson, d. Jan. 10,

1863, aged 75, m. (2) Aug. 14, 1863, by Rev. L. D. Hall, Sabra (Stackpole) Leigh, wid. of Thomas, d. Mar. 26, 1889, aged 65, dau. of Capt. Tobias.

GLINES, Asa, d. Sept. 30, 1882, aged 84, m. Aug. 7, 1825, by Rev. Jeremiah Shaw, Deborah Leonard, d. Feb. 19, 1869, aged 69.

GLINES, Capt. Nathaniel S., son of Nathaniel S., b. June 19, 1821, d. Aug. 22, 1876, m. int. Aug. 7, 1842, in Dover, Mary M. Lucas, b. Feb. 25, 1822, d. Mar. 26, 1886.

GLINES, Benjamin M., of Eaton, m. Feb. 3, 1866, by Rev. Asa Piper, Anna S. Rand, of Wakefield.

GLOVER, William P., b. Oct. 14, 1820, d. June 8, 1859, m. near 1841, Mary A. Lamos, b. May 10, 1825.

GLOVER, John, m. Sept. 20, 1841, in Lee, Betsey Lamos, both of Lee.

GLOVER, Thomas, m. Aug. 11, 1849, in Lee, Sarah Leathers, both of Lee.

GLOVER, Enoch, of Lee, b. near 1840, m. Feb. 27, 1868, in Lee, Mrs. Sarah E. Kenniston, of Nottingham, b. near 1830.

GOFF, William F., m. int. Nov. 1863, in Lee, Mary E. Burnham, b. 1843, both of Lee.

GOLDSMITH, Joshua, of Ossipee, son of William, m. Feb. 7, 1833, in Wolfeboro, Sally Haines, of Wolfeboro, d. Oct. 1877, aged 87, dau. of Joseph.

GOLDSMITH, William F., son of William, b. Feb. 18, 1829, d. Mar. 22, 1911, m. May 4, 1851, in Ossipee, Elizabeth A. Wiggin, b. Feb. 5, 1831, d. Jan. 28, 1912.

GOODRICH, Paul, m. Mar. 26, 1767, in S. Berwick, Me., Mary Guptill, b. July 3, 1754, dau. of Thomas.

3) **GOODWIN**, John, son of William, b. Sept. 2, 1694, m. June 12, 1715, Patience Willowby, b. 1696, dau. of William.

3) GOODWIN, Taylor, son of William, d. Aug. 2, 1773, m. Elizabeth Nason, bpt. Nov. 1, 1713, dau. of Benjamin.

4) GOODWIN, Cpl. Willowby, son of John, d. 1775, m. early as 1753, Lydia Knox.

GOODWIN, Thomas, bpt. Apr. 16, 1746, m. Aug. 17, 1769, by Rev. Matthew Merriam, Mehitable Goodwin, dau. of Elisha.

4) GOODWIN, Maj. Jedediah, of Berwick, Me., son of James, b. 1746, d. July 1, 1818, m. Oct. 7, 1771, Hannah Emery, b. 1756, dau. of Joshua.

4) GOODWIN, Ebenezer, son of Aaron, b. Aug. 9, 1747, d. Oct. 20, 1803, m. Dec. 12, 1771, by Rev. Jacob Foster, Abigail Hubbard, d. Oct. 25, 1828, aged 77, dau. of Philip.

5) GOODWIN, Jeremiah, son of Elisha, m. May 9, 1775, Mary Remick, b. Oct. 9, 1754, d. July 4, 1845, dau. of William.

NEW HAMPSHIRE MARRIAGES SUPPLEMENT

GOODWIN, Ens. James, b. 1754, m. Feb. 1, 1781, by Rev. Isaac Hasey, Sarah Copp.

GOODWIN, Moses, son of Ebenezer, d. May 31, 1838, aged 63, m. Mar. 12, 1795, by Rev. Jonathan Tompson, Sarah Lord, d. Apr. 17, 1861, aged 86.

GOODWIN, William, d. Sept. 12, 1817, m. Feb. 25, 1798, Betsy Chapman, b. Apr. 25, 1772.

GOODWIN, Silas, of Berwick, Me., m. (1) Isabella Bragdon, m. (2) Sept. 1, 1800, by Rev. Joseph Haven, Anna Clements, of Dover.

6) GOODWIN, Capt. Thomas, son of Daniel, b. Nov. 21, 1779, m. Feb. 12, 1804, by Rev. Jonathan Tompson, Sally Lord, d. June 23, 1804, aged 22, dau. of Mark.

GOODWIN, Thomas, Jr., m. (pub. Jan. 19, 1805, in Lebanon, Me.), Nelly Burrows.

5) GOODWIN, Maj. Andrew, son of Gen. Ichabod, d. Nov. 4, 1843, aged 60, m. (1) Dec. 18, 1814, by Rev. Jonathan Tompson, Betsey Tompson, d. June 10, 1817, aged 32, m. (2) Oct. 4, 1818, by Rev. Joseph Hilliard, Betsey Wallingford, of Berwick, Me., b. May 19, 1794, d. May 20, 1874, dau. of John.

GOODWIN, Daniel, Jr., m. Feb. 25, 1815, Kezia Hodgdon, bpt. Oct. 19, 1792, dau. of Thomas.

GOODWIN, Robert, m. Nov. 9, 1825, in Durham, Sarah Stilson, of Durham, b. Sept. 22, 1806, d. Feb. 7, 1843, dau. of William, Jr.

GOODWIN, Ivory, son of Moses, d. June 30, 1868, aged 60, m. Elizabeth Hill, b. May 27, 1811, d. Dec. 7, 1885, dau. of Samuel.

GOODWIN, Richard Hanson, son of Joseph, b. Dec. 1, 1808, m. May 14, 1836, by Rev. David Root, Mary Ann (Roberts) Plummer, wid. of James P., d. Apr. 1, 1859, aged 54

GOODWIN, Elder Lemuel, b. Apr. 7, 1804, d. May 2, 1881, m. (1) Mary -----, d. Oct. 1, 1839, aged 42, m. (2) July 13, 1841, by Rev. Elihu Scott, Ann Downs, b. Dec. 15, 1813, d. May 10, 1884.

GOODWIN, Shepard K., son of Joseph, b. 1822, d. Dec. 31, 1891, m. June 9, 1844, in Wolfeboro, Sophronia Jane Young, b. 1824, d. June 12, 1903, dau. of Isaac, both of Milton.

GOODWIN, Ichabod, son of Maj. Andrew, b. July 9, 1819, d. Dec. 7, 1869, m. Sept. 18, 1850, in S. Berwick, Me., Sophia Elizabeth Hayes, of S. Berwick, Me., b. Sept. 8, 1824, d. Mar. 25, 1905, dau. of William A.

GOODWIN, Jeremiah, m. Mar. 26, 1862, by Rev. James Rand, Esther A. Cooper.

GOODWIN, George M., m. Dec. 5, 1865, in Dover, Hannah Conacker.

GOODWIN, Samuel H., d. Jan. 13, 1918, aged 73, m. Apr. 3, 1866, in Dover, Helen E. Gowen.

GOODWIN, Frederick A., m. Nov. 20, 1866, by Rev. Ezra Haskell, Nellie Booker.
GOODWIN, Albion N., son of Asa, d. June 16, 1910, aged 65, m. Jan. 30, 1867, in Dover, Elma P. Glidden.
GOODWIN, Andrew, m. Dec. 4, 1867, in Dover, Louisa Weaver.
GOODWIN, Horace J., m. Mar. 17, 1869, in Dover, Electra J. Bragdon.
GOODWIN, Simeon, Jr., m. Nov. 12, 1869, in Dover, Mary E. Webster, d. Oct. 14, 1889, aged 43, dau. of Charles.
GOODWIN, Charles E., m. May 2, 1870, in Dover, Sarah F. Fall.
GOODWIN, John A., m. Aug. 13, 1870, in Dover, Abbie M. Tibbetts.
GOODWIN, Orrin, m. Nov. 26, 1873, in Dover, Hannah E. Neal, both of S. Berwick, Me.
GOODWIN, Rufus C., of Wells, Me., m. Dec. 18, 1873, in Dover, Alice I. Libbey.
GORDON, William, m. Dec. 18, 1862, in Dover, Agnes A. Nalty.
GORDON, E. H., Jr., m. Jan. 24, 1864, in Dover, Lucy A. Chapman.
GORDON, Charles C., m. Oct. 9, 1869, in Dover, Nellie G. Percy.
GOSS, Robert, m. Jan. 5, 1793, in Dover, Jane Berry.
GOSS, Cyrus, d. 1867, aged 75, m. Mar. 23, 1824, in Durham, Abigail Ballard, of Durham, b. Aug. 25, 1790, d. Feb. 1862, aged 70, dau. of Joseph.
GOUCH, Moses D., of Alton, m. int. Feb. 12, 1849, in Lee, Ann M. Davis, of Lee.
GOULD, A. M., m. Feb. 12, 1866, by Rev. James Drummond, Alice Mullen.
GOULD, Charles W., of Rollinsford, m. June 6, 1874, in Dover, Eliza A. Goodwin, of Eliot, Me.
GOWELL, John, son of Richard, b. Dec. 25, 1754, m. Dec. 5, 1776, Eleanor Hill, b. May 4, 1757, dau. of Joseph. (moved to Minot, Me.)
GOWELL, Lt. Timothy, d. 1827, aged 41, m. Mar. 24, 1818, by Rev. Joseph Haven, Sarah F. Haven, dau. of Rev. Joseph, both of Rochester.
GOWEN, George, 2nd, m. Jan. 19, 1828, in Lebanon, Me., Anna Abbott, both of Sanford.
GOWEN, Horace, m. (1) July 23, 1865, in Dover, Jennie A. Perkins, m. (2) July 6, 1869, in Dover, Sarah F. Roberts.
GRANT, Landers, b. 1726, d. 1802, m. (1) Sept. 3, 1745, by Rev. Jeremiah Wise, Amy Shorey, dau. of John, m. (2) June 26, 1776, by Rev. Matthew Merriam, Love Davis, dau. of Samuel, both of Berwick, Me.
GRANT, Capt. James, d. May 1826, aged 90, m. (1) Dec. 25, 1760, by Rev. Jacob Foster, Mary Hodsdon, m. (2) Lois -----.

GRANT, Nehemiah, m. Mar. 19, 1770, by Rev. Jacob Foster, Olive Goodwin, b. May 28, 1749, dau. of James.

GRANT, John, of Boston, Mass., b. Sept. 1, 1746, d. Nov. 3, 1825, m. Jan. 8, 1771, by Rev. Jacob Foster, Sarah Wise, dau. of Capt. John.

GRANT, Joshua, b. 1747, d. Nov. 22, 1831, aged 84, m. Apr. 25, 1771, by Rev. Matthew Merriam, Judith Fall, d. Aug. 20, 1825, aged 70.

GRANT, Peter, of Berwick, Me., b. 1757, d. 1836, m. Sept. 10, 1778, by Rev. Matthew Merriam, Elizabeth (Nason) Goodwin, wid. of Taylor, bpt. Nov. 1, 1713, dau. of Benjamin.

GRANT, Edward, b. 1754, m. Nov. 5, 1784, by Rev. Matthew Merriam, Shuah Holmes.

GRANT, Daniel, m. Dec. 8, 1785, by Rev. Isaac Smith, Lydia Bean, both of Gilmanton.

GRANT, Sgt. James, Jr., b. June 17, 1765, d. Aug. 31, 1851, m. July 26, 1792, by Rev. Jonathan Tompson, Patty Shackley.

GRANT, John, m. Apr. 13, 1794, by Rev. Matthew Merriam, Elizabeth Clark, both of Berwick, Me.

GRANT, John Jr., m. (1) Dec. 10, 1817, Suky Jones, d. Dec. 17, 1819, aged 21, m. (2) Mar. 15, 1821, by Elder John Blaisdell, Eunice Jones, d. June 17, 1877.

GRANT, Lucian H., son of Micah, m. (1) May 19, 1866, by Rev. James Rand, Emeline S. Witham, m. (2) Jan. 27, 1893, in Dover, Elizabeth Mullen.

GRANT, Henry, m. Nov. 21, 1867, by Rev. Robert S. Stubbs, Louisa H. Chase.

GRANT, Edward F., m. Feb. 6, 1869, by Rev. Robert S. Stubbs, Sarah Hurd.

GRAVES, Lyford T., m. Sept. 28, 1865, in Dover, Abbie F. Downs.

GRAY, Samuel, b. 1756, d. 1812, m. near 1780, Rebecca Otis, dau. of Stephen, both of Farmington.

GRAY, James, of Strafford, m. near 1797, Polly Twombly, b. 1777, dau. of Joshua.

GRAY, William, of Farmington, m. (pub. Sept. 25, 1813, in Barrington), Polly Gray, of Barrington.

GRAY, Levi L., d. Dec. 13, 1872, aged 65, m. (1) (pub. Nov. 29, 1831, in Strafford), Sally Clark, both of Strafford, d. Nov. 25, 1861, aged 54, m. (2) Aug. 7, 1862, in Rochester, Mrs. Lucy Horne, of Rochester, d. Sept. 27, 1898, aged 84.

GRAY, John, son of Samuel, d. Mar. 30, 1885, aged 85, m. near 1838, Dorothy Otis, d. Mar. 18, 1866, aged 67.

GRAY, Joseph, of Barrington, d. Dec. 24, 1908, aged 91, m. (pub. Dec. 17, 1839, in Rochester), Joan Berry, of Strafford.

GRAY, Ephraim, of Strafford, m. June 21, 1846, in Newmarket, Rebecca Foss, of Newmarket.
GRAY, Dennis, d. Apr. 12, 1908, aged 78, m. (1) int. Dec. 9, 1849, in Dover, Lydia Perkins, d. Nov. 10, 1861, aged 36, both of Dover, m. (2) Mary C. -----, d. Oct. 6, 1896, aged 65.
GRAY, George W., son of James, d. July 2, 1911, aged 74, m. (1) Nov. 29, 1855, in Dover, Laura A. Parker, both of Somersworth, m. (2) Jan. 27, 1894, in Lowell, Mass., Nancie C. Bedell, of Rollinsford.
GRAY, Smith W., son of John, d. July 8, 1910, aged 72, m. Mar. 15, 1862, by Rev. James Rand, Delia A. Tuttle.
GRAY, John W., m. May 9, 1863, in Dover, Addie Warren.
GRAY, Solomon S., m. Mar. 8, 1865, in Dover, Hannah J. Davis.
GRAY, Henry S., m. Oct. 9, 1869, in Dover, Fanny C. Libbey.
GRAY, Solomon S., m. June 6, 1870, in Dover, Sarah M. Randall.
GRAY, Eben T., son of William, d. July 3, 1888, aged 50, m. Jan. 30, 1871, in Rochester, Almira C. Howe.
GRAY, Lorenzo D., m. July 1, 1871, in Rochester, Lydia M. Witham.
GREELEY, Dr. Jonathan, of Dover, m. July 3, 1810, by Rev. Caleb Sherman, Susan Richardson, of Durham, d. June 2, 1812, aged 25, dau. of Capt. Joseph.
GREEN, Jonathan, m. Jan. 17, 1776, by Rev. Isaac Smith, Phebe Sargent.
GREEN, Jonathan, of Moultonboro, son of Nathan, b. 1815, d. Jan. 1, 1881, m. Feb. 22, 1843, Sarah Cuthbert Brackett, of Alton, b. May 1825, d. June 25, 1887, dau. of Benning.
GREEN, Frederick, m. Apr. 9, 1869, in Dover, Mary A. Young.
GREENLEAF, Albert F., son of Joshua, m. (1) Nov. 21, 1866, in Dover, L. F. Hartford, m. (2) June 1, 1890, in Dover, Mrs. Ella J. Blaisdell.
GRIFFIN, John b. June 17, 1782, d. Oct. 27, 1841, aged 59, m. in 1806, by Rev. John Osborne, Keziah Jenkins, of Lee, b. Apr. 11, 1786, d. Oct. 26, 1866, aged 80.
GRIFFIN, James J., of Lee, son of John, b. Oct. 1, 1813, m. (1) int. Sept. 3, 1838, in Lee, Lucinda Nutter, of Barnstead, m. (2) int. June 14, 1847, in Lee, Irena McDaniel, of Barrington.
GRIFFITH, Capt. Edward, of Dover, b. Aug. 30, 1781, d. May 31, 1858, m. (1) Nov. 22, 1804, Judith Taylor, d. Dec. 6, 1812, aged 28, m. (2) Dec. 3, 1813, Martha Bennett, of Durham, b. May 13, 1787, d. Nov. 14, 1875, dau. of Capt. Eleazer.
GRIFFITH, David P., son of Capt. Edward, b. Nov. 1818, d. Mar. 5, 1855, m. Feb. 1, 1846, by Rev. Daniel P. Cilley, Sarah E. Joy, b. July 23, 1821, d. Sept. 30, 1887, dau. of Ebenezer, both of Durham.

GRIMES, William, m. Nov. 21, 1865, in Dover, Mary C. Chase.
GROVER, Henry W. B., son of George, b. Dec. 28, 1805, d. June 22, 1882, m. Sept. 28, 1828, Rebecca Linscott, of Eaton, b. Sept. 7, 1805, d. Feb. 10, 1860.
4) **GUPPEY**, John, of Rochester, son of George, d. Jan. 27, 1842, aged 43, m. Dec. 9, 1827, in Dover, Mary Ann Dame, of Dover, d. Jan. 20, 1855, aged 55.
GUPPEY, James E., m. Oct. 21, 1866, in Dover, Ellen A. Quimby.
GUPPEY, John, m. Nov. 26, 1868, by Rev. Robert S. Stubbs, Annie M. Dearborn.
GUPPEY, Albert F., m. Nov. 1, 1873, in Dover, Rosanna Berry, both of Dover.
GUPTILL, Nathaniel, son of Nathaniel, bpt. Nov. 11, 1716, m. in 1732, in S. Berwick, Me., Mary Brawn.
GUPTILL, John, son of Nathaniel, bpt. May 29, 1726, m. Nov. 16, 1749, by Rev. Jeremiah Wise, Abigail Goodwin, dau. of William.
GUPTILL, James, son of Benjamin, bpt. Dec. 8, 1741, m. Jan. 21, 1760, by Rev. John Morse, Mary Stone, dau. of Paul.
GUPTILL, Ebenezer, son of Thomas, bpt. July 10, 1743, m. May 16, 1760, in Berwick, Me., Sarah Jellison.
GUPTILL, William, son of Benjamin, b. July 12, 1748, d. Aug. 4, 1812, m. Dec. 28, 1772, by Rev. Matthew Merriam, Dorcas Stone, b. Oct. 20, 1754, d. Feb. 20, 1843, dau. of Paul.
GUPTILL, Daniel, b. 1749, d. 1815, m. May 11, 1773, in N. Berwick, Me., Sarah Morrill.
GUPTILL, Daniel, of Berwick, Me., m. Dec. 7, 1827, in Lebanon, Me., Eunice Clark.
GUPTILL, George, son of James, b. Mar. 12, 1815, d. Aug. 22, 1899, m. Nov. 22, 1842, Sarah A. Butler, b. May 6, 1818, d. Mar. 5, 1904, dau. of Benjamin.
GUPTILL, George, of Berwick, Me., m. Aug. 17, 1845, in Lebanon, Me., Eliza Ricker, of Lebanon, Me.
GUPTILL, George, of Milton, d. June 2, 1889, aged 43, m. Mar. 25, 1866, Sarah F. Morgan, of Wolfeboro, d. Feb. 8, 1889, aged 43.
GUSHEE, E. M., m. June 8, 1864, in Dover, Lydia H. Low.
HACKETT, Ephraim, m. Dec. 2, 1782, by Rev. Isaac Smith, Sarah Sargent, of Loudon.
HACKETT, Richard, of Salisbury, Mass., m. June 8, 1806, in Barrington, Martha Balch, dau. of Rev. Benjamin.
HACKLEY, William, of Portsmouth, m. (pub. May 19, 1804, in Portsmouth), Nancy Cooper.
HADLEY, Albert H., m. Aug. 14, 1869, in Dover, Abbie M. Leighton.
HAINES, Simeon, m. July 15, 1781, Welthen Spencer, dau. of Abednego.

HALE, Stephen, m. Mar. 1802, by Rev. Robert Gray, Susan Waldron, dau. of Col. John.

HALE, Wright, m. Feb. 12, 1804, by Rev. Benjamin Balch, Sally Waldron.

HALE, Samuel, Jr., son of Samuel, of Barrington, m. Mar. 19, 1822, by Rev. J. W. Clary, Anne Weeks Rollins, d. Jan. 3, 1859, aged 66, dau.. of Daniel, both of Barrington.

HALE, Jacob Thomas, m. (1) Jan. 10, 1843, in Sanbornton, Elvira M. Sanborn, m. (2) Jan. 9, 1855, in Sanbornton, Hannah G. Sanborn.

HALE, Thomas W., son of William, d. Jan. 26, 1911, aged 85, m. Nov. 29, 1865, by Rev. Francis E. Abbott, Lizzie K. Hayes.

HALEY, John Parkman, of Lee, son of John, d. June 10, 1899, aged 78, m. June 22, 1843, in Nottingham, Lydia Ann Gile, dau. of Mark, d. Jan. 10, 1895, aged 71.

HALEY, Frank, of Lee, m. Nov. 27, 1877, in Lee, Sarah M. Libbey, of Nottingham.

3) **HALL**, Joseph, son of John, living in 1730, m. Nov. 3, 1707, by Rev. John Pike, Esther Beard, dau. of Thomas.

4) HALL, Rev. Avery, son of Theophilus, b. Dec. 2, 1737, d. Aug. 5, 1820, m. (1) Hannah (or Mary) Chesley, d. June 10, 1771, **(Tate)**, dau. of James, m. (2) May 17, 1772, by Rev. James Pike, Abigail Pike, b. Mar. 30, 1740, d. 1819, dau. of Rev. James.

4) HALL, Joseph, son of Joseph, d. Dec. 16, 1826, aged 85, m. in 1763, Mary Coe, d. May 18, 1822, aged 78.

4) HALL, Samuel, son of Joseph, d. Apr. 19, 1831, aged 84, m. (1) Aug. 26, 1763, Bridget Gilman, b. Nov. 4, 1748, d. June 18, 1781, dau. of Capt. Jeremiah, m. (2) in 1795, Hannah Leighton, of Barrington, d. May 7, 1845, aged 89, dau. of Isaac.

HALL, Paul, m. Jan. 29, 1783, in Berwick, Me., Sarah Neal.

HALL, William, m. May 30, 1785, in Berwick, Me., Sarah Roberts.

HALL, Elisha, d. 1829, aged 67, m. Aug. 1786, Lois Tasker, both of Madbury.

HALL, Silas, m. Mar. 15, 1787, in Berwick, Me., Hannah Neal.

HALL, Samuel, d. June 26, 1845, aged 70, m. Oct. 13, 1795, by Rev. Benjamin Randall, Charity Hall, d. Nov. 2, 1845, aged 71, both of Barrington.

HALL, John, b. 1744, d. 1827, m. (1) Nov. 30, 1797, in Berwick, Me., Lydia Rendall, m. (2) Mary -----.

HALL, Jeremiah, m. May 29, 1800, by Rev. Isaac Smith, Polly Gilman, both of Gilmanton.

HALL, Cyrus, m. 1802, in Berwick, Me., Nabby Guptill, d. Aug. 15, 1802, aged 22.

NEW HAMPSHIRE MARRIAGES SUPPLEMENT

HALL, Jonathan, son of Benjamin, b. Apr. 29, 1766, d. Mar. 24, 1852, m. Feb. 14, 1802, Abigail Tuttle, b. June 26, 1770, d. Jan. 23, 1858, dau. of Thomas.

HALL, Nathan, of Chester, m. Dec. 26, 1816, by Rev. Isaac Smith, Sally Boynton, of Gilmanton.

HALL, William, son of Ebenezer, d. Oct. 30, 1868, m. Aug. 31, 1820, by Elder Enoch Place, Susanna Cate, b. 1804, d. June 13, 1854, aged 50, both of Barrington.

HALL, Thomas B., of Portsmouth, b. Oct. 1, 1794, m. Mar. 11, 1821, Mehitable L. Bennett, of Newmarket, b. Jan. 15, 1802, d. May 8, 1839.

HALL, Samuel, m. Nov. 28, 1821, by Rev. William Demeritt, Mary Grover, dau. of George.

HALL, Hatevil, of Lee, m. int. Apr. 26, 1823, in Lee, Abigail Atkins, of Portsmouth.

HALL, Deac. Joseph, d. Mar. 20, 1874, aged 71, m. May 31, 1827, by Elder Enoch Place, Betsey Brock, d. May 28, 1849, aged 42, both of Strafford.

HALL, Jonathan, of Strafford, d. Jan. 11, 1871, aged 76, m. June 28, 1827, by Elder Enoch Place, Lydia M. Demeritt, of Barrington, d. Mar. 15, 1880, aged 77.

HALL, Israel, 3rd, d. May 18, 1877, aged 70, m. Nov. 3, 1830, by Elder Enoch Place, Lydia Hill, d. Jan. 25, 1881, aged 73, both of Strafford.

HALL, John C., of Lee, m. int. Apr. 30, 1831, in Lee, Martha Rand, of Epson.

HALL, Capt. Edward, son of Samuel, d. 1838, aged 31, m. (pub. Oct. 4, 1831, in Portsmouth), Elizabeth Walton Floyd, d. Apr. 13, 1896, aged 88, dau. of Capt. Benjamin.

HALL, Benajah, m. May 1, 1837, in Berwick, Me., Mary Augusta Hall.

HALL, William, m. Nov. 20, 1842, by Rev. John Winkley, Margaret Ham, both of Barrington.

HALL, Warren, of Barrington, d. Oct. 26, 1886, aged 65, m. (pub. Sept. 28, 1847, in Barrington), Thankful V. Dyer, of Roxbury, Mass., d. May 9, 1904, aged 82, dau. of Asa.

HALL, George W., son of Orange, m. Nov. 15, 1854, in Rollinsford, Lucinda Hall, d. Mar. 8, 1917, aged 90, dau. of Henry.

HALL, Charles F., son of John, d. July 25, 1920, aged 83, m. Oct. 12, 1856, in Rochester, Ellen P. Hall, both of Barrington.

HALL, Joseph L., b. Aug. 6, 1835, m. Nov. 10, 1859, in Strafford, Ellen E. Tuttle, b. Apr. 10, 1835, d. Sept. 5, 1897.

NEW HAMPSHIRE MARRIAGES SUPPLEMENT

HALL, George W., of Barrington, son of Nathaniel, d. Oct. 27, 1904, aged 76, m. Apr. 25, 1860, in Barrington, Georgio A. Lord, of Dover.

HALL, Stacy W., m. Nov. 7, 1864, in Dover, Hattie A. Chadbourne.

HALL, J. Milton, m. May 17, 1865, in Dover, Lizzie M. Chapman.

HALL, Thomas B., b. near 1795, m. Aug. 23, 1866, in Lee, Mrs. Mindwell A. York, b. near 1801, both of Lee, (Was this a second marriage?)

HALL, Asa A., m. Dec. 31, 1866, in Dover, Maria A. Stanton.

HALL, Stephen T., m. Sept. 29, 1867, in Dover, Martha J. Varney.

HALL, Charles B., m. May 20, 1869, in Dover, Nellie Meader.

HALL, John Freeman, m. Nov. 20, 1869, in Dover, Sarah E. Hussey.

HALLIBURTON, Andrew, m. July 6, 1823, in Portsmouth, Sarah Ann Manning, dau. of Thomas.

HALSTEAD, William W., m. Sept. 4, 1866, in Dover, Clara L. Watson.

3) **HAM**, Deac. Daniel, son of Joseph, b. July 24, 1714, d. Jan. 15, 1803, m. (1) near 1740, Sarah Downs, b. Nov. 25, 1712, dau. of Thomas, m. (2) near 1750, Mary Horne, dau. of Daniel.

3) HAM, Jonathan, b. June 8, 1720, d. 1793, m. near 1744, Elizabeth Ham, b. 1725, d. Oct. 1822, dau. of John.

4) HAM, Aaron, b. 1735, d. Apr. 11, 1817, m. near 1760, Lucy Watson, b. 1739, d.Apr. 2, 1817.

HAM, Col. Joseph, d. Nov. 13, 1825, aged 88, m. before 1761, Hannah Coffin, b. Nov. 24, 1732, dau. of Tristram.

HAM, Israel, of Rochester, son of Jonathan, b. Feb. 14, 1759, d. June 25, 1801, m. Sept. 23, 1784, by Dr. Belknap, Mehitable Hayes, of Madbury, b. 1766, d. May 23, 1817.

HAM, Ephraim, d. Apr. 1806, m. Mar. 24, 1785, Hannah Kelley, b. Mar. 22, 1765, d. June 4, 1849, dau. of John.

HAM, Dodavah, b. 1771, d. 1806, m. Dec. 20, 1797, by Rev. William Hooper, Nancy Tufts, d. Sept. 24, 1820, both of Barrington.

HAM, Capt. Moses, b. Nov. 14, 1769, d. Aug. 2, 1839, m. Mar. 29, 1798, in Dover, Mehitable Hanson, d. Jan. 9, 1852, aged 76, dau. of William.

5) HAM, Joshua, b. 1781, d. 1834, m. (1) July 1804, Mehitable Horne, d. Dec. 1824, aged 44, m. (2) Sept. 22, 1825, by REv. J. W. Clary, Susanna Y. Horne, b. 1795, d. Nov. 4, 1872.

HAM, Nathaniel, Jr., b. June 28, 1777, d. Aug. 22, 1820, m. May 10, 1807, in Rochester, Hannah Allen, of Rochester, d. Apr. 23, 1817, dau. of Maj. Samuel.

HAM, Samuel, son of George W., m. Nov. 7, 1820, by Rev. J. W. Clary, Rebecca Harty.

HAM, Solomon, son of William, b. Mar. 12, 1808, m. int. Feb. 18, 1829, in Dover, Lydia Gowell.

HAM, Rufus, of Somersworth, m. Oct. 22, 1849, by Rev. Thomas Bartlett, Elizabeth B. Peirce, of Barrington, d. Oct. 21, 1902, aged 87, dau. of Curtis.

HAM, Albert, of Amesbury, Mass., m. Mar. 14, 1852, by Rev. John Winkley, Charlotte Caverly, of Barrington.

HAM, James L., of Milton, m. Oct. 9, 1855, by Rev. John Winkley, Mary F. H. Blane, of Somersworth.

HAM, Joshua M., son of Walter, b. Apr. 1841, d. Nov. 19, 1888, aged 47, m. June 9, 1867, in Dover, Mary A. Wiggin, d. Jan. 17, 1929, aged 80, dau. of George.

HAM, John R., d. Oct. 31, 1920, aged 78, m. June 30, 1869, in Dover, Olive A. Dana, d. Apr. 1, 1921, aged 84, dau. of James W.

HAM, Edward B., m. Sept. 1, 1869, in Dover, Aramantha E. Ham.

HAMILTON, Solomon, son of Abial, bpt. Aug. 19, 1733, m. (1) Jan. 27, 1757, by Rev. John Morse, Sarah Keay, dau. of Peter, m. (2) Elizabeth Peirce.

HAMILTON, Rufus, b. Dec. 26, 1783, d. May 30, 1865, m. Dec. 8, 1814, Margery Gerrish, b. Apr. 1, 1792, d. Jan. 2, 1842.

HAMMETT, Ephraim, son of Ephraim, b. May 1, 1812, d. Jan. 22, 1899, m. (1) Anne Clark, b. Aug. 25, 1812, d. Nov. 11, 1877, m. (2) Mary (Clark) Warren, b. 1810, d. Dec. 18, 1894, dau. of Louis.

HAMMON, Squire B., m. Sept. 18, 1867, by Rev. Robert S. Stubbs, Patience T. Hammon.

HANSCOM, Uriah, son of Uriah, b. 1757, d. July 19, 1825, m. Aug. 21, 1789, Anne Barnes, d. Mar. 16, 1860, aged 90.

HANSCOM, Alpheus, son of Uriah, b. Apr. 19, 1794, d. Mar. 28, 1883, m. (1) Apr. 25, 1819, Joanna Stacy, d. Apr. 18, 1848, aged 48, m. (2) Mrs. Louisa Frost, wid. of James, b. July 7, 1811, d. Nov. 6, 1902.

HANSCOM, Samuel, son of Pelatiah, b. Nov. 1, 1804, d. Feb. 25, 1834, m. (pub. Dec. 4, 1832, in Milton), Eliza Hanson, of Lebanon, Me.

HANSCOM, James, son of Pelatiah, d. Jan. 29, 1890, aged 67, m. May 10, 1846, in Milton, Sarah Jones, d. Sept. 24, 1889, aged 68, dau. of Nathan.

HANSCOM, John F., m. July 18, 1862, in Dover, Julia F. Dore.

HANSCOM, Reuben, m. May 24, 1866, in Dover, Lizzie M. Earl.

HANSCOM, Isaac, m. Nov. 7, 1867, in Dover, Carrie J. Hayes.

4) **HANSON**, Ebenezer, son of Thomas and Hannah, b. Apr. 6, 1726, d. Dec. 6, 1782, m. near 1745, Anne Hodgdon, b. Sept. 25, 1728, d. Aug. 27, 1803.

4) HANSON, Joseph, son of Benjamin and Elizabeth, b. Dec. 15, 1714, d. Aug. 1798, m. Oct. 9, 1754, Margaret Hanson, dau. of Timothy and Kezia.
5) HANSON, Anthony, son of Benjamin, d. Dec. 15, 1806, m. Jan. 24, 1771, by Dr. Belknap, Hannah Davis.
5) HANSON, Solomon, son of Solomon, b. near 1749, d. Oct. 1805, m. (1) in 1776, Mary Chase, b. May 25, 1756, dau. of John, m. (2) June 1790, by Rev. William Hooper, Elizabeth Horne, b. 1740, d. Mar. 1802, (She may have been a widow), both of Dover.
5) HANSON, Jedediah, of Dover, son of Silas, b. July 4, 1759, d. July 23, 1822, m. Mar. 1787, by Rev. William Hooper, Mary Young, of Madbury, d. 1825, aged 56.
6) HANSON, Israel, Jr., b. Nov. 11, 1770, d. Feb. 21, 1844, m. (1) Sarah Howard, d. June 11, 1815, m. (2) Apr. 20, 1817, in Rochester, Eunice Twombly, of Rochester, b. Mar. 25, 1787, d. Mar. 26, 1853, dau. of Samuel.
5) HANSON, Shadrach, son of Ebenezer, b. Oct. 19, 1768, m. Nov. 4, 1792, in Dover, Hannah Patten, dau. of Stephen.
HANSON, Samuel, m. June 1795, in Dover, Hannah Plummer.
5) HANSON, Timothy, son of Timothy and Mary, of Dover, b. Sept. 23, 1763, d. Apr. 1806, m. Feb. 28, 1797, in Kittery, Me., Kezia Neal, dau. of James, of Kittery, Me.
6) HANSON, Elijah, son of Stephen, b. Mar. 12, 1771, d. Mar. 11, 1848, m. (pub. June 7, 1806, in Dover), Mary Ricker, b. Dec. 18, 1782, d. Apr. 9, 1868.
HANSON, Samuel, m. Jan. 26, 1807, in Dover, Sarah Watson, b. July 6, 1780, dau. of Benjamin.
HANSON, John, m. July 6, 1819, by Rev. Jeremiah Shaw, Olive Batchelder, d. Sept. 29, 1824, aged 30.
HANSON, Aaron, b. May 28, 1791, m. int. Feb. 5, 1832, in Lee, Deborah Jane C. Hall, b. Apr. 22, 1808, both of Lee.
HANSON, Capt. Rufus, of Wakefield, son of Jonathan, b. 1807, d. 1892, m. (1) Nov. 2, 1833, in Wakefield, Dolly Getchell, of Newfield, Me., m. (2) Mary S. Cook, b. 1813, d. 1894, dau. of Thomas.
HANSON, Nathaniel E., m. May 8, 1842, by Rev. John Winkley, Clarissa Ann Foss, both of Strafford.
7) HANSON, Tobias, Jr., of Brookfield, son of Tobias, b. Apr. 25, 1810, d. Sept. 27, 1855, m. (pub. June 27, 1843, in Ossipee), Mary Smith, of Ossipee, b. Aug. 22, 1813, d. Jan. 22, 1892, dau. of John.
HANSON, Moses C., of Barrington, son of Caleb, b. Mar. 14, 1824, d. Oct. 17, 1886, m. Mar. 27, 1845, by Rev. John Winkley, Eliza

Hanson, d. Mar. 13, 1896, aged 73, dau. of Nathaniel, 3rd, of Strafford.

HANSON, John, of Strafford, son of Caleb, d. June 16, 1892, aged 64, m. (1) Jan. 5, 1846, by Rev. John Winkley, Susan Hanson, d. Oct. 17, 1866, aged 41, dau. of Nathaniel, 3rd, m. (2) Oct. 1, 1867, Mary S. (Quimby) Brown, of Newburyport, Mass., d. Mar. 30, 1890, aged 52, dau. of Henry.

HANSON, James L., of Rochester, m. Nov. 10, 1852, in Newmarket, Lois A. Wentworth, of Milton.

HANSON, Ebenezer Freeman, son of John, d. Aug. 2, 1913, aged 84, m. Sept. 2, 1855, in Strafford, Lizzie J. James, both of Strafford.

HANSON, William H., son of Moses, d. Oct. 27, 1913, aged 79, m. Sept. 18, 1857, in Milton, Olive Hill, both of Lebanon, Me.

HANSON, Joseph, of Wakefield, son of Jonathan, b. 1811, d. 1889, m. Jan. 27, 1858, by Elder Joseph Spinney, Alice Pray, of Dorchester, Mass., b. 1815, d. 1865.

HANSON, John, of Newmarket, m. Apr. 17, 1860, in Newmarket, Lydia A. Frost, of Dover.

HANSON, Isaac, son of John, b. Jan. 21, 1826, d. Apr. 22, 1888, m. Mar. 14, 1861, Elizabeth A. Stillings, b. Oct. 1, 1840, d. Jan. 20, 1916, dau. of Peter.

HANSON, John C., m. Feb. 5, 1862, in Dover, Elizabeth A. Demeritt.

HANSON, Samuel G., m. Nov. 26, 1862, Ellen Sophia Emerson, b. Feb. 8, 1836, dau. of Timothy.

HANSON, James, m. Sept. 1, 1863, in Dover, Mary E. Clancy.

HANSON, Joshua M., m. May 9, 1864, in Dover, Alma J. Webber.

HANSON, Luther F., m. Nov. 12, 1864, in Dover, Martha A. Rogers.

HANSON, Jonathan A., m. Dec. 10, 1865, in Dover, Leonora A. Deland, d. Nov. 5, 1890, aged 53, dau. of John.

HANSON, William, m. Dec. 10, 1865, in Dover, Christine Daniels, d. Jan. 2, 1887, aged 83.

HARDING, Edward G., m. May 28, 1866, by Rev. Asa Piper, Mary A. Lombard.

HARDY, Capt. Washington W., son of Thomas, b. Mar. 15, 1838, d. Apr. 9, 1916, aged 78, m. Mar. 29, 1871, in Dover, by Rev. Geo B. Spaulding, Elizabeth Bickford, b. Mar. 6, 1842, d. Apr. 3, 1908, aged 66, dau. of Alphonso.

HARRIS, Samuel, m. Feb. 2, 1869, by Rev. J. C. Foster, Harriet M. Hutchinson.

HART, John, d. Feb. 9, 1854, aged 68, m. Nov. 17, 1811, in Wakefield, Elizabeth Nutter, of Milton, d. June 19, 1866, aged 80.

HART, Capt. Joshua B., of Dover, d. Nov. 13, 1826, aged 28, m. July 3, 1823, in Augusta, Ga., Eliza Olivia Powers, of Augusta, Ga.

HART, Edward, of Milton, son of John, b. Mar. 5, 1812, d. May 12, 1885, m. (pub. Oct. 10, 1843, in Acton, Me.), Sally T. Fox, b. July 3, 1820, d. May 22, 1847, dau. of Jonathan.

HART, John D., d. Jan. 3, 1896, aged 67, m. Dec. 28, 1860, in Milton, Mary A. Twombly, b. June 24, 1833, d. Sept. 13, 1891, dau. of James M.

HARTFORD, Nicholas, son of Nicholas, m. Jan. 29, 1731, Mary Ferguson, b. Mar. 18, 1705, d. in Mar. 1769, dau. of Alexander.

HARTFORD, John, b. 1771, d. Apr. 8, 1832, m. near 1795, in Strafford, Elizabeth Babb, d. Nov. 4, 1857, aged 77.

HARTFORD, Simon L., son of John, b. Mar. 15, 1804, d. Oct. 22, 1857, m. (pub. Feb. 13, 1827, in Somersworth), Olive Goodwin, d. Oct. 4, 1885, aged 85, both of Dover.

HARTFORD, Joseph, son of John, b. Mar. 19, 1815, d. 1905, m. Jan. 29, 1837, Rebecca Downs, b. Feb. 16, 1872, aged 56.

HARTFORD, Benjamin P., m. Sept. 4, 1855, in Lebanon, Me., Hannah S. Brown, both of Wakefield.

HARTFORD, James M., m. July 4, 1857, by Rev. John Winkley, Mahalia Hayes, both of Strafford.

HARTFORD, Lyman, m. Feb. 21, 1863, in Dover, Salome Whittier.

HARTFORD, Charles E., m. July 29, 1865, in Dover, Hattie S. Goodwin.

HARTFORD, Samuel B., m. Oct. 28, 1874, in Rochester, Jennie A. Seavey.

HARTHAN, Lucius, of Dover, m. int. Sept. 30, 1827, in Dover, Salome C. Cady, of Windsor, Vt.

HARVEY, John, of Northwood, m. Jan. 10, 1815, by Rev. J. W. Clary, Dorothy F. Wentworth, of Dover.

HARVEY, Richard James, m. Jan. 8, 1820, by Rev. William Demeritt, Abigail G. Hall, d. May 1825, aged 31.

HARVEY, John H., m. May 8, 1847, in Lee, Jane Gile, both of Nottingham.

HARVEY, Joseph P., of Nottingham, b. 1844, m. Nov. 27, 1877, in Lee, m. Lizzie Allen, of Lee, b. 1856.

HARWOOD, William F., m. June 1, 1867, in Dover, Augusta Pasho.

HASKELL, Jacob W., son of Asa, b. Feb. 8, 1821, d. Feb. 7, 1872, m. Dec. 17, 1851, by Rev. Thomas J. Greenwood, Mary Eliza Jordan, both of Portland, Me.

HASKELL, Rev. Ezra, son of Ezra, d. June 23, 1916, aged 81, m. Nov. 9, 1859, in Dover, Isabella Riley, of Dover, d. July 17, 1888, aged 56, dau. of Capt. John.

HATCH, Hosea, m. Nov. 21, 1776, by Rev. Isaac Smith, Elizabeth Edgerly.

NEW HAMPSHIRE MARRIAGES SUPPLEMENT

HATCH, Nathan, m. Oct. 11, 1804, by Rev. Isaac Smith, Phebe Thurston, both of Gilmanton.

HATCH, William, m. Feb. 3, 1819, in Milton, Keziah Hartford, both of Milton.

HAWKINS, Hosea, b. 1810, d. Oct. 15, 1889, m. Sept. 26, 1826, by Elder Enoch Place, Mary Caswell, b. 1806, d. May 21, 1894, both of Strafford.

4) HAYES, Ichabod, son of Ichabod, of Rochester, m. (1) Nov. 29, 1770, by Dr. Belknap, Tamson Hayes, of Barrington, m. (2) pub. Jan. 19, 1805, in Lebanon, Me.), Mehitable (Libbey) Pray, wid. of Nathaniel.

HAYES, Charles T., d. Jan. 31, 1861, aged 39, m. Apr. 12, 1846, by Elder Enoch Place, Betsey C. Foss, d. May 31, 1857, aged 31, dau. of George, both of Strafford.

HEARD, John, m. July 2, 1698, in Kittery, Me., Jane (Cole) Littlefield, wid. of Joseph, dau. of Nicholas.

HEARD, James, m. Sept. 20, 1716, in Berwick, Me., Martha Jackson.

HEARD, William, m. Dec. 15, 1717, in Berwick, Me., Margaret Warren.

HEARD, Nathaniel, m. Dec. 18, 1718, in Berwick, Me., Margaret Warren.

HEARD, Benjamin, b. 1744, d. Feb. 2, 1817, aged 73, m. Sept. 8, 1768, by Rev. Matthew Merriam, Molly Andrews, d. Sept. 23, 1819, aged 72.

HEARD, Jethro, bpt. May 10, 1753, d. Nov. 17, 1815, m. Nov. 23, 1769, by Dr. Belknap, Sarah Hartford, d. Dec. 1, 1815, aged 70.

HEARD, Shadrack, d. Aug. 19, 1860, aged 81, m. Sept. 7, 1797, by Rev. Joseph Haven, Lydia Hoitt, d. Aug. 10, 1850, aged 72, both of Rochester.

HEARD, Joshua, m. Jan. 1802, by Rev. Robert Gray, Hannah Chase.

HEARD, Seth, m. (pub. June 11, 1833, in Alton), Adaline M. Buzzell, d. Aug. 24, 1896, dau. of Hezikiah.

HEARD, (HURD), Edmund, son of Ichabod, d. June 4, 1869, aged 53, m. Oct. 1, 1837, in Lebanon, Me., Hephzibah H. Merrill, d. Oct. 24, 1880, aged 59.

HEARD, George W., of Dover, m. July 11, 1844, by Rev. Alvin Tobey, Lucinda Drew, of Durham, b. June 7, 1810, d. June 4, 1888, dau. of Shadrach.

HEARD, (HURD), Jonathan W., m. Apr. 22, 1861, in Rochester, Martha M. Foss, both of Rochester.

HEARD, (HURD), William, m. Oct. 8, 1864, in Dover, Mary A. Hosmer.

HEARD, (HURD), Samuel F., m. Jan. 4, 1865, in Dover, Charlotte B. Drew.

HEARD, (HURD), Ezekiel, m. Oct. 30, 1869, in Dover, Caroline (Torr) Cushing, d. Jan. 4, 1911, aged 84, wid. of Thomas H., dau. of Benjamin.

HEARD, (HURD), George R., of Rochester, m. May 5, 1874, in Rochester, m. May 5, 1874, in Rochester, Mrs. Sarah Austin, of Dover.

HEATH, Josiah, of Haverhill, Mass., m. July 19, 1671, Mary Davis, b. Nov. 6, 1647, dau. of Ens. John.

HEATH, Alonzo, m. (1) Oct. 24, 1855, by Elder Elias Hutchins, Susan A. Perkins, d. Feb. 8, 1861, aged 27, dau. of Solomon, m. (2) Aug. 11, 1866, in Dover, Sarah L. Williams.

HEATH, S. A., m. May 13, 1865, in Dover, Grace E. Brown.

HEATH, Alonzo, m. Aug. 11, 1866, in Dover, Sarah L. Williams.

HENDERSON, Stephen, b. 1785, d. Mar. 5, 1862, m. Feb. 22, 1807, by Rev. Joseph Haven, Sarah Roberts, d. Nov. 29, 1867, aged 82, both of Rochester.

HENDERSON, C. W., m. Nov. 7, 1864, in Dover, Martha J. Goodwin.

HENDERSON, Samuel, m. Nov. 14, 1871, in Rochester, Sarah E. Richardson.

HERSEY, William Jr., of Sanbornton, m. Nov. 26, 1807, by Rev. Isaac Smith, Ruth Bean, of Gilmanton.

HERSEY, Elijah, of Wolfeboro, son of Jonathan, d. Oct. 1, 1844, aged 62, m. (1) Apr. 25, 1810, in Tuftonboro, by Rev. Jeremiah Shaw, Hannah Tibbetts, of Tuftonboro, d. Aug. 17, 1834, aged 44, m. (2) Mar. 10, 1835, in Wolfeboro, Hannah Haines, d. Sept. 13, 1848, aged 54, both of Wolfeboro.

HERSEY, Capt. James G., b. 1816, d. 1872, m. (pub. Apr. 28, 1840, in Tuftonboro), Frances A. Hersey, b. 1817, d. 1880.

HERSEY, James P., b. Dec. 19, 1822, d. Jan. 7, 1892, m. Apr. 22, 1848, in Wolfeboro, Clara J. Willey, b. Aug. 30, 1826, d. Apr. 26, 1906, both of Wolfeboro.

HERSOM, John S., m. Nov. 19, 1864, in Lebanon, Me., Martha A. (Jones) Butler, wid. of Francis, b. May 2, 1845, dau. of James.

HERSOM, Oliver, m. Oct. 6, 1867, in Dover, Melissa A. Durgin.

HERSOM, John, m. Apr. 5, 1869, by Rev. Robert S. Stubbs, Mary Jane Varney.

HEWITT, Gilbert, m. Aug. 7, 1808, by Rev. Isaac Smith, Betsey Morgan.

HICKS, David, m. Dec. 12, 1824, by Rev. J. W. Clary, Mary Bickford, of Dover.

NEW HAMPSHIRE MARRIAGES SUPPLEMENT

HICKS, Nathaniel, of Wolfeboro, d. Feb. 17, 1885, aged 74, m. Nov. 12, 1840, by Elder John Chick, Betsey J. Watson, of New Durham, d. May 1, 1892, aged 78.

HIDDEN, Rev. Samuel, m. Nov. 29, 1792, by Rev. Isaac Smith, Mrs. Elizabeth Story Price.

HIGGINS, James T., m. Oct. 29, 1862, in Dover, Annie Dow.

HILDRETH, Levi, m. Dec. 31, 1778, by Rev. Isaac Smith, Sarah Darling.

HILDRETH, William E., m. Oct. 26, 1869, in Dover, Ellen Mack.

4) HILL, William, son of William, b. 1679, m. before 1723, probably near 1700, Judith -----.

4) HILL, William, Jr., son of William, d. 1760, m. (1) Hannah -----, m. (2) Aug. 21, 1729, Patience Drew, b. Jan. 1707, d. July 7, 1805, dau. of Thomas.

5) HILL, Henry, of Durham, son of William, m. early as 1738, Hannah Drew, b. Feb. 26, 1709, dau. of John and Rebecca.

HILL, Joseph, son of Samuel, m. Sept. 13, 1753, in Durham, Mary Bamford, both of Barrington.

HILL, Edward, b. 1724, d. July 1800, m. near 1758, Mary Willey, of Lee, dau. of Thomas.

4) HILL, Valentine, son of Samuel, b. 1730, d. Feb. 18, 1825, m. near 1760, Sarah Burley, b. 1743, d. Aug. 4, 1833.

HILL, Deac. John, of Berwick, Me., d. May 21, 1810, aged 72, m. Sept. 25, 1766, in Saco, Me., Elizabeth Scammon, of Saco, Me., d. Feb. 28, 1822, aged 74.

6) HILL, Amos, of Berwick, Me., son of Joseph and Mary, d. May 6, 1832, m. Dec. 30, 1790, in Berwick, Mercy Varney, b. Mar. 8, 1771, d. Oct. 31, 1840, dau. of Timothy.

5) HILL, Trueworthy, son of Benjamin, d. Aug. 22, 1856, aged 86, m. (1) Nov. 12, 1792, Hannah Drew, m. (2) in 1808, by Rev. John Osborne, Ruth Matthews, of Lee, dau. of Samuel.

HILL, James, m. Apr. 29, 1798, in Berwick, Me., Sally Guptill.

HILL, Daniel, m. Feb. 8, 1823, in Lebanon, Me., Sally Downs.

HILL, Samuel, of Epping, m. int. Apr. 24, 1824, in Lee, Mary Burleigh, of Lee.

HILL, Daniel, of Lebanon, Me., son of Jeremiah, d. Dec. 13, 1880, aged 83, m. Feb. 8, 1828, Sarah Downs, of Milton, d. Oct. 20, 1861, aged 59, dau. of John.

HILL, Azariah B., b. 1817, d. 1901, m. Apr. 4, 1839, by Elder Enoch Place, Hannah Hall, b. 1821, d. 1907, both of Strafford.

HILL, Maj. Alfred J., of Portsmouth, b. June 6, 1804, d. Apr. 1, 1889, m. Apr. 15, 1841, Elizabeth Peverly, b. 1819, d. Feb. 19, 1890, dau. of George.

HILL, Joseph M., b. 1824, d. 1902, m. (1) (pub. July 20, 1847, in Great Falls), Mary S. Boodey, b. 1831, d. 1874, both of Dover, m. (2) Florence L. Sherman, b. 1857, d. 1907.

HILL, John W., of Lee, son of Trueworthy, b. June 22, 1822, d. Apr. 20, 1899, m. July 7, 1850, Mary Jane Caldwell, of Barrington, b. Dec. 6, 1830, d. Dec. 6, 1910.

HILL, Daniel W., son of Daniel S., d. Jan. 13, 1903, aged 75, m. Mar. 11, 1855, in Milton, Betty Rankins, d. Dec. 23, 1902, aged 74, dau. of John.

HILL, Samuel, Jr., m. June 19, 1859, in Strafford, Lydia C. Parshley, d. Feb. 4, 1860, aged 25, dau. of Ebenezer, both of Strafford.

HILL, John, son of William L., d. Aug. 20, 1879, aged 58, m. Nov. 24, 1859, in Strafford, Mrs. Eliza A. (Smith) Hill, wid. of William, d. Mar. 11, 1905, aged 70.

HILL, John Tilton, m. Mar. 9, 1865, in Dover, Vienna O. Locke.

HILL, Newell, m. Apr. 19, 1865, in Dover, Hannah L. Clough.

HILL, Joseph W., m. (1) Apr. 3, 1866, by Rev. James Rand, Sarah E. Tibbetts, m. (2) (pub. June 11, 1874, in Rochester), Mrs. Sarah Berry.

HILL, Joseph C., m. Apr. 9, 1867, by Rev. James Rand, Addie Morrison.

HILL, Andrew S., m. Jan. 11, 1868, in Dover, Etta E. Chapman.

HILL, John T., m. Sept. 28, 1868, in Dover, Sarah A. Foss.

HILL, David, m. Jan. 17, 1874, in Northwood, Jennie Sanders, both of Pittsfield.

HILL, Horace C., m. Apr. 29, 1874, in Dover, Gracie Davis, both of Dover.

HILL, George J., of Haverhill, Mass., m. Sept. 29, 1874, by Rev. Asa Piper, Annie D. Guptill, of Cornish, Me.

HILLIARD, Rev. Joseph, of Berwick, Me., m. Jan. 1, 1821, in Lebanon, Me., Sally Hasey, of Lebanon, Me., dau. of Rev. Isaac.

1) **HILTON**, Edward, son of Edward, d. 1671, m. after 1650, Catherine (Shapleigh) Treworgie, wid. of James, d. May 29, 1676, dau. of Alexander.

5) HILTON, Winthrop, of Newmarket, son of Winthrop, b. Sept. 26, 1766, d. July 6, 1826, m. Dec. 1, 1795, by Rev. Nathaniel Ewer, Abigail Hilton, d. Dec. 20, 1861, aged 84, dau. of Capt. Edward.

HILTON, James, b. 1806, d. Dec. 21, 1873, m. Sept. 23, 1855, in Middleton, Adaline E. P. Davis, b. 1806, d. 1896, both of Middleton.

HILTON, Charles H., m. Oct. 22, 1864, in Dover, Lucy E. McCann.

HIXON, Jacob, m. (pub. Dec. 5, 1826, in Somersworth), Abigail Tilden.

HOAG, Benjamin, son of Joseph, m. Mary Scribner, d. Oct. 14, 1753, dau. of Thomas.

HOBBS, Sgt. Morrell, son of Henry, b. Nov. 23, 1753, d. Oct. 20, 1826, m. Feb. 26, 1778, by Rev. Matthew Merriam, Miriam Brackett, dau. of John, both of Berwick, Me.

HOBBS, Nathaniel, d. Nov. 12, 1852, aged 82, m. Aug. 30, 1792, by Rev. Matthew Merriam, Patience Nowell, d. 1828, aged 58.

HOBBS, George Frank, m. Nov. 19, 1873, in Dover, Emma J. Christie, both of Dover.

HOBBS, James, m. May 2, 1874, in Dover, Harriet M. Porter, both of S. Berwick, Me.

HODGDON, Benjamin, of Newington, d. Mar. 1823, aged 74, m. Feb. 25, 1771, by Rev. J. Adams, Hannah Sayward, of Dover.

HODGDON, Joseph, of Newington, son of John, b. June 21, 1755, m. Nov. 13, 1775, in Greenland, Sarah Peverly, b. July 21, 1754.

HODGDON, Charles, m. Mar. 27, 1794, by Rev. Isaac Smith, Abigail Thing.

HODGDON, George P., m. Nov. 23, 1826, by Elder Enoch Place, Phebe W. Shepard, d. Nov. 22, 1847, aged 41, both of Strafford.

HODGDON, Matthew, b. 1803, d. 1873, m. Apr. 26, 1834, by Rev. William Demeritt, Susan Snell, b. 1812, d. 1901, both of Lee.

HODGDON, George, m. 1849 or 1850, in Newmarket, Nancy H. Hanson.

HODGDON, Joseph H., of Dover, son of Samuel, b. Mar. 28, 1827, d. Nov. 3, 1914, aged 87, m. Sept. 17, 1853, in Dover, Melvina A. Bunker, of Durham, b. Mar. 24, 1838, d. June 17, 1922, aged 84, dau. of Ephraim.

HODGDON, Lyman, m. Apr. 4, 1866, in Dover, Hattie Delaney.

HODGDON, Darius, Jr., m. July 1, 1868, by Rev. James Rand, Maria E. Moody.

HODGDON, Alvin A., of Lee, m. Nov. 7, 1870, in Lee, Abby F. Hall, of Barrington.

HODGDON, Edwin, of Springfale, Me., m. Nov. 30, 1872, by Rev. Asa Piper, Mahala M. Day, of Newfield, Me.

HODGDON, John H., of Rollinsford, m. Dec. 24, 1873, in Dover, Bessie Chapman, of Lawrence, Mass.

HODGDON, Billings, of Biddeford, Me., m. Oct. 17, 1874, by Rev. Asa Piper, Laura Hasty, of Buxton, Me.

HODSDON, Capt. Thomas, Jr., b. 1738, d. Apr. 16, 1816, m. Oct. 30, 1763, by Rev. Jacob Foster, Margaret Goodwin, dau. of James.

HODSDON, Aaron H., d. Oct. 26, 1849, aged 34, m. Oct. 1, 1840, in Milton, Ann E. Hart, dau. of John, both of Milton.

HOITT, Nathan, m. Sept. 28, 1783, by Rev. Jeremiah Shaw, Martha Adams, d. Nov. 1814, aged 68.

HOITT, Jonathan, of Amesbury, Mass., m. Dec. 25, 1806, by Rev. Isaac Smith, Mary Currier, of Gilmanton.

HOITT, Gorham, of Lee, m. int. May 5, 1824, in Lee, Abigail P. Locke, of Barrington.

HOITT, Benjamin, m. (pub. Feb. 14, 1826, in Rochester), Betsey Pickering.

7) HOITT, Gen. Alfred, of Lee, son of Samuel, b. Jan. 11, 1806, d. Nov. 9, 1883, m. (1) Oct. 26, 1828, Susan Demeritt, of Nottingham, b. Dec. 22, 1806, d. Apr. 24, 1877, dau. of Paul, m. (2) June 6, 1879, Mary A. (Walker) Smart, wid. of Deac. James M., b. Apr. 13, 1834, d. Oct. 28, 1901.

HOITT, Gen. Nathaniel B., d. Sept. 5, 1866, aged 61, m. (1) Eliza L. Shaw, d. July 9, 1846, aged 38, dau. of Jeremiah, m. (2) (pub. Dec. 28, 1846, in Moultonboro), Susan Richardson, d. Aug. 14, 1888, aged 74, dau. of Joseph.

8) HOITT, Samuel Piper, of Lee, son of Gen. Alfred, b. Mar. 26, 1833, d. Apr. 20, 1902, m. (pub. Feb. 8, 1855, in Newmarket), Mary E. Doe, of Newmarket, b. Aug. 5, 1829, d. Dec. 15, 1901.

8) HOITT, Alfred Demeritt, of Durham, son of Gen. Alfred, b. Oct. 14, 1830, d. June 8, 1909, m. Aug. 24, 1858, in Charlestown, Mary E. Sawyer, of Dover, d. May 9, 1880, aged 46, dau. of Thomas E.

HOITT, Enoch P., m. Sept. 2, 1862, in Dover, Lavina M. Tasker.

HOITT, (HOYT), Calvin, m. Jan. 3, 1866, in Dover, Sarah A. Varney.

HOITT, Frank R., m. Dec. 31, 1867, by Rev. Alden Sherwin, Mrs. Isabella F. Giles.

HOITT, (HOYT), Arthur H., of Dover, m. Mar. 11, 1874, in Dover, Emma L. Jackson, dau. of Levi L.

HOLLAND, Josiah, m. (pub. July 26, 1825, in Waterville, Me.), Josephine Wright.

HOLMES, Joseph, m. Jan. 11, 1828, in Farmington, Abigail Babb.

HOLMES, Capt. John G., b. Nov. 18, 1823, d. Feb. 18, 1884, m. May 15, 1850, by Elder John C. Holmes, Eliza Jane Foss, b. May 11, 1829, d. Oct. 21, 1915, dau. of Eliphalet.

HOLMES, John F., m. May 1, 1859, Sarah A. Jones, b. July 4, 1840, dau. of Ebenezer.

HOLMES, William F., m. Sept. 16, 1865, by Rev. James Rand, Maria S. Daniels.

HOLMES, Charles W., m. Sept. 1, 1869, in Dover, Fanny M. Hooper.

HOLT, Joseph N., son of Asa, b. 1835, d. Feb. 19, 1913, m. (1) Aug. 18, 1855, in Dover, Caroline E. Fuller, b. 1833, d. Aug. 16, 1863, both of Dover, m. (2) Feb. 20, 1864, by Rev. James Rand, Sarah M. Jones, b. 1846, d. 1877.

HOOPER, William, b. 1719, d. 1809, m. Oct. 29, 1743, in Berwick, Me., Elizabeth Emery, b. Sept. 24, 1724, d. 1812, dau. of Daniel.
HOOPER, John, son of Samuel, b. July 8, 1732, m. Nov. 2, 1758, by Rev. Jacob Foster, Elizabeth Nason, dau. of Joseph.
HOOPER, Daniel, m. Sept. 24, 1781, in Berwick, Me., Hannah Heard, both of Berwick, Me.
HOOPER, Jacob, m. Apr. 18, 1805, in Berwick, Me., Mary Clements.
HOOPER, Samuel, of Madbury, m. Mar. 12, 1807, in Berwick, Me., Polly Clark.
HOOPER, Tristram, m. Aug. 12, 1810, in Berwick, Me., Elizabeth Pitts.
HOOPER, John, m. Nov. 7, 1822, in Berwick, Me., Mary Butler.
HOOPER, James G., m. Feb. 10, 1846, in S. Berwick, Me., Hannah Patterson.
HOOPER, Sylvester I., m. Nov. 4, 1868, in Dover, Mrs. Lucy J. Howe.
HOPE, Henry, m. Jan. 5, 1870, in Dover, Elzira Stirling.
HORACE, James, m. June 20, 1862, by Rev. James Rand, Mary A. Gerrish.
3) **HORNE**, William, son of John, d. Aug. 11, 1770, m. (1) Dec. 17, 1713, in Somersworth, Mary Varney, b. Apr. 6, 1693, d. Sept. 18, 1735, dau. of Ebenezer, m. (2) Rachel-----, m. (3) Elizabeth -----.
5) HORNE, Samuel Heard, son of William, b. Dec. 22, 1756, d. Apr. 29, 1847, m. (1) near 1775, Joanna Peverly, m. (2) Jan. 31, 1781, by Dr. Belknap, Hannah Ricker.
HORNE, Caleb, son of Samuel, b. May 26, 1757, d. June 1800, m. Feb. 11, 1777, by Dr. Belknap, Mary Randall, d. Feb. 12, 1835, aged 79, dau. of Samuel, both of Somersworth.
HORNE, Ebenezer, son of Samuel, b. Feb. 14, 1755, d. Jan. 20, 1847, m. (1), Mar. 21, 1780, by Rev. Joseph Haven, Lydia Canney, b. Apr. 8, 1757, dau. of William, m. (2) Lucinda Davis, d. Feb. 28, 1847, aged 44.
HORNE, William, m. June 4, 1780, by Rev. Joseph Haven, Lucy Thompson, d. Jan. 13, 1819, aged 77.
HORN, Benjamin, b. 1753, d. Nov. 7, 1834, aged 80, m. Nov. 8, 1781, by Rev. Matthew Merriam, Ruth Hanson, d. Aug. 8, 1844.
HORNE, Stephen Wentworth, d. Mar. 26, 1823, aged 69, m. Sept. 29, 1785, in Wolfeboro, Molly Martin, d. June 6, 1823, aged 62.
HORN, John, m. Nov. 15, 1785, by Rev. Jeremiah Shaw, Jane Rust, b. Nov. 19, 1763, d. July 15, 1843, dau. of Col. Henry, both of Wolfeboro.
HORNE, Andrew, of Somersworth, m. (pub. Dec. 29, 1804, in Dover), Lucy (Stackpole) Watson, wid. of William, b. 1742, dau. of Joshua.

HORNE, William, of Somersworth, d. Dec. 12, 1860, aged 60, m. in 1821, Olive Horne, of Dover, d. Nov. 12, 1873, aged 70.

HORNE, James T., of Wolfeboro, son of Jacob, d. June 17, 1886, aged 88, m. Nov. 12, 1822, in Wolfeboro, Sophia Nute, of Madbury, d. June 10, 1883, aged 80.

HORNE, Henry, of Wolfeboro, son of Jacob, b. Sept. 8, 1800, d. June 28, 1845, m. Jan. 4, 1825, in Wolfeboro, Nancy Nute, of Madbury, d. June 8, 1861, aged 65.

HORNE, John, of Somersworth, m. Jan. 4, 1827, Ruth Wentworth, of Dover, b. Mar. 30, 1802.

HORNE, Stephen, d. Aug. 18, 1867, aged 66, m. Dec. 14, 1829, in Wolfeboro, Mary Ann Orne, d. May 26, 1856, aged 77, both of Wolfeboro.

HORNE, Enoch, Jr., d. Oct. 1884, aged 75, m. Dec. 27, 1832, by Rev. Joseph Boodey, Louisa Littlefield, d. May 8, 1900, aged 87, dau. of John, both of Farmington.

HORNE, Ira, b. 1807, d. 1890, m. Dec. 21, 1835, in Wolfeboro, Eliza D. Mason, b. 1813, d. 1887, both of Wolfeboro.

HORNE, Thomas, son of Ebenezer, m. Oct. 18, 1840, by Elder John Parkman, in Gilford, Martha Davis, b. Feb. 3, 1813, d. Apr. 6, 1858, both of Moultonboro.

HORNE, Francis D., son of James, b. Sept. 12, 1815, d. Nov. 26, 1865, m. in 1841, Sarah D. Ricker, b. Apr. 21, 1818, d. June 24, 1890, dau. of Elmer.

HORNE, Spencer, of Orneville, Me., m. int. May 11, 1849, in Lee, Sarah R. Langley, of Lee.

HORN, Charles H., son of Gershom, d. Jan. 11, 1887, aged 80, m. (pub. Aug. 9, 1853, in Somersworth), Almira Varney.

HORN, Gershom H., son of Jesse, b. May 7, 1829, d. Nov. 24, 1896, aged 67, m. (1) (pub. Dec. 27, 1853, in Great Falls), Camilla A. Horn, d. July 25, 1887, aged 56, both of Rochester, m. (2) Dec. 3, 1887, in Dover, Mrs. Mary P. Stevens.

HORN, Nathaniel, son of Nathaniel, d. Feb. 11, 1911, aged 72, m. Oct. 29, 1863, in Dover, Martha Wilson, d. Apr. 5, 1916, aged 87, dau. of David.

HORNE, James F., m. Jan. 21, 1864, by Rev. James Rand, Leonora Varney, d. June 15, 1920, aged 76, dau. of George W.

HORNE, Charles A., m. Mar. 24, 1864, in Dover, Florence Allen.

HORNE, John C., m. June 13, 1866, in Dover, Sarah E. Tuttle.

HORNE, Gustavus H., m. Oct. 18, 1866, in Dover, Ellen Hampsen.

HORNE, Wilber F., d. May 31, 1908, aged 62, m. Jan. 4, 1871, by Rev. Elmer Hewitt, Mary L. Lowell.

HORNE, Moses W., m. (pub. July 24, 1873, in Great Falls), Hannah S. Maddox.

HORSUM, John, Jr., b. 1749, d. May 6, 1833, m. Dec. 27, 1770, by Rev. Matthew Merriam, Margaret Frost.

HOUGHTON, Josiah, m. (pub. Jan. 22, 1823, in Deerfield), Mary White, dau. of Col. N. White.

HOUSTON, Sylvester, m. Oct. 11, 1858, in Rollinsford, Mary T. Jacobs, d. May 25, 1910, aged 84, dau. of George, both of Sanford, Me.

HOVEY, Temple, son of Dr. Ivory, d. Aug. 23, 1811, aged 36, m. July 7, 1798, by Rev. John Thompson, Mary Lord, dau. of Mark.

HOVEY, George H., m. Nov. 6, 1862, in Dover, Melissa F. Davis.

HOWARD, Dr. David, m. (1) Mar. 31, 1814, in Tamworth, Mrs. Abigail Hull, widow, both of Eaton, m. (2) Jan. 28, 1822, in Parsonsfield, Me., Judith G. Chapman.

HOWARD, Henry H., m. (pub. Aug. 4, 1818, in Boston, Mass.), Eliza-Ann Tabor, of Boston, Mass.

HOWARD, John, m. Oct. 12, 1830, by Rev. John Winkley, Elizabeth Brown, both of Strafford.

HOWARD, Hanson, of Strafford, m. Sept. 27, 1837, by Rev. John Winkley, Mary Hanson, of Alton.

HOWARD, Alfred, m. Nov. 24, 1841, by Rev. John Winkley, Aline C. Goodwin, both of Somersworth.

HOWARD, George W., son of James, d. Jan. 13, 1895, aged 73, m. Apr. 8, 1845, by Elder Enoch Place, Sarah Ann Otis, b. 1823, d. 1889, dau. of Joshua, both of Strafford.

HOWARD, Joseph M., son of Jedediah, d. Nov. 18, 1921, aged 89, m. July 13, 1854, in Barnstead, Hannah A. Hill.

HOWARD, Elbridge W., m. June 10, 1861, in Rochester, Sarah E. Howard, both of Rochester.

HOWARD, Aldo B., m. Mar. 30, 1862, by Rev. John Winkley, Nancy Wallingford, both of Rochester.

HOWARD, Mathew, m. Sept. 14, 1867, by Rev. Robert S. Stubbs, Lydia A. Nute.

HOWARD, Ephraim O., m. Apr. 20, 1869, in Dover, Lucretia S. Wentworth.

HOWE, Deac. Jonathan, d. Dec. 21, 1866, aged 84, m. (1) Oct. 20, 1805, by Rev. Joseph Haven, Mehitable Twombly, b. July 26, 1782, d. Dec. 17, 1834, dau. of Samuel, m. (2) Abigail -----, d. Dec. 3, 1869, aged 80.

2) **HUBBARD**, Moses, b. July 8, 1700, d. 1757, m. Dec. 26, 1723, in Berwick, Me., Abigail Heard, b. Apr. 15, 1702, dau. of Capt. John.

HUBBARD, Capt. Philip, son of Philip, b. 1718, d. Aug. 8, 1792, m. near 1740, Hannah Plummer, b. 1722, d. 1792.

HUBBARD, Rufus, m. (pub. Nov. 28, 1826, in Portsmouth), Elizabeth Lake.

HUCKINS, Isaac, son of Robert, b. Feb. 22, 1747, m. Lydia Clay.
HUCKINS, John, son of Capt. John, d. Dec. 20, 1794, m. near 1750, Mary -----, d. Apr. 20, 1820, aged 90.
HUCKINS, John, m. July 18, 1784, by Rev. Isaac Smith, Hannah Mudgett, both of Gilmanton.
HUCKINS, Joseph, m. (1) Hannah Waldron, d. Dec. 15, 1825, aged 33, m. (2) Mar. 18, 1827, by Elder Enoch Place, Sarah Waldron, d. Aug. 9, 1878, aged 78, both of Strafford.
HUCKINS, Israel, m. (1) Mary Waldron, m. (2), June 4, 1827, by Elder Enoch Place, Susanna M. Boodey, d. Mar. 11, 1855, aged 44, both of Strafford.
HUCKINS, Jonathan D., of Lee, m. (1) int. Nov. 5, 1830, in Lee, Eleanor H. Page, of Rochester, d. Aug. 5, 1842, aged 42, m. (2) Nancy D. -----, d. Mar. 19, 1853, aged 34.
HUCKINS, Asa, b. 1808, m. Oct. 1835, by Rev. David Root, Eliza Seavey, b. Dec. 27, 1807, d. Jan. 7, 1894.
HUCKINS, Capt. Robert, of Lee, m. int. July 14, 1838, in Lee, Charlotte Perkins, of Loudon.
HUCKINS, John, b. 1815, d. 1889, m. Nov. 12, 1840, by Elder Enoch Place, Hannah Abbie, Hill, b. 1818, d. 1893, both of Strafford.
HUCKINS, George H., m. Dec. 10, 1870, in Dover, Sarah M. Tucker.
HUDSON, John, m. July 25, 1689, by Rev. John Pike, Mary Beard, dau. of Thomas.
HULBERT, A., m. Dec. 13, 1873, in Dover, Jennie Rolfe, both of Dover.
HULL, Alfred, m. Aug. 6, 1827, in Dover, Lydia Jones, both of Dover.
HUNT, John, m. Feb. 4, 1800, by Rev. Isaac Smith, Polly Runnels.
HUNT, Harry, m. Mar. 14, 1816, by Rev. Isaac Smith, Polly Moulton.
HUNT, Joseph St.(?) L., m. Oct. 26, 1826, in Durham, Lucy A. Perkins, both of Dover.
HUNTOON, George W., son of James, d. Nov. 17, 1906, aged 80, m. (pub. Aug. 3, 1847, in Somersworth), Melvina R. Drew, d. Oct. 2, 1906, aged 76, dau. of Solomon, both of Dover.
HUNTRESS, Christopher, of Newington, b. 1728, m. Sept. 22, 1750, by Rev. Jos. Adams, Elizabeth Pearson, of Hampton.
HUNTRESS, Christopher, Sr., of Newington, m. Aug. 9, 1770, by Rev. Jos. Adams, Mrs. Abigail Hodgdon, of Berwick, Me. (Was this a second marriage?).
HUNTRESS, Solomon, b. June 16, 1749, m. Mar. 17, 1777, by Rev. Nathaniel Ewer, Lucy Burleigh.
HUNTRESS, George, of Newington, son of Joseph, b. 1761, d. Mar. 12, 1836, m. 1783, Mary Peverly, b. 1761, d. Jan. 2, 1850, dau. of William.

HUNTRESS, Mark, d. Feb. 8, 1861, aged 60, m. Feb. 7, 1825, by
Rev. Jeremiah Shaw, Esther Clement, d. July 17, 1877, aged 81.
HUSSEY, Christopher, son of Paul and Hannah, of Biddeford, Me.,
b. Nov. 8, 1769, d. May 31, 1834, m. Nov. 27, 1794, in Berwick,
Me., Eunice Cole, b. Dec. 21, 1771, d. May 31, 1834, dau. of
John and Elizabeth, of Sanford, Me.
HUSSEY, Joseph, d. Jan. 11, 1871, aged 82, m. (1) Jan. 19, 1817,
Anna Wiggin, d. July 17, 1853, aged 57, m. (2) Susan E. -----, d.
Mar. 21, 1886, aged 51.
HUSSEY, Josiah W., d. Feb. 22, 1896, aged 78, m. Dec. 28, 1842, in
Milton, Pheobe S. Goodwin, d. Feb. 18, 1902, aged 77, dau. of
Jeremiah, both of Wakefield.
HUSSEY, William B., m. May 18, 1846, by Rev. Nathaniel Barker,
Sophia Applebee, d. Mar. 15, 1890, aged 64, both of Milton.
HUSSEY, Alexander T., d. Nov. 15, 1851, m. Aug. 17, 1851, in
Milton, Elizabeth Jane Chamberlain, b. Nov. 24, 1829, d. May 18,
1823, dau. of Samuel.
HUSSEY, Silas, son of Silas, b. 1828, d. Mar. 22, 1913, m. 1854,
Rosanna A. Hussey.
HUSSEY, Charles R., m. Oct. 31, 1862, in Dover, Clara A.
Wentworth.
HUSSEY, Timothy, of Dover, m. Nov. 27, 1862, by Rev. James Rand,
Sarah J. Chesley, b. Jan. 13, 1847, dau. of William J.
HUSSEY, Charles, m. Apr. 29, 1865, in Dover, Joanna Bodwell.
HUSSEY, Timothy, of Dover, son of Timothy, d. Feb. 1, 1922, aged
82, m. (pub. Jan. 2, 1874, in Berwick, Me.), Addie M. Nelson, of
Strafford.
HUSSEY, William Penn, m. Jan. 3, 1874, in Dover, Nellie Neal, both
of N. Berwick, Me.
HUSSEY, Charles M., m. May 13, 1874, in Great Falls, Caddie
Austin, both of Great Falls.
HUTCHINS, Joseph, m. Jan. 29, 1790, by Rev. Isaac Smith, Jerusha
Parker, of Loudon.
HUTCHINS, James, of Wakefield, m. in 1813, by Rev. John Osborne,
Temperance Snell, of Lee, dau. of John.
HUTCHINS, Elder Elias, d. Sept. 11, 1859, m. Dec. 24, 1846, by
Rev. Ransom Dunn, Mrs. Marilla Marks.
HUTCHINS, John S., of Wakefield, son of Stephen, d. 1863, m. (pub.
Aug. 7, 1849, in Brookfield), Betsey Lyford, of Brookfield.
HUTCHINS, Martin S., son of Remington, d. Oct. 15, 1918, aged 80,
m. Dec. 3, 1864, in Dover, Olive A. Champion, d. Oct. 17, 1909,
aged 68, dau. of John N.
HUTCHINS, George W., m. Aug. 27, 1866, by Rev. James Rand,
Sarah F. Hill.

HUTCHINS, George S., m. Aug. 8, 1867, by Rev. Alden Sherwin, Mary Jane Smith.
HUTCHINS, Mark S., m. Feb. 8, 1873, in Rochester, Mary J. Evans.
HUTCHINSON, Levi, m. June 5, 1783, by Rev. Isaac Smith, Esther Melcher, both of Gilmanton.
HUTCHINSON, Dudley, m. Jan. 31, 1788, by Rev. Isaac Smith, Lucy Rollins.
HUTCHINSON, Elijah, m. Sept. 18, 1791, by Rev. Isaac Smith, Elizabeth Bickford, both of Gilmanton.
HUTCHINSON, Dudley, m. Apr. 4, 1792, by Rev. Isaac Smith, Mehitable Folsom.
INGRAHAM, Orimel C., of Canada, b. May 18, 1822, d. Oct. 9, 1897, m. Sept. 22, 1845, by Rev. Samuel Sherburne, Mary S. Hanson, d. Nov. 24, 1904, aged 83.
JACKMAN, Moses, of Salisbury, Mass., m. June 22, 1860, Henrietta Grover, b. Jan. 1, 1840, dau. of Henry.
2) **JACKSON**, William, son of Walter, m. before 1700, Mary -----.
2) JACKSON, James, son of Walter, d. Mar. 3, 1718, m. near 1700, Sarah Rice, dau. of Henry.
3) JACKSON, William, Jr., son of William, b. in 1715, deposition, will 1757, proved 1760, m. (1) early as 1741, Abigail Follett, dau. of Ichabod, m. (2) Olive -----, d. Feb. 1, 1813, aged 88.
4) JACKSON, James, son of James, d. 1800, m. June 16, 1755, Abigail Hill, dau. of William.
JACKSON, Robert, d. Sept. 21, 1842, aged 87, m. June 1780, Lydia Jackson, d. Aug. 27, 1821, aged 56, both of Madbury.
4) JACKSON, Josiah, son of James, b. Mar. 3, 1767, d. Nov. 9, 1833, m. Feb. 10, 1798, by Rev. William Hooper, Abigail Thompson, b. Apr. 12, 1777, d. Apr. 1853, both of Durham.
JACKSON, Samuel, son of Caleb, b. in 1779, d. Nov. 21, 1846, m. (1) (pub. May 12, 1804, in Rochester), Sarah Hayes, m. (2) Mary Twombly, b. in 1785, d. in 1878, dau. of Isaac.
JACKSON, Samuel, Jr., of Belfast, Me., m. (pub. Jan. 22, 1823, in Portsmouth), Lydia J. Ackerman, dau. of Joseph, Jr.
5) JACKSON, Benjamin T., son of Josiah, b. Mar. 21, 1805, d. May 1, 1842, m. near 1826, Betsey Abbott, b. Dec. 24, 1809, d. Jan. 15, 1873.
JACKSON, Thompson, son of Josiah, b. Oct. 5, 1810, d. Apr. 6, 1871, m. (1) June 3, 1833, Mary Ann Page, m. (2) Aug. 29, 1842, Louisa J. (Chesley) Chesley.
JACKSON, Moses F., m. Dec. 14, 1867, in Dover, Elizabeth A. Merrow.
JAMES, John, son of John, b. Jan. 19, 1752, d. Feb. 6, 1844, m. Mar. 26, 1779, Lydia Door.

JAMES, Jabez, m. Apr. 10, 1783, by Rev. Isaac Smith, Joanna Hutchinson, both of Gilmanton.
JAMES, John, m. Oct. 5, 1789, by Rev. Isaac Smith, Anne Page, both of Pittsfield.
JAMES, Thomas, d. Apr. 10, 1855, aged 76, m. Nov. 20, 1803, by Rev. John Osborne, Sarah Dudley, of Lee, d. Sept. 14, 1859, aged 75.
JAMES, Henry, of Gilmanton, m. (pub. Sept. 18, 1829, in Danvers, Mass.), Caroline Manning, of Danvers, Mass.
JAMES, John, m. int. Aug. 7, 1830, in Lee, Sally Edgerly, both of Lee.
JAMES, Andrew D., of Lee, m. int. Feb. 22, 1847, in Lee, Lillis Bunker, of Durham, b. Apr. 6, 1816, d. Apr. 20, 1901, dau. of Samuel.
JAMES, John H., m. Feb. 3, 1868, in Dover, Roesa A. Roberts.
JELLISON, Nicholas, b. 1683, d. 1730, m. Dec. 23, 1707, Hannah Nason, dau. of John.
JELLISON, Joseph Jr., son of Joseph, b. Sept. 9, 1744, d. 1814, m. Dec. 5, 1771, by Rev. Jacob Foster, Abigail Pray.
2) **JENKINS**, Stephen, b. in 1653, killed July 18, 1694, m. (1) before 1682, Elizabeth Pitman, suicide in 1687 --drowning, dau. of William, m. (2) Anne Tozier, killed July 18, 1694, dau. of Richard.
3) JENKINS, Stephen, son of Stephen, m. before 1710, Elizabeth Dean, dau. of John.
4) JENKINS, William, son of Joseph, d. Dec. 10, 1785, m. before 1743, Phebe Hoag, of Hampton, d. Mar. 29, 1764, dau. of Joseph.
3) JENKINS, Joseph, son of Stephen, m. (1) Hannah -----, b. 1668, m. (2) Apr. 27, 1743, in Dover, Tabitha Weymouth, b. Oct. 14, 1698, d. Feb. 18, 1777, dau. of William, both of Dover.
5) JENKINS, William, son of William and Phebe, of Lee, b. Aug. 10, 1747, d. Dec. 4, 1809, m. Apr. 8, 1772, in Kittery, Me., Ruth Frye, b. Dec. 8, 1743, d. Oct. 20, 1841, dau. of Benjamin and Sarah, of Kittery, Me.
5) JENKINS, Joseph, son of William and Phebe, of Lee, b. Feb. 5, 1750, d. Oct. 19, 1826, m. July 30, 1777, in Dover, Catharine Austin, of Dover, b. Apr. 24, 1762, d. June 1782, dau. of Nathaniel and Sarah.
5) JENKINS, John, Jr., son of William and Phebe, b. Sept. 30, 1752, m. Abigail Varney, b. Apr. 7, 1768, dau. of Stephen and Deliverance.
JENKINS, John, son of William, b. Feb. 5, 1750, d. Aug. 16, 1834, m. near 1787, Sarah Clark, d. May 27, 1832, aged 61, dau. of Benjamin.
JENKINS, John, m. Oct. 5, 1789, in Gilmanton, Anna Page.

6) JENKINS, Ephraim, son of Jonathan and Mercy, of Madbury, b. Jan. 20, 1780, d. Apr. 23, 1857, m. Nov. 13, 1814, in Rochester, Mercy Varney, b. Aug. 28, 1786, d. June 5, 1859, dau. of Shubael and Sarah, of Dover.

6) JENKINS, Jonathan, son of Jonathan and Mercy, of Madbury, b. July 24, 1782, m. May 29, 1822, in Dover, Patience C. Hodgdon, d. Nov. 30, 1853, aged 53, dau. of Peter and Patience.

JENKINS, Joseph, m. int. Sept. 21, 1825, in Lee, Eliza Davis, both of Lee.

JENKINS, John, son of John, d. Jan. 20, 1861, aged 72, m. int. Dec. 23, 1834, in Lee, Hannah L. Dame, d. Feb. 23, 1892, aged 77, both of Lee.

7) JENKINS, Ephraim, Jr., of Madbury, son of Ephraim, b. Sept. 26, 1826, m. Nov. 23, 1854, by Rev. Alvin Tobey, Abby T. Jackson, of Durham, b. Mar. 23, 1828, d. Jan. 20, 1899, aged 70, dau. of Benjamin.

JENKINS, George W., of Milton, d. Nov. 25, 1866, aged 30, m. Jan. 1, 1857, in Lebanon, Me., Phebe F. Kendall, of Lebanon, Me., d. Apr. 14, 1867, aged 29.

JENKINS, Silas, son of Thomas, b. Mar. 31, 1840, m. Apr. 10, 1865, Anna M. Watson, b. Sept. 2, 1842.

JENKINS, George Henry, m. Oct. 11, 1865, in Dover, Melissa E. Thurston.

JENKINS, John S., of Lee, b. 1847, m. int. Nov. 18, 1865, in Lee, Maria Otis, of Newmarket, b. 1845.

JENKINS, Charles B., m. Jan. 4, 1869, by Rev. Robert S. Stubbs, Sarah F. Miles.

JENKS, Joshua E., m. Sept. 15, 1869, in Dover, Nettie C. Perkins.

JENNESS, John, m. Oct. 5, 1789, in Gilmanton, Anna Page.

JENNESS, Isaac, Jr., of Rochester, son of Jonathan, d. July 28, 1887, aged 82, m. Dec. 4, 1827, by Rev. Isaac Willey, Hannah Tebbetts, of Rochester, b. 1793, d. Mar. 15, 1887, dau. of Stephen.

JENNESS, John J., of Rochester, d. Mar. 21, 1842, aged 28, m. Apr. 29, 1835, by Elder Enoch Place, Abigail Berry, of Strafford, b. 1813, dau. of John, Jr.

JENNESS, Hiram, d. Feb. 1, 1870, aged 56, m. (1) July 28, 1835, in Middleton, Sarah Welch, both of Wakefield, m. (2) Sarah A. -----, b. 1841, d. 1911.

JENNESS, Joseph, b. Sept. 13, 1813, d. Feb. 27, 1886, m. May 2, 1841, in Wolfeboro, Eliza Jane Hawkins.

JENNESS, Aaron, of Durham, m. int. Sept. 2, 1848, in Lee, Eliza Wiggin, of Lee.

JENNESS, William B., of Rochester, m. Nov. 13, 1853, in Lebanon, Me., Emma J. Berry, d. Mar. 28, 1864, aged 31, dau. of John.

JENNESS, Samuel, b. 1838, d. 1903, m. (pub. Mar. 14, 1861, in Dover), Sarah A. Scruton, b. 1843, d. 1920, both of Strafford.

JENNESS, Franklin H., m. Jan. 13, 1862, by Rev. James Rand, Elvira B. Quimby.

JENNESS, Cyrus L., m. Nov. 12, 1873, in Dover, Sarah E. Holmes, both of Dover.

JENNESS, Charles H., of Dover, m. pub. Feb. 5, 1874, in Newmarket), Ida L. Smith, of Bangor, Me.

JEPSON, John W., m. Feb. 17, 1862, in Dover, m. Jennie Brackett.

JEWETT, James, merchant, d. Jan. 11, 1823, aged 75, m. Dorothy Frost, b. Feb. 27, 1759, d. May 9, 1838.

JEWETT, Nathaniel, d. June 2, 1847, aged 66, m. int. Dec. 24, 1809, in Milton, Nancy Rogers, d. Jan. 10, 1881, aged 93, both of Milton.

JEWETT, Thomas, of S. Berwick, Me., son of Dearborn, b. May 8, 1789, d. June 5, 1864, aged 74, m. Jan. 9, 1817, by Rev. J. W. Clary, Elizabeth Lord, of Somersworth, d. Nov. 10, 1867, aged 76.

JEWETT, Capt. Theodore F., son of Dearborn, d. Jan. 23, 1860, aged 72, m. (1) Olive Walker, d. July 15, 1826, aged 36, dau. of Tobias, m. (2) Mary Rice, d. Dec. 3, 1854, aged 69, m. (3) Feb. 28, 1856, in S. Berwick, Me., Mrs. Eliza S. Jewett, d. Feb. 9, 1870, aged 77.

JEWETT, Asa B., of Milton, son of Nathaniel, d. Apr. 17, 1883, aged 68, m. Oct. 31, 1837, by Rev. Nathaniel Barker, Mary Ann Richards, of Wakefield, d. Aug. 7, 1910, aged 97.

JEWETT, David, son of Nathaniel, b. June 1, 1825, d. May 30, 1881, aged 62, m. (pub. July 13, 1847, in Great Falls), Susan M. Fox, b. Apr. 26, 1824, d. Nov. 13, 1899.

JEWETT, William D., of S. Berwick, Me., son of Capt. Theodore, b. Apr. 4, 1813, d. Aug. 24, 1887, m. (pub. Mar. 29, 1855, in Kittery, Me.), Augusta M. W. Rice, of Kittery, Me., dau. of John.

JEWETT, William G., m. Jan. 18, 1868, by Rev. Robert S. Stubbs, Mary E. Ham.

JEWETT, Charles, m. July 9, 1868, by Rev. Alden Sherwin, Abbie E. Flagg.

JOHNSON, Benjamin, of Epping, m. int. Feb. 2, 1826, in Lee, Sally Watson, of Lee.

JOHNSON, Jeduthan, m. Feb. 9, 1826, in Dover, Almira Stickney, both of Newmarket.

JOHNSON, James, 3rd, of Strafford, d. Jan. 8, 1891, aged 78, m. Dec. 27, 1832, by Elder Enoch Place, Peggy Tuttle, of Barrington, d. Jan. 1, 1875, aged 62.

JOHNSON, Stephen, d. Feb. 7, 1864, aged 45, m. Sept. 22, 1839, by Elder Enoch Place, Catherine Johnson, d. Jan. 5, 1893, aged 73, both of Strafford.

JOHNSON, Joshua B., son of Brackett, d. Apr. 10, 1902, aged 89, m. Oct. 28, 1847, in Wolfeboro, Hannah R. Perkins, both of Wolfeboro.

JOHNSON, Daniel C., d. Nov. 1882, aged 57, m. int. July 29, 1849, in Dover, Mrs. Julia Ann (Drew) Streeter, wid. of Ethan, d. Aug. 8, 1880, aged 57.

JOHNSON, David, m. June 19, 1851, by Rev. John Winkley, Mary W. Carter, both of Somersworth.

JOHNSON, Oliver G., m. Sept. 14, 1851, by Rev. John Winkley, Eunice Saunders, both of Strafford.

JOHNSON, Plumer, d. Dec. 5, 1913, aged 79, m. Nov. 16, 1856, by Rev. John Winkley, Mary Ann Berry, d. Nov. 23, 1926, aged 92, both of Strafford.

JOHNSON, Ivory, b. 1837, d. 1892, m. Sept. 15, 1861, by Rev. John Winkley, Martha A. Otis, b. 1842, d. 1929, both of Strafford.

JOHNSON, Samuel F., m. Mar. 17, 1864, by Rev. James Rand, B. A. Hoitt.

JOHNSON, Levi, of Strafford, m. May 16, 1864, by Rev. Asa Piper, Melissa Young, of Wakefield.

JOHNSON, Henry, m. Sept. 9, 1865, by Rev. Asa Piper, Melissa M. Cotton.

JOHNSON, Charles, m. Aug. 12, 1867, in Dover, Delia P. Chick.

JOHNSON, Augustus, m. Jan. 1, 1868, in Dover, Abbie Dicey.

JOHNSON, George E., m. Jan. 20, 1870, in Dover, Jane A. Holden.

JOHNSON, Dennis A., son of Dennis, d. Nov. 12, 1919, aged 82, m. July 26, 1873, in Dover, Abbie E. Stevens, both of Dover.

JOHNSON, Sidney, m. Sept. 6, 1873, in Rochester, Georgie H. Hurd, both of Rochester.

2) **JONES**, Lt. Joseph, son of Ens. Steven, b. 1674, d. 1744, m. (1) Feb. 1706/7, Mary Spencer, dau. of Moses, m. (2) Ann Nutter, d. 1762, dau. of Anthony.

3) JONES, Ebenezer, son of Stephen, m. (1) Joanna Ham, d. May 4, 1745, aged 31, dau. of John, m. (2) Jan. 1, 1761, Mrs. Abigail Ham, wid. of John, d. Jan. 4, 1797.

4) JONES, Ebenezer, son of Ebenezer, d. Aug. 23, 1783, aged 48, m. Mary Beck Randall, d. Dec. 15, 1811, aged 69, dau. of Nathaniel.

JONES, Eliphalet, b. 1752, d. 1820, m. Apr. 20, 1775, by Rev. Matthew Merriam, Ruth Roberts, b. May 12, 1758, d. May 12, 1828, dau. of Joshua, both of Berwick, Me.

JONES, Stephen, b. Jan. 8, 1762, d. Mar. 1, 1846, m. Nov. 5, 1782, by Rev. Matthew Merriam, Martha Ricker, dau. of Noah, m. (2) Mehitable Moody.

JONES, Stephen Millet, son of Maj. Stephen, b. Sept. 10, 1763, d. Dec. 23, 1847, m. Nov. 23, 1785, Sally Emerson, b. Nov. 24, 1766, dau. of Col. Timothy, both of Durham.

JONES, Robert, of Newmarket, d. July 29, 1835, aged 70, m. (1) June 5, 1795, Elizabeth Edgerly, m. (2) (pub. Nov. 1, 1812), Lydia Edgerly.

JONES, William, of Berwick, Me., son of Ebenezer, b. Nov. 17, 1769, d. Jan. 26, 1845, m. June 13, 1798, Charlotte Cushing, of Dover, b. Jan. 3, 1779, d. Nov. 12, 1838.

JONES, Col. Levi, of Lebanon, Me., son of Ebenezer, b. Oct. 21, 1771, d. Aug. 18, 1847, aged 76, m. (1) Oct. 15, 1801, by Rev. Joseph Haven, Elizabeth Plummer, b. Oct. 20, 1779, d. Nov. 1, 1815, dau. of Joseph, m. (2) Nov. 23, 1831, by Rev. Isaac Willey, Sarah (Plumer) Wallingford, d. Jan. 12, 1863, aged 69, both of Milton.

4) JONES, Thomas, son of Maj. Stephen, b. Oct. 4, 1775, d. Mar. 26, 1848, m. Dec. 1804, Elizabeth Chesley, b. July 10, 1784, d. Oct. 23, 1874, dau. of Jonathan, both of Durham.

JONES, Nathan, of Milton, d. Sept. 14, 1855, aged 82, m. int. Apr. 12, 1807, in Milton, Susannah Davis, of Barnstead, d. Oct. 20, 1864, aged 81.

JONES, Jonathan, m. Feb. 13, 1812, by Rev. John Osborne, Lydia M. Smith, of Durham.

JONES, Amos, of Milton, b. Sept. 13, 1786, m. June 13, 1813, Martha Lord, of Berwick, Me., b. Nov. 9, 1789, d. May 26, 1844, aged 55.

JONES, Joshua, son of Ebenezer, b. Mar. 9, 1789, d. June 17, 1868, m. Dec. 10, 1818, by Rev. Paul Jewett, Sarah Cowell, b. May 6, 1793, d. Jan. 15, 1857, aged 84, dau. of Samuel.

5) JONES, Stephen, son of William, b. July 31, 1799, d. Dec. 9, 1881, m. June 2, 1822, by Elder Enoch Place, Louisa Foye, b. 1803, d. Oct. 6, 1876, both of Strafford.

JONES, Pelatiah, of Lee, b. June 3, 1797, d. Sept. 8, 1853, aged 56, m. Jan. 4, 1823, by Rev. John Osborne, Sophia T. Demeritt, of Nottingham, b. Jan. 8, 1804, dau. of John.

JONES, Daniel, m. Sept. 27, 1824, Mary Allen, d. June 24, 1870, aged 69, both of Milton.

JONES, Samuel, of Nottingham, son of John P., b. Aug. 23, 1805, d. Nov. 1847, m. Oct. 16, 1827, by Rev. John Osborne, Elizabeth J. Garland, of Durham, d. Mar. 16, 1883, aged 77, dau. of James.

JONES, Elijah C., of Farmington, m. in 1828, Mary E. P. Roberts, d. 1828, aged 24.
JONES, Samuel, of Lee, m. int. Nov. 21, 1828, in Lee, Augusta Wiggin, of Epping.
JONES, John, m. in 1829, in Gilmanton, Mary Moody.
JONES, Samuel, m. int. Dec. 24, 1837, in Lee, Susan Wentworth, both of Lee.
JONES, Ivory, son of Samuel, d. Mar. 2, 1890, aged 70, m. Jan. 21, 1841, by Rev. Elihu Scott, Harriet Parsons, both of Somersworth.
JONES, Joseph, b. 1819, d. 1895, m. May 2, 1841, by Rev. Nathaniel Berry, Druzilla E. Young, b. 1821, d. 1877, both of New Durham.
JONES, John P., of Milton, son of Nathan, d. Jan. 30, 1901, aged 82, m. Apr. 4, 1848, in Somersworth, Louisa Wentworth, of Somersworth, b. Mar. 10, 1820, d. Nov. 1, 1899, dau. of John.
JONES, Nathan, d. Apr. 29, 1897, aged 71, m. (pub. June 5, 1849, in Portsmouth), Charlotte Roberts, d. Feb. 1896, aged 67, dau. of Jonathan.
JONES, David R., of Milton, m. Aug. 3, 1850, by Rev. Nathaniel Barker, Frances D. Wentworth, dau. of John.
JONES, John, son of Pelatiah, b. Aug. 14, 1828, m. Dec. 16, 1850, by Elder Samuel Sherburne, Mary P. Rollins, b. 1823, d. 1898, both of Lee.
JONES, George Henry, son of Joshua, b. Apr. 6, 1826, d. Oct. 23, 1918, m. (pub. Aug. 12, 1851, in Farmington), Lucy Jane Varney, b. July 22, 1826, d. Mar. 20, 1897, dau. of Beard, both of Milton.
JONES, Jeremiah, son of James N., d. Oct. 28, 1911, aged 82, m. Nov. 3, 1855, in Alton, M. Ellen Sawyer, d. July 5, 1913, aged 77, dau. of Daniel.
JONES, George W., son of Eliphalet, d. Feb. 20, 1900, aged 66, m. (1) Mar. 16, 1856, in Milton, Lydia J. Corliss, both of Milton, m. (2) Feb. 29, 1860, in Milton, Charlotte Dixon, of Lebanon, Me., aged 19.
JONES, Washington F., b. 1835, m. int. Oct. 29, 1856, in Lee, Elizabeth Jones, b. 1831, both of Lee.
JONES, Thomas, of Amesbury, Mass., m. Mar. 11, 1862, in Rochester, Mrs. Mary Canney, of Rochester.
JONES, Charles H., b. 1838, m. int. Apr. 15, 1862, in Lee, Linda A. Snell, b. 1837, both of Lee.
JONES, George, m. July 5, 1865, by Rev. James Rand, Louisa A. Richards.
JONES, Eliphalet, m. June 10, 1866, in Dover, Emma D. Hardison.
JONES, Merrick R., m. June 17, 1868, in Dover, Anna A. Bagley.

JONES, Alphonzo, m. Sept. 7, 1870, in Lee, Lizzie A. Woodman, both of Lee.
JONES, Frank M., of Lee, m. in 1872, in Lee, Etta Stevens, of Boston, Mass.
JORDAN, Freeman B., m. June 24, 1865, in Dover, Abbie M. Johnson.
JORDAN, Henry N., m. Mar. 22, 1866, in Dover, Lydia A. Dacy.
JORDAN, Granville, m. Aug. 1, 1867, in Dover, Sarah E. Emerson.
JOY, Jacob, of Newmarket, son of Samuel, b. Feb. 17 1749, d. Mar. 12, 1805, aged 56, m. (1) Feb. 2, 1775, by Rev. Nathaniel Ewer, Hannah Cram, d. May 14, 1792, aged 37, dau. of James, m. (2) Lovey Thompson, d. Oct. 14, 1798, aged 34, dau. of Sgt. John, m. (3) Dec. 16, 1802, Alice Horn, d. 1850, aged 88.
JOY, Samuel, son of Samuel, b. Feb. 18, 1769, d. Dec. 15, 1849, aged 81, m. Dec. 21, 1794, Hannah Edgerly, d. 1838, aged 64, dau. of Jonathan.
JOY, James, son of Jacob, b. Mar. 4, 1778, d. July 14, 1859, m. Dec. 18, 1802, Sarah Pickering, b. Dec. 15, 1781, d. Dec. 14, 1858.
JOY, Jacob, Jr., son of Jacob, d. May 8, 1858, aged 78, m. Oct. 15, 1803, by Rev. Robert Gray, Elizabeth Hicks, d. May 28, 1872, aged 90, dau. of Joseph, both of Madbury.
JOY, Ebenezer, son of Samuel, b. May 30, 1785, d. Aug. 8, 1827, m. Jan. 16, 1815, Nancy Watson, d. Oct. 1, 1827, dau. of Henry.
JOY, Ebenezer, son of Timothy, b. Nov. 30, 1812, m. Feb. 28, 1833, Mehitable M. Doe, d. Mar. 11, 1906, aged 92.
JOY, Joseph, Hicks, son of Jacob, b. Aug. 9, 1814, d. Aug. 6, 1850, aged 36, m. Oct. 25, 1835, by Rev. William Demeritt, Jane Straw, d. Dec. 3, 1844, aged 36.
JOY, Samuel, of Durham, aged 33, m. Mar. 21, 1857, by Rev. Thomas J. Greenwood, Susan D. Smart, of Newmarket, aged 32.
JOY, Lovell E., m. Feb. 12, 1873, in Rochester, Jennie M. Preston.
JUNKINS, Rufus, of Wakefield, d. Apr. 1854, aged 60, m. (1) Sarah Hayes, d. July 12, 1828, aged 25, dau. of James, m. (2) (pub. July 21, 1829, in Milton), Temperance P. Adams, of Milton, d. Mar. 14, 1874, aged 74.
JUNKINS, Alexander, of Great Falls, son of Alexander, d. Mar. 8, 1900, aged 86, m. (pub. Apr. 25, 1837, in Eliot, Me.), Elizabeth L. Staples, of Eliot, Me., d. Jan. 15, 1902, aged 83, dau. of Oliver.
JUNKINS, Rufus A., son of Rufus, b. Jan. 28, 1825, m. (1) July 13, 1845, by Rev. Nathaniel Barker, Nancy M. Thurston, d. May 1848, both of Wakefield, m. (2) June 26, Abigail Sawyer, b. 1832, d. 1915, dau. of Admiral.

JUNKINS, James H., son of Rufus, b. 1823, d. 1896, m. Oct. 16, 1852, by Rev. Nathaniel Barker, Sally Wentworth, of Wakefield, b. 1830, d. May 23, 1903, dau. of Albra.
KEAY, William G., m. Aug. 14, 1849, by Rev. Tho. G. Salter, Olive J. Emery, d. Dec. 22, 1903, aged 74, dau. of Timothy, both of Dover.
KEITH, George H., m. May 7, 1863, in Dover, Lucy A. Wiggin.
KELLAM, A. N., m. July 20, 1864, by Rev. Ezra Haskell, Emma C. Drew.
KELLEY, Jacob, m. Dec. 1772, in Gilmanton, Deborah Page.
KELLEY, Macajah, m. Dec. 10, 1783, by Rev. Isaac Smith, Mary Gilman, both of Gilmanton.
KELLEY, Edward P., m. May 12, 1862, in Dover, Lizzie Bateman, d. Oct. 6, 1917, aged 70.
KENNARD, Daniel, of Plaistow, m. int. Nov. 15, 1834, in Lee, Sarah A. Garland, of Lee.
KENNISON, John, m. (pub. Dec. 12, 1807, in Newmarket), by Rev. John Osborne, Polly Kennison, of Newmarket.
KENNISON, Stephen, of Reedfield, Me., m. Dec. 8, 1845, in Lee, Sarah L. Burley, of Lee.
KENNISTON, James, of Greenland, m. Nov. 7, 1723, Elizabeth Drew, dau. of Francis.
KENNISTON, Francis, of Northfield, m. Nov. 25, 1802, by Rev. Isaac Smith, Sally Kenniston, of Gilmanton.
KENNISTON, Stephen, of Reedfield, Me., m. Dec. 5, 1845, in Lee, Sarah L. Burleigh, of Lee, d. Feb. 12, 1881, aged 75.
6) KENT, Richard, Jr., son of Richard, d. June 8, 1842, aged 77, m. (1) June 9, 1814, by Rev. John Osborne, Polly Crommett, of Durham, dau. of John, m. (2) Sept. 1821, by Rev. John Osborne, Love Bickford, b. Feb. 13, 1800, d. Feb. 6, 1888, aged 88, dau. of Robert.
KEPPEL, John F., m. Nov. 3, 1868, by Rev. Robert S. Stubbs, Georgia A. Welch.
5) KIMBALL, Ezra, son of Ezra, b. near 1739, d. Mar. 1817, m. Eleanor Horne, bpt. Apr. 18, 1742, dau. of John.
KIMBALL, John, m. Feb. 6, 1781, by Rev. Is. Smith, Sarah Crosby.
KIMBALL, John, m. Nov. 17, 1782, by Rev. Isaac Smith, Susanna Gill, both of Hopkinton.
KIMBALL, Trueworthy, m. Mar. 23, 1786, by Rev. Isaac Smith, Hannah Gilman, both of Gilmanton.
6) KIMBALL, Paul, son of Daniel, m. Sept. 3, 1801, by Rev. Joseph Haven, Lois Knight, b. 1780, d. June 10, 1858, dau. of William.
KIMBALL, Nathaniel, of Gilmanton, m. Aug. 22, 1802, by Rev. Isaac Smith, Dolly Towle, of Alton.

7) KIMBALL, Jesse, son of Ephraim, b. Apr. 19, 1781, m. Apr. 25, 1804, in Farmington, Abigail Varney, b. June 12, 1780, dau. of Nathaniel, lived in Hiram, Me.

7) KIMBALL, John, of Hiram, Me., son of Ephraim, b. Feb. 20, 1796, m. (1) May 26, 1817, in Rochester, Mrs. Sarah Howe, m. (2) Mehitable Bucknell, lived in Hiram, Me.

7) KIMBALL, Richard, of Somersworth, son of Nathaniel, b. Mar. 1, 1798, d. Dec. 20, 1886, aged 68, m. (1) Oct. 4, 1832, by Rev. Samuel Lothrop, Margaret Jane Pendexter, b. May 14, 1809, d. Mar. 25, 1843, aged 34, dau. of George, m. (2) Dec. 12, 1843, by Rev. Mr. Farwell, Elizabeth Hale, b. May 26, 1817, d. Oct. 27, 1844, dau. of Moses, m. (3) Elizabeth White Hale, b. Nov. 24, 1810, d. 1873.

KIMBALL, James French, m. June 14, 1840, in Gilmanton, Caroline Peabody Carr.

KIMBALL, Samuel A., d. Nov. 9, 1860, aged 40, m. Mar. 20, 1857, in Milton, Lucy D. Pinkham.

KIMBALL, John D., m. Jan. 14, 1864, by Rev. Arthur Caverno, Adaline Kelley.

KIMBALL, Benjamin, m. Aug. 18, 1867, by Rev. Alden Sherwin, Nellie L. Moulton.

KING, Samuel, of Pittsfield, m. Nov. 24, 1802, by Rev. Isaac Smith, Polly French, of Gilmanton.

KING, Thomas J., m. May 28, 1870, in Dover, Jennie A. Getchell.

KING, Benjamin, m. July 12, 1870, in Dover, Abby Pray.

KINGSBURY, James A., m. Sept. 2, 1864, in Dover, Georgiana D. Thomas.

KINGSBURY, Byron F., m. Dec. 25, 1867, in Dover, Caroline M. Chick.

KITTREDGE, John, m. June 30, 1864, in Dover, Harriet H. Peirce.

KNEELEY, Andrew, m. Apr. 3, 1780, by Rev. Isaac Smith, Mary Paine.

KNIGHT, Ephraim, of Tamworth, d. Feb. 4, 1823, aged 64, m. Sept. 28, 1783, by Rev. Jeremiah Shaw, Joanna Clark, of Moultonboro.

KNIGHT, Hatevil, son of Joseph, b. 1765, d. July 12, 1849, m. (1) Oct. 25, 1789, in Rochester, Polly Bryant, b. Oct. 4, 1768, d. June 28, 1801, dau. of Walter, m. (2) Aug. 29, 1805, in Rochester, Mary McDuffee, b. 1779, d. Feb. 25, 1849.

KNIGHT, Robert, d. Apr. 30, 1826, aged 60, m. Oct. 14, 1792, by Rev. Joseph Haven, Susanna Kimball, d. May 20, 1856, aged 86, both of Rochester.

KNIGHT, James F., m. Aug. 3, 1862, in Dover, S. A. Nelson.

KNIGHT, Gilman, m. Dec. 11, 1862, in Dover, Mary C. Pinder.

KNIGHT, John D., b. 1835, m. int. July 23, 1864, in Lee, Anna E. Cook, b. 1846, both of Lee.

KNIGHT, Moses B., m. Nov. 26, 1873, in Alton, Jennie M. Lougee, both of Great Falls.

KNOWLES, James, b. Feb. 26, 1720, d. 1802, m. (1) Oct. 11, 1744, Mary Libbey, b. Mar. 4, 1722, dau. of Isaac, m. (2) Comfort Wallis, m. (3) May 30, 1751, by Rev. Amos Main, Experience Chamberlain, b. 1727, dau. of William.

KNOWLES, John, m. Apr. 5, 1805, by Rev. Isaac Smith, Sakey Buzzell, both of Gilmanton.

KNOWLTON, Oliver, of Newmarket, m. Apr. 29, 1854, in Newmarket, Ellen K. Drew, of Durham, b. Sept. 20, 1833, dau. of Nicholas.

KNOWLTON, Charles T., m. May 4, 1869, in Dover, Martha Hodgdon.

KNOX, John, b. 1799, d. 1845, m. in 1827, in Lebanon, Me., Elizabeth Jones, b. Jan. 30, 1802, d. 1832.

KNOX, Jesse, of Lebanon, Me., d. Aug. 29, 1878, aged 76, m. (pub. July 24, 1827, in Milton), Lydia Dore, of Milton, d. Mar. 16, 1860, aged 59.

KNOX, Ira L., son of John, d. June 2, 1911, aged 81, m. Jan. 4, 1850, in Milton, Sarah A. Pinkham, b. 1828, d. 1917.

KNOX, Hosea B., son of Jesse, d. Oct. 2, 1895, aged 65, m. Feb. 29, 1852, in Milton, Belinda O. Leighton, b. 1836, d. Mar. 20, 1882, dau. of Jedediah.

KNOX, Asa W., m. July 4, 1865, in Dover, Abbie H. Chick.

LADD, Col. Eliphalet, d. Feb. 1806, aged 62, m. early as 1790, Elizabeth Bragg, d. Sept. 4, 1797, aged 31, sister of Samuel, Jr. (Was it his second marriage?) See *History of Exeter*.

LADD, Thomas, m. Dec. 11, 1806, by Rev. Isaac Smith, Eunice Lyford.

LADD, Jonathan, of Meredith, m. Feb. 20, 1807, by Rev. Isaac Smith, Rachel Prescott, of Gilmanton.

LAKE, Otis, m. (pub. May 12, 1804, in Dover), Abigail Ricker.

LAMOS, Nathaniel, of Oyster River, b. 1653, m. early as 1705, Deliverance Clark, d. July 2, 1706.

LAMOS, Moses, son of Samuel, m. Oct. 1791, Judith Hill, d. 1860, dau. of Edward, both of Lee.

LAMOS, Jonathan, son of Nathaniel and Abigail, b. Jan. 5, 1769, d. July 1806, m. (1) Sept. 23, 1795, in Dover, Susanna Hanson, b. Aug. 7, 1767, d. Jan. 12, 1797, dau. of Stephen and Mary, m. (2) about 1798, Keziah Austin, b. Aug. 7, 1778, dau. of Elijah, both of Dover.

LAMOS, Samuel, d. Aug. 20, 1872, aged 77, m. Dec. 1, 1819, by Rev. William Demeritt, Susan Langmaid.

NEW HAMPSHIRE MARRIAGES SUPPLEMENT

LAMOS, Nathaniel, m. int. Nov. 8, 1824, in Lee, Rhoda Ricker, both of Lee.

LAMOS, Samuel, m. int. Oct. 2, 1836, in Lee, Mrs. Polly Glover, both of Lee.

LAMOS, Horace A., m. Nov. 24, 1870, by Rev. Elmer Hewitt, Jennie Collins.

LAMPER, Samuel, m. Nov. 4, 1802, by Rev. Isaac Smith, Sally Burley, both of Gilmanton.

LAMPREY, Asa, b. Jan. 12, 1780, d. Sept. 6, 1865, m. Mar. 17, 1807, Nancy Shannon, b. June 7, 1789, d. May 17, 1855, dau. of Nathaniel.

LAMPSON, Ephraim H., m. Aug. 15, 1824, Elizabeth Clark, d. 1855.

LANE, John, b. Oct. 12, 1709, d. Feb. 13, 1784, m. (1) Sept. 28, 1732, in Rye, Hannah Lamprey, m. (2) Mar. 9, 1738, in Rye, Mary Knowles.

LANE, Daniel, of Gilmanton, m. Nov. 16, 1800, by Rev. Isaac Smith, Esther Fogg, of Exeter.

LANE, Otis, m. (pub. May 12, 1804, in Dover), Abigail Ricker.

LANE, William, son of John, d. Oct. 29, 1837, aged 38, m. Oct. 28, 1820, by Rev. John Osborne, Charlotte Hill, b. Apr. 1801, d. in 1855, dau. of William.

LANE, John, Jr., of Lee, d. Nov. 23, 1887, aged 83, m. Jan. 21, 1836, by Rev. Enoch Mack, Sarah Chesley, of Dover, b. Feb. 4, 1802, d. Jan. 16, 1849, dau. of Lemuel.

LANE, John, Jr., of Lee, m. Jan. 20, 1850, in Lee, Jane Cole, of Newmarket.

LANE, (LAYN), John, Jr., of Lee, m. Mar. 21, 1852, by Rev. Justin Spaulding, Patience S. Jenness, of Dover.

LANE, Charles H., of Lee, b. 1828, d. 1890, m. June 24, 1855, in Lee, Sophia Demeritt, of Durham, b. 1827, d. 1880.

LANE (LAYN), Samuel W., of Lee, d. Sept. 5, 1916, aged 83, m. Sept. 30, 1860, by Rev. Alvin Tobey, Susan P. Durgin, of Nottingham, d. Apr. 25, 1924, aged 85.

LANE, Edmund, b. 1841, m. int. Feb. 14, 1865, in Lee, Hannah M. Jenkins, b. 1840, both of Lee.

LANE, Samuel F., m. Apr. 17, 1867, by Ezra Haskell, Mary A. Fitzgerald.

LANE, Frank, m. July 31, 1868, by Rev. Asa Piper, Anna M. Bartlett, both of Wakefield.

LANG, Joseph W., m. (pub. June 21, 1825, in Tuftonboro), Mehitable C. Young.

LANG, John W., of Wakefield, m. Mar. 16, 1841, Joanna Drew, b. Dec. 23, 1820, d. May 29, 1903, dau. of Joseph.

NEW HAMPSHIRE MARRIAGES SUPPLEMENT

LANG, George, d. Sept. 18, 1882, aged 90, m. (1) Susan -----, d. Apr. 17, 1838, aged 45, m. (2) int. Sept. 18, 1841, in Lee, Mrs. Charlotte Lane, d. May 5, 1855, aged 54, both of Lee.

LANGDON, Joseph, Jr., m. Dec. 20, 1747, in Portsmouth, Mrs. Mary Hunkin.

LANGDON, Andrew J., m. Dec. 19, 1867, in Dover, Mary Ann Lane.

LANGLEY, Thomas, of Oyster River, son of Deac. James, d. 1778, m. (1) Sept. 7, 1743, by Rev. Jos. Adams, Sarah Trickey, of Newington, dau. of John, m. (2) Hannah Kent, dau. of Joseph, m. (3) July 9, 1773, in Portsmouth, Esther Ross.

LANGLEY, Thomas, son of Thomas, m. Jan. 29, 1759, Eleanor Libbey, dau. of Ephraim.

LANGLEY, John, son of Jonathan, m. Oct. 16, 1783, Mrs. Sarah Dearborn.

LANGLEY, Timothy, m. Oct. 1787, Abigail Jackson, dau. of Robert, both of Barrington.

LANGLEY, Thomas, m. Mar. 1790, Deborah Randall, b. Aug. 9, 1765, d. Aug. 14, 1806, both of Lee.

LANGLEY, John, of Lee, d. May 1825, aged 53, m. Oct. 2, 1800, by Rev. William Hooper, Temperance Ayers, of Barrington.

LANGLEY, Thomas, son of Joseph, b. Dec. 3, 1785, m. in 1807, by Rev. John Osborne, Lovey Thompson, of Lee.

LANGLEY, Capt. James, d. 25, 1862, aged 72, m. Feb. 27, 1812, Polly Garland, b. May 7, 1795, dau. of Gideon, both of Durham.

LANGLEY, Henry, son of John, b. Jan. 21, 1793, d. Aug. 11, 1872, m. (1) near 1815, Abigail (Tasker) Nelson, wid. of Samuel, Jr., b. Nov. 18, 1787, d. Oct. 13, 1852, dau. of Joseph, m. (2) Feb. 10, 1855, Elizabeth (Stilson) Shaw, wid. of John, b. Feb. 2, 1810, d. Nov. 4, 1891, dau. of William.

LANGLEY, Noah, m. Dec. 7, 1817, Hannah Jackson, b. June 17, 1798, dau. of Josiah.

LANGLEY, Jedediah, son of Obediah, b. Nov. 28, 1803, d. May 6, 1871, m. near 1822, Hannah Clay, b. July 14, 1802, d. Mar. 19, 1884, dau. of Daniel.

LANGLEY, Olando, of Lee, son of Levi, b. Jan. 19, 1797, d. Oct. 5, 1855, m. Jan. 16, 1823, by Rev. John Osborne, Harriet Walker, of Durham, b. May 13, 1802, d. Sept. 18, 1891, dau. of Seth.

LANGLEY, David, m. int. Dec. 11, 1824, in Lee, Lucy Grovesnor, both of Lee.

LANGLEY, Benjamin, m. Nov. 21, 1827, Mary Jackson, b. May 8, 1808, dau. of Josiah.

LANGLEY, Jonathan, of Lee, m. int. Oct. 23, 1829, in Lee, Mary Blaisdell.

LANGLEY, Job R., of Lee, b. July 4, 1802, d. Aug. 23, 1870, m. May 25, 1830, Deliverance Caldwell, of Barrington, b. Oct. 12, 1809, d. Mar. 14, 1871.

LANGLEY, John, son of Obediah, b. Nov. 15, 1812, d. Jan. 15, 1881, aged 69, m. (pub. Nov. 15, 1831, in Durham), Mary Willey, b. May 2, 1808, dau. of Robert.

LANGLEY, Samuel Nelson, son of Henry, b. Nov. 9, 1816, d. Jan. 8, 1889, m. (pub. Apr. 28, 1840, in Pittsfield), Abigail F. Hatch, both of Barnstead.

LANGLEY, John O., d. July 1, 1863, aged 42, m. July 4, 1850, by Elder Samuel Sherburne, Hannah T. Jones, d. May 24, 1868, both of Lee.

LANGLEY, John Henry, of Barnstead, son of Henry, b. 1825, m. (pub. Feb. 17, 1852, in Lyman, Me.), Mary S. Proctor, d. Dec. 21, 1875, of Lyman, Me.

LANGLEY, Henry, of Barnstead, m. Feb. 10, 1855, in Newmarket, Elizabeth Drew, of Durham.

LANGLEY, John C., of Madbury, d. Mar. 1857, aged 30, m. Jan. 4, 1857, by Elder Elias Hutchins, Martha A. Hanson, of Lee, b. 1836.

LANGLEY, George E., son of Alfred, b. Oct. 12, 1838, m. Oct. 17, 1861, by Rev. Alvin Tobey, Lydia M. Palmer, dau. of Ezekiel Leathers (Ezekiel changed his name to Palmer).

LANGLEY, John W., of Acton, Me., m. May 16, 1863, by Rev. Asa Piper, Nancy Dunnells, of Newfield, Me.

LANGLEY, Henry, of Natick, Mass., b. 1838, m. int. Aug. 18, 1864, in Lee, Hannah Kenniston, of Newmarket, b. 1835.

LANGLEY, Henry L., of Newfield, Me., m. Oct. 5, 1864, by Rev. Asa Piper, Jennie Puffer, of Concord.

LANGLEY, Alonzo B., m. Aug. 6, 1865, by Rev. Asa Piper, Charlotte D. Wood.

LANGLEY, Thomas J., m. July 11, 1867, by Rev. Robert S. Stubbs, Hannah Cook.

LANGLEY, George W., of Newfield, Me., m. Nov. 21, 1870, by Rev. Asa Piper, Julia A. Maddox, of Shapleigh, Me.

LANGMAID, Winthrop, d. Oct. 28, 1863, aged 83, m. (pub. May 11, 1805, in Barrington, Frances Kielley, d. Oct. 23, 1847, aged 66.

LANGMAID, Samuel, d. Oct. 4, 1891, aged 89, m. Apr. 9, 1827, by Rev. William Demeritt, Elizabeth Woodman.

LANGMAID, Minot Wesley, b. Sept. 30, 1811, d. Sept. 19, 1884, aged 73, m. (1) Apr. 15, 1832, by Rev. William Demeritt, Louisa Williams, m. (2) Priscilla Adams Chesley, b. June 30, 1837, d. Aug. 12, 1910, dau. of Rev. Alfred.

NEW HAMPSHIRE MARRIAGES SUPPLEMENT

LANGMAID, John, Jr., m. int. July 12, 1832, in Lee, Mrs. Ann Parker, both of Lee.

LANGMAID, Jacob H., son of Minot, d. Apr. 11, 1907, aged 70, m. Feb. 11, 1864, in Dover, Emma F. Davis, b. Mar. 21, 1841, d. Apr. 22, 1879, dau. of David.

LANGMAID, Charles A., m. Oct. 25, 1865, in Dover, Lizzie A. Bean.

LANGMAID, Alonzo E., m. Jan. 28, 1866, in Lee, Zetta W. Wiggin, both of Lee.

LARKIN, Samuel B., m. (pub. Apr. 30, 1823, in Portsmouth), Mary A. Lock.

LASKEY, William, son of John, b. Oct. 28, 1745, d. May 9, 1807, m. Oct. 17, 1769, Mary Randall, b. Aug. 19, 1753, d. Oct. 3, 1828, dau. of Nathaniel.

LASKEY, Jonathan, son of William, b. Mar. 25, 1771, d. 1811, m. July 21, 1796, Comfort Jones, d. Dec. 15, 1866, aged 90.

LASKEY, Pelatiah Jones, son of Jonathan, b. July 4, 1803, d. Dec. 26, 1856, m. Jan. 17, 1823, Judith Abbie Miller, b. July 6, 1804, d. Oct. 25, 1891, dau. of Henry.

LASKEY, William, son of Pelatiah, b. May 31, 1825, d. Sept. 1, 1866, m. July 4, 1848, Caroline Goodwin, d. May 21, 1868, aged 40.

LASKEY, Warren Pelatiah, son of Pelatiah, b. Dec. 8, 1834, d. Sept. 1, 1866, m. Sept. 4, 1857, in Milton, Roena Chick Mack.

LASKEY, Jonas S., of Milton, son of Pelatiah, b. Dec. 28, 1832, d. Dec. 6, 1911, m. Mar. 21, 1858, in Milton, Sarah Abby Vinall, of Dover, d. Mar. 21, 1910, aged 69, dau. of James.

LASKEY, Lewis B., son of John, b. Aug. 24, 1846, m. Nov. 19, 1868, in Dover, Lydia Tuttle.

LAWRENCE, Samuel, m. May 18, 1800, by Rev. Isaac Smith, Susanna Smith, both of Meredith.

LAWRENCE, Ethan C., of Somersworth, m. June 3, 1827, in Lebanon, Me., Rebecca Quint, of Sanford, Me.

LAWRENCE, Capt. Joseph C., of Lee, m. int. Oct. 14, 1827, in Lee, Harriet Nealley, of Northwood.

LAWRENCE, Benjamin F., b. 1834, m. int. Oct. 29, 1858, in Lee, Sarah F. Pease, b. 1838, both of Lee.

LAWRENCE, Joseph F., of Lee, m. Nov. 4, 1858, in Boscawan, Sarah F. Pease, of Meredith.

LAWRENCE, Rufus K., m. Apr. 19, 1864, by Rev. James Rand, Laura P. Davis.

LEACH, John Endicott, son of Dr. John B., d. May 8, 1908, aged 78, m. Apr. 13, 1854, in Somersworth, Eleanor Babb.

2) **LEATHERS**, William, "Senior," b. 1675, m. early as 1700, Abigail Willey, d. aged 104, dau. of Thomas.

117

4) LEATHERS, Robert, son of Edward, b. 1735, d. Apr. 13, 1814, m. Feb. 29, 1756, Deborah Follet, d. Mar. 6, 1820, dau. of Ichabod.
LEATHERS, Benjamin, m. Dec. 1782, Hannah Tuttle.
LEATHERS, Benjamin, son of William, m. in 1789, Margery McCoy, of Barrington, dau. of John.
LEATHERS, Levi, m. in 1825, S---- Green.
LEATHERS, Ezekiel, son of Joseph, b. Dec. 13, 1805, m. near 1827, Sally Butler, b. Oct. 30, 1804 (Ezekiel changed his name to Palmer).
LEATHERS, Daniel S., m. Jan. 13, 1828, Alvira Willey.
LEATHERS, Stephen, m. Oct. 22, 1835, Olive Patrick.
LEATHERS, Joseph, m. Dec. 6, 1865, in Dover, Mary J. Arlin.
LEATHERS, Levi, m. Aug. 3, 1869, in Dover, Emily M. Davis.
LEAVITT, William, of Sanford, Me., b. Mar. 31, 1752, d. Oct. 22, 1837, m. Nov. 27, 1788, in Wakefield, Elizabeth Hardy.
LEAVITT, Ephraim, m. Mar. 16, 1795, by Rev. Isaac Smith, Judith Cogswell, both of Gilmanton.
LEAVITT, William, of Wakefield, d. Sept. 4, 1820, aged 44, m. Mar. 28, 1798, in Wakefield, Polly Goodwin, of Rochester, d. Apr. 27, 1813, aged 34.
LEAVITT, Joseph, m. Feb. 1, 1801, in Lee, Mary Wiggin.
LEAVITT, Benjamin, m. Jan. 8, 1807, by Rev. Isaac Smith, Lydia Sanborn, both of Gilmanton.
LEAVITT, Capt. John C., d. Sept. 3, 1864, aged 47, m. Sept. 18, 1843, in Wolfeboro, Betsey S. Rust, d. Mar. 29, 1890, aged 66, both of Wolfeboro.
LEAVITT, Joseph, m. Dec. 13, 1873, in Northwood, Etta C. Babb, both of Strafford.
LEE, Ebenezer, b. 1729, d. 1808, m. Mar. 27, 1788, by Rev. Jeremiah Shaw, Mary Brown, d. Oct. 29, 1823, aged 73 (Was this a second marriage?).
LEE, Deac. Nathan, son of David, m. 1796, by Rev. Jeremiah Shaw, Mary Wiggin.
LEE, Charles E., m. Sept. 8, 1869, in Dover, Ellen S. Jerold.
LEGG, Frank W., m. Dec. 24, 1873, in Dover, Carrie M. Warren, both of Dover.
LEGRO, Daniel, son of Thomas, b. Feb. 7, 1795, d. Sept. 27, 1834, m. (1) Feb. 27, 1817, by Rev. Paul Jewett, Ruth Horne, d. Apr. 1, 1820, m. (2) int. July 9, 1822, in Lebanon, Me., Lydia Plummer, b. Jan. 25, 1798, d. Dec. 19, 1845.
LEGRO, David, son of David, b. Nov. 20, 1820, d. Nov. 3, 1904, m. Eunice Dore, b. Aug. 26, 1826, d. July 13, 1879.
5) **LEIGHTON**, Stephen, son of Gideon, d. July 6, 1824, aged 60, m. (1) June 16, 1794, by Rev. William Hooper, Polly Emery, d. Mar.

11, 1810, aged 35, both of Barrington, m. (2) Deborah -----, d. Feb. 13, 1860, aged 79.
6) LEIGHTON, Stephen, son of Stephen, b. 1813, d. Aug. 11, 1896, m. Oct. 24, 1833, by Elder Enoch Place, Susan Montgomery, b. 1813, d. Dec. 1, 1898, both of Strafford.
LEIGHTON, William S., of Epping, m. int. Aug. 11, 1834, in Lee, Betsey Stevens, of Lee.
LEIGHTON, John, m. Jan. 25, 1862, in Dover, Lavina S. Hussey.
LEVI, William A., m. May 18, 1869, in Dover, Sarah E. Horne.
LEWIS, William H., d. Feb. 7, 1858, aged 30, m. Oct. 18, 1849, by Rev. Charles N. Smith, Lydia Jane Emerson, b. May 1824, d. Jan. 25, 1911, dau. of Daniel, both of Dover.
LEWIS, William, m. Oct. 26, 1854, by Elder Israel Chesley, Mrs. Olive (French) Huckins, wid. of Ebenezer, both of Newmarket.
LIBBEY, Ephraim, of Kittery, Me., son of David, b. Feb. 2, 1702, d. 1777, m. Nov. 21, 1728, by Rev. Hugh Adams, Mary Ambler, of Oyster River, b. Feb. 1, 1709/10, dau. of John.
LIBBEY, Stephen, son of Nathaniel, b. 1741, d. May 8, 1793, aged 52, m. (1) Apr. 22, 1761, by Rev. John Morse, Alice Guptill, dau. of Samuel, m. (2) July 23, 1773, by Rev. Matthew Merriam, Hannah Young, both of Berwick, Me.
LIBBEY, Sgt. Charles, Jr., b. Dec. 16, 1749, d. 1791, m. July 16, 1772, by Rev. Matthew Merriam, Sarah Pray.
LIBBEY, Ephraim, m. Feb. 27, 1783, by Rev. Isaac Smith, Judith Page.
LIBBEY, Dr. Benjamin, b. Mar. 16, 1777, d. Sept. 17, 1821, m. Apr. 5, 1802, by Rev. Joseph Haven, Sukey Demeritt, b. May 3, 1789, dau. of Paul, both of Farmington.
LIBBEY, Oliver, of Eliot, Me., b. Jan. 6, 1799, m. Nov. 2, 1823, by Rev. J. W. Clary, Elizabeth Henderson, of Dover, d. June 5, 1871, aged 70.
LIBBEY, Dudley Leavitt, of Wolfeboro, d. Dec. 29, 1856, aged 53, m. Oct. 7, 1827, in Tuftonboro, Sarah Ann Wiggin, of Tuftonboro, b. 1798, d. 1888, dau. of Samuel.
LIBBEY, Joshua, d. Mar. 8, 1894, aged 81, m. (1) May 9, 1841, by Rev. John Winkley, Esther Tuttle, d. June 13, 1853, aged 38, both of Strafford, m. (2) Apr. 27, 1856, Martha Smith, of Strafford.
LIBBEY, Jacob, m. Apr. 23, 1849, by Elder Elias Hutchins, Rebecca K. Bunker, d. Oct. 18, 1860, dau. of James.
LIBBEY, Charles H., son of Joshua, d. Dec. 12, 1911, aged 79, m. (pub. Dec. 10, 1857, in Somersworth), Julia Ann, Legro, b. Apr. 10, 1839, dau. of Thomas, Jr., both of Lebanon, Me.
LIBBEY, Martin A., m. Feb. 26, 1870, in Dover, Mattie E. Leavitt.

LIBBEY, Benjamin F., m. June 18, 1870, in Dover, Almeda Webber.
LILLY, William, m. May 16, 1863, by Rev. John Brady, Mary Hart.
LITTLE, Paul, of Lee, m. June 22, 1800, Hannah Crawford, dau. of Daniel.
LITTLE, John, of Lee, m. July 4, 1802, Mary Crawford, dau. of Daniel.
LITTLEFIELD, Albert Haynes, of Boston, Mass., son of Ralph, d. Apr. 22, 1890, aged 68, m. Aug. 6, 1851, by Rev. Joseph Boodey, Sarah B. Locke, of Dover, b. 1821, d. 1893, dau. of Benjamin B.
LITTLEFIELD, Edward E., d. Nov. 17, 1905, aged 76, m. Aug. 17, 1852, in Dover, Hannah E. Leighton, d. Aug. 20, 1930, aged 97, dau. of William P., both of Dover.
LITTLEFIELD, Cyrus L., son of James, b. Jan. 27, 1837, d. Apr. 1, 1914, aged 77, m. May 10, 1860, by Rev. Francis E. Hicks, Harriet J. Webster, b. Jan. 1, 1844, d. May 4, 1910, dau. of William, both of Dover.
LITTLEFIELD, Seth J., m. May 21, 1866, in Dover, Minnie A. Putnam.
LITTLEFIELD, William H., m. Jan. 16, 1867, in Dover, Emma T. Hutchinson.
LITTLEFIELD, Alpheus, son of John, b. Feb. 2, 1845, d. Sept. 8, 1930, aged 84, m. Oct. 31, 1868, in Dover, Atsy L. Pierce, b. Oct. 29, 1840, d. Feb. 4, 1898.
LITTLEFIELD, Morris C., m. Aug. 29, 1870, in Dover, Elvira Thurston.
LOCKE, William, b. 1704, d. 1784, m. (1) Meribah Page, m. (2) Jan. 5, 1735, in Rye, Elizabeth Rand.
LOCKE, Joseph, m. Dec. 4, 1739, in Rye, Hannah Jenness, b. Nov. 1, 1712, dau. of John.
LOCK, James, m. Apr. 24, 1776, by Rev. Isaac Smith, Mary Bean.
LOCKE, John, of Barrington, m. Sept. 20, 1792, by Rev. Joseph Haven, Abigail Page, of Rochester, dau. of Daniel.
LOCKE, Jethro, d. Apr. 19, 1874, aged 75, m. Feb. 19, 1818, by Elder Enoch Place, Sukey Clark, both of Barrington.
LOCK, William, m. Feb. 25, 1830, by Rev. John Osborne, Sarah P. Dame, b. Mar. 21, 1811, d. Feb. 28, 1860, dau. of Israel, both of Lee.
LOCKE, Howard, son of Simon, d. Dec. 12, 1889, aged 79, m. (1) Eunice T. -----, d. 1852, aged 39, m. (2) (pub. Aug. 2, 1853, in Somersworth), Susan Wentworth, of Berwick, Me., dau. of Andrew.
LOCK, Henry W., son of Elisha, b. 1827, d. Mar. 19, 1895, m. (1) Elizabeth Whitehouse, b. 1826, d. May 9, 1855, dau. of Nicholas,

NEW HAMPSHIRE MARRIAGES SUPPLEMENT

m. (2) Evengline Hayes, b. 1839, d. Mar. 18, 1919, dau. of Watson.

LOCKE, William, of Lee, m. int. Mar. 14, 1844, in Lee, Nancy Judkins, of Kingston.

LOCKE, Charles D., son of Eben, d. Nov. 12, 1895, aged 70, m. May 12, 1853, by Rev. Samuel Sherburne, Ann M. Swain, both of Barrington.

LOCKE, Samuel S., son of Alfred, d. Nov. 27, 1913, aged 78, m. (pub. Sept. 24, 1857, in Barrington), Lydia A. Savory, both of Rochester.

LOCKE, Elisha E., m. Aug. 14, 1862, by Rev. John Winkley, Lucy M. Smallcorn, both of Barrington.

LOCKE, George W., m. Jan. 15, 1863, in Dover, Mary E. Dorr.

LOCKE, Ira W., m. May 27, 1869, by Rev. Jesse Meader, Mary A. Babb.

LOCKE, Alphonso B., m. Dec. 27, 1870, in Dover, Mary A. Waterhouse.

LOCKE, Israel H., m. June 28, 1873, in Dover, Annie McCharles, both of Peabody, Mass.

LOONEY, Francis, m. Feb. 22, 1848, by Rev. E. G. Page, Rhoda A. Leighton, d. June 22, 1896, aged 79, dau. of Thomas, both of Milton.

4) **LORD**, Nathan, son of Samuel, d. Feb. 3, 1792, aged 69, m. June 30, 1748, by Rev. Jeremiah Wise, Esther Perkins, d. Dec. 4, 1811, aged 90.

LORD, Nicholas, m. Sept. 28, 1765, in S. Berwick, Me., Elizabeth Chick.

LORD, Nathan, son of Ebenezer, and Martha (Emery), b. Jan. 26, 1756, d. Nov. 26, 1833, aged 83, m. (1) Mar. 26, 1781, by Rev. Matthew Merriam, Mercy (Knox) Downs, d. Nov. 22, 1810, aged 55, wid. of William, dau. of Benjamin, m. (2) Sarah Wingate.

LORD, Ichabod, son of Benjamin, d. 1812, m. May 23, 1782, by Rev. Matthew Merriam, Lydia Keay, dau. of William, both of Berwick, Me.

LORD, Pelatiah, m. May 21, 1783, in S. Berwick, Me., Mary Hurd.

LORD, Ichabod, son of Nathan, b. 1756, m. Apr. 29, 1784, by Rev. Jonathan Tompson, Louise Shackley.

LORD, Richard, son of Joseph, d. Aug. 18, 1833, aged 78, m. Oct. 1, 1787, by Rev. Jonathan Tompson, Mary Gerrish, d. Feb. 22, 1836, aged 75.

LORD, Samuel, b. Sept. 4, 1759, d. Feb. 8, 1855, aged 95, m. (1) early as 1791, Abigail Allen, d. Oct. 23, 1825, aged 63, m. (2) (pub. Sept. 19, 1826, in Dover), Mrs. Molly (Roberts) Wentworth, wid. of Thomas, d. May 1, 1858, aged 90.

LORD, Joseph, Jr., son of Joseph, b. 1764, d. Jan. 7, 1831, m. Aug. 11, 1791, by Rev. Jonathan Tompson, Olive Hodsdon, b. 1770, d. Aug. 1848.

LORD, Capt., Simeon, son of Nathan, b. Dec. 1750, d. Oct. 28, 1815, m. Aug. 18, 1791, by Rev. Matthew Merriam, Polly Frost.

LORD, John, m. (pub. Jan. 19, 1805, in Lebanon, Me.), Polly Ross.

LORD, John Perkins, son of John, b. Jan. 29, 1786, d. Dec. 5, 1877, m. (1) Sophia Ladd, d. July 8, 1830, aged 42, dau. of Col. Eliphalet, m. (2) in 1833, in Somersworth, Sarah Noble, d. June 15, 1897, aged 93, both of S. Berwick, Me.

LORD, William, m. Apr. 4, 1808, in Lebanon, Me., Diadamia Downs.

LORD, Benjamin, m. Oct. 5, 1811, in Lebanon, Me., Charlotte Downs.

LORD, John, m. (1) May 20, 1817, in Lebanon, Me., Elizabeth Downs, b. June 8, 1797, d. Jan. 1, 1822, dau. of Stephen, m. (2) May 15, 1825, Polly Lord, b. Mar. 7, 1804, d. Jan. 6, 1857, dau. of Stephen, m. (3) Ann (Downs) Legro, b. Aug. 24, 1799, d. Aug. 1889, wid. of Eben, dau. of Stephen.

LORD, John, m. May 25, 1825, in Lebanon, Me., Polly Downs.

LORD, John, of Brookfield, m. (pub. Nov. 15, 1825, in Wakefield), Mary Shortridge, of Wakefield.

LORD, Samuel, of Berwick, Me., m. (pub. Sept. 12, 1826, in Dover), Mrs. Molly Wentworth.

LORD, John H., son of Joseph, b. Oct. 5, 1793, d. Mar. 18, 1871, m. Feb. 18, 1830, Hannah Fernald, b. Apr. 9, 1807, d. Oct. 3, 1870, dau. of James.

LORD, Rev. Gershom, m. int. July 7, 1842, in Lee, Betsey Jane Langley, of Lee.

LORD, John S., of Newburyport, Mass., m. Aug. 3, 1850, in Newmarket, Nancy Sanborn, of Barnstead.

LORD, Charles E., son of Nathan, d. Nov. 17, 1896, aged 66, m. (1) Apr. 11, 1852, in Dover, Hannah Ham, d. July 19, 1861, aged 26, both of Dover, m. (2) Sept. 28, 1865, in Dover, Clara E. -----, d. Aug. 27, 1886, aged 54, m. (3) Jan. 16, 1888, in Dover, Mrs. Eva F. Goodwin.

LORD, Jeremiah, son of Jeremiah, d. Dec. 15, 1898, aged 64, m. (pub. Dec. 27, 1855, in Somersworth), Eliza Torrey.

LORD, George B., m. July 8, 1862, by Rev. James Rand, Lizzie C. Mott.

LORD, Charles E., m. Sept. 28, 1865, in Dover, Clara R. Stiles.

LORD, Henry W., m. Aug. 24, 1868, in Dover, Arabella M. Clark.

LORD, John A., m. Apr. 30, 1870, in Dover, Abby F. Baker, d. Sept. 10, 1890, aged 42, dau. of Otis.

LORD, Coleman F., m. Dec. 26, 1870, in Dover, Elizabeth A. Furber.

NEW HAMPSHIRE MARRIAGES SUPPLEMENT

LORD, Christie L., of Milton, m. (pub. July 10, 1873, in Great Falls), Helen A. Dow, of Great Falls.

LOTHROP, Daniel, of Somersworth, b. 1801, d. May 31, 1870, m. (1) in 1825, Sophia Horne, d. 1848, aged 46, m. (2) Sept. 9, 1849, in Brookfield, Mary E. Chamberlain.

LOUD, Wentworth, son of Solomon, b. Apr. 15, 1794, d. Mar. 30, 1872, m. (1) Jan. 28, 1818, Hannah Roberts, b. Apr. 11, 1794, d. Aug. 26, 1849, dau. of Love, m. (2) Martha Witham, b. Mar. 25, 1808, d. June 22, 1867, dau. of Josiah.

LOUD, Sylvester, son of Wentworth, b. May 10, 1819, d. Dec. 6, 1884, m. (1) May 4, 1843, Dorcas Hanson, b. Nov. 24, 1819, d. June 11, 1871, m. (2) Oct. 3, 1882, in Chelsea, Mass., Mary M. Elliott, of Taunton, Mass.

LOUD, Wentworth, of Acton, Me., son of Wentworth, b. Oct. 12, 1830, d. Apr. 7, 1871, m. (1) (pub. Dec. 2, 1851, in Acton, Me.), Martha Witham, of Milton, m. (2) May 7, 1855, in Acton, Me., Sarah E. Tasker, d. Oct. 8, 1915, aged 83, dau. of Nahum.

LOUGEE, Samuel, m. Feb. 6, 1779, by Rev. Isaac Smith, Sarah Rand.

LOUGEE, Gilman, m. Apr. 8, 1779, by Rev. Isaac Smith, Joanna Smith.

LOUGEE, Isaac, m. Mar. 4, 1801, by Rev. Isaac Smith, Judith Perkins, both of Gilmanton.

LOUGEE, John Jr., m. Apr. 1, 1801, by Rev. Isaac Smith, Betsey Marsh, both of Gilmanton.

LOUGEE, John 3rd, m. Aug. 16, 1801, by Rev. Isaac Smith, Nancy Jacobs, both of Gilmanton.

LOUGEE, John Fogg, m. Jan. 18, 1814, by Rev. Isaac Smith, Anna Smith, both of Gilmanton.

LOUGEE, Seth, m. July 12, 1814, by Rev. Isaac Smith, Joanna Kimball, both of Gilmanton.

LOUGEE, John 4th, m. Nov. 24, 1814, by Rev. Isaac Smith, Apphia Gilman.

LOUGEE, Cyrus T., of Effingham, d. Sept. 16, 1857, aged 26, m. Nov. 30, 1854, by Elder Elias Hutchins, Viannah M. Hanson, of Dover.

LOVEJOY, Joshua, m. May 1797, Sally Kimball, of Gilmanton.

LOVEJOY, Warren F., m. June 30, 1866, in Dover, Angeline Starbird.

LOVERING, Zebulon, of Loudon, m. Jan. 22, 1807, by Rev. Isaac Smith, Abigail Buswell, of Gilmanton.

LOVERING, Johnson, m. int. Jan. 16, 1831, in Lee, Caroline Glover, both of Lee.

NEW HAMPSHIRE MARRIAGES SUPPLEMENT

LOVEREN [LOVERING], Johnson, m. Feb. 24, 1831, by Rev. William Demeritt, Caroline Glover, both of Lee.

LOW, Dr. Nathaniel, of S. Berwick, Me., b. July 4, 1792, d. Apr. 2, 1883, m. Nov. 18, 1818, by Rev. J. W. Clary, Mary Ann Hale, of Dover, b. Nov. 11, 1798, d. Oct. 7, 1882, dau. of William.

LOW, John, m. int. July 11, 1865, in Lee, Susan Critcherson, both of Lee.

LOWE, George, m. Oct. 10, 1870, in Dover, Mary D. Gerrish.

LUCAS, James, m. June 21, 1862, in Dover, Celestia E. Powers.

LUCAS, John, of Milton, m. June 11, 1865, by Rev. Asa Piper, Sarah E. Trask, of Brookfield.

LUCAS, William T., d. July 10, 1912, aged 70, m. Sept. 13, 1867, in Dover, Minerva E. Pinkham.

LUCAS, George H., m. Jan. 30, 1869, by Rev. Robert S. Stubbs, Zelia Churchill.

LUCAS, Freeman D., of New Durham, m. Oct. 10, 1873, in Alton, Emma E. Whitehouse, of Farmington.

LYMAN, Capt. William B., of Milton, son of Theodore, b. Apr. 23, 1807, d. Nov. 13, 1889, m. Dec. 29, 1833, by Rev. Gibbon Williams, Lydia Jones, of Dover, d. Mar. 1, 1890, aged 76, dau. of John.

LYMAN, Theodore, son of Theodore, d. Aug. 1, 1891, aged 78, m. (pub. Jan. 30, 1838, in Milton), Betsey Bragdon, d. Sept. 21, 1864, aged 46, dau. of Samuel, both of Milton.

LYMAN, George, of Milton, son of Micah, b. Dec. 22, 1827, d. June 19, 1900, m. Nov. 27, 1851, in Rochester, Hannah Plummer, of Rochester, d. Nov. 16, 1886, aged 59, dau. of Jeremiah.

MACE, Richard, m. Apr. 7, 1862, in Dover, Theodate S. Rand.

MADDOX, William, of N. Shapleigh, Me., m. Sept. 14, 1871, by Rev. Asa Piper, Mary J. Fogg, of Limerick, Me.

MAIN, Josiah, Jr., son of Josiah, b. May 3, 1777, d. June 8, 1847, m. (1) June 16, 1799, by Rev. Joseph Haven, Elizabeth Harford, m. (2) Abigail Norwood, d. July 11, 1847, aged 72.

MAIN, Dr. Jacob, son of Josiah, b. Jan. 5, 1772, d. Oct. 14, 1807, m. (pub. June 21, 1806, in Portsmouth), Sarah Ann Cutter, of Portsmouth, dau. of Dr. Ammi R.

MAIN, William, of Rochester, m. (pub. Apr. 16, 1823, in Portsmouth), Susan R. Spinney.

MALEHAM, William A., of Wakefield, son of Joseph, b. 1818, d. 1896, m. (pub. Mar. 5, 1844, in Brookfield), Nancy W. Pike, of Brookfield, b. 1822, d. 1891, dau. of Robert.

MALOON, Lewis, of Newmarket, m. Mar. 18, 1846, in Newmarket, Fanny Atherton.

MANN, William, m. Mar. 8, 1810, by Rev. Isaac Smith, Hannah Evans, both of Northfield.

MANSON, Theodore, m. (1) Anna Cloutman, d. Nov. 28, 1803, aged 19, dau. of John, m. (2) Nov. 13, 1804, in Wakefield, Lydia Philbrook, of Brookfield, dau. of Eliphalet.

MANSON, John W., m. Aug. 29, 1862, in Dover, Sarah A. Moore.

MARBLE, James S., of Roxbury, Mass., m. (pub. Sept. 18, 1829, in Ossipee), Emily Ayers, of Ossipee.

MARCH, Jonas Clark, d. Aug. 19, 1820, aged 56, m. (1) Sept. 13, 1795, by Rev. Joseph Haven, Sarah Wingate, both of Rochester, m. (2) Oct. 11, 1814, by Rev. Joseph Haven, Lydia Wingate, of Rochester, d. Mar. 13, 1865, aged 87.

MARCH, Capt. Joseph W., of Portsmouth, d. Jan. 1823, aged 39, m. Jan. 30, 1811, by Rev. Caleb Sherman, Susan Sparhawk Atkinson, of Dover, d. Dec. 18, 1821, aged 29, dau. of William K.

MARDEN, James, Jr., d. Mar. 1817, aged 54, m. Oct. 16, 1783, by Rev. Joseph Haven, Frederica Seavey, d. Dec. 1837, aged 72.

MARDEN, John, m. Jan. 4, 1792, by Rev. Isaac Smith, Rachel Shaw, of Chichester.

MARDEN, Thomas L., d. June 16, 1830, aged 45, m. Feb. 1805, by Rev. Jeremiah Shaw, Rachel W. Morrill, d. Dec. 4, 1871, aged 84.

MARDEN, Hinkson, m. (pub. Dec. 19, 1812, in Barrington), Abigail Remick.

MARDEN, Jones, b. 1830, d. 1918, m. June 26, 1853, in Wolfeboro, Lucinda W. Warren, b. 1837, d. 1912, both of Wolfeboro.

MARDEN, Jacob K., m. May 6, 1871, in Dover, Augusta A. Chesley.

MARSH, Henry Jr., m. Jan. 8, 1792, by Rev. Isaac Smith, Hannah Folsom.

MARSH, John, m. Nov. 24, 1842, in Gilmanton, Hannah F. Page.

MARSHALL, David, d. Sept. 24, 1815, aged 41, m. before 1807, ----------.

MARSTON, John H., of Nottingham, d. Dec. 30, 1876, aged 75, m. Apr. 8, 1832, Mary Thompson, of Lee, b. July 4, 1806, d. June 8, 1845, dau. of Job.

MARSTON, Capt. James, of Gardiner, m. (pub. Mar. 18, 1815, in Milton), Mrs. Mary Plummer, of Boston, Mass.

MARSTON, Abram Fogg, m. Oct. 3, 1847, in Effingham, Catherine Redman Piper.

MARSTON, William W., m. May 9, 1874, in Dover, Mrs. Jennie S. Marston, both of Great Falls.

MARTIN, William, of Sandwich, m. in 1827, Betsey Horney Hill, b. Jan. 2, 1804, d. Mar. 1862, dau. of David.

MARTIN, Phineas A., of Effingham, m. Oct. 1, 1866, by Rev. Daniel Tappan, of Buxton, Me., Lizzie S. Babb, of Buxton, Me.

MASON, John, d. July 10, 1804, aged 49, m. Dec. 28, 1778, by Dr. Belknap, Rebecca Perkins, d. Dec. 24, 1847, aged 90.
MASON, Simeon, m. Nov. 13, 1783, by Rev. Isaac Smith, Abigail Buzzell, both of Gilmanton Gore.
MASON, John, m. Oct. 28, 1846, by Elder Elias Hutchins, Avis Reynolds, d. Oct. 9, 1887.
MASON, Benjamin E., b. Oct. 6, 1818, d. Jan. 26, 1893, m. Nov. 3, 1852, in Wolfeboro, Hannah R. Hersey, b. Mar. 27, 1834, d. Apr. 3, 1904, both of Wolfeboro.
MATHERSON, Joseph, m. June 5, 1876, in Dover, Addie S. Foye.
3) **MATHES**, Capt. Francis, son of Capt. Benjamin, d. 1755, m. Feb. 23, 1691/92, in Dover, Ruth Bennett, dau. of Arthur.
6) MATHES, Elder Robert, son of Samuel, b. May 19, 1772, d. Mar. 13, 1840, aged 68, m. (1) Sept. 24, 1795, Polly Meserve, b. Aug. 4, 1778, d. Feb. 18, 1801, m. (2) Apr. 14, 1803, by Rev. Joseph Haven, Sally Jones, b. July 3, 1778, d. Aug. 22, 1822, dau. of Ebenezer, both of Milton.
7) MATHES, Stephen Meserve, son of Robert, b. Apr. 13, 1797, d. May 13, 1857, m. (1) Aug. 24, 1823, by Rev. James Walker, Clarissa Watson, b. June 17, 1799, d. Jan. 16, 1824, m. (2) Feb. 5, 1826, Theodosha Grant, b. Aug. 5, 1797.
7) MATHES, Jesse Ingalls, son of Gideon, m. Oct. 9, 1828, by Rev. John Osborne, Adeline Elizabeth Osborne, both of Lee.
7) MATHES, Reuben, son of Gideon, b. Sept. 22, 1809, d. Mar. 13, 1886, m. (1) Dec. 11, 1831, by Rev. John Osborne, Lydia Ann Stevens, d. June 10, 1844, aged 33, dau. of Joseph, both of Lee, m. (2) (pub. June 11, 1850, in Newmarket), Sally Bartlett, dau. of Joseph, of Nottingham.
8) MATHES, Valentine, son of Valentine, b. Mar. 23, 1807, d. Aug. 1, 1883, m. (1) June 30, 1833, Frances Mathes, d. Aug. 5, 1854, dau. of John, m. (2) May 11, 1867, Emeline S. Chesley, (divorced), d. June 24, 1902, aged 74, dau. of Asa.
7) MATHES, John, son of Gideon, b. Feb. 20, 1810, d. June 8, 1882, m. int. Aug. 16, 1834, Emily Jane Cartland, b. 1813, both of Lee.
MATHES, Robert, son of Robert, b. June 5, 1812, d. July 31, 1894, m. (pub. June 12, 1838, in Dover), Mary Fogg Moulton, b. May 8, 1817, d. Sept. 10, 1907, aged 90, dau. of Josiah.
8) MATHES, John Mooney, son of Abraham, b. Aug. 30, 1821, d. Aug. 9, 1868, m. Eliza Kent, dau. of Ebenezer.
MATHES, Stephen M., of Rochester, son of Stephen, m. (1) May 10, 1843, in Milton, Lydia Watson, of Milton, d. Apr. 5, 1848, aged 39, m. (2) Apr. 29, 1849, Louisa F. Davis.

MATHES, Joseph, of Milton, son of Robert, b. Dec. 4, 1814, d. Feb. 1883, aged 68, m. July 7, 1844, by Rev. Nathaniel Barker, Martha A. Ricker, of Wakefield, d. Mar. 23, 1893, aged 67.

MATHES, George, m. Nov. 13, 1862, in Dover, Susan J. Bunker.

MATHES, Burnham, son of John, b. Aug. 20, 1836, d. Feb. 4, 1895, m. Elizabeth A. Stevens.

MATHES, Robert H., m. Apr. 28, 1866, by Rev. James Rand, Mary E. Cousens.

MATHES, John H., son of Samuel H., d. Sept. 26, 1912, aged 65, m. May 21, 1870, in Dover, Alice A. Brown.

MATHES, George, of Chicago, Ill., m. Nov. 30, 1871, in Lee, Martha Randall, of Lee.

MATHEWS, Reuben, of Lee, m. int. May 26, 1850, Sally I. Bartlett, of Nottingham.

MAXWELL, John S., m. Oct. 7, 1867, by Rev. James Rand, Hattie S. Wiggin.

MCBRIDE, Nathaniel B., m. Feb. 25, 1870, in Dover, Lydia H. Bickford.

MCCRILLIS, Dr. John, of Berwick, Me., m. Mar. 15, 1826, in Farmington, Betsey Furber, of Farmington, dau. of Gen. Richard.

MCCRILLIS, John R., b. 1818, m. Dec. 24, 1848, in Strafford, Maria Babb, b. 1823, d. Sept. 10, 1876.

MCCRILLIS, John, m. May 15, 1862, Mary Jane Emerson, b. Nov. 10, 1830, dau. of Timothy.

MCDANIEL, George, of Nottingham, m. int. Nov. 1, 1822, in Lee, Alice Osborne Williams Rollins, of Lee.

MCDANIEL, Samuel, of Nottingham, m. int. Dec. 15, 1823, in Lee, Betsey B. Rollins.

MCDANIEL, Levi C., of Lee, son of James S., b. Feb. 2, 1818, d. May 29, 1894, m. int. Mar. 24, 1864, in Lee, Ursula A. Wilson, of Newmarket, b. 1829.

MCDONALD, Alexander, of Newfield, Me., m. Dec. 22, 1869, by Rev. Asa Piper, Mary E. Davis.

2) **MCDUFFEE**, William, b. Sept. 1, 1728, d. July 9, 1804, m. Apr. 22, 1753, by Rev. Amos Main, Martha Allen, b. Aug. 29, 1729, d. Jan. 1, 1808.

MCDUFFEE, George, son of James, b. Apr. 2, 1801, m. June 15, 1823, Sarah F. Davis, b. Mar. 10, 1803, d. July 5, 1870, dau. of Nathaniel.

MCDUFFEE, Jacob, of Alton, m. (pub. Feb. 15, 1825, in Tuftonboro), Amanda Piper, of Tuftonboro.

MCDUFFEE, Franklin, of Alton, son of John, b. Aug. 27, 1832, d. Nov. 11, 1880, aged 48, m. Jan. 30, 1860, Hannah Willey, of Wolfeboro.

MCDUFFEE, Henry G., m. Jan. 14, 1867, by Rev. Ezra Haskell, Ellen A. Clarke.
MCDUFFEE, George C., m. June 3, 1869, by Rev. Jesse Meader, Abby E. Parsons.
MCINTIRE, Capt. Asa, m. Aug. 21, 1825, in York, Me., Caroline Brooks, dau. of Daniel.
MCINTIRE, Jefferson, m. Nov. 5, 1826, in Rochester, Mary Nute, b. June 27, 1802, d. June 24, 1840, dau. of Francis.
MCINTIRE, William, son of Joseph, d. Apr. 7, 1910, aged 88, m. Aug. 18, 1850, by Rev. Nathaniel Berry, Melissa B. Nute, b. near 1834, both of Alton.
MCINTIRE, John A., m. Sept. 2, 1868, by Rev. Robert S. Stubbs, Amanda M. Ford.
MCINTIRE, James F., m. Nov. 24, 1870, in Dover, Phebe P. Libbey.
MCNEAL, James, of Barrington, d. Apr. 1823, m. May 23, 1805, by Rev. William Hooper, Mary Hanson, of Madbury.
4) **MEADER**, Joseph, of Durham, son of Daniel, m. (1) Dec. 8, 1756, in Dover, Abigail Varney, of Dover, dau. of Joseph, m. (2) June 24, 1767, in Kittery, Me., Abigail Frye, of Kittery, Me., b. Jan. 26, 1741, d. Dec. 15, 1784, dau. of William, m. (3) Aug. 24, 1791, in Dover, Deliverance (Lamos) Varney, wid. of Stephen, b. near 1730, d. Oct. 12, 1814, dau. of Nathaniel and Abigail.
5) MEADER, Daniel, son of Daniel, b. May 10, 1749, d. Oct. 17, 1819, m. Oct. 1, 1772, Jerusha Wormwood, b. Dec. 9, 1751, d. May 21, 1843, dau. of Benjamin.
5) MEADER, Joseph, son of Joseph and Martha, of Rochester, b. Nov. 4, 1753, d. June 1820, m. (1) Aug. 8, 1773, Abigail Field, b. Jan. 19, 1756, d. Dec. 15, 1784, dau. of John, m. (2) Mar. 18, 1786, in Dover, Elizabeth Gould, b. Sept. 15, 1756, dau. of Samuel and Mary, of Berwick, Me.
5) MEADER, Timothy, son of Samuel, b. May 12, 1741, d. Jan. 1, 1819, m. Oct. 17, 1773, Joanna Springer.
5) MEADER, Ebenezer, son of Samuel, b. Oct. 22, 1748, d. July 28, 1826, m. (1) Dec. 26, 1773, Susanna Joy, b. Nov. 16, 1750, d. Feb. 5, 1803, dau. of Samuel, m. (2) Jan. 20, 1806, Sarah Young, of Durham, b. Mar. 1769, d. Apr. 25, 1855.
MEADER, Paul, son of Joseph, b. 1765, d. 1842, m. Nov. 20, 1787, Debbey Knight, bpt. Dec. 14, 1766, dau. of George, both of Durham.
MEADER, Francis, b. Jan. 14, 1757, d. Apr. 1825, m. Jan. 22, 1795, by Rev. Joseph Haven, Elizabeth Whitehouse, d. Oct. 14, 1839, aged 74, both of Rochester.

MEADER, Lemuel B., son of Lemuel, b. Apr. 12, 1771, d. May 19, 1839, m. May 24, 1798, by Rev. Joseph Haven, Mary Kimball, b. Apr. 17, 1779, d. July 24, 1845, dau. of Ephraim and Hannah.

5) MEADER, John Frye, of Lee, son of Joseph and Abigail, d. Nov. 24, 1825, m. Nov. 1, 1804, in Lee, Deliverance Varney, b. Mar. 27, 1778, d. Sept. 20, 1863, dau. of Stephen and Deliverance, of Dover.

5) MEADER, Otis H., son of Nathaniel and Mary, b. Apr. 21, 1794, d. July 25, 1833, m. (1) Apr. 3, 1817, in Rochester, Lydia Varney, b. May 24, 1791, d. June 28, 1871, dau. of Tobias and Eunice, both of Rochester, m. (2) ----- Mudge, d. June 28, 1871, aged 80.

5) MEADER, Elijah, son of Elijah, b. Oct. 19, 1787, d. 1872, m. (1) Hannah Dame, b. Aug. 6, 1797, d. Aug. 1831, dau. of Richard, m. (2) int. Jan. 7, 1834, Abigail (Brewster) Cate, wid. of Moses, b. 1796, d. May 8, 1866.

MEADER, Aaron, son of Stephen, d. 1842, m. July 1, 1830, Sarah Berry, of Salem.

7) MEADER, Valentine, son of Joseph and Mehitable, of S. Berwick, Me., b. Aug. 15, 1815, d. May 22, 1880, m. June 1, 1837, in N. Berwick, Me., Mercy Hussey, dau. of Ebenezer and Mercy, of Berwick, Me., b. Mar. 25, 1811, d. Feb. 27, 1885.

MEADER, Stephen, son of John, b. Jan. 1, 1820, m. (pub. Sept. 11, 1843, in Newmarket), Mary Jane Pinkham.

MEADER, James J., d. July 23, 1909, aged 69, m. Oct. 14, 1865, in Dover, Anna M. Johnson.

MEADER, Edward, m. Mar. 2, 1867, in Dover, Sarah E. Hanson.

MEADER, Dudley P., m. July 11, 1867, in Dover, Julia E. Hill.

MEADER, James D., m. Sept. 4, 1869, in Dover, Emma A. Perkins.

MEARS, Joseph, m. May 1, 1863, in Dover, Sarah J. Warren.

MELCHER, John, of Gilmanton, m. July 15, 1799, by Rev. Isaac Smith, Rebecca Grant, of Exeter.

MELCHER, Stephen, m. (pub. June 28, 1804, in Portsmouth), Sally Hayes.

MELLEN, John, b. Mar. 14, 1722, d. July 4, 1807, m. Nov. 30, 1749, Rebecca Prentiss, b. Sept. 22, 1727, d. Jan. 10, 1802.

MELLEN, Rev. John, son of John, b. June 27, 1752, d. Sept. 1828, m. May 27, 1784, Martha Fitch.

MELLEN, John Prentice, son of Henry, b. June 21, 1799, d. Mar. 16, 1877, m. Apr. 29, 1823, Mehitable S. Frost, b. Aug. 20, 1799, d. Mar. 27, 1879, dau. of George.

MELLEN, William Pepperrell, son of Henry, b. July 18, 1806, m. June 16, 1831, Sarah Carpenter Lewis, b. Nov. 26, 1812, d. Feb. 22, 1870.

MELLEN, William, m. July 21, 1866, in Dover, Mary F. Hurd.

MELOON, John, m. Dec. 19, 1793, by Rev. Isaac Smith, Abigail Richardson, both of Gilmanton.
MELVIN, George, m. Apr. 18, 1870, in Dover, Mary J. French.
MENDUM, Clement, of Kennebunk, Me., m. Sept. 18, 1827, in S. Berwick, Me., Lydia Roberts, of Somersworth.
MENDUM, John, b. 1828, m. Oct. 11, 1876, in Lee, Mrs. Susan Elliot, b. 1804, both of Lee.
MERCHANT, Job Harris, m. July 3, 1828, in S. Berwick, Me., Mary Parks.
MERRIAM, Matthew, of Gilmanton, m. (pub. Sept. 26, 1820, in Dover), Izetta Canney.
MERRILL, Lemuel, m. Aug. 10, 1795, by Rev. Isaac Smith, Hannah Thing, both of Gilmanton.
MERRILL, David B., m. Nov. 23, 1832, in Gilmanton, Almira Page.
MERRILL, Luther, of Newbury, Mass., m. int. Sept. 11, 1841, in Lee, Elizabeth A. Chesley, of Lee, b. Apr. 2, 1822, dau. of Thomas.
MERRILL, George W., son of Nathan, b. 1822, d. Mar. 7, 1907, aged 84, m. Apr. 18, 1854, in Milton, Rebecca Downs, b. 1829, d. Dec. 10, 1898, aged 69, dau. of Aaron.
MERRILL, George A., d. Aug. 28, 1917, aged 70, m. Feb. 23, 1871, by Rev. Elmer Hewitt, Emma Foss.
MERROW, Elisha, of Milton, d. May 8, 1893, aged 80, m. (1) July 5, 1838, by Rev. Samuel K. Lothrop, Maria Merrow, of Great Falls, m. (2) Apr. 10, 1863, in Milton, Mary (Ricker) Duntley, wid. of Ariel.
MERROW, Daniel Garland, m. in 1848, in Center Ossipee, Sarah Moody.
3) **MESERVE**, Lt. Clement, son of Daniel, b. in 1716, d. July 18, 1800, built Garrison House, m. Abigail Ham.
3) MESERVE, John, son of Clement, b. Mar. 21, 1708, d. 1792, m. before 1741, Jemima Hubbard, b. 1712, d. 1768.
4) MESERVE, Col. Ebenezer, son of Lt. Clement, b. 1746, d. Sept. 20, 1822, m. Eunice Torr, d. Mar. 28, 1826, aged 74, sister of Lois, dau. of Vincent.
4) MESERVE, Israel, son of Lt. Clement, b. Feb. 1767, d. Feb. 5, 1804, m. Oct. 1791, by Rev. William Hooper, in Madbury, Sarah Gerrish, b. June 1772, d. June 22, 1849, dau. of Benjamin.
5) MESERVE, Ebenezer, son of Col. Ebenezer, b. 1769, d. Oct. 12, 1842, m. Sept. 24, 1797, Joanna Smith, b. Apr. 4, 1781, d. Mar. 28, 1820, dau. of Maj. Daniel.
MESERVE, Clement, d. Dec. 1824, aged 40, m. Nov. 17, 1808, by Rev. William Hooper, Mehitable Coleman, both of Dover.
MESERVE, Stephen M. Y., son of Hopley, b. Feb. 26, 1811, d. May 15, 1876, aged 85, m. (1) Feb. 21, 1811, by Rev. Joseph Haven,

Susanna Henderson, both of Rochester, m. (2) int. Dec. 31, 1837, in Dover, Mary Jane Stackpole, d. Apr. 7, 1903, aged 83, dau. of Joshua.
6) MESERVE, George W., son of Samuel, b. 1816, d. July 25, 1846, aged 30, m. Mar. 6, 1840, Climena Chesley, d. July 25, 1855, aged 31, dau. of Paul.
6) MESERVE, Charles R., son of Samuel, b. July 24, 1825, d. Apr. 5, 1898, aged 72, m. (1) Jan. 8, 1846, in Dover, Sophronia R. Tucker, b. June 1, 1826, d. Sept. 18, 1876, aged 50, m. (2) July 4, 1888, by Rev. Ithamar W. Beard, Annie E. Brown, b. Dec. 25, 1864, d. July 20, 1893, dau. of William H., m. (3) Mar. 27, 1845, in Concord, Clara L. Nason.
MESERVE, George, m. July 4, 1864, in Dover, Hannah J. Bickford.
MESERVE, William N., m. Nov. 30, 1864, in Dover, Abby A. Hill.
MESERVE, William A., of Wakefield, m. May 30, 1866, by Rev. Asa Piper, Emma J. Grant, of Wakefield.
MESERVE, George, m. Sept. 3, 1867, by Rev. Jesse Meader, Emma J. Hiller.
MESERVE, John P., m. Dec. 23, 1868, in Lee, Annie M. Plumer, both of Lee.
MEYERS, Rudolph H., m. Dec. 14, 1866, in Dover, Hannah Bobbott.
MILES, Abraham, d. July 7, 1867, aged 66, m. Oct. 3, 1824, by Rev. J. W. Clary, Eliza H. Joy, b. Mar. 28, 1804, d. Aug. 9, 1879, aged 75, dau. of Jacob, both of Madbury.
MILES, Reuben M., m. Aug. 10, 1862, by Rev. James Rand, Susan L. Pray.
MILES, William H., m. Nov. 28, 1866, in Dover, Hattie C. Kendall.
MILLER, Robert C., d. Feb. 2, 1867, aged 65, m. July 17, 1825, in Dover, Mrs. Rebecca Poland, d. Apr. 10, 1868, aged 76.
MILLER, Tobias H., m. (pub. Nov. 8, 1825, in Portsmouth), Mary Moses.
MILLER, Mark C., of Alton, d. Nov. 24, 1863, aged 35, m. (pub. May 10, 1853, in Gilmanton), Ann E. Page, of Gilmanton, d. June 6, 1908, aged 71, dau. of Asa.
MILLER, Lt. Robert, d. Feb. 12, 1883, aged 49, m. July 22, 1854, in Lebanon, Me., Sarah M. Hodgdon, b. Nov. 18, 1836, d. Mar. 13, 1916, dau. of Isaac.
MILLER, Elias L., son of John, d. Feb. 24, 1905, aged 80, m. Mar. 12, 1863, Mary J. Pinkham, d. Aug. 23, 1921, aged 73.
MILLER, James A., m. July 4, 1866, by Rev. James Rand, Jane M. Berry.
MILLS, Jeremiah, son of Samuel, b. 1805, d. Sept. 26, 1882, aged 77, m. (1) Betsey -----, d. Jan. 6, 1836, aged 27, m. (2) Nov. 27,

1836, by Elder Enoch Place, Sarah Foss, b. 1812, d. June 10, 1852, both of Strafford.

MILLS, Francis H., of Wakefield, son of Elisha, d. May 1, 1873, aged 44, m. Oct. 6, 1853, in Haverhill, Mass., Mary J. Ellis, of Middleton, b. 1833, d. 1882.

MILLS, William F., m. Nov. 3, 1866, by Rev. James Rand, Nancy M. Hawkins.

MITCHELL, William, m. June 20, 1791, by Rev. Isaac Smith, Hannah Dow, both of Gilmanton.

MITCHELL, Ira W., of New Durham, son of Samuel, d. Aug. 24, 1913, aged 74, m. Oct. 6, 1859, in Dover, Martha A. Nute, of Alton.

MITCHELL, Alfred, m. May 5, 1866, in Dover, Mary E. Gilbert.

MONROE, James, d. Jan. 25, 1886, m. Apr. 23, 1862, Mary Helen Dame, b. May 25, 1827, d. Dec. 4, 1868, dau. of Capt. George.

MONTGOMERY, Moses, b. 1805, d. 1871, m. Mar. 5, 1829, by Elder Enoch Place, Sarah Ann Peavey, d. Nov. 17, 1843, aged 31, dau. of Hudson, both of Strafford.

MONTGOMERY, Capt. Nathaniel, d. July 19, 1856, aged 50, m. (pub. Feb. 7, 1832, in Strafford), Love Tuttle, d. May 12, 1875, aged 68, both of Strafford.

MONTGOMERY, Capt. David, m. Sept. 17, 1835, by Rev. John Winkley, Mary Ann Winkley, both of Strafford.

MONTGOMERY, Jonathan H., b. 1822, d. Apr. 21, 1855, m. Nov. 25, 1850, by Elder Elias Hutchins, Sarah E. Stiles, b. 1827, d. 1910, both of Strafford.

MOODY, John, m. Nov. 1, 1764, in Gilmanton, Abigail Swett.

MOODY, Gilman, m. Aug. 21, 1778, by Rev. Isaac Smith, Anne James.

MOODY, John Jr., m. Oct. 9, 1786, by Rev. Isaac Smith, Elizabeth Weeks, both of Gilmanton.

MOODY, Capt. John, m. Aug. 3, 1793, by Rev. Isaac Smith, Elizabeth White, both of Gilmanton.

MOODY, Elisha, m. Sept. 16, 1794, by Rev. Isaac Smith, Betsy Weymouth, both of Gilmanton.

MOODY, David, m. Dec. 18, 1799, by Rev. Isaac Smith, Jemmima Bean.

MOODY, Lewis B., m. Nov. 9, 1825, in Tamworth, Lucy A. French.

MOODY, Edwin, of Thomaston, Me., m. (1) June 6, 1827, by Rev. J. W. Clary, Elizabeth Watson, of Dover, m. (2) int. Apr. 20, 1834, in Dover, Nancy Watson.

MOONEY, Lt. Benjamin, son of Hercules, b. Jan. 6, 1740, d. 1798, m. Hannah Burnham, b. Jan. 28, 1745, dau. of Jeremiah.

NEW HAMPSHIRE MARRIAGES SUPPLEMENT

MOONEY, Lt. John, of Holderness, m. Mar. 8, 1791, by Rev. Isaac Smith, Sarah Smith, of Meredith.

MOONEY, Stephen, son of Lt. Benjamin, b. Feb. 5, 1773, m. Jan. 19, 1795, by Rev. Benjamin Randall, Lydia Horne, both of New Durham.

MOONEY, Jeremiah, son of Lt. Benjamin, d. Sept. 30, 1857, aged 68, m. Nov. 11, 1813, by Rev. Joseph Boodey, Jane Coffin, d. Mar. 31, 1875, aged 87, dau. of Jonathan, both of Alton.

MOONEY, Hiram, m. (pub. Dec. 23, 1845, in Farmington), Lucretia B. Tredick, d. Feb. 26, 1901, aged 78, dau. of William, both of Alton.

MORDOUGH, Robert, of Wakefield, m. Mar. 15, 1798, in Wakefield, Hannah Stanton, of Brookfield, d. Sept. 27, 1809, aged 28, dau. of John.

MOORE, William, d. Sept. 11, 1747, m. Jan. 16, 1723, Ann Goodwin, b. Feb. 16, 1704, d. Aug. 1, 1732, dau. of Daniel.

MOORE, Joshua, m. Nov. 5, 1789, by Rev. Isaac Smith, Dolly Moody, both of Gilmanton.

MOORE, Archelaus, of Loudon, m. May 21, 1801, by Rev. Isaac Smith, Nabby Fifield, of Gilmanton.

MOORE, Delmont, m. Nov. 29, 1864, in Dover, C. M. Varney.

MOORE, James A., m. May 18, 1868, in Dover, Mary F. Tanner.

MOORE, Samuel, m. July 4, 1868, in Dover, Hannah L. Smith.

MOORE, John B., m. Aug. 27, 1868, by Rev. James Rand, Sarah E. Rose.

MOORE, Moses H., m. Oct. 3, 1868, by Rev. Robert S. Stubbs, Nancy J. Kendall.

MORGAN, Jeremiah, m. Nov. 23, 1809, by Rev. Isaac Smith, Betsy Smith, both of Gilmanton.

MORGAN, Joseph M., son of Joseph, Jr., b. 1823, d. 1896, m. Apr. 7, 1843, in Wolfeboro, Mary W. Glidden, b. 1820, d. 1881, both of Wolfeboro.

MORGAN, Charles H., m. Oct. 27, 1867, in Dover, Augusta S. Moore.

MORRILL, Ephraim Jr., m. June 26, 1777, by Rev. Isaac Smith, Anna Weed.

MORRILL, Nathan, m. June 21, 1781, by Rev. Isaac Smith, Dorothy Weed.

MORRILL, Ephraim, of Gilmanton, m. Dec. 8, 1783, by Rev. Isaac Smith, Lydia Jackson, of Barnstead.

MORRILL, Joseph Jr., of Chichester, m. June 23, 1785, by Rev. Isaac Smith, Abigail Hinkson, of Gilmanton.

MORRILL, Timothy, of Northwood, m. Oct. 13, 1785, by Rev. Isaac Smith, Joanna Small, of Gilmanton.

MORRILL, David, of Loudon, m. Sept. 6, 1804, by Rev. Isaac Smith, Lydia Buswell, of Gilmanton.

MORRILL, Arch, m. in 1822, in N. Berwick, Me., Statira Chick, b. Dec. 3, 1797.

MORRILL, Winthrop, of Berwick, Me., b. Oct. 26, 1806, d. 1888, m. early as 1836, Cordelia Hanson, b. 1811, d. 1872.

MORRILL, Enoch, of Salisbury, m. Nov. 29, 1849, Martha A. Bunker, b. May 3, 1828, d. Mar. 24, 1895, dau. of William.

MORRILL, Tappen W., of Providence, R.I., m. July 13, 1856, in Dover, Frances Jane Gleason, of Durham, b. Dec. 14, 1834, dau. of John.

MORRILL, Alphonso, m. June 4, 1864, in Dover, Helen C. Twombly.

MORRILL, Edward H., m. Oct. 31, 1867, by Rev. Robert S. Stubbs, Jane E. Moore.

MORRILL, Daniel P., of N. Berwick, Me., m. Dec. 1, 1873, Hattie C. Randall, of Waterboro, Me.

MORRISON, Jonathan, m. Aug. 14, 1783, by Rev. Isaac Smith, Shuah Stevens, both of Gilmanton.

MORRISON, David, b. Aug. 27, 1763, d. Dec. 9, 1801, m. Mar. 27, 1788, by Rev. Joseph Haven, Mary Kimball, b. June 9, 1765, dau. of Daniel and Martha.

MORRISON, Samuel, m. Nov. 26, 1806, by Rev. Isaac Smith, Sally Kelley.

MORRISON, Jonathan, Jr., of Tuftonboro, m. Dec. 18, 1820, in Wolfeboro, Belinda Libbey, of Wolfeboro, dau. of Ichabod.

MORRISON, Nathan, d. Nov. 20, 1852, aged 38, m. Apr. 20, 1844, in Wolfeboro, Ann C. Fullerton, both of Wolfeboro.

MORRISON, John J., m. Apr. 28, 1844, by Rev. John Winkley, Sarah Bodge, both of Barrington.

MORSE, Dr. Caleb, d. May 2, 1843, aged 82, m. Sept. 28, 1783, by Rev. Jeremiah Shaw, Anna Ambrose, d. Mar. 30, 1841, aged 75.

MORSE, Caleb, son of Caleb, m. Dec. 12, 1809, by Rev. Jeremiah Shaw, Abigail Brown.

MORSE, Nathan, son of Dr. Caleb, d. Oct. 10, 1854, aged 65, m. Mar. 26, 1812, in Tamworth, Sally Gilman, d. Mar. 28, 1860, aged 71, both of Tamworth.

MORSE, Darwin, b. Mar. 26, 1813, d. Jan. 14, 1864, m. Oct. 4, 1847, in Milton, Phebe Ann Huntress, b. May 2, 1827, d. Dec. 21, 1907.

MOSES, George, m. Nov. 24, 1790, by Rev. Isaac Smith, Abigail Moses, both of Gilmanton.

MOSES, Mather, m. Nov. 14, 1792, by Rev. Isaac Smith, Molly Moulton.

MOSES, Timothy, of Lee, son of Timothy, b. 1747, d. Jan. 15, 1826, m. (1) Mary Glidden, d. July 1, 1821, dau. of William, m. (2) Oct. 11, 1824, by Rev. John Osborne, Elizabeth (Daniels) Moses, of Durham, wid. of Aaron, b. Mar. 30, 1742, dau. of Capt. Eliphalet.

MOSES, Thomas, of Portsmouth, son of Samuel, d. 1856, m. Apr. 4, 1811, in Rye, Margaret Huntress, b. Nov. 24, 1783, d. 1868, dau. of George.

MOSES, William, son of James, d. Jan. 1892, aged 84, m. (pub. July 5, 1831, in Portsmouth), Abigail A. Seavey.

MOSES, William, m. (pub. Aug. 25, 1835, in Portsmouth), Clarissa Waterman. (Was this a second marriage?)

MOSES, Dearborn B., of Epsom, m. int. Jan. 22, 1839, in Lee, Sarah H. Locke, of Lee.

MOSHIER, William, of Farmington, Me., m. (pub. Oct. 17, 1826, in Somersworth), Eliza Frost.

MOSLEY, Timothy, of Lee, m. int. Sept. 25, 1825, in Lee, Betsey Walker, of Durham.

MOULTON, Robert, m. Feb. 5, 1789, by Rev. Isaac Smith, Betty Gilman, both of Gilmanton.

MOULTON, Nathan Smith, m. 1805, by Rev. Jeremiah Shaw, Polly Robertson, d. July 22, 1812, aged 26.

MOULTON, Capt. Josiah, b. Oct. 13, 1778, d. Dec. 27, 1826, m. Dec. 10, 1811, in Wakefield, Mary Fogg Watson, b. Aug. 9, 1791, d. Apr. 5, 1850.

MOULTON, Joses, m. Dec. 16, 1813, by Rev. Isaac Smith, Hannah Dudley, both of Gilmanton.

MOULTON, Jonathan, m. Feb. 15, 1820, by Rev. Jeremiah Shaw, Nancy E. Moulton, b. 1799, d. 1867.

MOULTON, Thomas T., of Dover, b. Feb. 22, 1795, m. Feb. 1822, in Saco, Me., Sarah P. Pike, of Saco, Me.

MOULTON, Briscoe J., aged 18, m. int. Mar. 30, 1855, Ellen J. Huckins, of Lee, aged 19.

MOULTON, Orlando M., of Gilford, m. Dec. 18, 1862, in Rochester, Mary J. Curtis, of Brookfield.

MOULTON, Josiah S., d. Jan. 29, 1918, aged 74, m. Feb. 15, 1865, in Dover, Ella M. Mathes.

MOULTON, E. B., m. Sept. 2, 1865, in Dover, Sarah W. Hamilton.

MOULTON, Erastus, m. July 6, 1867, by Rev. Alden Sherwin, Georgia B. Chick.

MOULTON, Moses P., m. Feb. 9, 1869, by Rev. Robert S. Stubbs, Susan F. Hanson.

MOULTON, John F., of Parsonfield, Me., m. (pub. Feb. 19, 1874, in Great Falls), Martha A. Parsons, of Great Falls.

MUCHMORE, William, m. Sept. 1796, in Portsmouth, Elizabeth Kinsman Peverly, dau. of Kinsman.

MUCHMORE, Joseph C., m. (pub. Jan. 8, 1857, in Portsmouth), Ann Maria Stavers, d. Dec. 12, 1890, aged 66, dau. of Charles. (Was this a second marriage?)

MUDGETT, David, m. June 2, 1778, by Rev. Isaac Smith, Elizabeth Kenniston.

MUDGETT, Richard, m. Sept. 14, 1802, by Rev. Isaac Smith, Nancy Blake, both of Gilmanton.

MUDGETT, Samuel B. F., of Gilmanton, m. Dec. 26, 1843, by Rev. Samuel C. Gilbert, Susan L. Rundlett, of Lee.

MUIR, Capt. Samuel, of Portsmouth, m. (pub. Nov. 8, 1806, in Rochester), Sophia Dame, of Rochester, dau. of William.

MUNSEY, Joseph B., m. Jan. 5, 1837, by Rev. John Winkley, Sally Twombly, both of Barnstead.

MURRAY, Samuel, m. (1) Elizabeth -----, d. Dec. 27, 1760, m. (2) May 4, 1769, in Rye, Hannah Dalton.

MURRAY, Jonathan, m. Aug. 20, 1798, by Rev. Isaac Smith, Sally Avery, both of Pittsfield.

MURRAY, David, m. Aug. 16, 1820, by Rev. John Osborne, Elizabeth B. French, d. Aug. 1825, aged 25, both of Newmarket.

MURRAY, David, of Newmarket, m. Feb. 22, 1840, Sophia (Pendexter) Wiggin, of Durham, wid. of Capt. William.

MURRAY, Eusaph, m. Oct. 3, 1870, in Dover, Catherine Megan.

MURRAY, Moses D., m. Jan. 7, 1874, by Rev. Asa Piper, Sarah E. Miller, both of Acton, Me.

5) **NASON**, Stephen, son of Samuel, d. Mar. 7, 1842, aged 90, m. Sept. 25, 1776, by Rev. Jacob Foster, Molly Jellison, b. June 7, 1741, dau. of Thomas.

NASON, Amos, m. Nov. 22, 1822, Betsey Cole.

NASON, William Warren, son of Levi, d. Apr. 8, 1899, aged 81, of Great Falls, m. (pub. May 4, 1847, in Norwalk, Conn.), Susan Bigelow, of Ashland, Mass., d. July 1884, aged 64, dau. of John.

NASON, Josiah, son of Thomas, d. Mar. 13, 1900, aged 75, m. Dec. 13, 1855, in Alton, Martha M. Varney, d. May 24, 1923, aged 86, dau. of Joshua A.

NASON, Robert, m. Aug. 18, 1862, in Dover, Ellen E. Oxford.

NASON, Reuben, m. Apr. 23, 1863, in Dover, Vienna M. Davis.

NEAL, Moses L., from Derry, N.H., b. in 1767, d. Nov. 25, 1829, m. (1) early as 1795, Ruth Prentiss, d. Nov. 10, 1818, aged 44, dau. of John, m. (2) in 1820, Sarah Furbush, d. Sept. 12, 1871, aged 74.

NEAL, Samuel Adams, b. July 26, 1800, d. Oct. 10, 1870, m. Sept. 23, 1821, by Rev. William Hooper, Caroline Varney, d. Oct. 27, 1867, aged 66, both of Dover.

NEAL, George A., d. Nov. 2, 1880, aged 60, m. (pub. May 3, 1855, in Wakefield), Sarah Plummer, of Milton, d. Feb. 8, 1894, aged 72, dau. of Joseph.

NEAL, Robert, d. Feb. 1, 1895, aged 79, m. (pub. Aug. 23, 1860, in Dover), Mrs. Martha Ann (Lear) Curtis, wid. of Benjamin B, both of New Castle. (Was this a second marriage?)

NEAL, George W., m. Aug. 11, 1868, by Rev. George G. Field, Delia A. Henderson, d. Sept. 17, 1914, aged 71, dau. of Samuel H.

NEAL, Enoch B., m. (pub. Apr. 17, 1874, in Great Falls), Mrs. Nancy D. Tibbetts.

NEALEY, Benjamin M., d. Oct. 16, 1859, aged 74, m. in 1807, by Rev. John Osborne, Sarah Ford, of Nottingham, d. Sept. 7, 1849, aged 65.

NEALEY, Charles M. N., d. July 1, 1876, aged 59, m. pub. Nov. 3, 1840, in S. Berwick, Me.), Caroline Hanson, d. Nov. 29, 1862, aged 42.

NEALEY, Sylvester L., of Newmarket, aged 30, m. Aug. 20, 1857, by Rev. Alvin Tobey, Sarah A. Hanson, of Madbury, d. Dec. 24, 1906, aged 71, dau. of Sargent.

NEALLEY, Daniel S., m. int. Jan. 22, 1825, in Lee, Mary Jane Burley, both of Lee.

NEALLEY, Benjamin Frank, son of Benjamin M., d. Mar. 27, 1911, aged 71, m. Aug. 1, 1866, in Dover, Hattie R. Colby.

NELSON, Samuel, m. Jan. 13, 1777, by Rev. William Parsons, Abigail Tasker, d. 1830, dau. of Joseph.

NELSON, William, m. Apr. 10, 1794, by Rev. Isaac Smith, Sarah Sanborn, both of Gilmanton.

NELSON, Jonathan Jr., m. Apr. 1, 1806, by Rev. Isaac Smith, Lydia Warner Potter, both of Gilmanton.

NELSON, Josiah, m. June 16, 1806, by Rev. Isaac Smith, Jemima Folsom.

NELSON, Stephen Smith, m. Apr. 5, 1843, in Gilmanton, Elizabeth Page.

NEWELL, Maj. Daniel, d. June 12, 1857, aged 84, m. (1) Lydia -----, d. Nov. 23, 1827, aged 37, m. (2) Nov. 24, 1828, by Rev. Benjamin Hoyt, Elizabeth Tebbets, d. Sept. 12, 1853, aged 70, both of Dover.

NEWELL, Ebenezer S., m. Sept. 24, 1848, in Newmarket, Abia D. Wentworth, both of Somersworth.

NEWTON, William C., of Portsmouth, m. (pub. Nov. 22, 1853, in Newbury, Mass.), Mary Hodgdon, of S. Berwick, Me., d. July 28, 1899, aged 80, dau. of Robert.

NICHOLS, George, d. Mar. 6, 1866, aged 74, m. Aug. 26, 1804, by Rev. Isaac Hasey, Nabby Clark, d. Jan. 19, 1844, aged 64, dau. of Josiah.

NICHOLS, Stillman, of Woburn, Mass., b. 1830, m. int. June 13, 1855, in Lee, Hannah F. Durgin, b. 1835.

NIGHSWANDER, Jacob, m. Oct. 13, 1869, in Dover, Costilla Borton, d. June 17, 1911, aged 66, dau. of Charles H.

NOBLE, John, of Lee, m. int. Mar. 19, 1825, in Lee, Eliza Kelsey, of Nottingham.

NOBLE, Silas, of Lee, m. int. Aug. 28, 1831, in Lee, Mary Jane Dow, of Hopkinton.

NOBLE, Francis A., son of Clement, d. Jan. 29, 1919, aged 83, m. (1) Aug. 21, 1858, by Rev. Benjamin F. Parsons, Ann C. Anderson, d. Nov. 28, 1887, aged 47, dau. of Samuel, both of Kennebunk, Me., m. (2) Sept. 4, 1890, in Dover, Ellen Teressa Alvisio.

NORRIS, David, m. Nov. 15, 1804, by Rev. Isaac Smith, Theodate Hutchinson.

NORTON, John H., son of Samuel, d. Dec. 3, 1918, aged 72, m. Dec. 3, 1868, in Dover, Annie S. Bragdon, d. July 29, 1928, aged 82, dau. of Joel.

NORWOOD, Gorham, m. Nov. 17, 1870, in Dover, Julia Berry.

NOWELL, Samuel, of Derry, b. 1826, m. int. Sept. 13, 1857, in Lee, Augusta M. Rollins, of Lee, b. 1835.

NOYES, Milton, m. (pub. Jan. 9, 1827, in Somersworth), Sarah Peirce, of Berwick, Me.

NUDD, William, b. 1763, d. Dec. 25, 1837, m. Dec. 5, 1798, in Wolfeboro, Polly Moore, b. 1779, d. Oct. 5, 1844, both of Wolfeboro.

NUDD, Capt. Samuel, son of Samuel, d. Feb. 6, 1874, aged 86, m. (1) Apr. 4, 1816, in Wolfeboro, Nancy Perkins, both of Wolfeboro, m. (2) Aug. 14, 1828, in Middleton, Nancy Frances Whitten, b. Feb. 28, 1803, d. Mar. 26, 1867, dau. of Jesse, both of Wolfeboro.

NUTE, Jonathan, of Dover, m. Apr. 10, 1794, by Rev. Matthew Merriam, Abigail McCarrel, of Berwick, Me.

5) NUTE, Daniel, son of James, b. near 1753, d. after 1790, went to Bartlett, m. Apr. 25, 1776, by Dr. Jeremy Belknap, Lucy Tuttle, dau. of John.

5) NUTE, Isaac, Jr., son of Isaac, of Dover, m. Feb. 19, 1783, in Berwick, Me., Sarah Rowe, of Berwick, Me.

NUTE, Jeremiah, of Milton, son of Jotham, b. Oct. 25, 1788, m. May 31, 1810, by Rev. Joseph Haven, Martha Reynolds, of Dover.

NUTE, Jacob, of Milton, son of Jotham, b. July 16, 1790, d. Jan. 22, 1879, m. (1) May 29, 1815, by Rev. Joseph Haven, Hannah D. Young, of Madbury, d. Nov. 23, 1835, aged 45, m. (2) Susan H. -- ---, d. Oct. 21, 1859, aged 45, m. (3) Hannah (Fish) Nute, wid. of Israel.

6) NUTE, Hayes, son of Samuel, m. Nov. 7, 1819, in Lebanon, Me., Mehitable Goodwin, of Lebanon, Me., d. May 2, 1881, aged 88, dau. of Thomas.

NUTE, Daniel, of Milton, son of Jotham, b. June 19, 1799, d. Mar. 20, 1875, aged 75, m. July 23, 1820, by Rev. Joseph Haven, Mary Main, of Rochester, d. May 31, 1838, aged 40, dau. of Dr. Jacob.

NUTE, David, of Milton, son of Jotham, b. Apr. 30, 1797, d. Sept. 4, 1881, m. Dec. 9, 1824, in Wakefield, Lavina Cook, of Wakefield, b. July 17, 1801, d. Feb. 8, 1874, aged 72, dau. of Peter.

NUTE, Ivory H., of Milton, son of Jotham, b. Aug. 4, 1803, m. Mar. 14, 1826, by Rev. Isaac Willey, Phebe Heard, of Rochester.

NUTE, Luther, b. Nov. 25, 1806, m. Aug. 17, 1834, Susan Goodwin, b. Jan. 28, 1814.

NUTE, Thomas S., son of Thomas, b. 1809, d. Jan. 27, 1880, m. (1) June 23, 1838, in Wolfeboro, Adeline Nudd, b. 1817, d. May 12, 1860, both of Wolfeboro, m. (2) in 1860, Mary A. Goldsmith, b. 1815, d. Aug. 14, 1897.

NUTE, Rufus M., of Natick, Mass., m. (1) Feb. 20, 1845, in Middleton, Charlotte Ann Burrows, of Middleton, d. Mar. 28, 1848, aged 28, m. (2) (pub. Feb. 19, 1850, in Farmington), Abigail Burrows, of Middleton, d. May 19, 1852, aged 27, m. (3) int. Apr. 25, 1853, in Farmington, Lydia A. Dame, d. Oct. 6, 1855, aged 20.

NUTE, Paul, m. (1) Mar. 6, 1849, in Wolfeboro, Mary A. Nute, d. Oct. 12, 1854, aged 48, both of Wolfeboro, m. (2) June 14, 1857, in Wolfeboro, Mrs. Sarah Preble.

NUTE, Samuel Freeman, son of Ezekiel, b. July 8, 1827, d. Aug. 14, 1893, m. Aug. 25, 1853, in Portland, Me., Josephine W. Page, both of Wakefield.

8) NUTE, Othaniel Kenney, son of Joseph, b. June 24, 1839, m. (1) Aug. 9, 1857, in Milton, Rosella Knox, of Jackson, m. (2) Sept. 16, 1876, Sarah Johnson.

NUTE, John S., m. Mar. 15, 1866, by Rev. James Rand, Emma S. Moore.

NUTE, James, m. Sept. 10, 1866, in Dover, Emeline Stillings.

NUTE, Oliver, m. Nov. 19, 1867, in Dover, Catherine L. Moulton, d. Oct. 31, 1888, aged 64, dau. of Enoch.
NUTE, Charles Henry, m. Dec. 8, 1868, in Dover, Sarah Elizabeth Chesley, b. Oct. 8, 1849, d. Oct. 18, 1910, dau. of Daniel.
NUTE, John N., m. Feb. 18, 1871, in Dover, Sarah G. Busby.
NUTE, George A. m. (pub. July 10, 1873, in Dover), Annie L. Parsons, both of Rochester.
NUTTER, Jotham, d. Jan. 1, 1832, aged 84, m. Feb. 9, 1769, by Rev. Jos. Adams, Elizabeth Downing, d. Nov. 22, 1819, aged 77.
5) NUTTER, Hatevil, b. Dec. 1, 1748, d. Dec. 25, 1831, m. Susanna Shackford, b. Dec. 22, 1757, d. Nov. 13, 1848.
NUTTER, Mathias, m. Sept. 15, 1806, by Rev. Isaac Smith, Ruth Smith.
NUTTER, John Jr., b. 1782, d. Apr. 15, 1863, m. Nov. 18, 1810, Sarah Heard, b. 1788, d. Apr. 21, 1878.
NUTTER, Isaac, b. 1793, d. Jan. 13, 1873, m. Lydia Jeffers, b. 1798, d. Nov. 3, 1880.
NUTTER, John N., d. Mar. 10, 1856, aged 45, m. Oct. 7, 1841, by Rev. Aaron Ayer, Nancy Guptill, b. 1805, d. 1855.
NUTTER, John Leonard, son of John, b. 1815, d. Feb. 14, 1889, m. in 1843, Lydia Severance, d. Nov. 14, 1855, aged 31.
NUTTER, Noah K., son of John H., b. 1820, d. 1906, m. int. Aug. 18, 1844, in Dover, Joanna Buzzell, b. 1817, d. 1892, dau. of Joseph.
NUTTER, Alphonzo J., son of Isaac, d. Jan. 31, 1895, aged 77, m. July 27, 1845, by Elder Elias Hutchins, Elizabeth T. Taylor, d. Mar. 29, 1878, aged 56.
NUTTER, James W., son of Matthias, d. Dec. 21, 1892, aged 73, m. Mar. 5, 1850, in Milton, Ruth Varney, b. June 16, 1830, d. May 16, 1913, dau. of John H.
NUTTER, Charles A., of Newburyport, Mass., son of Thomas J., d. Aug. 3, 1910, aged 80, m. (pub. Dec. 20, 1855, in Portsmouth), Sarah O. Parker.
NUTTER, Enoch H., m. June 6, 1866, by Rev. Francis E. Abbott, Minnie Lockett, d. Dec. 16, 1926, aged 87.
NUTTER, James, m. Aug. 4, 1866, by Rev. James Rand, Flora E. Ford.
ODELL, Capt. Jacob, son of Jacob, m. Sept. 22, 1824, in Durham, Hannah Jenkins, of Lee, d. Oct. 10, 1875, aged 72, dau. of John.
ODIORNE, Capt. John, son of Benjamin, b. July 23, 1763, d. Nov. 29, 1811, m. Nov. 27, 1790, in Dover, Sarah Hanson, b. Dec. 18, 1772, d. June 14, 1847, dau. of John B.
ORDWAY, Walter S., m. July 3, 1866, in Dover, Charlotte W. Horne.
ORR, Frank H., of Rochester, m. July 14, 1873, in Stoneham, Me., Annie A. Ricker, of Stoneham, Me.

OSBORNE, Micajah, of Loudon, m. Nov. 6, 1805, by Rev. Isaac Smith, Polly Cogswell, of Gilmanton.

OSBORNE, Samuel D., d. July 9, 1866, aged 66, m. Dec. 29, 1821, by Rev. John Osborne, Sarah Christenson, d. Aug. 13, 1883, aged 82, both of Lee.

OSBORNE, Jere J., of Lee, m. int. Feb. 23, 1852, in Lee, Elizabeth L. Martin, of Limington, Me.

OSBORNE, Hiram S., of Louden, son of Green, d. Jan. 14, 1911, aged 79, m. (1) Aug. 30, 1856, by Elder Elias Hutchins, Jane N. Waldron, of Rochester, m. (2) May 12, 1864, in Dover, Mary E. Ham.

OSBORNE, Daniel G., m. Sept. 20, 1867, by Rev. James Rand, Clara Chase.

OSGOOD, Reuben, m. May 17, 1792, by Rev. Isaac Smith, Hannah Morrill, both of Gilmanton.

OSGOOD, John, m. Mar. 7, 1803, by Rev. Isaac Smith, Leah Prescott.

OSGOOD, Daniel, m. Nov. 12, 1804, by Rev. Isaac Smith, Betsy Osgood.

OSGOOD, Joseph, m. Oct. 7, 1813, by Rev. Isaac Smith, Betsy Gilman, both of Gilmanton.

OSGOOD, John H., m. Feb. 14, 1866, in Dover, Charlotte Bickford.

OSGOOD, John H., m. Apr. 22, 1871, in Dover, Lydia Ann Eastman.

OTIS, Samuel, b. 1802, d. Sept. 11, 1887, m. Feb. 5, 1824, by Elder Enoch Place, Lydia Smith, b. 1803, d. Feb. 29, 1875, both of Strafford.

OTIS, Thomas J., of Lee, d. Nov. 15, 1892, aged 86, m. int. Nov. 30, 1831, in Lee, Olivia Jane Goodwin, of Newmarket, d. Mar. 6, 1876, aged 66.

OTIS, Simeon, m. Jan. 26, 1832, by Rev. John Osborne, Mrs. Catherine (Pinkham) Jenkins, wid. of Timothy, b. Nov. 29, 1785, dau. of Joseph and Betsey, both of Lee.

OTIS, Howard L., son of Jethro, b. 1809, d. 1900, m. (1) int. Feb. 12, 1832, in Farmington, Jemima (Otis) Dickey, dau. of Lemuel, d. Mar. 20, 1863, aged 62, m. (2) ----- Hobbs, m. (3) Sarah Clark, d. Dec. 9, 1883, aged 76.

OTIS, Simon, Jr., son of Simon, b. Mar. 10, 1817, d. Nov. 26, 1846, m. int. Dec. 25, 1840, in Lee, Maria Wiggin, b. Aug. 9, 1814, d. Dec. 15, 1887, both of Lee.

OTIS, Asa Stevens, d. July 13, 1858, aged 33, m. (pub. Feb. 20, 1844, in Strafford), Mary Jane Gray, b. 1821, d. 1891.

OTIS, Moses, b. Jan. 8, 1823, m. Nov. 10, 1850, by Rev. John Winkley, Eliza C. Leighton, b. Aug. 21, 1831, d. May 26, 1862, both of Strafford.

OTIS, Joseph G., of Lee, b. 1818, m. May 30, 1856, by Elder Elias Hutchins, Abby D. Stanton, of Strafford, b. 1822.

OTIS, William T., m. May 23, 1864, by Rev. James Rand, Clara A. (Cole) Osgood, wid. of John, Jr.

OTIS, Charles S., of Lee, son of Thomas J., d. July 21, 1908, aged 61, m. (pub. Feb. 5, 1874, in Newmarket), Flora B. Nutter, of Alton.

PAGE, Andrew, m. in 1774, in Gilmanton, Elizabeth Page.

PAGE, Ebenezer Jr., m. (1) Mary -----, d. Sept. 1781, m. (2) Mar. 13, 1783, by Rev. Isaac Smith, Molly Tucker, both of Gilmanton.

PAGE, John, m. Feb. 10, 1791, by Rev. Isaac Smith, Anna Page, both of Gilmanton.

PAGE, True, m. May 1, 1791, in Gilmanton, Jemina Carr.

PAGE, Moses, m. Sept. 6, 1792, by Rev. Isaac Smith, Mrs. Rebecca Gilman, widow.

PAGE, Moses Jr., m. Feb. 20, 1794, by Rev. Isaac Smith, Rebecca Gilman, both of Gilmanton.

PAGE, Asa, m. Nov. 8, 1802, by Rev. Isaac Smith, Sally Lougee (Louger?), both of Gilmanton.

PAGE, Reuben, of Sandown, m. Oct. 1, 1805, by Rev. Isaac Smith, Mary Page, of Gilmanton.

PAGE, Benjamin, Jr., son of Daniel, b. 1794, d. 1870, m. (1) Elizabeth -----, d. Aug. 2, 1807, aged 44, m. (2) Mar. 21, 1824, by Rev. Thomas C. Upham, Hulda Hussey, b. 1797, d. 1845.

PAGE, Henry Jr., of Sandown, m. Dec. 28, 1813, by Rev. Isaac Smith, Sarah Page, of Gilmanton.

PAGE, Joseph, of Wakefield, d. Sept. 20, 1879, aged 84, m. Oct. 7, 1816, Lydia Staples Remick, b. May 11, 1795, d. Mar. 6, 1871, dau. of John.

PAGE, Ebenezer, m. Apr. 12, 1821, in Gilmanton, Joanna E. Small.

PAGE, Benjamin, m. Oct. 10, 1821, in Milton, Mary Ellen Witham.

PAGE, Henry, m. May 12, 1831, in Gilmanton, Hannah S. Sanborn.

PAGE, Adoniram, m. Nov. 24, 1834, in Gilmanton, Abigail Stevens.

PAGE, Winthrop D., m. Apr. 2, 1835, in Barnstead, Abigail Tuttle.

PAGE, Rev. Caleb Fessenden, of Bridgeton, Me., d. Nov. 6, 1873, aged 77, m. Aug. 3, 1844, by Rev. Nathaniel Barker, Mrs. Mary Coddington, of Wakefield.

PAGE, John, Jr., of Kensington, m. May 18, 1845, in Durham, Susan C. Stilson, of Durham, b. May 14, 1821, d. May 5, 1898, dau. of William, Jr.

PAGE, Arvilla, m. Sept. 25, 1845, in Gilmanton, Adino Page.

PAGE, Josiah E., m. July 27, 1864, by Rev. Asa Piper, Hannah E. Marsh, of Wakefield.

PAGE, Moses D., m. Nov. 10, 1864, in Dover, Emma L. Vickery.

PAGE, Jerome B., m. Apr. 22, 1874, in Dover, Annie B. Adams, both of Dover.

PAINE, Joshua, m. Oct. 29, 1798, Dorothy Wiggin.

2) PALMER, "Sargeant" William, son of Barnabas, b. Oct. 19, 1757, d. Apr. 28, 1815, aged 58, m. (1) Dec. 25, 1783, Susanna Twombly, d. Jan. 19, 1790, aged 26, m. (2) Aug. 30, 1791, Deborah Ham, b. near 1772, d. July 18, 1813, aged 47, dau. of Dodavah.

PALMER, Jonathan, m. Apr. 22, 1810, by Rev. Isaac Smith, Martha Prescott.

PALMER, Barnabas H., b. Aug. 1, 1789, d. July 27, 1850, m. Mar. 25, 1815, by Rev. Joseph Hilliard, at Berwick, Me., Elizabeth Higgins, of Berwick, Me.

PALMER, James, b. 1793, d. 1863, m. int. Dec. 20, 1823, in Lee, Sally Wood, b. 1793, d. 1876, both of Lee.

PALMER, Aaron, m. Oct. 11, 1867, in Dover, Myra Goodwin.

PALMER, E. Burritt, m. May 29, 1868, in Dover, Abby Y. Cate.

PALMER, Charles E., m. int. Nov. 29, 1869, in Dover, Sophia J. Ehlisher.

PALMER, Edger L., m. Nov. 1, 1874, in Rochester, Estella J. Wentworth.

PARISH, Dr. Obadiah, d. Nov. 16, 1794, aged 30, m. Dec. 4, 1793, by Rev. Isaac Smith, Hannah Badger, both of Gilmanton.

PARISH, Obediah B., m. Jan. 22, 1816, by Rev. Isaac Smith, Nancy Morgan.

PARKER, Benjamin, of N. Berwick, Me., d. Mar. 22, 1822, m. in 1798, in Berwick, Me., Nancy Nowell, d. in 1857, dau. of Silas.

PARKER, Henry Rust, son of MatthewStanley, d. Sept. 18, 1848, aged 70, m. Feb. 1804, in Wolfeboro, Hannah Horne Rust, b. 1784, d. 1870, both of Wolfeboro.

PARKER, Capt. Robert, d. Dec. 1819, aged 84, m. at age 73, Sept. 1805, by Rev. John Osborne, Hannah Chesley, aged 22, of Lee, dau. of Lemuel. (Was this a second marriage?)

PARKER, Humphrey, m. Apr. 10, 1808, by Rev. Isaac Smith, Polly Tilton, both of Gilmanton.

PARKER, Dr. David T., of Somersworth, d. Dec. 1, 1888, aged 75, m. (pub. Apr. 23, 1833, in Lebanon, Me.), Clarissa Chamberlain, of Lebanon, Me., d. Nov. 7, 1876.

PARKER, Dr. Alvah, of Lebanon, Me., d. June 3, 1851, m. May 8, 1836, Lucinda Jones, b. Nov. 17, 1817, dau. of Stephen.

PARKER, Daniel G., of Kittery, Me., m. Jan. 23, 1851, by Elder Enoch Place, Mary J. Tuttle, of Strafford, d. July 18, 1851, aged 21, dau. of James.

PARKER, Jeremiah L., m. Sept. 29, 1866, in Dover, Mrs. Emily J. Jones.
PARKER, Charles L., m. July 8, 1869, in Dover, Mary E. Roby.
PARKS, John L., d. Nov. 23, 1881, aged 70, m. Jan. 14, 1849, by Rev. James Pike, Elizabeth S. James, d. Apr. 10, 1885, aged 59, both of Newmarket.
PARKS, Charles E., m. June 26, 1865, in Dover, Annie A. Clifford.
PARMALEE, Horace, b. Aug. 20, 1780, d. 1825, m. Oct. 27, 1803, Polly -----.
3) **PARSHLEY**, John Banfill, d. Apr. 3, 1829, aged 84, m. near 1767, Sarah Otis, d. July 6, 1823, aged 73, dau. of Joshua.
3) PARSHLEY, George, d. Mar. 28, 1829, aged 78, m. (1) Mar. 5, 1778, in Barrington, Betty Demeritt, m. (2) Nov. 24, 1814, in Barrington, Mrs. Meribah Sloper, b. 1784, d. 1860.
PARSHLEY, Richard, m. Aug. 11, 1782, in Northwood, Anna Sloper.
PARSHLEY, Joshua, m. Nov. 20, 1793, in Gilmanton, Joanna Gilman, d. 1845, aged 72.
PARSHLEY, John, d. Nov. 24, 1856, aged 71, m. Nov. 26, 1811, in Barrington, Polly Parsley, d. Dec. 21, 1872, aged 90.
PARSHLEY, Richard, m. Jan. 31, 1814, in Barrington, Polly Caverly.
PARSHLEY, Timothy, 3rd, m. (pub. Jan. 25, 1825, in Strafford), Betsey Foss, both of Strafford.
PARSHLEY, John W., b. 1809, d. May 9, 1866, m. Mar. 15, 1836, by Elder Enoch Place, Mary A. Foss, b. 1810, d. May 13, 1868, both of Strafford.
PARSHLEY, Ebenezer James, son of Ebenezer, d. June 22, 1918, aged 86, m. Nov. 22, 1864, by Rev. James Rand, Lizzie K. Thompkins, d. Nov. 22, 1874, aged 37.
PARSHLEY, Sanborn, d. Mar. 1, 1895, aged 63, m. Nov. 16, 1866, by Rev. James Rand, Rufina Smith, d. Jan. 27, 1917, aged 76.
PARSONS, Ebenezer, m. Jan. 18, 1798, Sally Joy, b. Nov. 10, 1771, d. July 7, 1850, dau. of Samuel.
PARSONS, Josiah, m. May 10, 1808, by Rev. Isaac Smith, Judith Badger, both of Gilmanton.
PARSONS, Ebenezer, m. Nov. 30, 1809, by Rev. Isaac Smith, Hannah Ross, both of Gilmanton.
PARSONS, William Jr., m. May 2, 1810, by Rev. Isaac Smith, Mary Dudley.
PARSONS, Abraham, m. July 1, 1813, by Rev. Isaac Smith, Anna Dudley.
PARSONS, Solomon B. G., m. Apr. 2, 1864, in Dover, Eugenia F. Brown.
PATTEN, George W., m. June 23, 1870, in Dover, Hannah F. Leslie.

PATTERSON, Thomas P., of Anson, Me., b. 1831, m. Aug. 18, 1864, in Lee, Ellen Wither, of Lee, b. 1845.

PATTERSON, Willard, m. Aug. 22, 1867, in Dover, Mary A. Green.

6) **PAUL**, Stephen, son of Stephen, b. Mar. 15, 1769, m. Sept. 21, 1794, Mary Spinney, d. June 1815.

PAUL, Samuel, m. Nov. 1798, in Dover, Margaret Hanson.

PEAREY, Pomfhret, m. Dec. 10, 1843, by Rev. John Winkley, Sarah C. Smith, both of Barrington.

3) **PEARL**, Abraham, b. Apr. 5, 1726, d. 1812, m. June 23, 1748, in Rochester, Abigail Bickford, bpt. June 23, 1748, dau. of John.

PEARL, Paul, son of Abraham, b. 1748, d. 1777, m. Mary Howard Jones.

PEARL, Azaiah, son of Isaac, b. 1807, d. Jan. 5, 1882, m. Mary J. Watson, b. 1806, d. Apr. 2, 1887, dau. of John.

PEARSON, John, Jr., m. int. May 22, 1824, in Lee, Eliza Ann Simes, both of Lee.

3) **PEASLEE**, Amos, son of Robert and Anna, m. Feb. 6, 1785, by Dr. Belknap, Lydia Ham, d. July 22, 1823, aged 59, dau. of Samuel.

PEASLEE, William, m. Nov. 27, 1799, by Rev. Isaac Smith, Hannah Folsom.

PEASLEE, Stephen, of Meredith, m. Jan. 22, 1801, by Rev. Isaac Smith, Mehitable Ladd, of Gilmanton.

PEAVEY, Hudson, of Strafford, d. Jan. 18, 1864, aged 85, m. (1) in 1801, Hannah -----, d. Oct. 27, 1856, aged 77, m. (2) Nov. 24, 1857, by Rev. Alvin Tobey, Mrs. Hannah (Chesley), Young, of Durham, wid. of Daniel, b. Jan. 1, 1799, d. Feb. 26, 1881, dau. of Benjamin.

PEAVEY, John, Jr., b. 1791, d. 1864, m. Mar. 11, 1818, by Rev. Joseph Haven, Mary Caverly, b. 1800, d. Feb. 1, 1857, both of Barrington.

PEAVEY, Benjamin R., b. May 6, 1804, m. Jan. 5, 1826, Lydia Boice, b. Nov. 19, 1807.

PEAVEY, William, m. Jan. 22, 1843, by Rev. John Winkley, Matha Abiah Brown, both of Barrington.

PEAVEY, Robert B., son of John, b. 1824, d. 1895, m. (pub. Nov. 2, 1847, in Barnstead), Emily A. Montgomery, b. 1830, d. 1876, both of Strafford.

PEAVEY, Moses V., m. Jan. 21, 1863, in Dover, Sarah Hanscom.

PEEL, Charles F., m. June 1, 1867, by Rev. Alden Sherwin, Emma A. Howard.

PEIRCE, Nathaniel S., m. (pub. Oct. 26, 1805, in Portsmouth), Mrs. Sally Greenough.

PEIRCE, Deac. Andrew, of Dover, b. Dec. 18, 1785, d. Sept. 4, 1862, m. Aug. 27, 1809, by Rev. John Osborne, in Lee, Abigail Smith

Osborne, of Lee, b. Feb. 17, 1792, d. Mar. 5, 1875, dau. of Rev. John.

PEIRCE, Col. Joshua W., m. (pub. May 14, 1823, in Portsmouth), Emily Sheafe.

PEIRCE, Capt. Hall, of Barrington, d. Nov. 24, 1870, aged 57, m. (1) Mar. 4, 1838, by Elder Enoch Place, Sally Hall, of Strafford, d. Apr. 1867, aged 54, m. (2) Oct. 29, 1870, in Lee, Mrs. Sarah A. Woodman, of Lee, b. 1825.

PEIRCE, (PIERCE), Moses, m. Oct. 3, 1853, by Rev. Seth W. Perkins, Mrs. Martha F. (Gray) Young, wid. of Jonathan, both of Barrington.

PEIRCE, John I., of Barrington, son of Curtis, d. Dec. 27, 1898, aged 80, m. (pub. June 27, 1854, in Somersworth), Phebe H. Ham, d. Sept. 13, 1877, aged 55.

PEIRCE, (PIERCE), Daniel C. M., of Newmarket, b. 1831, m. int. Dec. 31, 1855, in Lee, Alvina A. Hoitt, of Lee, b. 1830.

PEIRCE, (PIERCE), William, m. Jan. 14, 1865, in Dover, Catherine E. Potter.

PEIRCE, (PIERCE), Ira M., m. May 31, 1866, in Dover, Fannie M. Ingraham.

PEIRCE, (PIERCE), Israel, m. Aug. 8, 1867, in Dover, Elizabeth Silvera.

3) **PENDERGAST**, Solomon, son of Stephen, b. Feb. 26, 1776, d. Dec. 3, 1860, m. Dec. 31, 1801, by Rev. John Osborne, Rebecca Sherburne, of Barrington, d. Feb. 5, 1865.

3) PENDERGAST, James, son of Stephen, b. 1784, d. Sept. 7, 1850, m. (1) in 1808, by Rev. John Osborne, Hannah Emerson, of Durham, b. June 25, 1790, d. Aug. 7, 1826, dau. of Capt. Smith, m. (2) Mar. 31, 1830, by Rev. John Osborne, Mary Hill, of Nottingham, b. 1783, d. Mar. 23, 1863.

3) PENDERGAST, Nicholas, son of John, m. (1) July 8, 1814, by Rev. John Osborne, Lois Emerson, of Lee, dau. of Joseph, m. (2) Hannah Emerson.

4) PENDERGAST, Thomas, son of Edmund, b. 1788, d. Apr. 16, 1865, m. Apr. 6, 1817, by Rev. John Broadhead, Charlotte Smart, b. 1799, d. 1879, dau. of Robert.

3) PENDERGAST, John, son of John, d. 1850, m. Aug. 13, 1819, by Rev. John Osborne, Mary Williams, both of Lee.

4) PENDERGAST, Solomon, son of Edmund, m. (1) Apr. 26, 1832, Lydia Wiggin, b. Nov. 6, 1811, d. Aug. 20, 1848, dau. of Capt. William, m. (2) (pub. June 11, 1850, in Newmarket), Judith Matilda Mathes, of Lee.

PENDERGAST, Nicholas D., m. int. Mar. 16, 1836, in Lee, Hannah Emerson, both of Lee.

NEW HAMPSHIRE MARRIAGES SUPPLEMENT

PENDERGAST, Alfred, m. July 29, 1838, Susan Day.
PENDERGAST, Nathaniel, of Durham, son of Edmund, m. (pub. Dec. 6, 1855, in Somersworth), Mehitable (Pendergast) Nelson, of Newmarket, b. 1819, dau. of Thomas.
PENDERGAST, Levi E., b. Apr. 26, 1824, d. Dec. 18, 1896, m. June 20, 1850, by Elder Samuel Sherburne, Sarah J. Jenness, b. Nov. 24, 1827, d. Sept. 21, 1909, both of Lee.
PENDEXTER, Edward, son of Thomas, b. Aug. 22, 1778, d. May 16, 1843, m. Apr. 3, 1803, in Madbury, Polly Joy, d. Dec. 30, 1871, aged 87, dau. of Jacob.
PENDEXTER, James, m. May 3, 1803, Polly Joy, d. Dec. 30, 1871, aged 87, dau. of Jacob.
PENDEXTER, Joseph B., of Barrington, son of Thomas, m. (1) July 28, 1809, by Rev. William Hooper, Lydia Killey, of Madbury, d. June 2, 1810, aged 29, dau. of Samuel, m. (2) in 1811, by Rev. John Osborne, Drusilla Burleigh, of Newmarket, b. Apr. 3, 1785, d. Feb. 12, 1814, m. (3) early as 1825, Lydia C. Bodge, b. in 1795, d. May 20, 1880.
PENDEXTER, John, b. 1786, d. 1863, m. Feb. 22, 1816, by Rev. Joseph Haven, Susan Davis, b. 1792, d. 1846, both of Farmington.
PENDEXTER, John, son of Thomas, m. Aug. 13, 1841, Hannah T. Piper.
PENDEXTER, Cyrus, son of Thomas, m. Nov. 25, 1847, Almira S. Parsons.
PENDEXTER, Frederick O., son of George, b. about 1820, d. Mar. 21, 1872, m. May 22, 1851, in New York City, Eliza Lawrence, b. June 1830, d. Apr. 1, 1909, dau. of David.
PERKINS, Jebez, of Wells, Me., m. Dec. 4, 1777, by Rev. Matthew Merriam, Joanna (Fernald) Pray, of Berwick, Me.
PERKINS, Joseph, m. Dec. 1779, Anne Canney, dau. of Ichabod, both of Madbury.
PERKINS, Shadrach, d. Apr 6, 1850, m. (1) Nov. 2, 1800, by Rev. Joseph Haven, Bridget Hartford, d. Apr. 1806, m. (2) (pub. Jan. 31, 1807, in Dover), Dorcas Plummer.
PERKINS, William, m. May 6, 1817, in Dover, Nancy Read, both of Dover.
PERKINS, Eri, son of William and Mercy, b. Apr. 11, 1795, d. Mar. 24, 1869, m. Dec. 10, 1818, in Dover, Mary Ann Hodgdon, b. July 20, 1796, d. July 19, 1867, dau. of Shadrack, both of Dover.
PERKINS, James, m. (pub. Nov. 8, 1825, in Rochester), Susan Downes.

PERKINS, Asa, b. 1809, d. May 7, 1888, m. Nov. 18, 1829, by Elder Enoch Place, Deborah Young, b. 1810, d. Mar. 6, 1906, both of Strafford.

PERKINS, Charles, b. 1813, m. Jan. 5, 1840, in Greenland, Louisa E. Peverly, b. 1822, dau. of George, both of Portsmouth.

PERKINS, Lemuel, son of Jonathan, d. Oct. 4, 1896, aged 77, m. Feb. 22, 1848, by Elder Elias Hutchins, Mahala Rogers, d. Jan. 26, 1906, aged 84 yrs., 8 mos., 29 das.

PERKINS, Hiram M., son of Hiram, m. (1) Jan. 26, 1860, in Dover, Martha A. Hoitt, m. (2) July 1, 1891, in Dover, Hattie M. Dowell, dau. of Samuel G.

PERKINS, Warren H., b. 1832, d. 1910, m. May 15, 1861, by Elder Enoch Place, Nancy L. Foss, b. 1841, d. 1919, both of Strafford.

PERKINS, Edmund R., of Strafford, m. July 9, 1864, by Rev. John Winkley, Lavina Sanders, of Laconia.

PERKINS, Samuel, m. Nov. 17, 1865, in Dover, Abby J. Goodwin.

PERKINS, James P., m. Dec. 20, 1866, by Rev. Francis E. Abbott, Helen F. Everett.

PERKINS, George A., m. May 25, 1869, in Dover, Lizzie A. Rothwell.

PERKINS, Winslow T., d. Jan. 15, 1920, aged 83, m. July 14, 1869, in Dover, Carrie S. Durant.

PERKINS, Edwin L., m. Feb. 19, 1870, in Dover, Emma I. Young.

PERKINS, John F., of Barrington, m. Aug. 17, 1873, in Dover, Mrs. Lavinia (Whidden) Canney, wid. of James, d. Feb. 27, 1898, aged 91.

PERKINS, William H., of Wakefield, m. June 28, 1874, by Rev. Asa Emeline Burns, of Saco, Me.

PERLIAM, Lemuel, of Dover, m. (pub. July 16, 1823, in Farmington, Me.), Mary Stoyles, of Farmington, Me., dau. of Dr. Aaron.

PERRY, Hosea, m. Feb. 19, 1829, by Rev. John Winkley, Susan Perkins, both of Strafford.

PERRY, Daniel, m. Nov. 26, 1829, by Rev. John Winkley, Hannah Babb, both of Strafford.

PERRY, Charles M., m. May 20, 1868, by Rev. Robert S. Stubbs, Etta C. Hill.

PETERS, John, of Boston, Mass., m. May 1, 1822, by Rev. Jonathan Thompson, Mary Haggins, of S. Berwick, Me.

PETERS, Timothy, m. Apr. 3, 1869, in Dover, Maria Card.

PETERSON, John A., m. Nov. 24, 1864, in Dover, Mary A. Stackpole.

1) **PEVERLY**, Thomas, b. 1623, d. June 1670, m. near 1644, Jane Walford, dau. of Thomas.

2) PEVERLY, John, son of Thomas, b. near 1649, d. 1731, m. ----- -----.

NEW HAMPSHIRE MARRIAGES SUPPLEMENT

3) PEVERLY, John, son of John, b. near 1688, m. Feb. 5, 1712/13, Deliverance Lang, dau. of Robert.
3) PEVERLY, Nathaniel, son of John, b. Mar. 14, 1690, d. May 20, 1769, m. Nov. 13, 1715, Elizabeth Cotton, b. Mar. 29, 1689, d. May 1765, dau. of Benjamin.
4) PEVERLY, William, son of John, m. (1) Elizabeth -----, m. (2) Feb. 1777, Joanna Viccar, dau. of John.
4) PEVERLY, George, son of John, d. Sept. 1774, m. Ann -----, d. 1810.
4) PEVERLY, Thomas, son of Nathaniel, b. Sept. 5, 1722, m. near 1746, Abigail Ham, dau. of Thomas.
5) PEVERLY, Kinsman, son of William, m. Nov. 30, 1768, Abigail Card.
4) PEVERLY, Nathaniel, son of Nathaniel, b. June 15, 1720, d. Sept. 24, 1799, m. early as 1769, Ann Jones, dau. of John.
5) PEVERLY, William, son of William, b. 1762, d. Jan. 7, 1852, m. Johanna -----, b. 1768, d. June 20, 1850.
5) PEVERLY, George, son of Nathaniel, b. May 12, 1773, d. Mar. 20, 1805, m. Mar. 19, 1799, Sarah Sherburne, b. Oct. 25, 1774, d. Apr. 27, 1836, dau. of George.
5) PEVERLY, Nathaniel, son of Nathaniel, b. Mar. 18, 1769, m. Jan. 3, 1802, Elizabeth Sherburne, b. Mar. 30, 1778, dau. of George.
5) PEVERLY, John, son of Nathaniel, b. July 17, 1770, d. Dec. 19, 1845, m. July 3, 1804, Elizabeth Sanborn, b. Mar. 24, 1774, d. June 20, 1849, dau. of Capt. John.
5) PEVERLY, Joseph, son of Thomas, d. Jan. 13, 1820, m. (1) --------, m. (2) Mar. 11, 1805, Hannah Farnham, widow.
5) PEVERLY, Thomas, son of Thomas, d. Dec. 20, 1842, aged 92, m. Joanna -----.
5) PEVERLY, Benjamin, son of Thomas, m. ----- -----.
6) PEVERLY, George, son of William, b. 1792, d. Dec. 24, 1856, m. July 26, 1816, Lois Adams, dau. of Joseph.
6) PEVERLY, Kinsman, son of William, b. 1799, d. Jan. 21, 1846, m. Harriet Nutter, b. 1802, d. Aug. 26, 1829, dau. of Matthias.
6) PEVERLY, Robert, son of William, b. Dec. 24, 1804, d. Jan. 18, 1870, m. Dec. 14, 1834, Jane Colbath Sherburne, b. Aug. 22, 1814, d. Sept. 20, 1903, dau. of Daniel.
6) PEVERLY, Freeman, son of William, b. 1808, d. May 1883, m. (1) Mary Seavey, widow, d. Oct. 1840, m. (2) (pub. Apr. 16, 1844, in Portsmouth), Mary Ann (Miles) Trickey, b. Dec. 15, 1813, wid. of George, dau. of Timothy, m. (3) Sept. 16, 1855, Hannah L. (Hodgdon) Merrill, wid. of Horace, b. Feb. 28, 1810, d. Apr. 13, 1898, dau. of Aaron.

NEW HAMPSHIRE MARRIAGES SUPPLEMENT

1) **PHILBRICK**, Thomas, d. 1667, m. Elizabeth -----, d. Feb. 19, 1663/64.
PHILBRICK, Samuel, of Groton, m. Jan. 15, 1804, by Rev. Isaac Smith, Sarah Jewett, of Gilmanton.
PHILBRICK, William, m. (pub. Oct. 18, 1836, in Lee), Abigail Williams, b. Oct. 18, 1814, d. Sept. 4, 1890, both of Newmarket.
PHILBRICK, Silas, m. int. May 22, 1842, in Dover, Maria Goodwin, d. Dec. 17, 1890, aged 68, dau. of Jedediah.
PHILBRICK, Charles E., of Alton, son of Ithiel, d. June 20, 1913, aged 77, m. (1) Mar. 9, 1864, in Dover, m. Augusta Burley, m. (2) Mar. 21, 1874, in Dover, Helen A. Drew, of Dover.
PHILLIPS, Albert O., m. Oct. 20, 1869, in Dover, Mary S. Frost.
PICKERING, John, bpt. Jan. 4, 1718, d. in 1790, m. Aug. 28, 1740, by Rev. Jos. Adams, Mary Nutter.
PICKERING, John Gee, b. Aug. 14, 1736, d. Aug. 15, 1795, m. June 10, 1773, by Rev. Jos. Adams, Deborah Mills, d. Oct. 1796, both of Newington.
PICKERING, Anthony, b. May 9, 1749, d. Mar. 4, 1825, m. in 1773, Lovey Hilton, d. Sept. 18, 1843, aged 91, dau. of Edward.
PICKERING, Capt. James, m. (pub. Dec. 30, 1828, in Newmarket), Mrs. Eliza Flanders.
PICKERING, Calvin, d. Oct. 24, 1856, aged 47, m. Sept. 30, 1832, by Rev. William Demeritt, Mary Bunker, b. Mar. 8, 1808, d. Oct. 23, 1890, dau. of Samuel.
PICKERING, Hazen, m. (1) (pub. Dec. 18, 1838, in Portsmouth), Elizabeth March, m. (2) Martha Ann Drew, b. June 19, 1819, dau. of Joseph L., d. Oct. 3, 1872, aged 53.
PICKERING, Thomas L., d. Oct. 3, 1872, aged 53, m. Dec. 25, 1842, in Milton, Ann L. Wiggin, d. July 24, 1894, aged 72, dau. of Daniel, both of Wakefield.
PICKERING, Ephraim, of Newington, d. July 4, 1809, m. (pub. Feb. 17, 1852, in Greenland), Margaret E. Henderson, dau. of Capt. Robert.
PICKERING, John C., m. int. Mar. 15, 1852, in Lee, Nancy D. Cotton, both of Lee.
PICKERING, John W., of Newmarket, aged 20, m. Oct. 9, 1854, in Rollinsford, Mary E. Cole, of Rollinsford, aged 18.
PICKERING, T. A., of New York, m. Dec. 9, 1862, in Rochester, Sarah M. Carter, of Rochester.
PIDGIN, William C., m. Nov. 4, 1868, by Rev. Robert S. Stubbs, Eunice A. Applebee.
PIKE, Daniel, b. Dec. 2, 1732, d. May 2, 1806, m. near 1756, Anne Carr.

PIKE, Amos, of Berwick, Me., m. Feb. 8, 1789, in Eliot, Me., Sally Stacy, of Kittery, Me.

PIKE, Joseph H., of Wakefield, son of Joseph, d. May 21, 1859, aged 58, m. Apr. 23, 1826, in Wakefield, Almira Lyford, of Brookfield, b. 1803, d. 1886, dau. of Robert.

PIKE, Jacob, m. May 3, 1862, by Rev. James Rand, Eliza A. Witham, d. Feb. 26, 1913, aged 72, dau. of Alexander.

PIKE, John G., m. July 18, 1867, in Dover, Alice W. Horn.

PIKE, George H., of Wakefield, m. Sept. 12, 1872, by Rev. Asa Piper, Lovey Sanborn, of Milton.

PILLSBURY, John C., of Strafford, m. (1) Mercy F. Caverno, d. Apr. 26, 1846, aged 32, dau. of Jeremiah, m. (2) May 17, 1848, by Rev. John Winkley, Lydia Jane Bennett, of Barrington.

PINKHAM, -----, m. Sarah Tebbetts, b. Aug. 18, 1725, d. June 1803.

PINKHAM, Daniel, b. in 1754, d. Mar. 14, 1822, m. May 1780, by Rev. William Hooper, Patience Ham.

PINKHAM, Samuel, m. Nov. 12, 1783, by Rev. Isaac Smith, Dorothy Ordway, of Loudon.

PINKHAM, Abijah, son of Abijah, b. July 22, 1763, d. July 8, 1815, m. Dec. 11, 1783, Sarah Spencer, b. Oct. 23, 1763, d. Mar. 16, 1814, dau. of Abednego.

PINKHAM, Otis, b. Jan. 13, 1765, d. Jan. 5, 1814, m. Hannah Young, d. Mar. 17, 1838, aged 68.

PINKHAM, Andrew, m. (pub. Jan. 3, 1806, in Boothbay, Me.), Mary Bickford, of Berwick, Me., dau. of Aaron.

PINKHAM, Daniel D., d. Aug. 4, 1848, aged 65, m. Jan. 17, 1811, by Rev. Moses Cheney, Alice Edgerly, both of New Durham.

PINKHAM, James Y., d. Feb. 23, 1844, aged 53, m. in 1818, Elizabeth Nute, b. July 15, 1798, d. June 5, 1835, dau. of Francis.

PINKHAM, Samuel, b. July 22, 1788, d. Apr. 1, 1825, m. Mar. 27, 1821, in Dover, Lydia Ham, b. Apr. 10, 1791, dau. of David.

PINKHAM, Capt. Daniel, son of Benjamin, b. May 30, 1797, d. Mar. 6, 1885, aged 87, m. Dec. 25, 1822, by Rev. J. W. Clary, Sophia Drew, b. Feb. 8, 1800, d. Aug. 22, 1878, aged 78, dau. of Daniel.

PINKHAM, Richard, of Madbury, son of Richard, d. May 15, 1858, aged 48, m. Apr. 4, 1835, by Rev. William Demeritt, Martha Clay, of Lee.

PINKHAM, Daniel, Jr., m. Sept. 24, 1837, by Rev. Samuel C. Gilbert, Mary Jane Davis, b. 1817, d. 1841.

PINKHAM, Eri, d. June 24, 1845, aged 30, m. (1) Nov. 8, 1840, by Rev. Lucian Hayden, Mary Susan Jones, d. Jan. 31, 1841, aged 21, m. (2) Dec. 7, 1842, by Rev. John Parkman, Eliza J. Jones.

PINKHAM, Edward J., son of Samuel, d. July 8, 1890, aged 67, m. Oct. 7, 1844, by John Wilde, Mary Ann Lee, d. Apr. 30, 1881, aged 56.

PINKHAM, Samuel W., of Farmington, m. Mar. 17, 1847, in Milton, Mary Cook, of Milton, b. Nov. 21, 1806, dau. of Jeremiah.

PINKHAM, Nathaniel G., son of James, d. May 29, 1906, aged 71, m. Oct. 28, 1855, in Milton, Emily Corliss, d. Jan. 27, 1913, dau. of John.

PINKHAM, Alonzo, of Dover, d. Mar. 20, 1900, aged 70, m. (1) Nov. 24, 1859, in Dover, Clara D. Nute, of Durham, d. Feb. 19, 1866, aged 28, dau. of Greenleaf, m. (2) Apr. 8, 1874, in Dover, Mrs. Amanda A. Cater, of Barrington.

PINKHAM, Charles H., m. Apr. 10, 1862, in Dover, Alice J. Foss.

PINKHAM, Nicholas, m. Oct. 22, 1865, by Rev. James Rand, Betsey Morrison.

PINKHAM, George N., son of Luther H., d. Nov. 12, 1888, aged 46, m. Feb. 6, 1869, by Rev. Robert S. Stubbs, Olive A. Hurd.

PINKHAM, Asa J., m. Jan. 1, 1870, in Dover, Mary A. Brownell.

PINKHAM, William T., m. Sept. 6, 1870, in Dover, Lizzie A. Ricker.

PIPER, Rev. Asa, of Acton, Mass., son of Josiah, b. Mar. 7, 1757, d. May 17, 1835, m. (1) Mary Cutts, of Portsmouth, b. 1766, d. Jan. 4, 1802, m. (2) Sarah Little, of Kennebunk, Me., b. 1765, d. Oct. 15, 1827.

PIPER, Reuben, m. Oct. 13, 1791, by Rev. Isaac Smith, Sally Hannaford, both of Gilmanton.

PIPER, Moses Clark, m. Nov. 18, 1820, in Wolfeboro, Eunice Baker, b. Oct. 9, 1797, d. Sept. 30, 1878, both of Wolfeboro.

PIPER, Deac. Edward Cutts, son of Rev. Asa, b. Dec. 30, 1791, d. Feb. 27, 1881, aged 90, m. (pub. June 3, 1828, in Wakefield), Mrs. Sally (Jones) Swasey, of Portsmouth, b. Mar. 18, 1790, d. Jan. 13, 1866, both of Wakefield.

PIPER, Benjamin Y., of Lee, son of John, b. Apr. 29, 1816, d. 1901, m. (1) Hannah -----, d. Oct. 5, 1856, aged 36, m. (2) Apr. 6, 1858, in Marblehead, Mass., Sarah Bell Evans, of Marblehead, Mass., b. May 9, 1823, d. Jan. 21, 1897.

PIPER, Nathan, m. Mar. 23, 1837, in Gilmanton, Sarah Buzzell.

PIPER, Thatcher William, son of Samuel, b. May 9, 1824, m. Nov. 27, 1845, in Tuftonboro, Nancy Mahaley Allen.

PIPER, Edward Cutts, Jr., son of Edward C., b. July 23, 1830, d. Nov. 22, 1862, m. Aug. 16, 1852, Henrietta Cox, b. 1830, d. Aug. 19, 1865.

PIPER, Jonas W., b. Mar. 11, 1832, d. Oct. 31, 1909, m. (pub. Nov. 7, 1861, in Wolfeboro), Martha A. Getchell, of Alton, b. Oct. 15, 1841, d. Aug. 7, 1921.

PIPER, George Francis, son of Edward C., b. Sept. 6, 1833, m. June 13, 1866, Mary Jenness, b. Sept. 21, 1842.

PITCHER, George F., m. Oct. 1, 1866, in Dover, Catherine L. Knox.

PITMAN, Ezekiel, of Portsmouth, son of Lt. Ezekiel, m. July 13, 1740, Elizabeth Peverly, b. Oct. 8, 1716, dau. of Nathaniel.

PITMAN, Alonzo J., m. June 26, 1870, in Dover, Sarah A. Legg.

PLACE, John, son of James, b. 1729, d. 1816, m. Apr. 12, 1750, by Rev. Amos Main, Lucy Jenness, b. 1728, d. Feb. 9, 1821.

PLACE, George, son of James, b. 1734, d. Nov. 1797, m. Aug. 21, 1755, by Rev. Amos Main, Kezia Knight.

PLACE, Paul, son of Richard, b. 1767, d. Mar. 5, 1845, m. Nov. 29, 1787, by Rev. Joseph Haven, Judith Brown, b. 1770, d. Oct. 31, 1841, both of Rochester.

PLACE, Isaac, of Rochester, m. (pub. Feb. 8, 1806, in Barrington), Betsey Babb, of Barrington.

PLACE, Rev. Enoch, son of James, b. July 13, 1786, d. Mar. 23, 1865, m. Sept. 29, 1808, Sally Demeritt, d. Jan. 1, 1880, aged 91, dau. of Capt. Daniel.

PLACE, Leonard H., m. (1) Mary E. -----, b. Mar. 26, 1817, d. Feb. 3, 1855, m. (2) (pub. Oct. 25, 1855, in Somersworth), Marie S. Nutter, d. June 17, 1866, aged 29, both of Rochester.

PLAISTED, John, d. Feb. 8, 1824, aged 71, m. Nov. 29, 1775, by Rev. Matthew Merriam, Martha Lord, b. Nov. 21, 1754, d. Mar. 28, 1847, aged 92, dau. of Ebenezer, both of Berwick, Me.

PLAISTED, William, m. Nov. 29, 1781, by Rev. Isaac Smith, Hannah Huckins.

PLAISTED, Samuel, m. Nov. 29, 1781, in Gilmanton, by Rev. Isaac Smith, Margery Huckins.

PLATTS, John L., m. Feb. 24, 1870, in Dover, Elizabeth A. Champion.

PLUMER, John, of Rochester, son of Richard, d. Nov. 19, 1815, aged 96, m. (1) Elizabeth Titcomb, b. Apr. 21, 1728, d. Jan. 26, 1770, dau. of Daniel, m. (2) Lydia Dennett, d. Aug. 4, 1812, aged 84.

PLUMMER, Sgt Richard, b. 1751, m. near 1770, Patience Neal, dau. of John.

PLUMMER, Capt. Beard, of Milton, son of John, b. Aug. 12, 1754, d. Oct. 7, 1816, m. Sept. 7, 1780, by Rev. Joseph Haven, Susanna Ham, d. Feb. 20, 1803, dau. of Jonathan.

PLUMMER, Deac. Samuel, d. Oct. 31, 1824, aged 86, m. Jan. 22, 1786, by Rev. Joseph Haven, Abigail Tebbetts, b. May 30, 1745, dau. of Edward, both of Rochester.

PLUMMER, Ephraim, son of Samuel, b. Apr. 30, 1766, d. May 4, 1843, m. Feb. 25, 1790, by Rev. Joseph Haven, Nancy McDuffee, b. May 1, 1768, d. Dec. 26, 1851, both of Rochester.

PLUMMER, Samuel, m. Feb. 11, 1799, by Rev. Isaac Smith, Betsy Norris, both of Gilmanton.
PLUMER, Joseph, m. Jan. 20, 1803, in Gilmanton, Hannah Elkins.
PLUMER, Joseph, son of Bard, b. Aug. 13, 1786, d. Jan. 3, 1826, m. Oct. 9, 1810, in Milton, Sally Brown, b. Mar. 26, 1785, d. July 25, 1867, dau. of Nathaniel.
PLUMER, James, son of Ephraim, b. June 28, 1800, d. 1831, m. (1) in 1822, Mary Ann Beedle, d. Oct. 22, 1824, m. (2) Jan. 10, 1828, Mary Ann Roberts.
PLUMMER, Jeremiah, d. Aug. 12, 1855, aged 55, m. Tamson Twombly, b. 1801, d. Dec. 26, 1878.
PLUMER, John, m. in 1823, in Farmington, by Rev. Samuel K. Lothrop, Mary Tasker.
PLUMMER, Richard, son of Ephraim, b. Mar. 26, 1792, d. Sept. 20, 1869, m. July 11, 1825, Mary Clark, b. May 18, 1792, d. Jan. 2, 1876.
PLUMER, Capt. John P., b. Mar. 31, 1807, d. Apr. 26, 1884, m. Oct. 1829, by Rev. Samuel K. Lothrop, Harriet Putnam, both of Dover.
PLUMMER, Enoch W., son of Joseph, b. Apr. 4, 1815, d. June 18, 1896, m. June 1840, by Rev. Nathaniel Barker, Orinda Ayers, of Wakefield, b. Aug. 6, 1817, d. Apr. 18, 1895, dau. of Joseph.
PLUMMER, Hiram, of Danvers, Mass., m. Nov. 22, 1840, by Rev. Rufus O. Williams, Sarah Ann Demeritt, of Lee.
PLUMER, Allen, of Dover, b. Feb. 3, 1812, d. May 4, 1892, m. Jan. 23, 1842, by Elder Samuel Sherburne, Abigail J. Pendergast, of Lee, d. Dec. 5, 1885, aged 74, dau. of Nicholas.
PLUMER, Joseph, of Milton, b. Mar. 11, 1820, d. Mar. 5, 1907, m. Oct. 30, 1844, by Rev. Isaac Willey, Adeline F. Baker, of Somersworth, d. June 30, 1858, aged 38, dau. of Moses.
PLUMMER, Richard Clark, of Milton, son of Richard, b. Mar. 8, 1826, m. (pub. Feb. 6, 1849, in Farmington), Mary Jane Wiggin, of Farmington, d. Sept. 28, 1851, aged 30.
PLUMER, Charles E., m. Apr. 7, 1853, in Gilmanton, Mary H. Moody.
PLUMER, John C., son of Daniel, d. Sept. 20, 1902, aged 73, m. (1) June 17, 1855, in Milton, Lydia Augusta Durrell, b. Nov. 4, 1823, d. Aug. 22, 1859, aged 35, both of Milton, m. (2) June 15, 1862, in Dover, Amelia C. Witherell, b. May 3, 1831, d. May 16, 1898.
PLUMER, John Porter, m. Nov. 22, 1855, in Freedom, Cordelia A. Bennett.
PLUMER, Daniel, son of Daniel, b. July 5, 1836, d. Feb. 1884, m. Aug. 3, 1856, in Acton, Me., Sarah E. Clements, d. Feb. 23, 1920, aged 83, dau. of Samuel.

PLUMER, Albert B., b. 1843, m. int. Sept. 1865, in Lee, Mary A. Critcherson, b. 1847, both of Lee.
PLUMER, Frank J., m. Nov. 27, 1868, in Dover, Abbie D. Knowles.
PORTER, Samuel, of Windham, m. Aug. 24, 1837, by Rev. John Winkley, Patience Brown, of Strafford.
PORTER, Charles, m. Nov. 27, 1866, in Dover, Sarah E. Applebee.
POTTER, Joseph, m. Dec. 26, 1782, by Rev. Isaac Smith, Mary Gilman, both of Gilmanton.
POTTER, Thomas, d. Mar. 14, 1816, m. Sept. 29, 1793, by Rev. Isaac Smith, Shuah Gale, d. July 1809, both of Gilmanton.
POWELL, Keys B., d. Nov. 1, 1841, aged 54, m. June 30, 1825, by Elder Enoch Place, Lydia Lougee, b. near 1786, d. June 10, 1852, aged 66, dau. of John, both of Strafford.
POWERS, William C., m. Dec. 14, 1868, by Rev. Robert S. Stubbs, Maggie H. Lytle.
PRATT, Seth, m. (pub. May 19, 1804, in Portsmouth), Hannah Dixon.
PRATT, Olney, m. (pub. Sept. 30, 1815, in Dover), Lavinia Taylor.
5) **PRAY**, Capt. Joseph, son of Samuel and Dorothy, bpt. Apr. 27, 1743, d. 1803, m. (1) Mar. 21, 1765, by Rev. Jacob Foster, Mary Libbey, m. (2) Apr. 16, 1787, Mary Hight.
5) PRAY, Joshua, d. Oct. 21, 1823, aged 81, son of John, m. near 1766, Sarah Roberts, d. Nov. 3, 1821, aged 78, of Somersworth.
PRAY, Samuel, Jr., b. Sept. 21, 1755, d. Apr. 14, 1837, m. Sept. 3, 1785, by Rev. Matthew Merriam, Sally Fernald, b. 1766, d. 1848, dau. of Thomas.
PRAY, Capt. Joseph, m. Apr. 16, 1787, by Rev. John Thompson, Mary Hight, both of Berwick, Me.
PRAY, Charles, of Berwick, Me., m. Nov. 17, 1793, by Rev. Matthew Merriam, Sally Garvin, of Somersworth.
PRAY, Moses, Jr., of Lebanon, Me., m. Apr. 10, 1794, by Rev. Matthew Merriam, Rachel McCarrel, of Berwick, Me.
PRAY, Sylvester, m. Aug. 30, 1862, in Dover, Martha S. Twombly.
PRAY, Thomas J. W., son of Moses, d. Dec. 7, 1888, aged 69, m. June 1, 1870, in Dover, Martha A. Mathews.
PREBLE, William E., m. Mar. 11, 1863, in Dover, Nellie A. Neal.
PRESCOTT, Jonathan, m. Dec. 28, 1785, by Rev. Isaac Smith, Molly Sargent.
PRESCOTT, John M., m. Nov. 24, 1811, in Belmont, Judith Clough, both of Gilmanton.
PRESCOTT, Samuel, m. in 1814, Jane Pendergast, dau. of John.
PRESCOTT, George B., m. May 31, 1864, by Rev. Thomas G. Salter, Malvina A. Swain, d. Oct. 28, 1928, aged 90, dau. of Israel.
PRESCOTT, Benjamin F., m. Oct. 20, 1865, in Dover, Rebecca Foss.

PRESCOTT, John R. S., m. Jan. 27, 1867, by Rev. James Rand, Phymelia A. Hutchins.
PRESCOTT, John W., m. Oct. 25, 1870, in Dover, Addie Jewett.
PRESTON, Nathaniel, of Haverhill, Mass., m. (pub. Sept. 14, 1852, in Barrington), Margaret J. Ham, of Barrington, d. Nov. 2, 1899, aged 72, dau. of James.
PRICE, John, m. Nov. 25, 1806, by Rev. Isaac Smith, Sally Parsons.
PRICE, William, m. Oct. 17, 1811, by Rev. Isaac Smith, Betsy Rand, both of Gilmanton.
PRICE, Stephen, m. Nov. 21, 1811, by Rev. Isaac Smith, Betsy Hutchinson.
PRIME, Hiram, d. Sept. 12, 1838, aged 40, m. Nov. 9, 1820, by Rev. Jeremiah Shaw, Betsey Moulton, d. Feb. 18, 1867, aged 66.
PRIME, Joseph, m. Mar. 11, 1829, by Rev. Benjamin Hoyt, Mahala Vickery, both of Dover.
PROCTOR, John D., of Barnstead, son of Thomas, m. Feb. 2, 1832, by Rev. Nathaniel Berry, Salina Drew, of Alton, b. Nov. 12, 1807, d. Dec. 1886, dau. of Joseph.
PROCTOR, Tyler B., son of John, d. June 28, 1887, aged 39, m. Jan. 1, 1871, in Dover, Clara B. Leighton.
PURINTON, John T., of Sandwich, d. July 1825, aged 29, m. Jan. 22, 1821, by Rev. Jeremiah Shaw, Betsey Ambrose, of Moultonboro.
QUARLES, Col. Samuel, d. July 7, 1846, aged 78, m. (1) near 1795, Lydia Very, d. Feb. 3, 1809, aged 35, m. (2) Abigail -----, d. Sept. 10, 1872, aged 91.
QUIMBY, Daniel M., d. Feb. 1, 1873, aged 62, m. int. Aug. 25, 1833, in Dover, Sophia Downs, d. July 24, 1866, aged 54, dau. of John.
QUIMBY, Henry, m. Dec. 5, 1833, by Rev. John Winkley, Phoebe Vanduzza, of Barrington.
QUINCY, John, of Durham, m. (1) Mar. 4, 1819, in Lee, Jane Clay, of Nottingham, m. (2) Feb. 27, 1836, in Lee, Lydia Clay, of Lee.
QUINT, Dr. Alonzo Hall, son of George, b. Mar. 22, 1828, d. Nov. 4, 1896, m. Jan. 30, 1854, in Boston, Mass., Rebecca Page Putnam, of Salem, Mass., b. May 14, 1829, d. Jan. 3, 1913.
RACKLEY, Gen. Benjamin Franklin, son of Jason, b. 1834, d. Apr. 26, 1890, m. Jan. 7, 1861, by Rev. Francis E. Hicks, Matilda J. Frye, b. 1836, d. Jan. 4, 1928, dau. of James, both of Dover.
RADCLIFFE, George K., m. May 5, 1864, in Dover, Annie M. Durgin.
RAITT, William F., m. Nov. 24, 1866, in Dover, Carrie C. Gage.
RAND, William, m. July 19, 1787, by Rev. Isaac Smith, Mary Gale, both of Gilmanton.

RAND, Lemuel, m. Nov. 4, 1799, by Rev. Isaac Smith, Judith Gilman.

RAND, Samuel, of Barnstead, m. Sept. 4, 1800, by Rev. Isaac Smith, Polly Hill, of Barrington.

RAND, Daniel, of Barnstead, m. in 1813, by Rev. John Osborne, Polly Kent, of Durham, dau. of Richard.

RAND, Bickford, b. Apr. 29, 1818, d. Feb. 21, 1895, of Rochester, m. (1) Mar. 15, 1838, by Elder Enoch Place, Abigail Berry, of Strafford, b. 1820, d. Dec. 22, 1871, m. (2) in 1873, Melissa Brown.

RAND, Leonard S., m. Nov. 23, 1862, by Rev. James Rand, Elizabeth H. Sawyer.

RAND, Ira, m. Jan. 25, 1864, in New Durham, Mrs. Clarrie A. Savage, both of New Durham.

RAND, John E., m. Apr. 20, 1865, by Rev. James Rand, Lizzie S. Randall.

RAND, Mark F., m. Nov. 9, 1869, in Dover, Laura A. Hurd.

RAND, John C., m. Sept. 23, 1870, in Dover, Mary Perkins.

2) **RANDALL**, John, son of Richard, m. June 22, 1718, in Berwick, Me., Mary Chick, dau. of Thomas.

RANDALL, John, of Durham, m. Jan. 16, 1755, Abigail Huckins, dau. of Robert.

RANDALL, Arthur, m. May 22, 1815, in Lebanon, Me., Patience Young.

RANDALL, Thomas, m. int. Aug. 23, 1823, in Lee, Mary Leighton.

RANDALL, Hiram Joseph, b. July 22, 1810, d. Apr. 18, 1851, m. Aug. 2, 1840, by Rev. Rufus O. Williams, Betsey Ham, b. Jan. 13, 1807, d. Apr. 14, 1892, dau. of Joseph.

RANDALL, Daniel S., son of Josiah, b. Sept. 10, 1818, d. Apr. 10, 1873, m. (pub. Jan. 3, 1843, in Newmarket), Abigail (Williams), Philbrick, wid. of William.

RANDALL, Isaac, d. Nov. 1, 1873, m. June 16, 1844, by Rev. Ransom Dunn, Mrs. Abigail Randall.

RANDALL, Richard, of Lee, d. Mar. 13, 1878, aged 53, m. Dec. 25, 1844, by Elder Samuel Sherburne, Betsey Freeman, of Barrington, d. Jan. 3, 1903, aged 71.

RANDALL, Luke L., m. Dec. 31, 1849, in Lee, Mary S. Wigglesworth, both of Lee.

RANDALL, Jeremiah D., b. 1838, m. (1) Nov. 4, 1858, in Dover, Mary E. Merrill, d. Aug. 30, 1860, aged 19, dau. of John, both of Dover, m. (2) int. Apr. 10, 1862, in Lee, Susan F. Bartlett, b. 1833.

RANDALL, Aaron W., of Berwick, Me., m. June 13, 1864, by Rev. Asa Piper, Emily S. Colomy, of Newfield, Me.

RANDALL, Charles D., m. Apr. 22, 1866, in Lee, Mrs. Cynthia A. Thompson, both of Lee.
RANDALL, Andrew R., of New Durham, m. July 2, 1868, by Rev. Asa Piper, Mrs. Sophia Driscoll, of Alton.
RANDALL, John H., m. Apr. 26, 1869, in Dover, Elizabeth F. Card.
RANDALL, Frederick H., m. Oct. 14, 1869, in Dover, Julia A. C. Sheridan.
RANDALL, Milton N., m. (pub. Apr. 17, 1874, in Great Falls), Nellie J. Foote.
RANDALL, Frank D., of Lee, m. Sept. 24, 1877, in Lee, Laura A. Chesley, of Durham.
RANSOM, Richard, of Dover, b. in 1774, d. May 26, 1851, m. (1) Abigail Canney, d. Mar. 1820, m. (2) July 1, 1822, Ruth Quimby, of Berwick, Me., b. near 1795.
RANSOM, Ebenezer, of Alton, b. Sept. 10, 1780, d. Feb. 26, 1847, m. (1) Mar. 21, 1771, by Dr. Belknap, Lydia Buzzell, d. Apr. 14, 1799, m. (2) Sarah Babb, b. Sept. 27, 1790, d. Sept. 29, 1867, aged 77.
RANSOM, George W., m. int. Oct. 19, 1834, in Dover, Sophia Bunker, of Durham, d. Jan. 7, 1894, aged 86, dau. of John.
2) **RAWSON**, Jonathan Augustus, d. Sept. 1819, aged 32, m. Dec. 11, 1815, by Rev. Joseph W. Clary, Rebecca G. Hodgdon, b. in 1794, d. June 5, 1816, aged 22.
READ, Robert, m. Apr. 4, 1839, Sarah Demeritt, b. Aug. 30, 1787, d. Aug. 15, 1854, dau. of Israel.
READ, David, m. Dec. 7, 1867, by Rev. Jesse Meader, Letitia Brooks.
REDLON, Eugene, m. Oct. 6, 1864, in Dover, Susan M. Harmon.
REED, Augustus H., m. Oct. 21, 1867, in Dover, Hannah E. Moore.
REMICK, John, son of Benjamin, d. June 25, 1823, aged 76, m. Jan. 14, 1773, in Kittery, Me., Susannah Cole, b. Mar. 15, 1749, d. Aug. 25, 1824, aged 74, dau. of Abner.
REMICK, John, Jr., of Eliot, Me., son of William, b. Apr. 17, 1771, d. Sept. 12, 1840, m. (1) Aug. 24, 1794, in Eliot, Me., Mary Butler, of Portsmouth, b. May 18, 1771, d. Oct. 17, 1825, dau. of Capt. Edward, m. (2) Feb. 9, 1826, in Wakefield, Sally Nudd, of Wakefield, d. Nov. 23, 1845, aged 67.
REMICK, Thomas, son of Stephen, d. Feb. 18, 1856, aged 84, m. (1) Nov. 28, 1799, in Kittery, Me., Lydia Remick, b. Sept. 15, 1778, d. Feb. 1, 1812, m. (2) near 1812, Olive L. Abbott, d. Dec. 7, 1882, aged 92.
REMICK, Joseph, m. (pub. Jan. 19, 1805, in Lebanon, Me.), Dolly Burrows.
REMICK, John L., m. Dec. 29, 1811, in Wakefield, Abra Applebee, of Milton, dau. of Thomas.

REMICK, George W., d. Dec. 28, 1903, aged 79, m. (pub. Jan. 12, 1847, in Great Falls), Rebecca A. Stevens, d. May 25, 1901, aged 76.

REMICK, Moses Howe, son of Thomas, b. Feb. 6, 1820, d. Apr. 22, 1892, m. June 27, 1847, Clarissa Wentworth, b. Sept. 9, 1828, d. Aug. 29, 1906, dau. of Levi.

REMICK, Alpheus, d. Oct. 12, 1887, aged 72, m. Mar. 4, 1851, in Milton, Harriet Walker, d. Apr. 30, 1892, aged 74, dau. of Joseph.

REMICK, Andrew J., son of Nathaniel, b. Dec. 3, 1835, d. Feb. 22, 1895, m. (pub. Dec. 16, 1858, in Great Falls), Lydia A. Hart, b. June 2, 1826, d. June 17, 1906, both of Milton.

REMICK, Colby, m. Aug. 24, 1870, in Dover, Isabel Goodwin.

REMICK, George E., m. (pub. Nov. 21, 1873, in Rochester), Etta Brown, both of Great Falls.

RENDALL, Charles C., d. in New Orleans, La., m. May 14, 1849, in Wolfeboro, Charlotte B. Cotton, b. 1827, d. 1864, both of Wolfeboro.

REYNOLDS, Capt. Daniel, son of Col. Daniel, d. Oct. 24, 1809, aged 39, m. Aug. 6, 1797, Elizabeth Leighton, b. Apr. 19, 1778, d. Sept. 12, 1851, dau. of James.

REYNOLDS, Daniel, b. July 9, 1799, m. Nov. 24, 1825, by Rev. J. W. Clary, Sarah Watson, b. May 26, 1803, both of Dover.

REYNOLDS, Asa, of Lee, m. int. May 3, 1829, in Lee, Mary Ann Haley, of Newmarket.

REYNOLDS, Andrew T., d. May 29, 1868, aged 33, m. Aug. 25, 1855, in Farmington, Elvina A. Reynolds, both of Milton.

REYNOLDS, James O., of Dover, son of Paul, d. Mar. 9, 1900, aged 73, m. Nov. 12, 1856, in Great Falls, Mary E. Cook, of Wakefield, b. 1831, dau. of Samuel.

REYNOLDS, Hambleton, of Lowell, Mass., m. (pub. July 30, 1857, in Alton), Corisand S. Glines, of Alton, d. Oct. 29, 1923, aged 85, dau. of Rev. Josiah (divorced).

REYNOLDS, James A., son of Stephen, d. May 11, 1919, aged 82, m. Mar. 16, 1864, by Rev. James Rand, Miriam S. Hanson.

REYNOLDS, George, of Lee, b. 1805, m. int. Nov. 26, 1865, in Lee, Mrs. Sarah York, of Pittsfield, b. 1804.

REYNOLDS, Benjamin O., d. May 28, 1923, aged 86, m. Apr. 19, 1871, in Dover, Martha Dodge White, d. May 3, 1891, aged 49, dau. of John H.

RICE, Richard, m. (pub. Sept. 29, 1804, in Portsmouth), Maria Ball.

RICE, David Hall, m. Feb. 25, 1868, by Rev. Alden Sherwin, Elizabeth H. Garland.

RICHARDS, John, son of John, b. 1754, d. Mar. 7, 1834, m. Sarah Bickford, b. 1754, d. Dec. 23, 1821, aged 67.

RICHARDS, George J., of Somersworth, son of Lambert, d. Jan. 23, 1894, aged 72, m. (pub. Jan. 22, 1844, in Portsmouth), Eunice J. Roberts, of Portsmouth.

RICHARDS, Charles C., m. Apr. 13, 1870, by Rev. Asa Piper, Kesiah F. Quimby, both of Newfield, Me.

RICHARDSON, William, m. July 22, 1745, in Rochester, Abigail Place.

RICHARDSON, Jeremiah Jr., m. Aug. 29, 1784, by Rev. Isaac Smith, Molly Rand, both of Gilmanton.

RICHARDSON, Joseph, m. July 7, 1793, by Rev. Isaac Smith, Polly Rand.

RICHARDSON, Lt. Josiah, of Moultonboro, d. Apr. 17, 1849, aged 72, m. Dec. 1812, by Rev. Jeremiah Shaw, Mary Burbank, of Tuftonboro, d. Nov. 2, 1824, aged 35.

RICHARDSON, Joseph, Jr., d. Jan. 20, 1855, aged 65, m. Mar. 7, 1820, by Rev. Jeremiah Shaw, Dolly B. Moulton, d. May 16, 1861, aged 69.

RICHARDSON, Louis B., m. July 17, 1825, in Dover, Lucy Cox.

RICHARDSON, John A., of Durham, m. (pub. July 10, 1829, in Kittery, Me.), Marcia A. Rice.

RICHARDSON, Joseph, m. (pub. Sept. 1, 1840, in Barrington), Elizabeth Hall, d. Apr. 30, 1898, aged 81, dau. of David, both of Dover.

RICHARDSON, George, of Northwood, b. May 12, 1835, m. (pub. Sept. 12, 1854, in Northwood), Lydia C. Durgin, of Lee, b. Mar. 24, 1833, d. June 4, 1859, dau. of Benjamin.

RICHARDSON, George A., m. Jan. 23, 1866, in Dover, Mary J. Rothwell.

RICHARDSON, Orlando, m. June 24, 1869, in Dover, Abbie L. Trafton.

RICHARDSON, James Herbert, m. July 5, 1873, Jettie Farrar, both of Dover.

RICKER, Samuel, of Somersworth, m. Oct. 1751, by Rev. Amos Main, Mary Frost, of Dover.

4) RICKER, Nicholas, son of Ephraim, b. in 1735, d. in 1801, inherited the Twombly Garrison at Littleworth, m. Eleanor Twombly, b. 1727, d. Aug. 9, 1816, dau. of William.

4) RICKER, Jebez, son of Joseph, b. 1742, m. May 14, 1761, by Rev. John Morse, Mary Wentworth, d. Dec. 1813, aged 80.

4) RICKER, Daniel, son of John, b. Apr. 9, 1740, d. May 3, 1823, m. early as 1762, Lucy Cromwell, dau. of Eliphalet.

5) RICKER, Simon Emery, son of Noah, m. Mar. 6, 1777, by Rev. Matthew Merriam, Mary Hooper, b. Mar. 14, 1749, dau. of Samuel, both of Berwick, Me.

RICKER, Cpl. Reuben, son of Richard, b. Dec. 9, 1758, d. July 14, 1846, m. Mary Styles, d. Jan. 11, 1848, aged 91 yrs., 8 mos.

5) RICKER, Capt. Ebenezer, Jr., of Somersworth, son of Capt. Ebenezer, b. July 15, 1762, d. 1827, m. Apr. 4, 1782, by Rev. Matthew Merriam, Molly Bodwell, of Berwick, Me., b. Jan. 30, 1762, d. 1852.

RICKER, Joseph, d. Feb. 7, 1838, aged 76, m. Dec. 9, 1784, by Rev. Joseph Haven, Sarah H. Trickey, d. Oct. 23, 1841, aged 77.

RICKER, Jeremiah, d. Mar. 9, 1816, aged 36, m. Jan. 1802, by Rev. Robert Gray, Elizabeth Drew.

RICKER, Isaac, m. May 1803, in Dover, Nancy Dame.

5) RICKER, David, Jr., son of David, b. Sept. 6, 1776, m. (pub. Nov. 26, 1803, in Dover), Lydia Chase, dau. of Enoch.

RICKER, Charles, son of Ebenezer, b. June 7, 1784, d. Sept. 15, 1836, aged 52, m. Mar. 11, 1810, by Rev. Joseph Haven, Mary Lord, both of Milton, d. Feb. 21, 1880, aged 91.

RICKER, Capt. Timothy, d. Feb. 9, 1832, aged 39, m. (1) July 15, 1813, in Dover, Abigail Varney, d. June 18, 1826, aged 32, m. (2) Oct. 25, 1828, Elizabeth C. Clark, d. Jan. 15, 1839, aged 36.

RICKER, Ezekiel, son of Ezekiel, b. Nov. 26, 1789, d. May 13, 1864, m. int. Oct. 29, 1814, in Lebanon, Me., Nancy N. Coffin, d. Apr. 5, 1877, aged 82.

RICKER, Harber, m. Feb. 26, 1824, in Milton, Elizabeth Corson, both of Somersworth.

RICKER, William W., b. 1814, d. 1870, m. Dec. 24, 1849, in Milton, Sarah Ann Downs, d. Oct. 17, 1863, aged 41.

RICKER, Charles E., son of Charles, d. Feb. 10, 1913, aged 79, m. May 29, 1851, in Milton, Sarah E. Hill, d. Oct. 12, 1865, aged 30.

RICKER, Joshua Morrill, m. (pub. Nov. 1, 1860, in Great Falls), Harriet A. Brock, d. Mar. 14, 1868, aged 29.

RICKER, Joel B., m. Jan. 31, 1866, in Dover, Pamelia A. Mullen, d. Nov. 16, 1908, aged 87.

RICKER, Albert M., m. Oct. 9, 1866, in Dover, Julia A. J. Howe, d. Jan. 10, 1909, aged 60.

RICKER, George K., m. Nov. 28, 1866, in Dover, Emma P. Newell.

RICKER, Oliver P., m. Dec. 22, 1866, in Dover, Susan A. Corson.

RICKER, William H., m. Aug. 28, 1867, by Rev. Robert S. Stubbs, Sarah M. Berry.

RICKER, D. W., of Acton, Me., m. Dec. 31, 1872, by Rev. Asa Piper, Emma Murrow, of Newfield, Me.

RIGGS, William F., m. (1) Apr. 20, 1864, in Dover, Hannah P. Sampson, m. (2) Feb. 19, 1897, by Rev. James Thurston, Elizabeth V. Sturtevant.

RINES, Henry, son of Henry, b. July 1830, d. Oct. 15, 1815, m. Nov. 26, 1761, Mary Fall, b. Jan. 1733, d. May 17, 1823, dau. of John.

RINES, Nathaniel, m. (1) Aug. 8, 1800, by Rev. William Hooper, Martha Wiggin, both of Dover, m. (2) Apr. 13, 1828, in Middleton, Nancy Cook, d. Oct. 10, 1855, aged 68, both of Middleton.

RINES, Joseph, son of Henry, b. Feb. 15, 1784, d. Aug. 19, 1861, m. Nov. 20, 1806, in Wakefield, Sally Remick, of Milton, b. Dec. 27, 1785, d. Feb. 12, 1855, dau. of John.

RINES, Mark, son of Henry, m. May 9, 1824, in Milton, Hannah Applebee, b. 1799, d. 1826, dau. of Thomas.

RINES, Samuel Fall, son of Joseph, b. May 23, 1818, d. Dec. 18, 1897, m. Dec. 24, 1840, Susan Remick, b. Apr. 13, 1820, d. Sept. 23, 1889, dau. of John.

RINES, Nathaniel, son of Joseph, b. 1816, d. Dec. 15, 1900, aged 84, m. Nov. 24, 1842, in Milton, Olive Remick, both of Milton, b. July 18, 1822, d. Aug. 28, 1908, dau. of Thomas.

RINES, James H., son of Harris, b. 1831, d. 1890, m. Jan. 12, 1852, in Milton, Milisse Boston, b. 1834, d. 1888, dau. of Joseph.

RINES, Joseph G., son of Joseph, b. May 12, 1824, d. June 10, 1907, aged 83, m. Aug. 7, 1853, in Milton, Sarah J. Sanborn, b. 1836, d. Aug. 28, 1816, dau. of William, both of Milton.

ROBBINS, Edwin, m. May 6, 1861, by Rev. James Rand, Frances M. Hill.

ROBBINS, William T., m. Apr. 15, 1865, in Dover, Mrs. Mary J. Daniels.

ROBERTS, John, Jr., of Somersworth, b. 1741, d. 1819, m. Dec. 13, 1768, by Rev. Jacob Foster, Elizabeth Hodgdon, b. 1740, d. 1825, dau. of Thomas.

ROBERTS, John, b. May 19, 1758, d. July 20, 1837, m. Aug. 1, 1782, by Rev. Joseph Haven, Ruth Rogers, b. 1756, d. Aug. 19, 1839.

ROBERTS, Timothy, Jr., son of John and Susanna, b. Aug. 3, 1759, d. Aug. 3, 1835, m. Nov. 28, 1782, by Rev. Joseph Haven, Elizabeth Hayes, b. July 25, 1757, d. Mar. 11, 1849, dau. of Wentworth.

ROBERTS, Samuel, m. Mary Estes, b. Sept. 5, 1760, d. Jan. 21, 1804, dau. of Elijah and Sarah.

ROBERTS, Joshua, (John?), b. 1760, d. 1817, m. Jan. 15, 1787, by Rev. Jonathan Tompson, Tamson Smith, d. Aug. 30, 1845, aged 78.

ROBERTS, David, m. Oct. 27, 1796, Hannah Meader, b. Apr. 27, 1763, dau. of Benjamin.

ROBERTS, Jedediah N., of Shapleigh, Me., b. 1777, d. 1860, m. Mar. 13, 1803, in Wakefield, Betsey Goodwin, of Milton, b. 1781, d. 1828.

ROBERTS, James, son of Timothy and Elizabeth, b. Dec. 24, 1783, d. July 5, 1839, aged 56, m. July 2, 1804, by Rev. Joseph Haven, Mercy Wentworth, b. Dec. 17, 1784, d. Sept. 10, 1845, dau. of John, both of Milton.

ROBERTS, John, b. Feb. 4, 1788, m. near 1807, Polly Davis, b. Nov. 25, 1789.

ROBERTS, John, Jr., b. May 19, 1797, d. Nov. 26, 1847, aged 60, m. Jan. 19, 1815, by Rev. Joseph Boodey, Abigail Wingate, b. Aug. 18, 1791, d. Apr. 6, 1873, aged 83, both of Farmington.

ROBERTS, John, Jr., son of John, d. Sept. 19, 1861, aged 72, m. Aug. 31, 1815, by Rev. Joseph Haven, Lois Dame, d. Apr. 9, 1858, aged 61, both of Rochester.

6) ROBERTS, Capt. Aaron, son of Daniel, b. May 27, 1797, d. June 15, 1874, m. (1) Aug. 22, 1823, in Wolfeboro, Mary Bickford, d. Sept. 16, 1835, aged 33, m. (2) (pub. May 2, 1837, in Wakefield) Maria A. Gage, of Wakefield, d. Dec. 14, 1875, aged 69, dau. of Moses.

ROBERTS, James Cutts, son of James, b. Mar. 27, 1810, d. Mar. 3, 1865, m. Nov. 16, 1834, in Milton, Lydia J. Scates, d. May 3, 1896, aged 59.

ROBERTS, Owen Swain, son of James, b. Apr. 4, 1813, d. 1853, m. (pub. Jan. 23, 1838, in Milton), Harriet L. Foss, b. 1814, d. 1895.

ROBERTS, Christopher, of Strafford, m. Feb. 7, 1841, by Rev. John Winkley, Mehitable C. Hanscom, of Barrington.

ROBERTS, Robert, m. (pub. Oct. 19, 1841, in Portsmouth), Mrs. Adeline Tremills, d. Oct. 28, 1892, aged 82.

ROBERTS, John Franklin, son of John, Jr., b. Oct. 31, 1820, d. Feb. 16, 1854, m. May 12, 1844, by Rev. Benjamin G. Willey, Lydia McDuffee Jones, d. Jan. 20, 1846, aged 22, dau. of Joseph.

ROBERTS, Hezekiah Wentworth, son of James, b. Feb. 26, 1826, d. July 20, 1852, m. May 30, 1846, in Milton, Persis B. Broughton, both of Somersworth.

ROBERTS, Col. John Y., of Somersworth, d. May 22, 1864, aged 37, m. (pub. Sept. 11, 1848, in Concord), Tamson M. Hayes, of Farmington, d. Feb. 2, 1870, aged 44.

ROBERTS, Jonathan, of Lowell, Mass., m. May 8, 1850, by Elder Elias Hutchins, Avis Jane Bodge, of Dover.

ROBERTS, Henry, m. in 1854, in Dover, Cynthia Chick.

ROBERTS, John R., son of John, b. Dec. 6, 1823, d. May 20, 1879, m. July 3, 1856, in Rollinsford, Ellen B. Johnson, b. May 15,

1833, d. Sept. 27, 1903, aged 70, dau. of David, both of Rochester.

ROBERTS, Alexander, son of George W., b. May 7, 1832, d. May 16, 1874, aged 42, m. Oct. 21, 1857, in Rollinsford, Caroline H. Plumer, d. May 16, 1874, aged 37, dau. of William, both of Rollinsford.

ROBERTS, William Estes, m. Dec. 5, 1865, in Dover, Rosetta Marie Chesley, b. Dec. 12, 1845, dau. of Daniel.

ROBERTS, William P., m. Oct. 5, 1866, by Rev. Asa Piper, Mae F. Campernell, both of Wakefield.

ROBERTS, Henry K., m. Mar. 16, 1867, by Rev. James Rand, Ellen A. Kimball.

ROBERTS, Lyman, m. Aug. 20, 1867, by Rev. Alden Sherwin, Susan F. Roberts.

ROBERTS, John F., m. May 18, 1876, in Dover, Ada M. Thompson.

ROBERTSON, Samuel, m. Oct. 5, 1834, in Eaton, Mary Snell.

ROBINSON, Gideon, m. Sept. 2, 1777, by Rev. Isaac Smith, Hannah Weed.

ROBINSON, Zebulon, m. (pub. May 2, 1807, in Portsmouth), Mary Turner.

ROBINSON, Ebenezer C., of Brookfield, m. Dec. 6, 1821, by Rev. Asa Piper, in Wakefield, Joann Swasey, of Wakefield.

ROBINSON, Noah, of Lee, m. int. Oct. 8, 1842, in Lee, Betsey Haley, of Epping.

ROBINSON, William F., son of Aaron, d. Jan. 31, 1914, aged 78, m. Jan. 13, 1861, in Barrington, Mary S. Ayers, both of Barrington.

ROBINSON, Richard L., m. Aug. 4, 1864, in Dover, Cornelia C. Danforth.

ROBINSON, William, m. Sept. 15, 1865, in Dover, Margaret Gallager.

ROBINSON, Edward H., son of William, d. Feb. 17, 1914, aged 76, m. Nov. 24, 1867, in Dover, Emma B. Wallace, d. July 19, 1917, aged 69, dau. of Jasper G.

ROBINSON, Joel F., m. July 3, 1869, in Dover, Martha H. Deering.

ROBINSON, George H., m. Oct. 29, 1870, in Dover, Fannie Leighton.

ROBINSON, Francis W., m. Nov. 14, 1870, in Dover, Mary M. Nutter.

ROBINSON, James R., m. July 4, 1873, in Rochester, Adelia A. Jordan, both of Cambridge, Mass.

ROBINSON, Albert O., m. Dec. 24, 1875, by Rev. Asa Piper, Clara E. Davis, both of Wakefield.

ROGERS, Charles, son of James, m. Nov. 12, 1747, in Rochester, Mary McDuffee.

ROGERS, James, son of James, m. Nov. 26, 1747, in Rochester, Lydia Leighton.

ROGERS, Daniel Jr., m. Jan. 13, 1803, by Rev. Isaac Smith, Polly Norris, both of Moultonboro.

ROGERS, Capt. Robert, d. Apr. 21, 1841, aged 66, m. Dec. 2, 1810, by Rev. Caleb Sherman, Rebecca Patten, d. Jan. 18, 1834, aged 46, dau. of Stephen, both of Dover.

ROGERS, Paul, of Berwick, Me., m. (pub. Feb. 24, 1816, in Salem, Mass.), Elizabeth Purinton, of Salem, Mass.

ROGERS, Alphonzo, m. Sept. 13, 1829, in Dover, Huldah Hatch, both of Great Falls.

ROGERS, David R., son of Nathaniel, b. 1827, d. 1890, m. Jan. 10, 1850, Sarah E. Clark, b. 1827, d. 1886, dau. of Enoch, both of Wolfeboro.

ROGERS, Tyler, m. Aug. 24, 1865, by Rev. James Rand, C. Felch.

ROGERS, Amasa A., m. Jan. 15, 1870, in Dover, Allie W. Blaisdell.

ROGERS, Charles H., m. Jan. 20, 1870, by Rev. Asa Piper, Abbie Tibbetts, both of Newfield, Me.

ROLLINS, Thomas, b. Apr. 22, 1755, m. Feb. 22, 1776, Sarah -----, b. Apr. 27, 1760.

3) ROLLINS, Sgt. Joseph, son of Thomas, d. Jan. 20, 1749, m. (1) Hannah -----, m. (2) Lydia (Heard) Norris, widow.

5) ROLLINS, James, d. Dec. 1813, aged 58, m. (1) Aug. 20, 1777, Hannah Carr, b. Dec. 9, 1754, d. July 1789, aged 33, dau. of Dr. Moses, m. (2) near 1800, Lucy Gerrish, d. Oct. 1815, aged 55.

ROLLINS, Reuben, m. Oct. 4, 1778, by Rev. Isaac Smith, Betty Smith.

ROLLINS, Ichabod, of Chichester, m. Aug. 29, 1793, by Rev. Isaac Smith, Sarah Leighton, of New Durham Gore.

ROLLINS, Jonathan, son of Thomas, b. Dec. 30, 1780, m. near 1806, Elizabeth -----, of Portland, Me., b. Sept. 16, 1781.

ROLLINS, Moses, m. Oct. 6, 1808, by Rev. Isaac Smith, Betsy Osgood, both of Gilmanton.

ROLLINS, Enoch, m. int. Nov. 1, 1821, in Lee, Betsey Ladd, both of Lee.

5) ROLLINS, Frederick A. C., son of Col. John, b. Oct. 1, 1799, d. July 1847, m. (1) Jan. 22, 1822, Abigail Miller, b. May 9, 1800, m. (2) int. Apr. 1826, in Lee, Mary Patrick, d. Apr. 1868, aged 79, both of Lee.

ROLLINS, Calvin, of Somersworth, d. Jan. 1, 1887, aged 72, m. Aug. 25, 1844, by Rev. Jacob Stevens, Rebecca Thompson, of Dover, d. Jan. 2, 1888, aged 77, dau. of Daniel.

6) ROLLINS, Isaac C., son of John, Jr., b. Feb. 26, 1829, d. June 16, 1862, m. Sept. 27, 1846, in Alton, Me., Abigail J. Watson, d. Oct. 5, 1916, aged 85, dau. of Samuel.

ROLLINS, Levi D., m. int. Feb. 20, 1847, in Lee, Grace Ellis, both of Lee.
6) ROLLINS, Amos L., son of Ichabod, b. Dec. 11, 1826, d. Feb. 22, 1900, m. (1) Dec. 24, 1851, in Alton, Sarah E. Kimball, d. Apr. 23, 1871, dau. of Nehemiah, both of Alton, m. (2) June 14, 1872, Permelia A. Pendergast, dau. of Thomas.
ROLLINS, George, b. 1842, m. int. Jan. 1, 1863, in Lee, Huldah McCoy, b. 1839, both of Lee.
ROLLINS, John J. P., b. 1835, m. Mar. 17, 1863, in Lee, Mary Redford, b. 1843.
ROLLINS, Charles, of Lee, b. 1845, m. int. July 18, 1864, in Lee, Angelissa Haines, b. 1846, of Newmarket.
ROLLINS, Charles C., m. Sept. 30, 1866, in Dover, Anne Danforth.
ROLLINS, John, of Ossipee, m. May 30, 1874, by Rev. Asa Piper, Sarah Ballard, of Wakefield.
ROSS, Jonathan, son of William, m. Aug. 1, 1771, by Rev. Matthew Merriam, Joanna Ricker.
ROSS, Jonathan, m. Oct. 31, 1782, by Rev. Isaac Smith, Sarah Dudley, both of Gilmanton.
ROSS, Daniel, m. Feb. 28, 1813, by Rev. Isaac Smith, Sally Morrill, both of Gilmanton.
ROSS, Joseph B., m. Apr. 30, 1867, by Rev. Alden Sherwin, Mary E. Johnson.
ROSS, William J., son of James M., d. Jan. 1, 1907, aged 73, m. Aug. 20, 1870, in Dover, Linna H. Thurlow.
ROSS, Joseph H., m. Nov. 24, 1870, in Dover, Mary A. Goodale.
ROSS, Albert, m. (pub. Feb. 19, 1874, in Great Falls), Matilda Chaney, both of Great Falls.
ROWE, Lazarus, b. 1725, d. Sept. 14, 1829, m. Oct. 11, 1752, by Rev. John Adams, Mary Webber, b. 1725, d. 1828, both of Greenland.
ROWE, Richard, m. Nov. 6, 1799, by Rev. Isaac Smith, Deborah Kelley, both of Gilmanton.
ROWE, Washington, m. Jan. 2, 1832, by Rev. John Winkley, Sarah Brown, both of Barrington.
ROWE, John F., m. Mar. 9, 1854, by Elder Samuel Sherburne, Nancy D. Heath, d. May 16, 1916, aged 84, dau. of Nathaniel, both of Barrington.
ROWE, David P., m. Jan. 24, 1856, by Rev. John Winkley, Elizabeth Ann Howard, both of Strafford.
ROWE, Levi, m. Mar. 24, 1866, in Dover, Amanda J. Nute.
ROWELL, Joseph, m. July 23, 1814, by Rev. Isaac Smith, Alice Williams, both of Barrington.
RUEE, Thomas, m. Mar. 6, 1870, in Dover, Laura J. Tibbetts.

RUMNEY, Moses, of Effingham, m. int. Feb. 22, 1823, in Lee, Martha Brackett, of Lee.

RUMNEY, Deac. Ezra T., d. May 31, 1865, aged 58, m. Apr. 30, 1829, by Rev. Benjamin Hoyt, Charlotte Lougee, dau. of Pitt, both of Dover.

RUNDLETT, Charles Jr., m. Apr. 7, 1801, by Rev. Isaac Smith, Nancy Osgood, both of Gilmanton.

RUNDLETT, Noah, son of Charles, m. Apr. 7, 1801, by Rev. Isaac Smith, Rachel Osgood.

RUNDLETT, Henry, son of Charles, m. May 23, 1807, by Rev. Isaac Smith, Sally Rogers, both of Gilmanton.

RUNDLETT, Nathaniel, m. in 1811, by Rev. John Osborne, Abigail Rollins, of Lee, d. Oct. 22, 1835, aged 46.

RUNDLETT, Daniel, m. July 5, 1815, by Rev. Isaac Smith, Mittee Leavitt Prescott, both of Gilmanton.

RUNDLETT, Nathaniel F., m. Oct. 23, 1816, by Rev. Isaac Smith, Nancy Boynton, both of Gilmanton.

RUNDLETT, Greenleaf, of Lee, m. int. Dec. 15, 1821, in Lee, Martha Haley, of Epping.

RUNDLETT, William, m. (pub. Jan. 22, 1823, in Portsmouth), Frances W. Brierley, d. 1825, aged 20, dau. of Benjamin.

RUNDLETT, Charles P., of Lee, son of David, b. Sept. 13, 1802, d. July 9, 1889, m. int. Sept. 30, 1827, in Lee, Mary G. Hilton, of Newmarket, b. Sept. 11, 1802, d. Oct. 16, 1882, dau. of Richard.

RUNDLETT, Nathaniel, of Lee, m. int. Feb. 17, 1836, Mary G. Simpson, of Nottingham.

RUNDLETT, Daniel, of Lee, m. int. Jan. 29, 1842, in Lee, Betsey F. Carter, of Louden.

RUNNELS, John, m. Nov. 1, 1820, in Berwick, Me., Lydia Guptill, b. 1793.

RUNNELS, Hosea, m. Dec. 3, 1842, in Milton, Tryphena Davis, both of Wakefield, b. 1812, d. 1871, dau. of Miles.

RUSSELL, Thaxter, m. Sept. 23, 1826, Mary Ann Joy, b. May 14, 1808, d. Nov. 11, 1835, dau. of Jacob.

RUSSELL, George H., m. Mar. 15, 1864, in Dover, Mary Esther Babb.

RUST, Rev. Henry, d. Mar. 20, 1749, m. in 1719, Anne Waldron, b. Aug. 29, 1698, d. 1734, dau. of Col. Richard.

RUST, Henry, d. Nov. 12, 1844, aged 90, m. Feb. 24, 1784, by Rev. Jeremiah Shaw, Hannah Horne, d. Oct. 4, 1843, aged 81, dau. of Ebenezer, both of Wolfeboro.

RUST, Nathaniel, son of William, d. Aug. 1, 1859, aged 69, m. (1) Jan. 21, 1816, in Wolfeboro, Lydia Folsom, d. Feb. 27, 1819, dau. of Jacob, both of Wolfeboro, m. (2) Apr. 12, 1820, in Wolfeboro, Fanny A. Wiggin, d. May 2, 1845, aged 4<u>8</u>, of Wolfeboro.

RYAN, Edmund, of Durham, <u>son of Michael, b. May 3, 1782</u>, d. Apr. <u>24</u>, 1834, <u>aged 52</u>, m. <u>Feb. 28</u>, 1805, by Rev. John Osborne, Hannah Thompson, of Lee, b. Feb. 22, 1779, d. June 23, 1849, dau. of Robert.

SABIN, Nathaniel, of Brookfield, Mass., <u>d. Aug. 1825, aged 62</u>, m. Aug. 5, 1798, in Wakefield, Mary Clay, of Brookfield, N.H.

ST. CLAIRE, Bernard, m. Feb. 7, 1867, by Rev. George G. Field, Melissa Emery.

SALTER, Thomas, of Barnstead, m. Mar. 10, 1808, by Rev. Isaac Smith, Anna Dudley, of Gilmanton.

SAMPSON, Ivory P., <u>son of Jonathan, d. May 21, 1912, aged 86</u>, m. Nov. 29, 1846, by Rev. Hezekiah D. Buzzell, Mary M. French, both of New Durham.

SANBORN, <u>Deac.</u> John, of Newmarket, b. July 16, 1730, d. Oct. 4, 1812, m. Dec. 26, 1754, by Rev. John Adams, Mary Glidden, of Durham, <u>d. Apr. 15, 1806, aged 72</u>.

SANBORN, Elisha, m. Aug. 29, 1790, by Rev. Isaac Smith, Agnes Moore, both of Sanbornton.

SANBORN, Benjamin, m. June 17, 1792, by Rev. Isaac Smith, Judith Tilton.

SANBORN, Jonathan, m. Nov. 10, 1802, by Rev. Isaac Smith, Sally Kelley, both of Gilmanton.

SANBORN, Jonathan, m. Nov. 3, 1803, by Rev. Isaac Smith, Hannah Page.

SANBORN, William, m. Nov. 24, 1806, by Rev. Isaac Smith, Betsy Sanborn.

SANBORN, Theophilus, m. (1) ----- -----, d. 1805, m. (2) Jan. 4, 1807, by Rev. Isaac Smith, Sally Smith, both of Gilmanton.

SANBORN, Samuel, m. Feb. 3, 1814, by Rev. Isaac Smith, Lucy Thurston, both of Gilmanton.

SANBORN, Asa, of Brookfield, <u>d. Aug. 1825, aged 42</u>, m. Feb. 24, 1824, by Rev. John Brodhead, Judith Burleigh, of Newmarket.

SANBORN, John, of Shapleigh, Me., b. 1800, d. 1876, m. Dec. 23, 1824, Mehitable Witham, of Milton, b. <u>Nov. 5</u>, 1803, d. 1881, <u>dau. of Josiah</u>.

SANBORN, John F., of Kingston, m. int. Oct. 27, 1827, in Lee, Hannah Sawyer, of Lee.

SANBORN, Edwin <u>A., son of Jacob, d. Apr. 14, 1895, aged 71</u>, m. int. Oct. 20, 1855, in Rollinsford, Abby D. Chase, both of Rollinsford.

SANBORN, Hiram M., m. Apr. 16, 1862, in Rochester, Ellen Henderson, both of Rochester.
SANDERS, George, m. Aug. 9, 1832, by Rev. John Winkley, Polly Twombly, both of Stratham.
SANDERS, John, b. 1812, d. Apr. 9, 1896, m. Nov. 21, 1833, by Elder Enoch Place, Maria L. Gray, b. 1815, d. July 31, 1897, dau. of Barber, both of Strafford.
SANDERS, Obed, m. Apr. 21, 1842, Maria Fields, b. Mar. 15, 1817, dau. of John.
SARGENT, Isaac, of Loudon, m. Aug. 16, 1798, by Rev. Isaac Smith, Jenny Moses, of Gilmanton.
SARGENT, Joseph, of Loudon, m. Dec. 7, 1813, by Rev. Isaac Smith, Betsy Buswell, of Gilmanton.
SARGENT, Cyrus M., of Amesbury, Mass., m. Jan. 20, 1850, in Lee, Hannah M. Davis, of Lee.
SARGENT, Jethro, of S. Berwick, Me., m. Aug. 30, 1873, in Salmon Falls, Hattie M. Stewart, of N. Berwick, Me.
SAVAGE, Maj. Joseph, b. June 14, 1756, d. Jan. 20, 1814, m. m. (1) ---- ----, m. (2) Dec. 16, 1793, by Rev. Jonathan Tompson, Catherine Hubbard.
2) **SAWYER**, Moses, son of Stephen and Sarah, of Newbury, Mass., b. Sept. 30, 1721, d. Apr. 1806, m. (1) Nov. 5, 1744, in Dover, Huldah Hill, of Kittery, Me., b. 1722, dau. of Samuel and Hannah, of Kittery, Me., m. (2) Aug. 28, 1766, in Dover, Rebecca Swain, of Dover, d. Dec. 13, 1816, dau. of Richard and Margaret.
SAWYER, John, m. (pub. July 7, 1804, in Portsmouth), Hannah Perkins.
SAWYER, Alfred J., of Dover, m. int. Aug. 30, 1829, in Dover, Nancy Davis, of Lowell, Mass.
SAWYER, David, of Lee, m. int. June 26, 1830, in Lee, Mrs. Susannah Chesley, of Durham.
SAWYER, Jefferson, of Lee, son of David, b. 1817, d. 1894, m. int. Oct. 3, 1840, in Lee, Elizabeth Jane Knowles, of Northwood, b. 1818, d. 1895.
SAWYER, Luther D., of Ossipee, son of Timothy, d. July 1884, aged 81, m. Feb. 1, 1843, by Rev. Mr. Leach, Lydia Hanson, of Sandwich.
SAWYER, Samuel B., b. Aug. 8, 1820, d. Dec. 23, 1898, m. June 20, 1844, by Rev. Charles Olin, Susan Maleham, b. July 29, 1809, d. June 10, 1896, both of Wolfeboro.
SAWYER, Franklin, of Lee, m. int. Feb. 8, 1850, in Lee, Lydia A. Perkins, of Greenland.

SAWYER, George William, son of William, b. 1831, d. 1890, m. (1) Aug. 12, 1850, in Milton, Hannah C. Young, d. 1871, aged 44, m. (2) Lucy Bickford, b. 1841, d. 1910.

SAWYER, Alonzo Havington, son of Daniel, b. May 17, 1827, d. July 17, 1885, m. Nov. 7, 1850, Martha J. Shapleigh, b. Feb. 17, 1831, d. May 18, 1918, dau. of Samuel.

SAWYER, Bitfield, of Strafford, m. May 1859, by Rev. John Winkley, Emily Arlin, of Barrington.

SAWYER, Charles Henry, son of Jonathan, b. 1840, d. Jan. 18, 1908, m. Feb. 8, 1865, in Dover, Susan Ellen Cowan, b. 1839, d. Apr. 20, 1899.

SAWYER, Jacob M., m. Jan. 11, 1868, in Dover, Maria D. Barber.

SAWYER, Franklin, of Lee, b. near 1833, m. Feb. 6, 1868, in Lee, Sarah P. Fernald, of Waltham, Mass., b. near 1833.

SAWYER, Frank P., of Lee, m. Dec. 29, 1877, in Lee, L. Etta Pusbeck (?), of Boston, Mass.

SCATES, John, m. June 30, 1745, in Rochester, Abigail Hayes, d. Aug. 18, 1782.

SCATES, Ithiel, of Rochester, son of John, m. Oct. 9, 1793, by Rev. Matthew Merriam, Ruth Clark, of Berwick, Me.

SCATES, John, son of Benjamin, b. 1777, d. Jan. 25, 1857, m. (1) Nov. 25, 1798, by Rev. Jos. Haven, Mary Worster, d. Jan. 28, 1828, aged 52, dau. of Lemuel, both of Rochester, m. (2) Abigail Walker, d. Jan. 20, 1858, aged 59.

SCATES, Isaac, son of Benjamin, b. Apr. 24, 1785, m. Dec. 1, 1811, in Wakefield, Betsey Worster, of Milton, b. May 10, 1785, d. Nov. 12, 1839, dau. of Lemuel.

SCATES, Benjamin, Jr., son of Benjamin, d. Nov. 10, 1862, aged 67, m. Jan. 27, 1820, by Rev. Joseph Haven, Lovey Lyman, b. Feb. 11, 1800, d. Sept. 13, 1855, aged 55, dau. of Theodore C., both of Milton.

SCATES, Zimri, of Ossipee, son of John, m. Dec. 23, 1830, in Effingham, Susan W. S. Clark, of Effingham, d. Mar. 28, 1859, aged 50, dau. of Dr. David W.

SCATES, Levi A., m. July 21, 1864, in Dover, Ellen A. Reed.

SCATES, Henry B., of Milton, son of Benjamin, b. Feb. 10, 1831, d. Oct. 31, 1919, m. Aug. 15, 1865, Ellen M. Dixon, of Lebanon, Me., b. Oct. 21, 1844, d. Mar. 17, 1930.

SCEGGEL, Benjamin, m. May 11, 1781, by Rev. Jeremiah Shaw, Judith Conner, of Wolfeboro.

SCOLLY, Thomas, of Westbrooke, Me., m. Jan. 1825, by Rev. J. W. Clary, Deborah Coffin, of Dover.

SCRIBNER, Benjamin, of Sandwich, d. 1829, aged 83, m. near 1769, Huldah Scribner.

SCRIGGINS, John, m. Jan. 3, 1759, Keziah Willey.
4) **SCRUTON**, William, son of Jonathan, b. Nov. 30, 1788, d. June 30, 1865, m. May 30, 1811, Mary Yeaton, b. 1794, d. Feb. 1, 1871, dau. of John.
SCRUTON, Joseph, m. Apr. 1, 1838, by Rev. John Winkley, Lavina Brock, both of Strafford.
SCRUTON, Charles D., of Strafford, d. Jan. 8, 1915, aged 78, m. Nov. 25, 1858, in New Durham, Hannah E. Scruton, of Alexandria, d. Sept. 20, 1891, aged 56.
SCRUTON, Stephen B., m. Nov. 25, 1863, by Rev. James Rand, Martha A. Wallingford.
SEAVEY, Ebenezer, of Rochester, d. Nov. 4, 1842, aged 77, m. (1) Hannah -----, d. 1836, aged 51, m. (2) Aug. 2, 1837, by Elder Enoch Place, Dorothy (-----) Seavey, of Farmington, wid. of Samuel, b. 1780, d. Nov. 24, 1859.
SEAVEY, Daniel, m. Oct. 20, 1830, by Rev. John Winkley, Betsey Brown, both of Strafford.
SEAVEY, James Frank, son of Samuel F., d. Aug. 15, 1920, aged 82, m. Apr. 20, 1863, in Dover, Sarah F. Webster, d. Mar. 26, 1900, aged 61.
SEAVEY, Charles H., m. Aug. 5, 1863, in Dover, Julia A. Seavey.
SEAVEY, Augustus, m. Dec. 7, 1865, in Dover, Annie L. Hussey.
SEAVEY, William, m. Feb. 9, 1871, in Dover, Caroline L. Brock, d. Jan. 2, 1903, aged 78.
SEAWARD, Horace E., son of Richard, d. Mar. 21, 1929, aged 87, m. Aug. 28, 1865, in Dover, Clara A. Nutter.
SELLER, John H., b. 1846, d. 1916, m. Apr. 8, 1869, in Dover, Annie E. Brown, b. 1845, d. 1924.
SENTER, Daniel, m. (pub. May 17, 1842, in Portsmouth), Mary Elizabeth Senter, d. Jan. 1894, aged 85.
SENTER, Levi, m. Dec. 31, 1870, in Tuftonboro, Adriana Dame.
SHACKFORD, Samuel, d. Oct. 21, 1843, aged 92, m. early as 1781, Anna Walker.
SHACKFORD, Josiah, of Barnstead, son of Capt. Samuel, b. Jan. 21, 1767, m. Jan. 27, 1796, Lydia Dennett, b. June 19, 1773, d. July 5, 1859, dau. of Jeremiah.
SHACKFORD, Samuel, son of Samuel and Anna, b. Feb. 8, 1782, d. Oct. 12, 1833, m. Jan. 28, 1806, Nancy Buzzell, b. Jan. 8, 1787, d. June 9, 1873, aged 87.
SHACKFORD, Nathaniel, of Newington, m. (pub. Dec. 6, 1825, in Somersworth), Abigail Coleman.
SHACKFORD, Charles B., b. Dec. 28, 1840, d. Jan. 2, 1881, m. Oct. 26, 1869, in Dover, Caroline Cartland, b. July 6, 1847, d. Nov. 21, 1897, dau. of Moses.

2) **SHANNON**, William, son of Cutt, b. Jan. 6, 1747, d. July 2, 1816, m. (1) Aug. 29, 1782, by Dr. Belknap, Eleanor Gerrish, d. Jan. 17, 1806, aged 51, dau. of Capt. Samuel, m. (2) in 1809, Jane Jordan.

SHANNON, Nathaniel, of Portsmouth, son of Nathaniel, b. 1764, d. Feb. 5, 1826, m. June 24, 1784, in Greenland, Ann Elizabeth Peverly, d. Feb. 9, 1850, dau. of George.

3) SHANNON, Lt. William, son of Capt. Thomas, d. in 1813, aged 34, at Sackett's Harbor, m. Sept. 27, 1801, Mary Waldron, of Barrington, dau. of Isaac.

SHANNON, George, of Gilmanton, son of Nathaniel, b. Oct. 4, 1786, d. Apr. 8, 1868, m. Sarah Tibbetts, b. 1785, d. June 5, 1872, dau. of Ephraim.

SHANNON, John Sherburn, of Gilmanton, son of Nathaniel, b. 1791, d. Aug. 4, 1868, m. 1815, Abigail Rand, b. 1797, d. Sept. 12, 1868, dau. of Moses.

SHANNON, Samuel, of Gilmanton, son of Nathaniel, b. May 15, 1793, d. Jan. 7, 1833, m. Aug. 15, 1816, Mary Burnham Caswell, of Northwood, b. Feb. 25, 1799, d. Nov. 13, 1893, dau. of Elijah.

SHANNON, William Cogswell, son of Nathaniel, b. Apr. 26, 1805, m. (1) in 1829, Maria M. Smith, b. 1808, d. Feb. 1, 1850, m. (2) Nancy Lamprey.

SHAPLEIGH, Richard, b. July 31, 1795, d. Dec. 8, 1869, m. (1) int. May 1, 1819, in Lebanon, Me., Shuah Ferguson, of Eliot, Me., b. Aug. 15, 1792, d. Apr. 2, 1828, m. (2) int. Aug. 17, 1828, in Lebanon, Me., Sarah Bragdon, of Milton, b. Nov. 30, 1806, d. Dec. 26, 1893, dau. of Samuel.

SHAPLEIGH, Samuel, m. Oct. 29, 1863, in Dover, Susan A. White.

SHAPLEIGH, Forrest E., m. Mar. 1, 1870, in Dover, Emily I. Cousins.

SHARP, William K., m. Sept. 3, 1870, in Dover, Ann J. Lapsley.

SHAW, Rev. Jeremiah, of Hampton, son of Edward, b. Jan. 28, 1747, d. Oct. 20, 1834, m. Apr. 21, 1773, in Seabrook, Hannah Moulton, d. Mar. 26, 1824, aged 76.

SHAW, Jeremiah, Jr., son of Rev. Jeremiah, b. July 24, 1778, d. Dec. 7, 1854, m. 1798, by Rev. Jeremiah Shaw, Rachel Warren, b. Dec. 15, 1778, d. Mar. 21, 1865.

SHAW, Levi, m. Apr. 22, 1805, by Rev. Isaac Smith, Mary Gilman.

SHAW, Dr. Ichabod, of Moultonboro, son of Rev. Jeremiah, b. Oct. 15, 1781, d. Jan. 16, 1836, aged 54, m. (1) May 18, 1809, in Tamworth, Eliza Little, of Cambridge, m. (2) Oct. 9, 1825, by Rev. J. W. Clary, Susan Buzzell, of Rochester.

SHAW, Hilliard, m. Oct. 1, 1811, by Rev. Isaac Smith, Betsy Witham, both of Nottingham.

SHAW, Benjamin, of Northport, Me., m. Feb. 24, 1815, by Rev. Isaac Smith, Elizabeth Kelley.
SHAW, John, of Epping, d. Mar. 15, 1846, aged 50, m. July 25, 1820, by Rev. John Osborne, Abigail Runnels, of Lee.
SHAW, Elihu, of Lee, m. int. July 26, 1827, in Lee, Abigail Nay, of Brentwood.
SHAW, Jackson, of Freedom, d. Feb. 18, 1907, aged 78, m. (1) June 8, 1861, in Dover, by Rev. D. P. Leavitt, Hannah S. Foss, of Rochester, m. (2) Nov. 2, 1865, in Dover, Lorinia N. Foss.
SHAW, Aratus B., son of Aratus, b. Mar. 20, 1841, d. July 21, 1909, m. Mar. 29, 1863, Sarah E. Rines, b. July 6, 1843, d. Oct. 15, 1933, dau. of Samuel, both of Milton.
SHAW, Harris M., m. Sept. 9, 1875, in Rochester, Jane H. Varney.
SHEPARD, John, m. Mar. 27, 1776, by Rev. Isaac Smith, Betsy Page.
SHEPARD, Benjamin, of Fair-Haven, m. July 1802, Polly Bell, of Dover.
SHEPARD, Daniel, b. 1811, d. 1883, m. Dec. 20, 1840, in Wolfeboro, Hannah Estes, b. June 18, 1810, d. Dec. 11, 1894, aged 83, dau. of Elijah.
SHERBURNE, Samuel, m. Nov. 20, 1775, Sally Hill, d. 1785, dau. of Benjamin.
SHERBURNE, Elder Samuel, son of Gideon, d. Aug. 8, 1861, aged 58, m. July 12, 1831, by Rev. William Demeritt, Elizabeth Swain, dau. of Deac. Daniel, both of Barrington.
SHERBURNE, Warren P., of Northwood, m. June 13, 1832, Elizabeth B. Demeritt, of Lee, b. June 14, 1807, dau. of Andrew.
SHERBURNE, John, m. May 18, 1836, by Rev. William Demeritt, Nancy (Buzzell) Shackford, wid. of Samuel, b. Jan. 8, 1787, d. June 9, 1873, aged 87.
SHERBURNE, Andrew, of Portsmouth, m. (pub. June 12, 1843, in Barnstead), Hannah R. George, of Barnstead, d. Mar. 1, 1900, dau. of Enos.
SHERBURNE, Isaac S., d. Feb. 3, 1907, aged 73, m. Dec. 16, 1858, by Elder Elias Hutchins, Hannah R. Woodman, d. Dec. 5, 1898, aged 67, both of Barrington.
SHERMAN, Edward B., m. Oct. 16, 1868, by Rev. Alden Sherwin, Hannah A. Wallace.
SHOREY, Lyford, of Wolfeboro, son of John, d. Oct. 15, 1879, aged 95, m. (1) int. Oct. 1813, in Tuftonboro, Mercy Wiggin, of Tuftonboro, d. Dec. 2, 1837, aged 47, m. (2) Jan. 14, 1839, in Wolfeboro, Betsey Willey, of Wolfeboro.

SHOREY, Samuel, d. Mar. 30, 1893, aged 77, m. Aug. 20, 1838, in Wolfeboro, Nancy Drew, d. Dec. 30, 1866, aged 55, both of Wolfeboro.
SHOREY, Timothy, m. Aug. 1, 1852, in S. Berwick, Me., Sarah C. Bennett, d. June 22, 1858, aged 27, both of S. Berwick, Me.
SHOREY, Gilbert, of Salmon Falls, son of Simeon, d. Aug. 4, 1899, aged 72, m. (pub. Apr. 17, 1856, in S. Berwick, Me.), Abby Miller, of S. Berwick, Me., d. Apr. 19, 1909, aged 73, dau. of Webster.
SHOREY, Albra, son of John W., m. (1) (pub. Oct. 23, 1856, in N. Berwick, Me.), Lucy J. Shorey, both of S. Berwick, Me., m. (2) July 25, 1866, in Dover, Eliza J. Keyes, d. July 14, 1880, aged 48.
SHORT, James, m. (pub. Sept. 5, 1843, in Durham), Catharine W. Bickford, b. Aug. 3, 1815, d. Jan. 11, 1857, dau. of Robert.
SHORTRIDGE, Capt. Richard, bpt. Dec. 13, 1762, d. June 5, 1811, m. in 1756, Mary Pitman, dau. of Benjamin.
SHOTWELL, Caleb, m. Mar. 2, 1779, by Rev. Isaac Smith, Phebe Glidden.
SHUTE, Dr. Samuel Addison, of Weare, m. (pub. Oct. 30, 1827, in Great Falls), Ruth Whittier.
SHUTE, Albert T., b. Sept. 11, 1846, d. Feb. 10, 1896, m. June 4, 1867, by Rev. James Rand, Josephine A. Dame, b. 1854, d. Sept. 25, 1936.
SHUTE, Henry P., m. Aug. 24, 1867, in Dover, Alfarata M. Perkins.
SIBLEY, William, m. July 27, 1786, by Rev. Isaac Smith, Lydia Hopkinson, both of Gilmanton.
SIBLEY, Mark, son of Mark, d. July 2, 1881, aged 74, m. Apr. 17, 1831, in Wakefield, Mehitable H. Wiggin, b. Aug. 27, 1806, d. Dec. 4, 1877, dau. of David, both of Wakefield.
SIMES, Bray W., of Milton, d. July 15, 1885, aged 84, m. June 4, 1828, in Middleton, Martha Spinney, of Wakefield, b. 1808, d. 1891.
SIMES, William, of Milton, son of Bray W., d. Dec. 17, 1907, aged 76, m. (1) Jan. 3, 1858, in Wakefield, Sarah E. Churchill, of Brookfield, d. May 24, 1863, aged 25, dau. of Eben C., m. (2) Feb. 26, 1865, in Dover, Amanda Vickery.
SIMES, Eben H., m. May 31, 1862, by Rev. James Rand, Olive A. Brown.
SIMES, John J., m. Oct. 1, 1863, in Dover, Nancy R. Jewett.
SIMMONS, William R., m. Dec. 27, 1865, by Rev. James Rand, Martha C. Rust.
SIMPSON, John, son of Theophilus, b. 1820, d. 1896, m. in 1851, Mary Elizabeth Hubbard, b. Oct. 4, 1828, d. Aug. 18, 1892, dau. of John.

NEW HAMPSHIRE MARRIAGES SUPPLEMENT

SINCLAIR, George H., m. Oct. 21, 1871, in Rochester, Addie Billings.

SISE, Edward F., m. May 8, 1825, in Portsmouth, Ann Simes.

SKILLIN, Lorenzo D., m. Feb. 6, 1868, by Rev. Robert S. Stubbs, Elizabeth M. (Hayes) Townsend, wid. of Jonas D.

SLADE, Thomas, of Hanover, m. Feb. 22, 1801, by Rev. Isaac Smith, Elizabeth Thurston, of Gilmanton.

SMALL, Samuel, son of Francis, b. 1666, m. Elizabeth Heard, dau. of James.

SMALL, Elder Carlton, of Limington, Me., m. Aug. 5, 1832, by Rev. Davis, Sarah L. Drew, of Ossipee, d. 1862, aged 61, dau. of George.

SMALL, Clement E., m. July 11, 1865, in Dover, Louisa S. Jordan.

SMART, John, m. (pub. Dec. 12, 1807, in Newmarket), by Rev. John Osborne, Mehitable Cheswell, dau. of Wentworth.

SMART, Dr. Burleigh, of Kennebunk, Me., m. July 2, 1821, by Rev. J. W. Clary, Abigail Cogswell, of Dover, b. Oct. 29, 1791, d. June 21, 1827.

SMART, Deac. James Monroe, of Durham, son of James, b. Nov. 27, 1829, d. Mar. 18, 1875, m. (pub. June 12, 1856, in Portsmouth), Mary A. Walker, b. Apr. 13, 1834, d. Oct. 28, 1901.

SMEELIE, John, d. Feb. 13, 1924, aged 86, m. Apr. 8, 1869, in Dover, Martha Southwick.

SMITH, Robinson, m. Mar. 24, 1785, by Rev. Isaac Smith, Meriam Glidden, both of Gilmanton Gore.

SMITH, Daniel Jr., of Meredith, m. July 10, 1791, by Rev. Isaac Smith, Sally Dow, of Gilmanton.

SMITH, Joseph, m. Nov. 4, 1792, in Durham, Abigail Bennett, b. June 19, 1773, dau. of John.

SMITH, Edward, of Gilmanton Gore, m. Nov. 11, 1792, by Rev. Isaac Smith, Mary Dow.

SMITH, Joseph, m. Mar. 28, 1793, by Rev. Isaac Smith, Molly Morrill.

SMITH, Joseph, m. Feb. 23, 1794, by Rev. Isaac Smith, Hannah Fifield, both of Gilmanton.

SMITH, Stephen, m. Aug. 10, 1794, by Rev. Isaac Smith, Comfort Wallace.

SMITH, Timothy, m. Nov. 24, 1806, by Rev. Isaac Smith, Betsy Rundlett.

SMITH, Caleb, d. 1813, aged 32, m. Mar. 29, 1807, by Rev. Jeremiah Shaw, Mary Burnham, d. 1840, aged 63.

SMITH, Joseph, m. Mar. 8, 1810, by Rev. Isaac Smith, Alice Gilman, both of Gilmanton.

SMITH, Joseph, of Dover, m. (pub. Nov. 24, 1810, in Haverhill, Mass.), Mary Emerson, of Haverhill, Mass.

SMITH, Valentine, m. (1) Jan. 4, ----, Mary Joy, b. Oct. 8, 1780, d. Oct. 10, 1810, dau. of Samuel, m. (2) Sept. 16, 1819, Betsey Ballard, b. June 7, 1786, dau. of Joshua.

SMITH, Charles C., m. Mar. 16, 1817, by Rev. Isaac Smith, Hannah Parsons.

SMITH, Joshua, b. June 3, 1784, d. Mar. 26, 1871, m. Aug. 14, 1819, Abigail Fall, b. May 17, 1793, dau. of Stephen.

SMITH, Ebenezer, of Brentwood, m. int. Aug. 23, 1828, in Lee, Katharine French, of Lee.

SMITH, John C., of Providence, R.I., m. (pub. Sept. 9, 1828, in Great Falls), Elizabeth M. Stanwood, of Great Falls.

SMITH, Remembrance C., of Barrington, m. Feb. 21, 1831, by Rev. John Winkley, Sarah Ann Bunker, of Strafford.

SMITH, George J. O., son of John, b. in 1808, d. Nov. 14, 1888, m. Abigail A. Downs, b. in 1810, d. in 1900, dau. of Jonathan.

SMITH, Deac. Ebenezer, Jr., of Strafford, son of Ebenezer, d. Jan. 13, 1894, aged 83, m. Apr. 6, 1834, by Elder Enoch Place, Mary Smith, of Barrington, d. Dec. 6, 1887, aged 74.

SMITH, Sherburne, of Loudon, m. June 2, 1835, by Rev. William Demeritt, Abigail P. Rundlett, of Lee.

SMITH, Charles M., m. Nov. 8, 1835, Betsey Jones.

SMITH, Ansel, of Canton, Mass., b. 1802, d. 1881, m. June 11, 1836, in Wakefield, Elizabeth Drew, of Somersworth, b. 1799, d. 1868, dau. of John.

SMITH, John M., d. Jan. 16, 1848, aged 31, m. Oct. 28, 1841, by Rev. Elihu Scott, Comfort York, b. July 19, 1820, d. 1860, dau. of Daniel, both of Newmarket.

SMITH, Winthrop, son of Winthrop, b. 1820, d. May 23, 1904, m. Aug. 9, 1843, by Rev. Samuel Sherburne, Nancy Hall, d. July 23, 1880, aged 58, both of Barrington.

SMITH, David M., of Strafford, m. May 5, 1844, by Rev. John Winkley, Mary Perry, of Barrington.

SMITH, Joseph, of Barrington, m. Oct. 6, 1846, by Rev. John Winkley, Martha B. Taylor, of Salmon Falls.

SMITH, James F., m. (pub. Mar. 9, 1847, in Alton), Jerusha Glidden, d. Jan. 1, 1897, aged 73, dau. of John, both of Farmington.

SMITH, Cyrus G., of Newmarket, m. Sept. 12, 1847, in Newmarket, Eliza Chapman, of Durham.

SMITH, Samuel A., m. Dec. 3, 1848, in Gilmanton, Maria L. Nute.

SMITH, Joshua S., son of Joshua, b. July 7, 1823, d. Nov. 27, 1894, m. (pub. Jan. 30, 1849, in Great Falls), Mary A. Page.

SMITH, Jacob B., of Bradford, Mass., b. 1818, d. Dec. 30, 1888, m. May 3, 1849, by Elder Enoch Place, Mary Ann Parshley, of Strafford, b. 1818, d. Oct. 18, 1870.

SMITH, Joseph Harris, aged 26, born in Meredith, m. June 26, 1850, by Elder Enoch Place, Olive Ann Foss, aged 20, born in Strafford, d. Dec. 25, 1852, aged 22, dau. of Isaac.

SMITH, Gilbert W., of Newmarket, m. Nov. 27, 1856, in Newmarket, L. Copp, of Durham.

SMITH, Dr. Jeremiah, b. July 14, 1837, m. (1) Oct. 10, 1858, in Dover, Angeline Horn, both of Dover, m. (2) int. Apr. 5, 1865, in Lee, Hannah M. Webster, of Dover, b. Jan. 29, 1835.

SMITH, Wesley G., m. Feb. 25, 1864, in Dover, Lizzie T. Carle.

SMITH, Charles B., d. Jan. 28, 1868, aged 24, m. Aug. 7, 1864, in Dover, Sarah W. Kimball, d. Sept. 30, 1873, aged 27.

SMITH, John A., m. Dec. 12, 1864, in Dover, Mary E. Davis.

SMITH, John Q. A., m. Jan. 3, 1865, by Rev. Ezra Haskell, Lucretia Riley,d. Feb. 20, 1916, aged 86.

SMITH, William, m. June 2, 1866, by Rev. James Drummond, Mary Carberry.

SMITH, John M., m. Aug. 8, 1867, by Rev. Alden Sherwin, Elvira R. Hanson.

SMITH, John W., son of Henry, d. Jan. 1, 1925, aged 83, m. June 28, 1868, by Rev. Robert S. Stubbs, Sarah J. Embry, d. Sept. 6, 1889, aged 53, dau. of Josiah.

SMITH, George W., son of John, d. Jan. 13, 1911, aged 67, m. Sept. 8, 1869, in Dover, Martha G. Smith.

SMITH, David F., m. Nov. 25, 1869, in Dover, Nellie F. Chick.

SMITH, Charles A., m. Aug. 31, 1872, in Lee, Sarah F. Tilton, both of Nottingham.

SMITH, Albion A., m. Aug. 12, 1874, in Rochester, Sarah L. Brown.

SNELL, Samuel, dead in 1648, m. before 1648, Martha Matthews, dau. of Francis.

SNELL, John, son of John, m. Oct. 8, 1801, by Rev. John Osborne, Lydia Leathers, of Lee, d. Oct. 8, 1860, aged 94.

SNELL, Abraham B., of Lee, son of William, d. Jan. 3, 1849, aged 38, m. July 26, 1831, by Rev. William Demeritt, Olive Gear, d. Sept. 11, 1877, aged 69.

SNELL, Paul Giles, son of John, b. 1791, d. 1876, m. Oct. 18, 1831, by Rev. William Demeritt, Lydia Swain Tebbetts, d. May 4, 1883, aged 74, dau. of Israel.

SNELL, Nathaniel, son of John, d. Aug. 16, 1863, m. Feb. 6, 1832, by Rev. William Demeritt, Avis Williams, d. Feb. 26, 1862, both of Lee.

SNELL, Alfred, m. int. June 19, 1853, in Lee, Emily A. Page, both of Lee.

SNELL, Rev. Nehemiah C., of Lee, son of Paul, b. Dec. 19, 1831, d. May 17, 1893, m. Dec. 14, 1858, in Barrington, Mrs. Martha A. Langley, of Madbury, b. Apr. 18, 1836, d. June 4, 1920.

SNELL, Timothy D., of Dover, m. Mar. 4, 1868, by Rev. John Winkley, Mary R. Foss, of Barrington.

SNELL, George C., m. May 14, 1868, in Dover, Hannah M. Pierce.

SPAULDING, Alanson, m. July 30, 1866, in Dover, Clara M. Philpot.

SPENCER, Abednego, of Durham, son of Ebenezer, m. Oct. 14, 1752, "Old Stile," by Rev. John Adams, Welthean Huckins, of Dover, dau. of Capt. John.

SPENCER, William, Jr., b. 1760, d. 1834, m. May 26, 1785, by Rev. Jonathan Tompson, Eleanor Cooper.

SPENCER, Levi, son of Abednego, m. Nov. 26, 1788, Molly Johnson.

3) **SPINNEY**, David, son of Samuel, b. Sept. 12, 1706, d. 1745, m. in 1731, in Kittery, Me., Jerusha Cole.

SPINNEY, Ephraim, d. June 24, 1807, m. Feb. 11, 1796, by Rev. William Hooper, Deborah Pendexter, both of Durham.

SPINNEY, Parker, of Wakefield, son of David, d. Aug. 1, 1874, aged 71, m. Oct. 13, 1825, in Middleton, Mary Dearborn, of Milton, d. Feb. 10, 1856, aged 51.

SPINNEY, Nicholas, m. Feb. 10, 1833, in Eliot, Me., Eleanor A. Cole.

SPINNEY, Oliver P., m. Nov. 23, 1837, by Rev. Eleazer Smith, Nancy Ann Whitehouse, d. Oct. 1897, aged 84, dau. of Samuel, both of Dover.

SPINNEY, Capt. David, of Wakefield, b. 1769, d. 1848, m. (1) Lydia Paul, b. 1780, d. 1842, m. (2) (pub. Jan. 3, 1843, in Wakefield), Sally Chamberlain, of Milton.

SPINNEY, Robert, m. Nov. 12, 1846, in Eliot, Me., Martha Jane Cole, b. 1818, dau. of Robert.

SPINNEY, John P., m. Jan. 24, 1867, in Dover, Annie S. Merrill.

SPRINGER, George H., m. Mar. 16, 1868, in Dover, Cynthia E. Blanchard.

SPURLIN, Hanson, son of Jonathan L., d. Oct. 19, 1883, aged 53, m. (1) Aug. 18, 1852, in Dover, Abby Freeman, both of Dover, m. (2) Mar. 13, 1862, in Dover, Lydia Whitehouse.

SPURLIN, Charles P., m. Dec. 8, 1869, in Dover, Mary E. Tucker.

SPURLIN, Charles F., son of Thomas T., d. Oct. 19, 1916, aged 73, m. Sept. 5, 1870, by Rev. James Thurston, Mary Eliza Cook, b. Feb. 10, 1851.

SPURLING, George A., b. Nov. 16, 1844, d. Sept. 28, 1931, m. Nov. 11, 1866, in Dover, Ellen A. Hall, d. Dec. 2, 1882, aged 34.

STACKPOLE, Joseph, of Somersworth, m. (pub. Feb. 13, 1827, in Somersworth), Lydia Wentworth, of Dover.

STACKPOLE, Charles, d. June 21, 1878, aged 79, m. Dec. 21, 1845, in Wolfeboro, Mary H. Cook, d. Jan. 19, 1895, aged 85, both of Wolfeboro. (Was this a second marriage?)

STACKPOLE, George L., m. Aug. 4, 1866, by Rev. James Rand, Martha A. McDuffee.

STACKPOLE, Charles H., m. Mar. 15, 1868, in Dover, Annie M. Carter.

STACKPOLE, Dominicus, m. Sept. 23, 1868, in Dover, Laura Gould.

STACKPOLE, Simon R., m. Oct. 31, 1869, by Rev. Ezra Haskell, Martha J. Horne.

STACKPOLE, Albert F., son of Col. John, b. Dec. 2, 1848, d. Oct. 11, 1923, m. Nov. 12, 1873, in Dover, Lizzie H. Emery, both of Dover.

STACY, Oliver C., m. Jan. 30, 1866, in Dover, Lydia A. Emery, b. May 7, 1851, d. Aug. 19, 1921, dau. of King.

STANLEY, Phineas, m. Sept. 27, 1850, in Moultonboro, Mary Hannah Wiggin.

STANTON, Benjamin, m. Dec. 15, 1748, by Rev. Amos Main, Hannah Jones, of Somersworth.

STANTON, Isaac, m. Apr. 7, 1757, by Rev. Amos Main, Patience Hartford.

STANTON, William P., b. June 22, 1826, d. Nov. 8, 1907, m. (pub. Jan. 14, 1858, in Strafford), Lizzie H. Brock, b. Jan. 23, 1834, d. June 6, 1890.

4) **STAPLES**, Solomon Jr., of Kittery, Me., son of Solomon, m. near 1754, Lydia Knight.

STAPLES, John, m. Oct. 29, 1827, in Berwick, Me., Joanna Heard.

STAPLES, Joseph, m. Sept. 14, 1845, in Berwick, Me., Roxanna B. Hurd.

STAPLES, John W., m. June 8, 1867, by Rev. Robert S. Stubbs, Nellie M. Hawkins.

STARBIRD, Stephen, d. Dec. 15, 1869, aged 80, m. (1) Jan. 18, 1818, by Rev. Federal Burt, Tamson Nute, m. (2) Caroline (Teague) Davis, wid. of Daniel.

STEARNS, William, m. Dec. 12, 1826, by Rev. R. Porter, in Barrington, Martha Winkley, of Barrington.

STEEL, Dr. Richard, son of Jonathan, b. Jan. 6, 1797, d. June 13, 1869, m. (1) in 1824, in Durham, Harriet King Pierce, m. (2) in 1825, in Durham, Mary Amanda Smith, d. June 23, 1867, aged 57.

STEEL, James C., m. Apr. 2, 1862, in Dover, Sarah A. Spinney.

STERLING, Capt. Henry H., b. 1849, d. 1917, m. Sept. 18, 1867, in Dover, Mary A. Buzzell, b. 1849, d. Feb. 4, 1926, dau. of Miles R.

STERLING, Truman, of Dover, m. Jan. 8, 1874, in Dover, Sarah C. Chadwick, of Holden, Me.
STEVENS, Ebenezer, m. Dec. 31, 1776, by Rev. Isaac Smith, Molly Sanborn, both of Gilmanton.
STEVENS, Moses, m. Oct. 16, 1783, by Rev. Isaac Smith, Molly Lougee, both of Gilmanton.
STEVENS, Benjamin, m. Mar. 2, 1784, by Rev. Isaac Smith, Elizabeth Dow, both of Gilmanton.
STEVENS, Joseph, of Salisbury, Mass., m. Dec. 2, 1784, by Rev. Isaac Smith, Meriam Tucker, of Gilmanton.
STEVENS, Daniel, m. May 5, 1788, by Rev. Isaac Smith, Rachel Hilliard, both of Gilmanton.
STEVENS, Jonathan, Jr., of Lee, b. 1773, d. Apr. 12, 1854, m. Feb. 15, 1798, Patty Davis, d. May 9, 1853, aged 77, dau. of David.
STEVENS, Benjamin, m. May 4, 1804, in Lebanon, Me., Mercy Downs.
STEVENS, Samuel, of Salisbury, Mass., m. (pub. June 22, 1805, in Barrington), Joanna Balch, of Barrington.
STEVENS, John, of Waldon, m. Feb. 13, 1806, by Rev. Isaac Smith, Ella Gilman, of Gilmanton.
STEVENS, Moses, m. Sept. 29, 1814, by Rev. Isaac Smith, Mrs. Nancy (Jacobs) Lougee, wid. of John 3rd.
STEVENS, Parker, son of Jonathan, b. June 16, 1799, m. in 1820, Mary D. Willey, b. Mar. 6, 1799.
STEVENS, Alpha, of Dover, m. int. June 7, 1829, in Dover, Sarah Bancroft, of Boston, Mass.
STEVENS, William J., son of Parker, b. June 9, 1821, m. Dec. 8, 1838, Mary J. S. Smith, d. July 24, 1851, aged 30, dau. of Rev. Daniel.
STEVENS, Federal Burt, son of Jonathan, m. Aug. 20, 1843, in Durham, Mary Ann Willey, dau. of Mark, both of Durham.
STEVENS, David, son of Jonathan, Jr., b. Jan. 16, 1826, m. July 8, 1845, Hannah Lee, b. Apr. 22, 1828.
STEVENS, Parker, son of Parker, b. Dec. 14, 1827, m. int. Mar. 7, 1847, in Dover, Clara A. Willey.
STEVENS, Daniel D., son of Samuel, b. Nov. 22, 1822, d. Dec. 8, 1896, m. June 18, 1848, Hannah J. Cook, b. Sept. 8, 1831, d. May 12, 1907, dau. of Lewis.
STEVENS, Abial C., d. Oct. 8, 1864, aged 38, m. (1) Sept. 29, 1850, Angeline Fall, of Lebanon, Me., d. Apr. 15, 1857, aged 30, dau. of Isaac, m. (2) June 12, 1862, in Dover, Ada B. Chamberlain.
STEVENS, Alvin W., m. Feb. 22, 1851, in Newmarket, Emily C. Wiggin, both of Somersworth.

STEVENS, Nathaniel Jr., of Newmarket, m. Sept. 19, 1852, in Newmarket, Elizabeth F. York, of Durham.
STEVENS, James, m. Nov. 4, 1854, by Elder Israel Chesley, Sophia D. Cloutman, both of Durham.
STEVENS, Thomas J., son of Isaac, b. Mar. 10, 1826, d. Jan. 7, 1917, m. Oct. 21, 1855, in Milton, Mary E. Whitehouse, b. July 23, 1836, d. Sept. 26, 1901, both of Middleton.
STEVENS, Benjamin L., of Lee, m. July 3, 1867, in Lee, Lydia S. Ellison, of Nottingham.
STEVENS, Charles A., m. Sept. 14, 1868, by Rev. Robert S. Stubbs, Laura A. Blake.
STEVENS, Lorenzo, m. Nov. 24, 1870, in Dover, Augusta T. Reynolds.
4) **STEVENSON**, Joseph, of Durham, son of Joseph, m. (1) Jan. 17, 1753, by Rev. Jos. Adams, Ann Buzzell, of Dover, dau. of John, m. (2) Anna (Bunker) Drew, wid. of Lemuel, dau. of Joseph.
5) STEVENSON, James, of Tamworth, son of Thomas, b. Aug. 28, 1766, d. May 25, 1842, aged 77, m. Mar. 10, 1793, in Tamworth, Mary Remick, d. May 29, 1842.
5) STEVENSON, Thomas, son of Joseph, b. 1777, d. 1864, m. Apr. 7, 1805, in Wakefield, Sally Johnson, of Brookfield, d. Dec. 4, 1866, aged 84.
STEVENSON, Richard, son of Bartholomew, b. Dec. 1805, m. Sept. 4, 1828, by Rev. William Demeritt, Sally Wentworth.
STEVENSON, Samuel J., son of Thomas, b. Sept. 24, 1810, d. Mar. 19, 1905, m. Mar. 29, 1840, in Wolfeboro, Mary Ann Rines, b. Nov. 17, 1808, d. Sept. 3, 1870, dau. of John, both of Wolfeboro.
STEVENSON, Thomas, m. Mar. 16, 1864, in Dover, Elizabeth L. Clements.
STICKNEY, Alexander H., of Somersworth, m. June 23, 1827, Elizabeth Chesley, b. Apr. 12, 1809, d. June 28, 1886, dau. of Capt. Joseph.
STICKNEY, Joseph, d. May 16, 1893, aged 84, m. in 1833, by Rev. David Root, Mary Jane Middleton.
STILES, Samuel, of Durham, m. Nov. 24, 1754, Mary Huckins, dau. of Robert.
STILES, Daniel, m. Sept. 25, 1771, in Middleton, Sarah Averill.
STILES, Samuel, m. Nov. 26, 1778, in Durham, Anna Foss.
STILES, Samuel, m. Oct. 23, 1810, by Rev. Isaac Smith, Susan Hewitt.
STILES, Lewis, b. 1821, d. 1894, m. Jan. 29, 1845, by Elder Enoch Place, Hannah S. Sloper, b. 1823, dau. of William, both of Strafford.

STILES, Tobias, of Strafford, m. Oct. 10, 1854, by Rev. John Winkley, Rosamond Smith, of Shapleigh, Me.

STILES, William L., Jr., m. Apr. 27, 1864, in Dover, Mary A. Glines.

STILLINGS, Alfred, m. Oct. 11, 1865, by Rev. James Rand, Leonora L. Hayes.

STILSON, William, Jr., of Durham, b. June 23, 1780, d. Mar. 25, 1842, m. in 1805, by Rev. John Osborne, Nancy Chapman, of Newmarket, b. Jan. 1, 1785, d. Feb. 5, 1854, dau. of David.

STILSON, Daniel B., m. (1) Jan. 22, 1827, by Rev. John Osborne, Mary Jane French, both of Lee, m. (2) int. Nov. 3, 1834, in Lee, Adaline French, of Nottingham.

STILSON, Daniel C., of Newmarket, son of William, Jr., b. Mar. 25, 1830, d. Aug. 20, 1899, m. Apr. 18, 1855, by Rev. Alvin Tobey, Ellen R. Davis, of Durham, b. Dec. 23, 1831, dau. of Clement M.

STIRLING, Walter S., son of James, d. Aug. 23, 1908, aged 73, m. Dec. 31, 1868, by Rev. Robert S. Stubbs, Abby Coleman, b. 1838, d. Oct. 22, 1906.

STODDARD, Henry R., m. July 10, 1850, in Wolfeboro, Sophia Nute, d. Mar. 4, 1903, aged 71, dau. of James, both of Wolfeboro.

STOKES, Joseph, of Exeter, m. int. Oct. 8, 1836, in Lee, Ruth Mathes, of Lee.

STONE, Horace, b. Nov. 8, 1836, d. Apr. 9, 1926, m. Nov. 22, 1864, in Dover, Mary Ridgway Emerson, b. Jan. 2, 1840, d. June 24, 1908.

STONE, Edwin A., m. Jan. 22, 1866, by Rev. Francis E. Abbott, Jennie P. Clement.

STONE, Thomas B., of Newfield, Me., m. July 12, 1867, by Rev. Asa Piper, Louise R. Adams.

STORER, John, m. Dec. 15, 1868, by Rev. Asa Piper, Ida Copp, both of Wakefield.

STOTT, Joseph H., m. June 7, 1867, in Dover, Emma F. Foss.

STRACHAN, William, d. Oct. 5, 1894, aged 81, m. (1) Jan. 1, 1839, in Strafford, Eleanor Foss, d. Dec. 7, 1849, aged 32, dau. of Ebenezer, both of Strafford, m. (2) (pub. Jan. 12, 1860, in Strafford), Mrs. Sarah A. Trask, of Rochester, d. Nov. 26, 1917, aged 84.

STRATTON, Jonathan D., d. Aug. 18, 1894, aged 70, m. Nov. 19, 1848, by Elder Elias Hutchins, Nancy B. Tetherly, d. Jan. 16, 1892, aged 70.

STREETER, Ethan, m. Feb. 9, 1843, by Rev. Elijah Mason, Julia Ann DRew, d. Aug. 8, 1880, aged 57, both of Dover.

STURTEVANT, Hosea, son of Church, b. Feb. 14, 1762, d. Apr. 20, 1850, m. Oct. 20, 1784, by Rev. Jeremiah Shaw, Mary (or Sarah) Paine, d. Feb. 1, 1835, aged 69.

STURTEVANT, Hosea, of Center Harbor, son of Hosea, d. Dec. 7, 1882, aged 91, m. Jan. 26, 1815, by Rev. Jeremiah Shaw, Joanna Lee, of Moultonboro, d. Dec. 15, 1878, aged 84.

STURTEVANT, George, son of Josiah C., b. Oct. 6, 1817, d. Apr. 3, 1909, m. Dec. 1, 1845, in Moultonboro, Lucy M. Brown, b. Mar. 21, 1820, d. Sept. 25, 1892.

1) **SULLIVAN**, John, Protestant emigrant from Limerick, Ireland, son of Donall, b. June 17, 1690, d. June 20, 1795, m. 1734, by Dr. Moody, Margaret Browne, b. 1714, d. 1801.

2) SULLIVAN, James, b. Apr. 22, 1744, d. Dec. 10, 1808, m. (1) June 26, 1768, Mehitable Odiorne, of Durham, b. June 26, 1748, d. Jan. 26, 1786, dau. of William, m. (2) Martha (Langdon) Simpson, d. Aug. 26, 1812.

3) SULLIVAN, Capt. John, son of John, b. Apr. 1, 1773, m. in 1803, Mary Yeaton, b. 1779, d. Sept. 1813, dau. of Samuel.

SUMNER, Joseph, Lubec, Me., m. Mar. 25, 1821, in Newmarket, Sally Wiggin, of Newmarket, dau. of Barker.

SWAIN, John, m. Apr. 8, 1789, by Rev. Isaac Smith, Abigail Sibley, both of Gilmanton.

SWAIN, Daniel, b. Jan. 14, 1766, d. Dec. 20, 1843, m. June 15, 1789, Elizabeth Ayers, b. Oct. 20, 1770, d. Nov. 27, 1856.

SWAIN, John, m. Aug. 5, 1792, by Rev. Isaac Smith, Mary Richardson.

SWAIN, Benjamin, of Hopkinton, m. Jan. 27, 1803, by Rev. Isaac Smith, Mary Sweat, of Gilmanton.

SWAIN, Jacob, of Northwood, m. Nov. 5, 1807, by Rev. Isaac Smith, Dorothy Chandler, of Gilmanton.

SWAIN, Stephen Jr., m. July 28, 1814, by Rev. Isaac Smith, Sally Nelson.

SWAIN, Jeremiah W., m. Sept. 18, 1825, in Somersworth, Melinda M. Aspinwall, b. June 4, 1803, d. Jan. 29, 1844, dau. of Ellis.

SWAIN, John, m. Nov. 4, 1838, by Rev. John Winkley, Mary W. Gray, both of Strafford.

SWAIN, Joel, m. Mar. 2, 1840, by Rev. John Winkley, Abigail Swain, both of Strafford.

SWAIN, Daniel, of Strafford, m. Apr. 29, 1841, by Rev. John Winkley, Lucy Ham, of Dover.

SWAIN, Moses C., d. Feb. 9, 1901, aged 84, m. (1) Mary Ann ----, d. Dec. 1850, aged 30, m. (2) (pub. May, 20, 1851, in Dover), Emma Gowell, d. Apr. 14, 1899, aged 72, dau. of Charles, both of Somersworth.

SWAIN, Truman C., son of Daniel, b. Dec. 10, 1863, aged 22, m. Aug. 23, 1862, in Dover, Lizzie Mitchell.

SWAIN, Edmund M., b. Sept. 8, 1828, d. Feb. 28, 1902, m. Nov. 23, 1864, in Dover, Susan F. Clark, b. Apr. 4, 1837, d. Mar. 6, 1910, dau. of William H.

SWAN, E. M., m. Nov. 23, 1864, in Dover, S. F. Clark.

SWASEY, Nathaniel, d. Nov. 2, 1803, aged 37, m. before 1787, Sarah -----, d. Aug. 27, 1850, aged 82.

SWASEY, Philip B., of Barnstead, m. Nov. 14, 1805, by Rev. Isaac Smith, Sally Kelley, of Gilmanton.

SWASEY, Asa, of Milton, b. Feb. 9, 1794, d. Aug. 31, 1825, m. Jan. 4, 1816, by Rev. J. W. Clary, Mehitable Baker, b. Apr. 7, 1793, d. Sept. 25, 1825, of Dover, dau. of Ebenezer.

SWASEY, Dr. Charles, of Milton, son of Nathaniel, d. Apr. 16, 1860, aged 72, m. Mar. 22, 1820, by Rev. J. W. Clary, Eunice Paul, of Somersworth, d. Feb. 29, 1864, aged 72.

SWEAT, Thomas Rogers, m. Aug. 3, 1786, by Rev. Isaac Smith, Abigail Cram, both of Pittsfield.

SWEATT, Stephen, m. Sept. 25, 1799, by Rev. Isaac Smith, Lois Sanborn, both of Gilmanton.

SWEATT, Jeremiah, m. Nov. 24, 1802, by Rev. Isaac Smith, Sally French, of Gilmanton.

SWEATT, Paul, m. Dec. 18, 1803, by Rev. Isaac Smith, Judith Currier.

SWEETSER, George E., m. Aug. 5, 1864, in Dover, m. Alice Holey.

SWINERTON, Charles, m. Oct. 23, 1864, by Rev. Asa Piper, Abby C. Wentworth.

SYKES, George, m. July 20, 1868, by Rev. Alden Sherwin, Mary E. Flack.

SYMMES, William, m. Feb. 22, 1847, by Rev. Mr. Greely, Nancy G. Hanson, d. Nov. 3, 1901, aged 72, both of Somersworth.

SYMMES, Charles M., m. June 3, 1866, in Dover, Sarah M. Morrill.

TABOR, John, Jr., m. (pub. May 15, 1849, in Somersworth), Sarah Thompson, b. Jan. 20, 1832, d. June 28, 1907, dau. of Samuel.

TALBOT, Edwin R., m. July 1, 1869, in Dover, Mary A. Wentworth.

TANNER, George, m. July 3, 1869, in Dover, Ellen Young.

TAPLEY, John, of Danvers, Mass., b. Dec. 14, 1790, d. Aug. 28, 1831, m. May 12, 1817, by Rev. J. W. Clary, Lydia Reade, of Dover, b. July 14, 1793, d. Dec. 16, 1859, dau. of Michael.

TAPPAN, Daniel D., m. (pub. Apr. 30, 1823, in Portsmouth), Catharine E. R. Whidden.

TARBOX, Charles, of Hollis, Me., m. July 29, 1869, by Rev. Asa Piper, Nellie S. Berry.

TASH, Joseph H., d. Aug. 29, 1829, aged 40, m. May 10, 1820, by Rev. John Osborne, Lucy Maria Walker, d. Nov. 26, 1861, aged 63, dau. of Seth.

TASH, Edwin S., of Dover, d. Mar. 16, 1895, aged 57, m. (1) Mar. 3, 1860, in Great Falls, Ann M. Leavitt, of Tuftonboro, d. Feb. 7, 1875, aged 38, m. (2) Belle F., b. 1854, d. 1881, m. (3) Ellen M. (James) -----, b. 1890, d. Nov. 7, 1917, dau. of Joseph.

TASH, George W., b. 1827, d. 1896, m. (1) May 30, 1865, in Dover, Eliza J. Webster, b. 1831, d. 1870, m. (2) June 19, 1873, in Dover, Marianna Webster, b. 1850, d. Feb. 21, 1887, dau. of Daniel K., both of Dover.

3) **TASKER**, John, son of Capt. John, d. Dec. 1805, m. near 1750, Mary Young, b. Dec. 30, 1725, d. Apr. 29, 1806.

4) TASKER, James, son of William, b. Feb. 6, 1757, d. Feb. 2, 1837, m. Mar. 4, 1786, Charity Church, both of Barrington.

TASKER, Nahum, of Dover, son of Nathaniel, d. July 12, 1888, aged 81, m. Apr. 1825, in Milton, Mary Wallingford, of Milton, d. Jan. 5, 1868, aged 69, dau. of David.

6) TASKER, Paul, son of William, b. Oct. 22, 1812, d. Oct. 12, 1887, m. Mar. 20, 1836, by Elder Enoch Place, Polly Hill, b. 1813, both of Strafford.

TASKER, Deac. Alfred Q., b. 1817, d. Mar. 13, 1886, m. Mar. 29, 1840, by Elder Enoch Place, Mary Margaret Hill, b. 1822, d. Dec. 25, 1880, dau. of Andrew, both of Strafford.

TASKER, Curtis C., m. Feb. 26, 1843, by Rev. Elijah Mason, Emeline L. Joy, b. Oct. 22, 1812, d. July 26, 1845, aged 33, dau. of Jacob, both of Madbury.

TASKER, John C., b. 1844, d. Jan. 2, 1919, m. Mar. 26, 1865, by Rev. Robert S. Stubbs, Mary F. Winkley, b. 1840, d. 1881.

TASKER, Charles W., m. Oct. 9, 1869, in Dover, Maria B. Newcomb, d. Jan. 8, 1926, aged 82.

TATE, Robert, son of "Master" Joseph, b. Aug. 10, 1744, d. Nov. 1827, m. (1) near 1766, Margaret Wallingford, dau. of Capt. Thomas, m. (2) Aug. 22, 1776, Alice Spinney, b. Mar. 27, 1753, dau. of Nicholas.

3) **TAYLOR**, Benjamin, son of Benjamin, d. Apr. 14, 1768, m. (1) before 1726, Elizabeth Wiggin, d. Jan. 18, 1749, dau. of Bradstreet, m. (2) Patience -----.

TAYLOR, Thomas, m. Sept. 17, 1761, in Newmarket, Abigail Piper.

TAYLOR, Jonathan, m. Feb. 3, 1789, by Rev. Isaac Smith, Judith Badger, both of Gilmanton.

TAYLOR, Nicholas, of Salisbury, m. Apr. 5, 1804, by Rev. Isaac Smith, Sally Eastman, of Gilmanton.

TAYLOR, William, m. Sept. 27, 1810, by Rev. Caleb Sherman, Sarah Phillips Gilman, of Dover, dau. of John P.

TAYLOR, Larkin, of Exeter, m. int. July 6, 1822, in Lee, Betsey Wedgewood, of Lee.

TAYLOR, Nathaniel L., of Dover, m. (pub. Jan. 24, 1854, in S. Berwick, Me.), Mary F. Preble, of Ossipee, b. 1831, d. Aug. 2, 1905.
TAYLOR, Priestley, of S. Berwick, Me., b. Dec. 13, 1838, d. Sept. 23, 1903, aged 64, m. Feb. 4, 1860, in Dover, Mary M. Renshaw, of Dover, b. Feb. 24, 1829, d. Sept. 20, 1910, aged 80.
TAYLOR, Hiram B., m. Apr. 23, 1863, in Dover, Almira Ham.
TAYLOR, Truman J., b. 1834, d. 1871, m. May 30, 1866, by Rev. James Rand, Caroline E. Wortman, b. 1844, d. June 17, 1913, dau. of Capt. Richard.
TAYLOR, William D., m. June 18, 1873, in Dover, Nettie Keay, both of Dover.
4) **TEBBETS**, Edward, son of Henry, b. Feb. 2, 1702, d. Oct. 19, 1790, will of 1790, m. early as 1734, Mary -----.
TEBBETS, Jeremiah, d. Feb. 1804, aged 94, m. before 1744, Martha -----.
6) TEBBETS, Ichabod, son of Samuel, d. May 1810, m. (1) early as 1771, Hannah Tebbets, b. Feb. 10, 1754, m. (2) Jan. 25, 1779, Judith Tebbets, of Berwick, Me.
TEBBETS, Jeremy, m. Oct. 23, 1796, in Dover, Abigail Kelley.
TEBBETS, Benjamin, b. Jan. 9, 1775, m. Jan. 21, 1798, by Rev. Joseph Haven, Elizabeth Walker, b. 1774, d. Feb. 4, 1843, dau. of Richard, both of Rochester.
TEBBETS, James, of Barnstead, m. Oct. 20, 1800, by Rev. Isaac Smith, Abigail Coffin, of Alton.
TEBBETS, Bradbury, of Canterbury, m. Feb. 15, 1802, by Rev. Isaac Smith, Polly Clough, of Gilmanton.
TEBBETS, Isaac, of Canterbury, m. Oct. 26, 1802, by Rev. Isaac Smith, Betsy Clough, of Gilmanton.
TEBBETS, Nathaniel, of Dover, b. Apr. 8, 1794, d. July 24, 1867, m. Oct. 30, 1823, in Somersworth, Ann W. Hodgdon, of S. Berwick, Me., d. May 12, 1871, aged 68.
TEBBETS, Levi, of Tuftonboro, m. int. Aug. 1826, in Tuftonboro, Charlotte Clark, of Wolfeboro, d. July 1, 1850, aged 66.
TEBBETS, Ephraim, m. int. Oct. 21, 1831, in Lee, Mrs. Hannah Wiggin, both of Lee.
TEBBETS, Asa, of Brookfield, d. Nov. 26, 1857, aged 45, m. (pub. June 26, 1838, in Ossipee), Esther F. Abbott, of Ossipee, b. July 6, 1815, d. Dec. 13, 1905.
TEBBETS, Winthrop B. (or Wentworth B.), m. Dec. 25, 1840, in Wolfeboro, Olive A. Rollins, d. Nov. 20, 1864, aged 43.
TEBBETS, Dudley, m. Nov. 11, 1841, in Berwick, Me., Martha Guptill.

TEBBETS, Eri, son of Edward, b. near 1827, d. May 15, 1885, m. (1) Oct. 1, 1848, by Rev. Joseph Boodey, Elvira Colbath, both of Farmington, m. (2) int. Sept. 29, 1859, in New Durham, Eliza B. Pinkham, b. near 1837, of New Durham.

TEBBETS, Thomas J., Jr., b. June 6, 1825, d. July 10, 1887, m. Nov. 26, 1849, in Wolfeboro, Sarah E. Locke, b. May 21, 1828, d. May 22, 1918, both of Wolfeboro.

TEBBETS, William, d. Jan. 2, 1894, aged 71, m. June 29, 1851, in Wolfeboro, Lucinda G. Plummer, d. Oct. 12, 1872, aged 61, dau. of Reuben, both of Wolfeboro.

TEBBETS, George W. O., m. Nov. 24, 1864, in Dover, m. Abby Cotton.

TEBBETS, George S., m. Feb. 24, 1865, in Dover, Hattie S. Roberts.

TEBBETS, George H., m. Dec. 15, 1867, in Dover, Ellen E. Young.

TETHERLY, Oliver C., of Alton, son of Oliver, d. Jan. 24, 1907, aged 70, m. Nov. 6, 1856, by Rev. Hezekiah D. Buzzell, Mary E. Rines, d. Apr. 5, 1912, aged 74, dau. of Harris.

THAYER, Ephraim, of Dover, d. Apr. 15, 1875, aged 67, m. (pub. Aug. 14, 1827, in Brookfield), Maria Giles, of Brookfield.

THING, Jeremiah B., of Gilford, m. Sept. 21, 1843, Hannah L. Davis, b. Nov. 24, 1818, d. Sept. 15, 1858, dau. of Nathaniel.

THING, Charles Y., of Alton, son of Mark, d. Dec. 5, 1915, aged 80, m. Oct. 24, 1857, in Barnstead, Lucy I. Ayers, of Barnstead.

THOMAS, John, d. before 1768, m. Dec. 24, 1733, Abigail (Hodgdon) Gear, wid. of Samuel.

THOMAS, Samuel, of Dover, d. Jan. 1825, aged 33, m. Sept. 4, 1823, in Berwick, Me., Lucretia Hersom, of Berwick, Me.

THOMPSON, Alexander, son of Isaac, m. Aug. 12, 1754, by Rev. Jeremiah Wise, Abigail Shorey, dau. of Thomas.

4) THOMPSON, Ens. Jonathan, son of Jonathan, b. 1718, d. 1792, m. Dec. 14, 1755, Susanna (Runnels) Thompson, wid. of Samuel, dau. of Job.

4) THOMPSON, Nathaniel, son of John, b. May 29, 1726, d. June 1785, m. near 1760, Elizabeth Stevens, dau. of Deac. Hubbard.

THOMPSON, Joseph, b. Nov. 29, 1737, d. Feb. 6, 1805, m. Nov. 12, 1772, Hannah Chesley, b. May 12, 1742, dau. of George.

5) THOMPSON, Lt. Col. Ebenezer, son of Ebenezer, b. July 12, 1762, d. Feb. 4, 1828, m. (1) Jan. 1, 1786, Martha Burleigh, b. Aug. 29, 1769, d. Apr. 11, 1796, dau. of John, m. (2) May 4, 1797, Mary Weeks, b. Mar. 8, 1770, d. Nov. 15, 1813, dau. of William, m. (3) Elizabeth Hale, d. 1826, aged 58, dau. of Maj. Samuel.

5) THOMPSON, Nathaniel, of Holderness, son of Nathaniel, b. Apr. 21, 1765, m. Apr. 11, 1786, by Rev. Isaac Smith, Olive Dow, of Gilmanton.

5) THOMPSON, Jonathan, son of Ens. Jonathan, m. Nov. 15, 1789, Jane Kelsey, d. Mar. 27, 1849, aged 81.
THOMPSON, Robert, b. Mar. 22, 1798, m. int. Nov. 4, 1821, in Lee, Kesiah R. Thompson, b. May 5, 1797, both of Lee.
THOMPSON, Noah, of Lee, m. int. Oct. 11, 1822, in Lee, Sukey Kelsey, of Nottingham.
THOMPSON, William, of Epping, d. Dec. 14, 1868, aged 77, m. int. Nov. 26, 1825, in Lee, Deborah Davis, of Lee, d. Nov. 10, 1880, aged 82, dau. of Obadiah.
THOMPSON, Joseph, Jr., m. (pub. Oct. 17, 1826, in Somersworth), Mary McIntire.
THOMPSON, Hugh, of Lee, son of Jonathan, b. May 2, 1800, m. in 1827, Mary Scates, of Nottingham, b. Feb. 22, 1803, d. 1879, dau. of Samuel.
THOMPSON, Samuel, of Lee, m. int. Aug. 12, 1827, in Lee, Nancy Elliot, of Portsmouth.
THOMPSON, Mark, b. Nov. 27, 1807, d. Feb. 7, 1864, m. int. Sept. 29, 1829, in Dover, Prudence Church, of Barrington, b. June 2, 1803, d. Mar. 4, 1895, aged 91.
6) THOMPSON, Stephen J., son of Edmund, b. Mar. 6, 1803, d. June 9, 1851, m. Feb. 22, 1830, by Rev. John Osborne, Nancy Griffin, b. Feb. 27, 1808, d. July 18, 1840, aged 32, dau. of John, both of Lee.
THOMPSON, George W., of Durham, m. (1) Feb. 19, 1832, by Rev. William Demeritt, Harriet P. Sheppard, of Lee, m. (2) Apr. 18, 1833, by Rev. Jacob Cummings, Mary Wingate, of Stratham.
6) THOMPSON, William F., son of Edmund, b. Feb. 23, 1809, d. Oct. 7, 1884, m. June 3, 1838, Hannah J. Griffin, b. Mar. 7, 1816, d. Jan. 26, 1899, dau. of John, both of Lee.
THOMPSON, Hezekiah, son of Noah, d. June 13, 1902, aged 88, m. (1) Mar. 10, 1839, Martha Susan Critchett, d. Aug. 1, 1843, aged 20, m. (2) Lucy A. -----, d. Dec. 11, 1903, aged 77.
7) THOMPSON, Abraham, son of Levi, b. Dec. 24, 1813, m. (1) May 24, 1840, Deborah Chesley, m. (2) ----- -----, m. (3) Aug. 4, 1891, in Dover, Annie (Newbury) Wiggin, dau. of Daniel.
THOMPSON, Jacob B., m. (pub. Jan. 5, 1841, in Durham), Ann Carr Stilson, b. 1820, dau. of William, both of Durham.
THOMPSON, Capt. Stephen J., of Barnstead, m. Apr. 17, 1842, by Rev. Silas Curtis, Lucy Y. Foss, of Dover, d. Sept. 29, 1886. (Was this a second marriage?).
THOMPSON, Samuel R., b. May 28, 1815, d. Dec. 26, 1892, m. July 7, 1844, by Rev. Eben Francis, Louisa M. Cilley, b. Oct. 12, 1822, d. July 13, 1900, dau. of Joseph.

THOMPSON, Benjamin F., m. Sept. 17, 1848, by Elder John Pinkham, Mrs. Hannah Wiggin, wid. of Eliphaz, d. July 30, 1871, aged 68, both of Wolfeboro.
7) THOMPSON, Samuel, son of Jonathan, b. Apr. 17, 1823, d. Apr. 30, 1900, m. 1850, Rhoda Davis, d. Apr. 22, 1909, aged 82.
THOMPSON, Jonathan, Jr., of Lee, m. int. June 22, 1852, in Lee, Lucy Moore, of Andover, Mass.
THOMPSON, Charles A. C., of Durham, d. Dec. 4, 1868, aged 33, m. Dec. 25, 1855, in Dover, Louisa J. Davis, of Dover, b. July 21, 1834, d. May 31, 1901, aged 66, dau. of Capt. James.
THOMPSON, Job, b. 1806, d. Apr. 21, 1891, aged 83, m. (1) Adaline -----, d. Feb. 25, 1853, aged 48, m. (2) Dec. 13, 1856, in Epping, Emma E. Demeritt, of Lee, d. Mar. 17, 1878, aged 61.
THOMPSON, Stephen, son of Jonathan, b. Sept. 20, 1833, m. Jan. 1859, Sarah (Gray) Lamos, wid. of Moses.
THOMPSON, George Weeks, son of Benjamin, b. Mar. 31, 1837, d. July 28, 1863, m. Feb. 25, 1859, in Rochester, Hannah M. Furber, both of Farmington.
THOMPSON, George W., of S. Berwick, Me., son of Isaac, d. Mar. 28, 1892, aged 53, m. July 21, 1861, in S. Berwick, Me., Susan L. Cooper, of York, Me.
THOMPSON, Josiah D., b. Oct. 17, 1836, d. Apr. 18, 1911, m. (1) Oct. 1866, in Lee, Sarah Hamilton, both of Lee, m. (2) May 10, 1876, in Lee, Susan E. Davis, of Lee, b. Oct. 13, 1844, d. Dec. 16, 1913.
THOMPSON, Charles E., m. Dec. 18, 1868, in Dover, Ellen L. Simpson.
THOMPSON, Edward F., son of Mark, b. Aug. 31, 1844, d. Aug. 23, 1890, aged 45, m. June 14, 1870, in Dover, Augusta M. Wentworth, b. Mar. 9, 1849, d. Nov. 5, 1835.
THOMPSON, William, m. Aug. 18, 1873, in Great Falls, Mary Morgan, both of Great Falls.
THOMPSON, Bert P., m. Nov. 7, 1876, in Lee, Mary V. Jenness, both of Lee.
THOMPSON, Charles F., of Lee, b. 1857, m. Apr. 2, 1877, in Lee, Ellen G. Cartland, of Dover, b. 1854.
THURSTON, Moses, m. Feb. 11, 1728/29, in Stratham, Sarah Jones, d. Nov. 28, 1748.
THURSTON, Samuel, m. Apr. 11, 1775, by Rev. Isaac Smith, Elizabeth Moulton.
THURSTON, John, m. June 14, 1779, by Rev. Isaac Smith, Lucy Moulton.
TILTON, Nathan, of Loudon, m. Oct. 19, 1780, by Rev. Isaac Smith, Susannah Gale, of Gilmanton.

TILTON, Nathaniel, m. Mar. 1, 1787, by Rev. Isaac Smith, Sarah Sanborn.
TILTON, David, m. Sept. 10, 1787, by Rev. Isaac Smith, Sarah Foster, both of Gilmanton.
TILTON, Samuel, m. Feb. 28, 1788, by Rev. Isaac Smith, Betty Folsom.
TILTON, Asa, m. June 18, 1801, by Rev. Isaac Smith, Lucy Lamper, of Gilmanton.
TILTON, John G., of Newburyport, Mass., m. Oct. 23, 1823, by Rev. J. W. Clary, Mary Ann Hanson, of Dover.
TILTON, Jefferson, m. Aug. 9, 1857, in Rochester, Submit B. Hatch, d. Feb. 6, 1897, dau. of Reuben, both of Rollinsford.
4) **TITCOMB**, Col. Benjamin, son of Daniel, b. June 12, 1743, d. June 4, 1799, m. Dec. 30, 1773, by Dr. Belknap, Hannah Hanson, b. in 1746, d. Jan. 23, 1816, dau. of Isaac and Ann.
TITCOMB, Moses, m. Jan. 26, 1826, in Tamworth, Mrs. Hannah (Gilman) Whitman, wid. of Simeon, both of Tamworth.
TITCOMB, George W., of Haverhill, Mass., m. Apr. 25, 1850, by Rev. Thomas J. Greenwood, Jane M. Thompson, d. July 12, 1862, aged 36, dau. of Noah.
TOMPSON, William J., of S. Berwick, Me., m. Apr. 5, 1819, by Rev. Federal Burt, Abigail M. Wentworth, of Somersworth, d. Feb. 8, 1873.
3) **TORR**, Lt. Andrew, b. Aug. 25, 1744, d. Mar. 8, 1817, m. (1) early as 1777, Mary Jones, d. Sept. 10, 1808, aged 56, dau. of Joseph, m. (2) Oct. 22, 1809, by Rev. William Hooper, Deborah (Ham) Hicks, of Madbury, wid. of Joseph, b. 1754, dau. of Joseph.
TOWLE, Col. Gardner, of Lee, m. (1) Elizabeth Fogg, b. 1795, d. 1827, dau. of Jonathan, m. (2) May 12, 1831, by Rev. King, Hannah Ela, of Portsmouth.
TOWLE, George W., d. Dec. 16, 1837, m. Aug. 1, 1833, Ann E. Mosley, both of Lee.
TOWLE, John F., m. int. Jan. 5, 1846, in Lee, Abigail D. Davis, both of Lee.
TOWNSEND, Joseph, of Milton, b. 1828, d. 1897, m. (pub. Feb. 12, 1850, in Milton), Ruth P. Wentworth, of Acton, Me., b. 1826, d. 1901, dau. of Nathaniel.
TRACY, Capt. Daniel, m. Dec. 24, 1812, by Rev. J. W. Clary, Abigail Watson, d. Sept. 25, 1822, aged 52, dau. of William.
TRASK, John B., m. (1) June 13, 1857, by Rev. Benjamin F. Parsons, Mary Jane Clark, both of Dover, m. (2) Sept. 22, 1866, in Dover, Elizabeth Moore.
TRASK, John B., son of Gardner, b. Apr. 21, 1842, m. Sept. 22, 1866, in Dover, Elizabeth Moore.

TRAVETT, Dr. Joseph, m. May 8, 1803, in Barrington, Eliza Noble.

TREDICK, Thomas T., of Dover, son of Henry, d. Nov. 18, 1888, aged 88, m. (1) in 1825, Mary Stavers, of Portsmouth, d. Aug. 4, 1842, aged 40, dau. of Capt. William, m. (2) June 1, 1845, by Rev. Mr. Peabody, Martha Stavers, d. Dec. 22, 1889, aged 80, dau. of Capt. William.

TREDICK, William O., of Alton, m. Mar. 15, 1850, Mary A. Durgin, of Lee, b. Aug. 13, 1828, dau. of Benjamin.

TREFETHEN, Joseph, m. in 1837, in Rye, Olivia B. Marden, d. Apr. 1889, aged 73, dau. of Josiah.

TREFETHEN, John W., son of Capt. Archelaus, b. 1841, d. 1886, m. May 8, 1870, in Dover, Francenia Runnels, b. 1852, d. May 15, 1927, dau. of Alvah.

4) **TRICKEY**, John, son of Thomas, b. near 1710, d. 1781, m. Rebecca Chamberlain, b. Dec. 28, 1722, d. Nov. 1815, dau. of Capt. William.

TRICKEY, Jonathan, m. (pub. Mar. 24, 1810, in Dover), Elizabeth Swaine.

TRICKEY, Charles H., son of Lemuel, b. 1833, d. Feb. 2, 1896, m. Dec. 4, 1869, in Dover, Ada J. Bond, b. 1835, d. 1893.

TRIPP, William, m. Sept. 16, 1865, by Rev. Francis E. Abbott, Nancy E. Perkins.

TRUE, Simeon S., d. Mar. 20, 1845, aged 43, m. Oct. 24, 1822, Lucy S. -----, b. Aug. 26, 1802, d. Jan. 28, 1886.

TRUE, John S., m. Sept. 1850, Lucy S. (-----) True, wid. of Simeon S., b. Aug. 26, 1802, d. Jan. 28, 1886.

TRUE, John S., d. Feb. 1, 1911, aged 70, m. Nov. 25, 1867, by Rev. Robert S. Stubbs, Alice Rothwell, d. Jan. 21, 1914, aged 73, dau. of Richard N.

TRUE, Samuel, Jr., of Salisbury, Mass., b. 1812, m. Dec. 1869, in Lee, Sarah C. Bartlett, of Lee, b. 1816.

TUCK, Capt. Henry, of Manchester, Mass., m. Apr. 12, 1810, by Rev. Mr. Thurston, Joanna H. Drew, of Somersworth.

TUCKER, Hugh, m. Nov. 25, 1717, in Kittery, Me., Dorcas Heard.

TUCKER, John, m. July 17, 1781, by Rev. Isaac Smith, Betty Page.

TUCKER, James, m. June 8, 1845, in Somersworth, Mary Elizabeth Hale.

TUCKER, Daniel H., of S. Berwick, Me., son of John, m. (1) July 2, 1860, in Dover, Maria M. Ham, of N. Berwick, Me., m. (2) Jan. 1, 1890, in Ogunquit, Me., Annie H. Littlefield.

TUCKER, Frank J., m. Jan. 31, 1861, in Rochester, Mary Jane Tuttle, both of Rochester.

TURNER, Louis, of Bangor, Me., b. June 11, 1808, d. Nov. 19, 1844, m. Apr. 7, 1839, by Rev. Francis Pike, Caroline Hale, of

NEW HAMPSHIRE MARRIAGES SUPPLEMENT

Rochester, b. June 2, 1811, d. Apr. 11, 1873, aged 58, dau. of Moses.
4) **TUTTLE**, John, son of Ens. John, b. May 8, 1704, d. Feb. 1774, m. (1) Oct. 30, 1728, in Berwick, Me., Elizabeth Nute, b. Dec. 28, 1706, dau. of James and Prudence, m. (2) early as 1771, Anne Nute, b. in 1750, d. July 27, 1819, dau. of James and Anne.
5) TUTTLE, Benjamin, son of Elijah and Esther, b. in 1742, d. Dec. 12, 1812, m. May 24, 1772, by Dr. Belknap, Mary Hussey, d. June 1825, aged 77.
5) TUTTLE, Stephen, son of James, of Dover, d. Oct. 1804, m. Jan. 1779, by Rev. William Hooper, in Madbury, Abigail Foss, of Barrington.
5) TUTTLE, Samuel, son of Elijah and Esther, b. in 1747, d. Oct. 8, 1807, m. June 22, 1780, in Rochester, Martha Varney.
TUTTLE, Joseph, m. Oct. 25, 1786, in Durham, Sarah Bennett.
6) TUTTLE, Elijah, son of Elijah, b. 1774, d. May 24, 1866, m. (1) Apr. 5, 1798, Sally Tasker, b. June 16, 1783, d. Feb. 3, 1819, dau. of Samuel, m. (2) Polly -----, d. Feb. 26, 1841, aged 66.
TUTTLE, Asa, m. Oct. 25, 1812, in Madbury, Elizabeth Bickford.
TUTTLE, Samuel, d. Mar. 13, 1827, aged 50, m. Nov. 12, 1812, by Rev. William Hooper, Hope Tuttle, b. Nov. 15, 1786, d. Jan. 11, 1819, dau. of Ebenezer and Deborah, both of Dover.
TUTTLE, Joseph, d. Sept. 13, 1877, aged 89, m. Jan. 1, 1815, by Rev. John Osborne, Mrs. Sarah Furber, of Lee, d. Mar. 24, 1862, aged 72.
TUTTLE, Levi, m. July 30, 1821, by Rev. John Osborne, Abigail (Stokes) Wiggin, both of Durham.
TUTTLE, James, Jr., d. Dec. 6, 1823, aged 24, m. Aug. 30, 1821, by Elder Enoch Place, Lavina Tuttle, d. Jan. 8, 1881, aged 78, both of Strafford.
TUTTLE, William, b. Apr. 9, 1802, d. Jan. 8, 1859, m. Oct. 3, 1822, by Elder Enoch Place, Mary Starbard, b. Nov. 5, 1797, d. Aug. 14, 1858, both of Strafford.
TUTTLE, Asa H., d. Dec. 5, 1868, aged 54, m. Nov. 23, 1824, by Rev. John Winkley, Louisa M. Colby, b. 1815, d. 1901, both of Strafford.
TUTTLE, Daniel C. of Strafford, b. 1798, d. June 24, 1864, m. Sept. 27, 1825, by Elder Enoch Place, Sarah Drew, of Barrington, b. in 1800, d. Nov. 28, 1864.
TUTTLE, Daniel, m. Oct. 9, 1827, by Rev. John Osborne, Nancy Scales, of Nottingham, b. Aug. 18, 1803, d. 1872, dau. of Samuel.
TUTTLE, Joseph, m. int. June 14, 1828, in Lee, Olive Marden, both of Lee.

TUTTLE, Joseph, of Lee, m. int. Oct. 8, 1828, in Lee, Mrs. Elizabeth Roles, of Barnstead.

TUTTLE, Samuel, b. 1799, d. Feb. 23, 1859, m. Sept. 2, 1830, by Elder Enoch Place, Sarah Ann Perkins, b. 1810, d. Feb. 8, 1897, both of Strafford.

TUTTLE, John C., of Nottingham, m. int. Nov. 5, 1832, in Lee, Martha Rollins, of Lee.

TUTTLE, John, of Barrington, d. Mar. 5, 1886, aged 69, m. Dec. 17, 1835, by Rev. John Winkley, Sally Hill, of Strafford, d. Apr. 24, 1909, aged 90.

TUTTLE, Thomas, of Lee, d. Oct. 4, 1851, aged 53, m. (pub. Mar. 15, 1836, in Barnstead), Christiana B. C. Robinson, d. Apr. 4, 1852, aged 51.

TUTTLE, Loammi, of Lee, m. int. May 28, 1836, in Lee, Susan W. Willey, of Durham.

TUTTLE, Elijah, of Barrington, d. Mar. 2, 1878, aged 62, m. Apr. 11, 1842, by Elder Enoch Place, Hannah Hanson, of Strafford, b. 1821, d. Jan. 10, 1869, dau. of Nathaniel.

TUTTLE, Hezekiah F., son of Enoch, b. Oct. 30, 1811, d. June 3, 1871, m. (1) Maria -----, b. Jan. 23, 1813, d. Sept. 5, 1837, m. (2) May 17, 1842, by Rev. John Walker, Sarah R. Tuttle, b. Sept. 2, 1812, d. May 7, 1887, both of Strafford.

TUTTLE, Asa, m. Nov. 24, 1842, by Rev. John Winkley, Clarissa Caverly, d. Nov. 15, 1888, aged 70, dau. of Ephraim, both of Strafford.

TUTTLE, Hendrick, m. int. Apr. 6, 1844, in Lee, Mary M. Gilman, both of Lee.

TUTTLE, Jerome Bonneparte, of Lee, son of Joseph, b. Apr. 15, 1815, d. Oct. 29, 1900, m. int. Nov. 9, 1845, in Dover, Hannah Watson, b. Jan. 27, 1824, d. Nov. 2, 1909, dau. of Winthrop.

TUTTLE, John F., m. Feb. 3, 1846, by Elder Alexander Tuttle, Abigail D. Davis, both of Lee.

TUTTLE, James, of Barrington, m. Apr. 24, 1846, by Rev. John Winkley, Deborah H. Howard, of Strafford.

TUTTLE, Joseph, b. 1826, m. July 13, 1848, by Elder Enoch Place, Mahala Howard, b. Feb. 7, 1825, d. Sept. 10, 1890, both of Wakefield.

TUTTLE, Timothy W., d. Sept. 6, 1875, aged 56, m. (pub. Mar. 18, 1851, in Barrington), Mary S. Buzzell, b. 1825, d. Dec. 29, 1898, dau. of Samuel E.

TUTTLE, Lorenzo D., of Nottingham, m. Aug. 8, 1854, by Elder Israel Chesley, Olive L. Taylor, of Stratham.

TUTTLE, Oliver B., of Nottingham, b. 1833, m. int. Sept. 25, 1855, in Lee, Eliza Ann Rayner, of Wilton, Me., b. 1836.

TUTTLE, Darias W., b. July 18, 1835, m. July 13, 1856, by Rev. John Winkley, Lavina Perkins Thompson, b. July 21, 1838, d. Sept. 22, 1926, dau. of Solomon, both of Strafford.
TUTTLE, James M., of Strafford, son of Enoch, b. Dec. 16, 1834, m. Aug. 12, 1861, in Strafford, Mary Cooper, of Clinton, Me.
TUTTLE, Charles H., b. 1834, m. int. Mar. 30, 1862, in Lee, Sarah L. Langley, of Newmarket, b. 1844.
TUTTLE, Alonzo F., m. Mar. 31, 1863, in Dover, Fannie L. Tuttle.
TUTTLE, Joseph E., m. Dec. 22, 1863, in Dover, Caroline H. Paul.
TUTTLE, Charles C., b. 1844, m. int. Dec. 5, 1865, in Lee, Mary F. Eastman, b. 1838, both of Nottingham.
TUTTLE, Monroe C., b. 1845, m. int. Dec. 5, 1865, in Lee, Sarah E. Harvey, b. 1847, both of Nottingham.
TUTTLE, H. Freeman, d. Apr. 17, 1882, aged 35, m. Dec. 25, 1865, by Rev. John Winkley, Jennie Caswell, both of Strafford.
TUTTLE, John T. G., son of John W., d. Apr. 21, 1923, aged 81, m. Apr. 4, 1866, in Dover, Mrs. Hannah Waldron.
TUTTLE, Horace, son of Ami, m. Sept. 25, 1866, by Rev. Francis E. Abbott, Anna Kerby.
TUTTLE, Joseph W., m. May 18, 1867, by Rev. Jesse Meader, Nellie J. Hodgdon.
TUTTLE, Richard H., d. July 19, 1915, aged 69, m. Apr. 2, 1868, in Dover, Carrie F. Meserve.
TUTTLE, Henry O., m. Nov. 18, 1869, in Dover, Nettie G. Cummings.
TWOMBLY, John, m. Oct. 29, 1769, Sarah Twombly, d. 1827, aged 75, dau. of Ens. Benjamin, of Somersworth.
5) TWOMBLY, Stephen, son of Samuel, d. Sept. 1800, m. Oct. 25, 1787, by Rev. Joseph Haven, Elizabeth Hanson, b. Oct. 21, 1768, d. July 27, 1802, dau. of Timothy.
6) TWOMBLY, Ephraim, son of Ezekiel, b. 1768, d. Nov. 6, 1843, m. (1) Dec. 27, 1792, by Rev. Matthew Merriam, Joanna Wentworth, b. 1774, d. 1799, dau. of Samuel, m. (2) Mar. 22, 1801, in Berwick, Me., Hannah Guptill, b. 1781, d. Sept. 10, 1826, m. (3) June 3, 1828, in Berwick, Me., Abigail Chadbourne, b. 1781, d. Aug. 26, 1843, dau. of Humphrey.
TWOMBLY, John, Jr., d. July 16, 1824, aged 47, m. May 7, 1798, by Rev. Joseph Haven, Abigail Meserve, both of Rochester.
TWOMBLY, James, of Rochester, son of Benjamin, d. June 28, 1835, aged 58, m. June 24, 1799, by Rev. Matthew Merriam, Sally Guptill, of Berwick, Me., d. May 15, 1821, aged 42.
TWOMBLY, Reuben, m. June 1803, in Portsmouth, Jane Casey.
TWOMBLY, Israel, m. (pub. June 23, 1804, in Kensington), Mary Richards, both of Madbury.

TWOMBLY, Ralph, of Madbury, d. Apr. 1823, m. Aug. 24, 1804, by Rev. John Osborne, Nancy Richards, of Lee.
TWOMBLY, Isaac, m. Oct. 17, 1816, by Rev. Joseph Haven, Sarah Foye, d. Sept. 6, 1823, aged 34, both of Barrington.
TWOMBLY, Silas, son of Samuel, b. Dec. 22, 1798, d. July 29, 1865, m. Mar. 28, 1822, by Elder Enoch Place, Sally Caverly, b. Sept. 2, 1794, d. Sept. 9, 1875, both of Strafford.
TWOMBLY, James, of Madbury, b. May 15, 1800, m. Aug. 28, 1827, in Saco, Me., Sarah R. Hart, of Durham, b. June 16, 1810.
6) TWOMBLY, Stephen, son of Stephen, b. Jan. 13, 1800, d. Oct. 15, 1839, m. Oct. 28, 1827, by Rev. Isaac Willey, Olive Plumer, b. 1794, d. Oct. 25, 1860, both of Rochester.
TWOMBLY, Martin Luther, son of Paul, b. June 21, 1806, d. May 16, 1889, m. Nov. 25, 1830, by Elder Simeon Swett, Deborah Bunker, both of Farmington.
TWOMBLY, J. Plumer, of Barrington, m. Oct. 1, 1831, by Rev. John Winkley, Lois Clark, of Strafford.
6) TWOMBLY, Samuel, son of Tobias, of Somersworth, d. Aug. 1877, aged 75, m. June 13, 1833, by Rev. David Root, Nancy Worcester, b. May 18, 1811, d. Mar. 2, 1871, aged 60, dau. of Ezekiel.
TWOMBLY, John, m. Oct. 30, 1834, Martha Varney.
TWOMBLY, John, of Madbury, m. (1) Dec. 7, 1837, by Rev. Silas Green, Susan H. Colbath, of Farmington, d. Nov. 24, 1840, aged 22, dau. of Hunking, m. (2) in 1842, Charlotte Drew, b. 1818, dau. of John.
TWOMBLY, John, m. Feb. 2, 1839, by Rev. John Winkley, Abigail Berry, both of Strafford.
TWOMBLY, Benjamin F., m. Jan. 1, 1841, by Rev. John Winkley, in Dover, Rosamond W. Colby.
TWOMBLY, Charles, m. Oct. 2, 1842, Martha Ann Twombly, both of N. Berwick, Me.
7) TWOMBLY, James B., son of James, d. Nov. 1, 1894, aged 75, m. (pub. May 14, 1844, in Portsmouth), Abigail Brown, d. Dec. 30, 1889, aged 74, dau. of Joseph.
TWOMBLY, Silas M., of Strafford, m. Oct. 10, 1854, by Rev. John Winkley, Ann M. Twombly, of Barrington.
TWOMBLY, Harrison, son of Silas, b. Sept. 5, 1820, d. Apr. 17, 1905, m. Nov. 29, 1855, in Strafford, Harriet Adeline Caverly, b. Apr. 12, 1838, d. Dec. 3, 1887, aged 50, both of Strafford.
TWOMBLY, Charles H., b. June 5, 1837, d. July 21, 1891, m. Apr. 3, 1862, by Rev. James Rand, Eliza C. Snell, b. Oct. 31, 1834, d. Nov. 18, 1894, dau. of Col. Samuel.

TWOMBLY, James M., d. Oct. 25, 1885, aged 82, m. May 7, 1862, in Milton, Lydia M. Jenness, b. 1829, d. Apr. 8, 1912, both of Milton.
TWOMBLY, William H. H., m. June 4, 1865, in Dover, Esther Hall.
TWOMBLY, John, m. Oct. 29, 1866, in Dover, Melissa J. Burleigh.
UPHAM, Nathaniel, of Deerfield, son of Rev. Timothy, d. July 10, 1829, aged 55, m. Mar. 22, 1798, Judith Cogswell, d. Apr. 18, 1832, aged 63, dau. of Thomas.
UPHAM, Rev. Thomas C., of Rochester, m. May 18, 1825, in Kennebunkport, Me., Phebe Lord.
UPHAM, Henry B., m. Sept. 10, 1867, in Dover, Mary H. Clark.
UTLEY, James m. Mar. 26, 1862, in Dover, Martha T. Dunlap.
VALLEY, Frank, d. Aug. 16, 1888, aged 42, m. Sept. 25, 1869, in Dover, Julia A. Weeks.
4) **VARNEY**, Nathaniel, son of Stephen and Mercy, b. Mar. 31, 1725, d. Feb. 4, 1808, m. Nov. 4, 1761, in Dover, Abigail Tuttle, b. Feb. 25, 1735, d. Jan. 19, 1793, dau. of Thomas and Mary.
VARNEY, Peter, son of Moses, b. in 1731, m. Feb. 7, 1770, in Dover, Mehitable -----.
4) VARNEY, Isaac, son of Ebenezer and Elizabeth, b. Apr. 1752, d. Aug. 23, 1826, m. (1) Dec. 10, 1772, in Dover, Mehitable Buffum, m. (2) Nov. 28, 1781, in Dover, Lydia (Hanson) Rogers, of Madbury, wid. of Aaron, b. Nov. 6, 1761, dau. of Timothy and Mary.
VARNEY, Elijah, d. Apr. 15, 1822, aged 72, m. in 1774, Anna Hayes, b. 1753.
4) VARNEY, Hanson, son of Ebenezer and Elizabeth, of Dover, d. Oct. 29, 1815, aged 80, m. Dec. 4, 1777, at Berwick, Me., Elizabeth Jenkins, of Berwick, Me., b. Jan. 26, 1758, d. Dec. 19, 1826, dau. of Elijah and Mehitable.
VARNEY, Elijah, m. Nov. 25, 1779, in Dover, Sarah Roberts.
VARNEY, Ichabod, m. Feb. 3, 1785, in Dover, Abigail Conant.
VARNEY, William, m. Dec. 18, 1785, in Somersworth, Mary Mason.
VARNEY, James, of Dover, son of James, d. June 1815, aged 56, m. (1) June 7, 1787, in Rochester, Martha Wentworth, of Rochester, dau. of William, m. (2) Elizabeth Clark, d. Jan. 22, 1817, aged 51.
VARNEY, Davis, m. Sept. 6, 1790, in Berwick, Me., Martha Goodwin.
VARNEY, Stephen, m. Feb. 1791, in Dover, Mary Rand.
VARNEY, John, son of James, d. July 11, 1806, aged 57, m. Oct. 1, 1793, by Rev. Joseph Haven, Mary Wentworth, b. Oct. 8, 1756, d. Oct. 2, 1836, dau. of William, both of Rochester.
VARNEY, Elijah, m. Dec. 3, 1799, in Eliot, Me., Anne Brooks.
VARNEY, Dudley, m. Nov. 4, 1810, in Rochester, Hannah Hussey.

VARNEY, John, m. Feb. 28, 1811, in Dover, Anna Beede, b. May 19, 1792, dau. of Jonathan.

6) VARNEY, George Dillwyn, of Somersworth, son of Samuel, b. Dec. 6, 1790, m. June 2, 1813, Sarah Whittier, of Somersworth, b. July 7, 1791, dau. of Obadiah and Sarah.

VARNEY, Hopley, son of James, d. Feb. 13, 1854, aged 62, m. Nov. 25, 1813, by Rev. Joseph Haven, Lydia Varney, d. May 7, 1877, aged 87, dau. of Aaron, both of Milton.

VARNEY, Ebenezer, of Dover, son of Richard, b. Feb. 26, 1782, m. June 1, 1814, in China, Me., Ruth Hussey, b. Nov. 6, 1794, d. Apr. 30, 1820, dau. of Stephen.

VARNEY, James, m. June 5, 1815, in Dover, Sarah Allen.

VARNEY, Nicholas, m. Dec. 27, 1815, in Durham, Me., Sarah Langdon.

VARNEY, Charles, m. (pub. July 6, 1816, in Dover), Charlotte Varney.

5) VARNEY, George C., son of Amos, of Rochester, b. July 11, 1792, d. June 14, 1826, m. Oct. 31, 1816, in Rochester, Betsey Varney, b. Aug. 20, 1794, dau. of Daniel and Susanna, of Rochester.

VARNEY, Simeon, son of Joseph, b. Dec. 15, 1795, m. Nov. 26, 1817, in Dover, Zerviah Buffum.

VARNEY, John C., son of Moses, b. July 17, 1796, d. Nov. 26, 1882, m. Oct. 14, 1819, Hannah Varney, b. Jan. 25, 1801, d. Mar. 18, 1882, dau. of John.

6) VARNEY, Mordecai, son of Jacob and Dorothy, b. Sept. 24, 1796, d. Apr. 12, 1864, m. Mar. 27, 1822, in Dover, Mary Worster.

VARNEY, Elder Moses, m. Dec. 26, 1824, in Lebanon, Me., Betsey Blaisdell, d. Nov. 22, 1844, aged 42.

VARNEY, Andrew, b. June 30, 1788, d. Feb. 10, 1876, m. May 19, 1825, in Durham, by Rev. Federal Burt, Susanna Footman, d. Jan. 17, 1866, aged 60.

5) VARNEY, Elias, son of Shubel, d. Oct. 29, 1867, aged 78, m. (1) Hannah H. -----, d. Aug. 8, 1830, aged 41, m. (2) May 1, 1831, by Elder Enoch Place, Mary Foss, d. June 8, 1878, aged 80, dau. of Maj. Samuel, both of Barrington.

VARNEY, Rufus C., son of Elias, d. June 14, 1900, aged 86, m. (pub. Jan. 6, 1835, in Barrington), Sally Foss, d. Jan. 24, 1888, aged 75, both of Barrington.

VARNEY, Josiah, m. Jan. 30, 1835, in North Berwick, Me., Lydia Cole, b. July 20, 1811, dau. of Caleb.

VARNEY, Solomon, d. Nov. 14, 1888, aged 77, m. Nov. 25, 1835, by Elder Enoch Place, Rachel Felker, d. June 10, 1892, aged 84, dau. of William, both of Barrington.

VARNEY, Hiram, son of Aaron, d. Sept. 8, 1855, aged 51, m. in 1836, in Milton, Emeline Walker, d. Aug. 25, 1881, aged 81, dau. of Joseph.

VARNEY, David Tibbetts, b. June 21, 1810, d. Feb. 6, 1888, m. (1) Mar. 13, 1838, in Lebanon, Me., Emily Lord, d. Mar. 30, 1857, m. (2) Caroline -----, b. Jan. 10, 1822, d. Mar. 19, 1888.

VARNEY, Andrew, son of Dominicus, b. Aug. 17, 1818, d. Mar. 14, 1896, m. Nancy Watson, d. Mar. 14, 1896, dau. of Winthrop.

VARNEY, Seth W., son of John C., b. Dec. 23, 1819, m. Dec. 23, 1842, Abbie Varney, dau. of Joel.

VARNEY, Moses E., son of Isaac, b. Nov. 23, 1819, m. Apr. 27, 1844, in Lebanon, Me., Sarah Ann Blaisdell.

VARNEY, Eli H., b. Aug. 30, 1823, d. Oct. 9, 1906, m. (1) Mar. 1, 1846, in Milton, Mary Ann Rines, d. Aug. 28, 1857, aged 29, of Milton, m. (2) Mary H. -----, b. Mar. 3, 1836, d. Sept. 31, 1921.

VARNEY, Elias, Jr., d. July 27, 1850, aged 27, m. Nov. 7, 1846, by Rev. Samuel Kelley, Eliza A. Foss, both of Barrington.

VARNEY, Jacob, d. May 7, 1854, aged 35, m. Oct. 15, 1848, in Milton, Sarah A. Varney, both of Milton.

VARNEY, Alfred N., d. Sept. 18, 1860, aged 38, m. Dec. 30, 1849, by Elder Elias Hutchins, Almira N. Foss, d. Mar. 1, 1903, aged 74.

VARNEY, Eli, son of John C., b. Mar. 30, 1831, d. Nov. 29, 1894, m. (1) Feb. 10, 1853, Sarah H. Place, of Farmington, d. May 30, 1871, aged 43, dau. of Aaron, m. (2) Dec. 19, 1871, Abigail (Ellis) Moore, wid. of Samuel, dau. of Robert.

VARNEY, Jonas March, son of Beard, m. Oct. 27, 1853, in Milton, Mary E. Jones.

VARNEY, Andrew J., son of Paul, d. July 30, 1906, aged 76, m. (pub. Dec. 18, 1856, in Alton), Loella Woodman.

VARNEY, Ezekiel, m. Nov. 25, 1857, in N. Berwick, Me., Lucretia Kelly.

VARNEY, Freeman, b. Dec. 6, 1836, d. Feb. 24, 1917, m. Aug. 24, 1859, in Somersworth, Mary Ham Hayes, b. June 7, 1836, d. Mar. 11, 1900.

VARNEY, Charles Ayer, son of John H., b. May 19, 1834, m. May 18, 1860, by Rev. Benjamin F. Parsons, Sophia J. Nute, both of Milton.

VARNEY, Edwin H., m. Mar. 19, 1865, in Dover, Rebecca A. Young.

VARNEY, Thomas G., m. May 21, 1865, in Dover, Lydia J. Trickey.

VARNEY, Eben, m. May 20, 1867, by Rev. James Rand, Mrs. Eliza A. Benn.

VARNEY, George H., son of Samuel, d. July 22, 1918, aged 75, m. June 16, 1867, by Rev. Francis E. Abbott, Jennie E. Hodgdon.

NEW HAMPSHIRE MARRIAGES SUPPLEMENT

VARNEY, Nehemiah E., m. Jan. 1, 1868, by Rev. Alden Sherwin, Mrs. Marcia O. Brock.
VARNEY, Robert, m. Feb. 19, 1870, in Dover, Caroline H. Locke.
VARNEY, John S., m. Sept. 23, 1873, in Farmington, Mrs. Nancy D. Knox, both of Wolfeboro.
VARNEY, Alvord O., m. Aug. 14, 1875, in Rochester, Henrietta Jones.
VAUGHAN, Capt. Daniel, m. Aug. 25, 1831, in Portsmouth, Sarah Ann Moses, d. Feb. 18, 1890, aged 83, dau. of Benjamin.
VICKERY, William H., son of John S., d. Mar. 10, 1916, aged 77, m. Mar. 11, 1869, by Rev. Robert S. Stubbs, Fanny Evans.
VICKERY, Frank, m. Nov. 2, 1870, in Dover, Augusta Leach.
VINTON, Josiah O., m. Dec. 10, 1867, in Dover, Mary S. Page.
WADLEIGH, George A. P., m. July 20, 1865, in Dover, Frances Gordon.
WAKEFIELD, Albert, d. Feb. 15, 1868, aged 51, m. (pub. Dec. 15, 1846, in Great Falls), Rhoda P. Tetherly, d. July 20, 1888, aged 76, dau. of Andrew.
WAKEHAM, Simeon L., d. Mar. 26, 1859, aged 31, m. Mar. 16, 1851, in Milton, Mary Ann Wentworth, b. Sept. 4, 1824, dau. of Ebenezer.
WALDO, Godfrey, m. Jan. 3, 1804, by Rev. Isaac Smith, Eliza Carpenter.
1) **WALDRON**, Richard Canney, b. in 1719, (ancestry not known), a soldier at Louisburg in 1745, of Dover, m. near 1746, Mary Clarke, dau. of Abraham and Anna, lived in Dover and had children:
   2) Col. Isaac, b. Mar. 16, 1747, d. May 3, 1841, aged 94, in Barrington, m. (1) Sarah Boodey, b. Mar. 8, 1755, d. 1799, dau. of Azariah, m. (2) Tirzah Noble.
   2) Aaron, b. Aug. 1, 1749, d. Dec. 9, 1820, aged 71, in Strafford, m. Hannah Boodey, b. 1758, d. Feb. 7, 1830, dau. of Azariah.
   2) David, d. Apr. 26, 1840, aged 83, in Barrington, m. Maria -----, d. Feb. 14, 1843, aged 85.
   2) Martha, b. Oct. 28, 1759, d. May 29, 1855, aged 95, in Barnstead, m. Nov. 1780, David Drew, b. July 2, 1758, d. Jan. 14, 1852, son of David.
     2) Abraham, administration granted on estate Jan. 17, 1803.
     2) Patience, m. Nov. 26, 1780, Robert Hanson.
     2) Lovey, m. ----- Daniels.
     2) Abigail, b. Jan. 31, 1765, m. June 22, 1786, John Heard, Jr.
5) WALDRON, William, son of Westbrook, b. June 8, 1756, d. Sept. 18, 1793, m. Apr. 16, 1779, by Dr. Belknap, Susanna Ham, d. Jan. 10, 1804, aged 48, dau. of Ephraim.

NEW HAMPSHIRE MARRIAGES SUPPLEMENT

WALDRON, Richard, Jr., of Dover, m. (1) Dec. 11, 1785, by Dr. Belknap, Sarah Titcomb, dau. of Maj. John, m. (2) (pub. Oct. 11, 1825, in S. Berwick, Me.), Mrs. Amy Lord, of S. Berwick, Me.

WALDRON, George, m. May 1803, in Portsmouth, Mrs. Rebecca Holland.

WALDRON, Robert S., of Rye, d. 1826, aged 40, m. July 10, 1814, by Rev. John Osborne, Martha Lang, of Lee.

WALDRON, Solomon, m. Sept. 27, 1818, by Rev. Joseph W. Clary, Nancy Remick.

WALDRON, Daniel, of Lee, m. int. Jan. 19, 1822, in Lee, Lois D. Glass, of Nottingham.

WALDRON, Richard, d. Oct. 17, 1839, aged 44, m. Nov. 21, 1824, by Elder Enoch Place, Rhoda Keniston, d. June 5, 1858, aged 64, both of Strafford.

WALDRON, Zachariah, d. Oct. 27, 1827, aged 28, m. Dec. 30, 1824, by Elder Enoch Place, Polly Willey, b. 1803, d. 1877, both of Strafford.

WALDRON, Jonathan C., b. 1817, d. 1898, m. Apr. 2, 1846, by Elder Enoch Place, Emeline S. Parshley, b. 1818, d. Nov. 20, 1881, aged 64, both of Strafford.

WALDRON, Hiram R., of Wakefield, son of Stephen, b. 1825, d. 1906, m. Nov. 11, 1847, Sarah Woodman, of Somersworth, b. 1829, d. 1896.

WALDRON, William W., b. 1822, d. 1908, m. Aug. 27, 1848, by Elder P. S. Burbank, Mary E. Peavey, b. 1828, d. 1903.

WALDRON, William H., of Dover, son of Jeremiah, m. (1) ----- -----, m. (2) (pub. May 27, 1849, in Boston, Mass.), Jane A. Hitchcock, of Boston, Mass., m. (3) Dec. 15, 1891, in Dover, Sarah E. Clough, dau. of Philemon.

WALDRON, Dudley B., m. (pub. Mar. 6, 1874, in Rochester), Celia C. Waldron.

3) **WALKER**, Seth, bpt. Oct. 9, 1726, m. Apr. 2, 1752, by Rev. Jos. Adams, Anna or (Nancy) Tripe, both of Newington.

4) WALKER, Col. Seth, of Portsmouth, son of Seth, b. Aug. 29, 1756, d. Oct. 8, 1838, m. Jan. 13, 1777, Temperance Peverly, b. Mar. 29, 1758, d. Mar. 30, 1841, dau. of George.

WALKER Cpl. John, of Rochester, b. May 4, 1750, d. July 21, 1827, m. Dec. 4, 1777, by Dr. Belknap, Hannah Emerson, b. June 28, 1753, d. Sept. 9, 1852, dau. of Samuel.

WALKER, Joseph, son of Richard, b. Feb. 12, 1769, d. Jan. 22, 1850, aged 81, m. Nov. 10, 1796, by Rev. Isaac Hasey, Sarah Pray, d. Apr. 16, 1868, aged 91, dau. of Joshua.

WALKER, Nathan, m. in 1823, Sophia Dore, of Milton, d. Dec. 7, 1873, aged 69.

WALKER, John S., of Lee, d. Jan. 21, 1890, aged 83, m. (1) int. Apr. 14, 1833, in Lee, Elizabeth Hilton, of Newmarket, dau. of Col. Richard, m. (2) Emma ----, d. Jan. 10, 1892, aged 52.

WALKER, Nathan P., son of Independence, b. Apr. 4, 1809, d. Oct. 9, 1889, m. (1) int. Jan. 19, 1834, in Dover, Martha Hicks, d. Dec. 7, 1873, aged 69, m. (2) Eliza H. (Joy) Miles, wid. of Abraham, d. Aug. 9, 1879, aged 75.

WALKER, Nathaniel K., b. Jan. 1807, d. May 25, 1880, m. (pub. Nov. 13, 1838, in Portsmouth), Ann Pray, dau. of Capt. Samuel.

WALKER, Edward, b. 1810, d. Mar. 11, 1882, m. Oct. 28, 1841, by Elder Kimball, Pauline S. Caswell, b. 1810, d. Sept. 3, 1875, aged 65, both of Strafford.

WALKER, Henry, m. Aug. 15, 1864, by Rev. James Rand, Annette Gilman.

WALKER, B. T., m. July 18, 1867, in Dover, Fannie C. Smith.

WALKER, Joseph H., m. Oct. 11, 1868, by Rev. Alden Sherwin, Elizabeth S. Tibbets, d. Dec. 14, 1914, aged 70.

WALLACE, John, of Pittsfield, m. Jan. 5, 1804, by Rev. Isaac Smith, Phebe Rand, of Barnstead.

WALLACE, Edwin, m. Jan. 17, 1861, in Rochester, Mrs. Mary E. (Horne) Wallace, wid. of Charles D., both of Rochester.

WALLACE, Sylvester B., m. Oct. 2, 1862, in Dover, Maggie I. Hoitt.

WALLACE, James S., m. Sept. 3, 1864, in Dover, Esther Tucker.

WALLACE, George F., m. Nov. 27, 1865, in Dover, Sarah Austin.

WALLINGFORD, John, Jr., m. Nov. 23, 1755, by Rev. Amos Main, Lydia Garland, of Somersworth, dau. of John.

6) WALLINGFORD, Samuel, son of David, d. 1825, m. Nov. 12, 1815, by Rev. Joseph Haven, Sarah Worster, b. Oct. 7, 1816, dau. of Lemuel, both of Milton.

WALLINGFORD, David, of Dover, d. July 20, 1879, aged 78, m. Sept. 21, 1828, by Elder Enoch Place, Mary Ann Tasker, of Strafford, b. 1805, d. 1887.

WALLINGFORD, Granville C., of Berwick, Me., son of John, b. Jan. 28, 1799, m. Mar. 4, 1829, in Alfred, Me., Mary Rogers, of Alfred, Me.

WALLINGFORD, Ira, d. Nov. 18 (13?), 1853, aged 30, m. May 13, 1848, by Rev. J. G. Forman, Delania Thompson, d. Jan. 28, 1860, aged 33, dau. of Samuel, both of Dover.

WALLINGFORD, John O., m. Oct. 4, 1864, in Dover, Nellie P. Cook, d. May 24, 1911, aged 67, dau. of Jedediah.

WALLINGFORD, Joseph D., m. Dec. 10, 1866, in Dover, Nellie D. Hutchins.

WARBURTON, Edward H., m. Aug. 30, 1868, by Rev. Robert S. Stubbs, Mary E. Shorey.

WARD, Freeman J., m. June 24, 1869, in Dover, Nettie J. Flagg.
WARNER, Daniel, of Portsmouth, m. Dec. 15, 1720, Sarah Hill, d. Nov. 11, 1783, dau. of Capt. Nathaniel.
WARNER, Thomas, m. (pub. Nov. 28, 1826, in Dover), Elizabeth McGooch.
WARNER, Eri, son of Samuel, d. Sept. 15, 1908, aged 86, m. Jan. 1, 1855, in Dover, Mary A. Doe, both of Boston, Mass.
WARREN, George, of Portsmouth, d. July 3, 1792, m. Aug. 14, 1754, by Rev. Jos. Adams, Elizabeth Hodgdon.
WARREN, Francis, son of Benjamin, b. Dec. 5, 1744, d. Oct. 1800, m. near 1763, Elizabeth Field.
WARREN, Cpl. William Cotton, of Scarboro, Me., b. 1752, d. Oct. 19, 1824, aged 73, m. July 17, 1777, by Rev. Matthew Merriam, Dorcas Smith, of Berwick, Me.
WARREN, Benjamin H., d. Oct. 1, 1846, aged 67, m. July 10, 1801, in Lebanon, Me., Achsah Nute, d. Aug. 23, 1876, aged 95.
WARREN, William, of Farmington, d. July 24, 1857, aged 82, m. Oct. 27, 1803, by Rev. Joseph Haven, Susanna Roberts, d. Jan. 24, 1856, aged 75.
WARREN, Thomas R., d. Jan. 21, 1881, aged 69, m. (1) Susan -----, d. Dec. 10, 1857, aged 44, m. (2) Apr. 25, 1858, in Milton, Asenath Ricker.
WARREN, Edwin, m. Dec. 25, 1861, in Dover, Sarah J. Scully.
WARREN, Charles E., m. June 9, 1866, in Dover, Mary E. Dyer.
WARREN, Timothy, m. Sept. 7, 1867, in Dover, Charlotte Bell.
WARREN, Charles W., m. July 18, 1868, by Rev. Robert S. Stubbs, Sarah F. Bedell.
WASHBURN, Alden, b. 1759, d. Apr. 14, 1826, m. Oct. 23, 1782, by Rev. Jeremiah Shaw, Sarah Gannet.
WATERHOUSE, Arthur, m. Jan. 15, 1737/38, Hannah Bickford, dau. of Henry.
WATERHOUSE, Samuel, m. Oct. 16, 1760, Hannah Bickford, dau. of Thomas.
WATERHOUSE, Benjamin, m. Sept. 17, 1833, by Rev. John Winkley, Lydia Tuttle, both of Barrington.
WATERHOUSE, Daniel, b. June 16, 1814, d. July 11, 1880, born in Barrington, m. Sept. 6, 1850, by Elder Enoch Place, Mrs. Delia Corson, b. July 25, 1818, d. Dec. 4, 1894, born in Raynham, Mass.
WATERHOUSE, John, m. Sept. 9, 1855, by Rev. John Winkley, Betsey Gray, both of Rochester.
WATERMAN, M., m. Sept. 16, 1861, in Dover, Margaret Neil.
WATSON, William, d. Jan. 1800, aged 67, m. Mar. 1, 1757, Christian Willey, dau. of John.

5) WATSON, Capt. Samuel, son of Benjamin, b. July 7, 1774, d. Apr. 14, 1847, m. Sept. 19, 1803, in Dover, Priscilla Hodgdon, b. Jan. 31, 1779, d. Oct. 31, 1822, dau. of Caleb.

WATSON, Capt. William, d. Oct. 28, 1815, aged 34, m. Oct. 21, 1811, Catherine Riley, b. Mar. 15, 1783, d. Sept. 23, 1870, dau. of John.

WATSON, Samuel, m. (pub. Dec. 28, 1811, in Somersworth), Priscilla Clark, both of Dover.

WATSON, David, Jr., of Newmarket, m. int. Mar. 13, 1830, in Lee, Eliza Ann Robinson, of Lee.

WATSON, Nathaniel, of Dover, son of Samuel H., d. Nov. 15, 1887, aged 59, m. Mar. 24, 1860, in Great Falls, Anna Chick, of Great Falls.

WATSON, Bernard G., d. Sept. 20, 1910, aged 73, m. Mar. 28, 1864, by Rev. John Brady, Mary Battles.

WATSON, John, m. July 17, 1865, in Dover, Mrs. Clara A. Carleton.

WATSON, George E., m. May 11, 1868, by Rev. Ezra Haskell, Nellie Crook, of Somersworth, dau. of William.

WEAVER, Robert, m. Aug. 24, 1869, in Dover, Harriet A. Partridge.

WEBBER, Benjamin, m. May 30, 1753, by Rev. Amos Main, ----- Allen, of Lebanon, Me.

WEBBER, Francis, m. (pub. June 2, 1804, in Portsmouth), Hannah Kennard.

WEBBER, John T., m. May 9, 1864, by Rev. James Rand, Julia E. Pierce.

WEBBER, Charles H., m. Oct. 25, 1867, by Rev. Alden Sherwin, Laura E. Hutchins.

WEBSTER, Davidson, m. July 5, 1801, in Durham, Lucy Chesley Drew, b. Sept. 13, 1786, dau. of Elijah.

WEBSTER, William Gage, son of Ebenezer, b. Aug. 26, 1803, d. Oct. 4, 1877, m. May 15, 1828, by Rev. Benjamin Hoyt, Hannah Jane Foss, d. Nov. 23, 1881, aged 77.

WEBSTER, Augustus A., son of Matthias, b. Sept. 9, 1829, d. July 24, 1919, m. July 29, 1850, in Lebanon, Me., Eliza A. Shorey, b. May 18, 1832, d. Nov. 4, 1902, both of Rochester.

WEBSTER, George A., son of John, d. Mar. 13, 1911, aged 71, m. Feb. 27, 1865, in Dover, Annie E. Young.

WEEDEN, Charles K., of E. Northwood, m. Oct. 28, 1876, in Lee, Carrie W. Comings, of Lee.

2) **WEEKS**, Capt. Joshua, d. June 13, 1758, aged 84, m. Comfort Hubbard, d. Mar. 20, 1750, aged 76, dau. of Richard.

WEEKS, John Jr., m. Oct. 10, 1786, by Rev. Isaac Smith, Hannah Moody, both of Gilmanton.

WEEKS, Mathias Jr., m. May 26, 1794, by Rev. Isaac Smith, Mary Bennett.
WEEKS, William, of Strafford, m. May 12, 1842, by Rev. John Winkley, Meriah Clark, of Barrington.
WEEKS, William B., m. Sept. 21, 1843, Rhoda O. Davis, b. Mar. 26, 1825, d. Sept. 22, 1908, dau. of Nathaniel.
WEEKS, Benjamin, m. Oct. 22, 1864, in Dover, Mary E. Downs.
WEEKS, George B., m. Oct. 29, 1864, in Dover, Catherine E. Shields.
WEEKS, Albert O., m. Feb. 8, 1870, in Dover, Dorrinda M. Davis.
WEEKS, John W., m. Apr. 22, 1874, in Great Falls, Lizzie F. Lord, dau. of John O.
WEEKS, Nathan O., m. Nov. 20, 1875, by Rev. Asa Piper, Abbie M. Lang, both of Wakefield.
WELLS, Stephen, of Ipswich, Mass., m. June 16, 1839, by Rev. John Winkley, Louisa Stiles, of Strafford.
WELLS, Brenton R., m. Jan. 10, 1870, in Dover, Abby W. Kittredge.
1) **WENDELL**, John Perkins, b. Feb. 28, 1777, d. Dec. 7, 1854, m. (1) Oct. 14, 1804, by Rev. Robert Gray, Sarah Ann Bickford, b. July 27, 1784, d. June 6,, 1822, aged 37, m. (2) Dec. 25, 1823, Patience Peavey, of Milton, b. June 15, 1804, d. June 20, 1833, aged 29.
WENTWORTH, Hiram Varney, m. July 6, 1840, in Rochester, Mary J. Nute.
WENTWORTH, John C., son of Daniel, b. Aug. 17, 1822, d. Aug. 17, 1864, m. Olive Downs, b. Aug. 20, 1822, d. Apr. 3, 1888, dau. of James.
WENTWORTH, Nahum, m. June 14, 1848, in Dover, Abby Ann Varney.
WENTWORTH, Andrew, of Wakefield, m. Feb. 26, 1868, by Rev. Asa Piper, Victoria E. Dicey, of Newfield, Me.
WENTWORTH, James E., of Conway, m. Jan. 4, 1869, by Rev. Daniel Tappan, Clara E. Wentworth, of Lowell, Mass.
WENTWORTH, Jacob C., b. 1837, m. Sept. 22, 1877, in Lee, Josephine Huckins, both of Newmarket.
WESCOTT, Henry H. H., m. July 2, 1868, in Dover, Nellie A. Hussey.
WESLEY, John, m. Aug. 21, 1864, in Dover, Frances A. Hyde.
WEST, Charles E., of Brookfield, m. Sept. 3, 1876, by Rev. Asa Piper, Hannah Dyer, of Wakefield.
WESTERN, Charles E., m. Jan. 28, 1867, in Dover, Rhoda B. Libbey.
WEYMOUTH, James, m. Apr. 13, 1807, by Rev. Isaac Smith, Polly Chase, both of Gilmanton.

NEW HAMPSHIRE MARRIAGES SUPPLEMENT

WEYMOUTH, Bradley, of Lee, m. int. May 24, 1828, in Lee, Mary Langley, of Nottingham.

WHEAT, Solomon, of Newmarket, m. int. Apr. 28, 1830, in Lee, Deborah Ryan, of Lee, b. Jan. 5, 1807, dau. of Edmund.

1) **WHEELER**, Dr. John, of Dover, b. May 17, 1770, d. Apr. 3, 1840, m. (1) Mar. 12, 1793, in Malden, Mass., Rebecca Harris, b. Apr. 15, 1770, d. Jan. 28, 1804, m. (2) Nov. 17, 1805, Elizabeth Neil, d. Sept. 6, 1807, aged 27, dau. of William, m. (3) June 5, 1810, Elizabeth Crosby, of Bellerica, Mass., b. July 30, 1782, d. June 5, 1857.

WHEELER, John S., m. June 12, 1866, by Rev. James Rand, Emma Frost.

WHIDDEN, Parson, m. Nov. 2, 1780, Hannah Doe, b. Apr. 14, 1761, dau. of Sampson.

1) **WHITE**, Timothy, Jr., (his father, Timothy, Sr., died Feb. 24, 1765, aged 64 yrs., 3 mos.), b. Oct. 29, 1733, d. 1803, m. Mar. 26, 1761, by Rev. Samuel Hill, of Rochester, Lydia Main, b. in 1738, d. Mar. 9, 1826, dau. of Rev. Amos.

WHITE, Samuel, of Deerfield, m. int. Oct. 24, 1835, in Lee, Sophia Chesley, of Lee.

WHITEHOUSE, Enoch, son of Turner, d. Oct. 1804, m. Sally Smith.

WHITEHOUSE, Joseph P., of Farmington, son of Moses, b. May 20, 1808, d. Oct. 23, 1877, m. Sept. 25, 1831, by Elder Enoch Place, Drusilla Brock, of Strafford.

WHITEHOUSE, George Washington, son of George L., b. Aug. 3, 1812, d. 1842, aged 30, m. (pub. July 19, 1836, in Brookfield), Eleanor Horn, d. Jan. 1888, aged 78.

WHITEHOUSE, Henry, m. int. Aug. 29, 1847, in Dover, Emeline S. Hanscom, d. Mar. 10, 1890, aged 63, dau. of Ezra.

WHITEHOUSE, Charles Carrol, son of George, b. May 20, 1825, d. Oct. 3, 1866, aged 41, m. Feb. 4, 1849, in Alton, Susan A. Jones, d. Mar. 12, 1858, aged 28, both of Farmington.

WHITEHOUSE, Charles S., of Rochester, son of Nicholas, b. Sept 3, 1827, d. Mar. 4, 1899, aged 71, m. (pub. Oct. 5, 1852, in Lowell, Mass.), Frances Ellen Foster.

WHITEHOUSE, Leonard, m. (pub. Feb. 15, 1853, in Barrington), Eliza Jane Brown, d. Jan. 22, 1912, aged 75, both of Barrington.

WHITEHOUSE, Jacob Powell, son of Samuel H., b. June 29, 1832, of Middleton, d. Mar. 25, 1908, aged 75, m. Mar. 23, 1853, in Milton, Mary Jane Hayes, d. Sept. 3, 1905, aged 71, dau. of George.

WHITEHOUSE, George W., m. (1) May 22, 1853, in New Durham, Lydia M. Ransom, both of Dover, m. (2) Apr. 10, 1862, by Rev. James Rand, Fannie Carpenter.

WHITEHOUSE, William, m. Nov. 20, 1860, in Rochester, Mrs. Betsey Watson, both of Rochester.
WHITEHOUSE, John M., m. May 25, 1862, in Dover, Sarah A. Foye.
WHITEHOUSE, Benjamin F., of Wakefield, m. Feb. 26, 1866, by Rev. Asa Piper, Delia F. Langley, of Wakefield.
WHITEHOUSE, Elihu B., m. July 28, 1866, in Dover, E. Jennie Nutter.
WHITEHOUSE, Daniel F., m. May 28, 1868, in Dover, Annie E. Scott.
WHITEHOUSE, Benjamin F., m. Sept. 20, 1870, by Rev. Ezra Haskell, Harriet A. Young.
WHITING, Isaac, of Fryeburg, Me., m. int. Dec. 10, 1826, in Lee, Olive Allen, of Lee.
WHITMAN, Josiah, m. Nov. 27, 1872, by Rev. Asa Piper, Georgianna Sanborn, both of Wakefield.
WHITNEY, Leonard P., m. Feb. 26, 1862, in Dover, Emma A. Griffin.
WHITNEY, Edward H., m. Nov. 29, 1866, by Rev. Ezra Haskell, Jennie H. Hooper, d. Nov. 29, 1918, aged 72.
WHITTEN, Jesse, son of Jesse, b. Mar. 18, 1801, d. Dec. 5, 1854, m. May 19, 1835, in Middleton, Betsey Drew, both of Wolfeboro.
2) **WHITTIER**, Moses, son of Obadiah, b. May 19, 1789, d. Dec. 17, 1857, m. (1) Dec. 1814, Gertrude Frye, d. Dec. 9, 1818, m. (2) Mar. 1, 1821, in Durham, Me., Sarah H. Jones, of Brunswick, Me., d. Jan. 23, 1837, aged 43, m. (3) Sept 25, 1842, by Rev. Elijah Mason, Deborah Burnham, d. Dec. 28, 1890, aged 87, dau. of Moses and Zipporah.
WHITTIER, Horace P., m. Nov. 10, 1864, in Dover, Emma D. Freeman.
3) **WIGGIN**, Col. Andrew, of Hampton, son of Andrew, b. Jan. 6, 1671/72, d. Jan. 23, 1756, m. (1) Sept. 2, 1697, by Rev. John Pike, Abigail Follet, of Dover, dau. of Nicholas, m. (2) Jan. 4, 1737, Rachel Freese, of Hampton, wid. of Jacob, d. June 14, 1771.
4) WIGGIN, Lt. Simon, son of Capt. Simon, b. Aug. 12, 1701, d. Aug. 11, 1757, m. May 16, 1728, Susannah Sherburne, b. Mar. 13, 1703, d. July 9, 1763, dau. of Henry.
4) WIGGIN, Andrew, son of Jonathan, b. Mar. 27, 1719, m. (1) Anna Ross, m. (2) Mehitable Moody, d. Nov. 30, 1749, m. (3) Sept. 12, 1751, Dorothy Sweat, b. Feb. 26, 1727, d. Sept. 20, 1754.
WIGGIN, Capt. Jonathan, b. Jan. 19, 1740, d. Feb. 1827, m. (1) Oct. 10, 1761, Mary Little, b. 1739, d. Aug. 14, 1771, m. (2) Mehitable -----, d. Nov. 14, 1784.
WIGGIN, David, son of Simeon, b. July 20, 1780, d. May 5, 1820, m. near 1796, Polly Hanscom, b. Sept. 11, 1777, d. May 21, 1850.

WIGGIN, Lt. David, Jr., d. Nov. 8, 1866, aged 95, m. (1) Nov. 17, 1796, Elizabeth Dame, d. Aug. 13, 1804, aged 30, dau. of George, m. (2) 1805, Olive Wiggin, d. May 29, 1815, aged 42, m. (3) Dec. 25, 1815, by Rev. John Osborne, Drusilla Young, of Newmarket, d. Nov. 29, 1879, aged 95.

WIGGIN, Josiah, son of Isiah, d. June 1, 1806, aged 31, m. Nov. 6, 1797, in Wakefield, Marjory Willard, of Wakefield, d. Jan. 14, 1844, aged 74.

WIGGIN, Capt. William, d. Jan. 16, 1831, aged 55, m. (1) Feb. 5, 1801, Lydia Chesley, d. July 9, 1820, aged 34, dau. of Maj. Joseph, m. (2) Dec. 25, 1823, Sophia Pendergast, b. Sept. 23, 1790, d. Mar. 30, 1849, dau. of Edmund.

WIGGIN, Samuel, b. Aug. 15, 1782, d. Aug. 30, 1836, m. Dec. 8, 1805, at Rochester, Susanna Fisher, b. Jan. 15, 1788, d. Mar. 8, 1862, dau. of Col. Janvrin.

WIGGIN, Porter Kimball, son of Joseph, b. 1789, d. 1870, m. Jan. 21, 1814, in Wakefield, Elizabeth Gerrish Piper, of Wakefield, b. July 1789, d. May 1881, dau. of Rev. Asa.

WIGGIN, Nathan, m. Apr. 17, 1816, in Northwood, Hannah Fellows, both of Dover.

WIGGIN, John, b. 1790, d. 1874, m. (1) Olive C. -----, b. 1790, d. 1816, m. (2) in 1818, in Moultonboro, Hannah Doten, b. 1789, d. 1849.

WIGGIN, David, m. Dec. 5, 1816, by Rev. Isaac Smith, Betsy Pervier.

WIGGIN, Simeon, son of David, d. Feb. 11, 1857, aged 54, m. May 6, 1824, Sarah Wentworth, d. Apr. 2, 1885, dau. of Samuel.

WIGGIN, George Jerry, of Durham, son of Lt. Davis, b. Oct. 14, 1801, d. 1891, m. (1) Apr. 17, 1827, Abigail Thompson, of Lee, b. Dec. 12, 1800, d. Feb. 2, 1872, dau. of Edmund, m. (2) Mrs. Alice Ann (Jones) Smart, wid. of Samuel.

WIGGIN, James L., of Durham, m. int. Sept. 25, 1831, in Lee, Abigail Wilson, of Lee.

WIGGIN, Oliver T., of Brookfield, m. (pub. Jan. 31, 1837, in Dover), Lydia J. Drew, of Durham, b. Oct. 13, 1796, dau. of Andrew.

WIGGIN, Leonard, of Lee, son of Theophilus, b. Nov. 10, 1808, d. Apr. 30, 1894, m. Aug. 7, 1838, by Rev. Mr. Chesley, Sarah Daniels, of Durham, b. July 28, 1806, d. Mar. 28, 1888.

WIGGIN, Issachar, d. July 7, 1886, m. int. Mar. 26, 1840, in Lee, Mary Ann Daniels, d. May 22, 1904, aged 81, both of Lee.

WIGGIN, Nathaniel P., b. Oct. 11, 1818, d. Mar. 22, 1897, m. (pub. May 4, 1841, in Barrington), Abigail Langley, b. Nov. 13, 1819, d. May 2, 1892, both of Lee.

WIGGIN, Asa Piper, son of Porter, m. Jan. 1, 1842, by Rev. Nathaniel Barker, Lucy Copp, dau. of George W. Copp.

WIGGIN, Theophilus, Jr., of Lee, m. (pub. July 3, 1849, in Durham), Sarah B. Jenness, of Durham.
WIGGIN, Theophilus, of Lee, m. Jan. 27, 1850, in Lee, Sarah Robie, of Raymond.
WIGGIN, John Goudy, son of Joshua, b. Dec. 6, 1831, m. Sept. 1851, in Moultonboro, Lovina Elizabeth Merrow.
WIGGIN, Charles, m. in 1851, in Tamworth, Mary Folsom.
WIGGIN, Joseph H., m. Feb. 5, 1862, in Dover, Susan Ann Rogers.
WIGGIN, Russel B., son of Benjamin, b. Nov. 25, 1836, d. Nov. 14, 1886, m. Mar. 27, 1862, in Dover, Emily J. Paul, b. Apr. 13, 1839, d. Dec. 23, 1890.
WIGGIN, Benaiah, m. Nov. 23, 1862, in Dover, Jennie M. Hall.
WIGGIN, James M., m. Apr. 18, 1863, in Dover, Angie A. Osborne.
WIGGIN, Joseph D., of Lee, b. 1841, m. int. Dec. 17, 1863, in Lee, Hannah M. Beardslee, of Salem, b. 1844.
WIGGIN, John H., m. Dec. 4, 1866, by Rev. James Rand, Sarah E. Tibbetts.
WIGGIN, Lyford M., m. Mar. 2, 1867, in Dover, Hattie E. Rogers.
WIGGIN, Daniel C., b. 1831, d. Oct. 24, 1898, m. June 3, 1869, in Dover, Abby H. Snell, b. 1837, d. Dec. 16, 1919.
WIGGIN, Alpheus, of Wakefield, m. Aug. 18, 1869, by Rev. Asa Piper, Caroline Sanborn, of Acton, Me.
WIGGIN, James M., of Lee, son of Isaachar, d. Apr. 5, 1835, aged 92, m. Sept. 7, 1872, in Lee, Matilda A. Bennett, of Barrington, d. Dec. 13, 1922, dau. of Frank.
WIGGIN, Frank, of Lee, m. Dec. 25, 1873, in Deerfield, Eva Tilton, of Deerfield.
WIGGIN, Charles H., of Wakefield, m. Mar. 31, 1876, by Rev. Asa Piper, Lizzie M. Gerald, of Brookfield.
WIGGLESWORTH, Dr. Samuel, b. Aug. 25, 1734, d. 1800, m. Sept. 9, 1779, by Dr. Belknap, Mary Waldron, dau. of George.
WILDES, Alpheus, of Kennebunkport, Me., m. (pub. May 21, 1823, in Brunswick, Me.), Hannah Cushing, of Rochester.
WILKINSON, James, m. Sept. 9, 1832, Lydia D. Goodrich, both of Berwick, Me.
WILKINSON, George W., m. Oct. 4, 1866, in Dover, Martha B. Smith.
2) **WILLAND**, Paul, d. Nov. 18, 1818, aged 76, m. near 1764, Elizabeth -----.
3) WILLAND, Nathaniel, d. Sept. 11, 1856, aged 80, m. (pub. Aug. 20, 1803, in Dover), Elizabeth Holden, dau. of Fabyan.
WILLAND, Edward A., son of Nathaniel H., d. July 8, 1915, aged 69, m. Dec. 25, 1870, in Dover, Calista A. Chesley, d. July 17, 1915, aged 66, dau. of Samuel.

NEW HAMPSHIRE MARRIAGES SUPPLEMENT

WILLAND, Noah, m. (pub. June 11, 1874, in Rochester), Mary A. Wentworth.
WILLARD, Samuel, of Alfred, Me., m. (pub. Sept. 18, 1829, in Somersworth), Eliza Durant, of Somersworth.
WILLEY, Josiah, son of William, b. June 10, 1762, m. Mar. 1782, Sally Drew, d. Mar. 15, 1847, aged 82.
WILLEY, William, m. Nov. 17, 1791, by Rev. Benjamin Randall, Phebe Taylor, d. Nov. 15, 1854, aged 84, both of New Durham.
5) WILLEY, Samuel, son of Samuel, b. Nov. 16, 1766, d. Nov. 10, 1826, m. Jan. 7, 1796, by Rev. Benjamin Randall, Elizabeth Bennett, b. May 13, 1776, d. Feb. 26, 1839, dau. of Capt. Benjamin, both of New Durham.
WILLEY, Phinehas, of Newmarket, d. Mar. 1825, aged 27, m. Mar. 25, 1818, by Rev. John Brodhead, Welthern Sias, b. Jan. 8, 1794, d. May 17, 1830, dau. of Maj. Nathaniel.
WILLEY, Josiah, Jr., son of Josiah, d. Sept. 29, 1864, aged 66, m. June 15, 1823, in Wolfeboro, Abigail Tibbetts, d. Sept. 30, 1879, aged 78, both of Wolfeboro.
WILLEY, Charles, m. int. Apr. 9, 1825, in Lee, Mrs. Comfort Elliot, widow, both of Lee.
WILLEY, Lemuel (or Samuel) B., son of Samuel, b. Mar. 19, 1804, d. June 21, 1842, m. Nov. 23, 1826, by Elder Enoch Place, Love Hanscomb, b. 1805, d. 1843, both of Barrington.
WILLEY, William A., son of Eliphalet, b. 1815, d. 1893, m. Sept. 27, 1837, by Rev. Eleazer Smith, Mercy Ann Roberts, d. May 7, 1874, aged 60.
WILLEY, Moses W., b. May 8, 1823, d. Nov. 8, 1875, aged 52, m. Aug. 17, 1845, by Rev. Samuel Kelly, Hannah D. Meader, b. Apr. 23, 1821, d. July 29, 1898, both of Rochester.
WILLEY, George W., d. June 20, 1911, aged 86, m. (pub. Oct. 21, 1845, in Rochester), Mary Jane Berry, both of Barrington.
WILEY, Charles R., m. Nov. 28, 1866, by Rev. James Rand, Mrs. Olivia Worthing.
WILEY, Frank J., son of Enoch, d. Dec. 19, 1926, aged 82, m. Mar. 1, 1869, by Rev. Robert S. Stubbs, Mary E. Willey.
WILEY, Elijah, m. Sept. 30, 1869, in Dover, Elizabeth E. Ashton.
WILEY, Alanson R., m. Mar. 22, 1870, in Dover, Emma C. Cary.
WILLIAMS, John, of Barrington, m. Nov. 7, 1838, by Rev. William Demeritt, Sally G. Doe, of Lee, dau. of Francis.
WILLIAMS, Charles, m. Sept. 2, 1865, in Dover, Ellen F. Perkins.
WILLIAMS, Frank G., d. Aug. 12, 1911, aged 68, m. Jan. 7, 1867, by Rev. Ezra Haskell, Hattie A. Thompson.
WILLIS, Richard, m. May 3, 1874, in Dover, Arabelle E. Paul, dau. of Ivory, both of Dover.

WILSON, Warren, m. Mar. 6, 1783, by Rev. Isaac Smith, Anna Berry.
WILSON, Capt. Parker H., m. int. Apr. 29, 1826, in Lee, Harriet Watson, both of Lee.
WILSON, Samuel G., b. Oct. 13, 1808, m. (pub. Sept. 9, 1834, in Lee), Elizabeth Towle, b. Oct. 10, 1811, d. Feb. 5, 1852, aged 40, dau. of Col. Gardiner.
WILSON, Tristram, d. June 1, 1860, aged 43, m. Aug. 28, 1839, Mary D. Cloutman, d. Jan. 6, 1859, aged 45.
4) **WINGATE**, Moses, bpt. Aug. 2, 1738, dead in 1769, m. before June 27, 1769, Elizabeth Bennett, d. Dec. 24, 1806.
WINGATE, Stephen, of Madbury, m. (pub. July 5, 1806, in Barrington), Abigail Cate, of Barrington.
5) WINGATE, Jeremy, of Farmington, son of Aaron, b. June 7, 1785, d. Mar. 27, 1864, m. May 25, 1818, by Rev. J. W. Clary, Mary Titcomb, b. July 1795, d. Apr. 16, 1822, dau. of John.
5) WINGATE, Aaron, d. Aug. 10, 1828, m. Aug. 31, 1826, by Rev. J. W. Clary, Phebe T. Lamos, both of Madbury.
WINGATE, Cyrus, son of John, b. Aug. 15, 1822, d. Sept. 20, 1896, m. Sarah Abbie Canney, b. near 1827, d. Nov. 20, 1868, aged 40, dau. of Jacob.
WINGATE, Jerry Y., m. Nov. 23, 1870, in Dover, Arvilla S. Clements.
WINKLEY, Francis, d. Apr. 7, 1855, aged 81, m. (1) near 1800, Sara Drew, d. Mar. 26, 1846, aged 68, dau. of Capt. John, m. (2) (pub. Feb. 2, 1847, in Madbury), Abigail (Peirce) Church, wid. of Benjamin, d. May 14, 1865, aged 63, dau. of Israel.
WINKLEY, David, m. July 1802, by Rev. Benjamin Balch, Anna Hussey.
WINKLEY, Rev. John, 3rd, b. 1795, d. Oct. 9, 1868, m. Nov. 9, 1815, by Elder Enoch Place, Susan Otis, b. Jan. 3, 1793, d. Jan. 4, 1873, dau. of Lt. Stephen, both of Barrington.
WINKLEY, Jeremiah, of Lowell, Mass., m. int. Sept. 4, 1831, in Lee, Maria Jane Langley, of Lee.
WINKLEY, Dennis, m. Nov. 11, 1865, in Dover, Betsey M. Hawkins.
WINKLEY, John L., m. Mar. 15, 1870, in Dover, Ellen T. Young.
WINKLEY, John F., son of Joseph, d. Oct. 30, 1908, aged 62, m. July 9, 1870, in Dover, Lucinda Ladd.
WINSLOW, Rev. Hubbard, m. int. May 3, 1829, in Dover, Susan W. Cutler.
WITHAM, John, of Kittery, Me., b. Feb. 10, 1765, m. Oct. 8, 1787, by Rev. Isaac Hasey, Mehitable Courson, of Lebanon, Me., b. Dec. 15, 1766.
WITHAM, Josiah, b. Dec. 2, 1768, m. Aug. 5, 1792, in Wakefield, Mehitable Jones, of Rochester, b. Mar. 20, 1770, d. May 10, 1863.

WITHAM, Josiah Norton, son of Josiah, b. Nov. 25, 1815, d. June 22, 1884, aged 68, m. Nov. 24, 1844, in Middleton, Susan Place, both of Milton.

WITHAM, Charles E., m. Aug. 19, 1870, in Dover, Mary Irvin.

WITHERAL, John, m. July 30, 1755, by Rev. Amos Main, Rebecca Clark.

WITHERAL, John, of Lebanon, Me., son of Thomas, b. Jan. 25, 1758, d. June 12, 1854, m. Mar. 28, 1778, by Rev. Matthew Merriam, Mary Morrill Gerrish, dau. of William.

WOOD, Eliphalet, of Rindge, m. June 12, 1788, by Rev. Isaac Smith, Elizabeth Tilton, of Loudon.

WOOD, John P., m. Nov. 14, 1869, by Rev. Asa Piper, Mary Dunnels, both of Newfield, Me.

WOODBURY, Jonathan, of Barrington, m. Feb. 9, 1814, in Northwood, Eliza Buzzell, of Northwood.

WOODES, John H. C., son of Samuel, d. Mar. 20, 1909, aged 66, m. May 19, 1866, by Rev. James Rand, Jennie N. Decatur, d. Aug. 11, 1916, aged 74, dau. of William.

4) **WOODMAN**, Joshua, son of Lt. Jonathan, b. Oct. 25, 1703, m. (1) early as 1742, Elizabeth Doe, dau. of John, m. (2) Rachel -----.

5) WOODMAN, Capt., Archelas, son of Joshua, b. Aug. 18, 1737, d. May 3, 1808, m. before 1762, Sarah Joy, dau. of Samuel.

6) WOODMAN, Andrew, son of Joshua, b. Mar. 29, 1760, d. Sept. 8, 1849, m. Oct. 25, 1789, Mary Woodman, b. Sept. 25, 1768, d. July 20, 1847, dau. of Capt. Jonathan.

6) WOODMAN, Moses, of Durham, son of Jonathan, b. 1779, d. Feb. 14, 1852, m. Oct. 13, 1817, by Rev. John Osborne, Elizabeth Snell, of Lee, d. Mar. 21, 1838, aged 52, dau. of John.

6) WOODMAN, Nathan, son of Jonathan, b. Dec. 9, 1789, d. Mar. 2, 1869, m. near 1818, Abigail H. Chesley, b. Aug. 21, 1799, d. Jan. 6, 1864, dau. of Samuel.

WOODMAN, Josiah, of Nottingham, m. (pub. June 2, 1829, in lee), Eliza D. Williams, of Lee.

WOODMAN, Joshua, b. 1802, d. Nov. 20, 1882, m. (1) Almira -----, d. Aug. 3, 1831, aged 27, m. (2) Jan. 22, 1834, by Elder Enoch Place, Martha Jane Huckins, b. 1813, d. Mar. 7, 1895, aged 82, both of Strafford.

WOODMAN, Jeremiah, of Alton, son of Samuel, b. 1814, d. Aug. 6, 1888, m. (pub. Dec. 24, 1839, in Alton), Mary P. Clough, of Gilmanton, b. Feb. 26, 1818.

WOODMAN, William, m. int. Aug. 28, 1842, in Lee, Abigail Buzzell, both of Lee.

WOODMAN, Charles C., b. 1814, d. 1895, m. Nov. 23, 1842, by Rev. John Winkley, Martha Ann Boodey, b. 1824, d. 1903, both of Strafford.

WOODMAN, Joseph C., of Boston, Mass., son of Joseph, b. Feb. 27, 1819, d. Sept. 22, 1869, m. Sept. 29, 1845, in Wolfeboro, Sarah Ann Demeritt, of Wolfeboro.

WOODMAN, John S., son of Nathan, b. Sept. 6, 1819, d. May 9, 1871, m. int. Nov. 26, 1848, in Dover, Ann Mary Pendexter, of Durham, b. May 1, 1833, d. Dec. 15, 1884, dau. of Stephen P.

WOODMAN, True William, son of Joseph, b. July 25, 1817, d. Oct. 18, 1880, aged 61, m. (pub. Feb. 16, 1849, in Great Falls), Harriet N. Thompson, d. Dec. 1873, aged 44.

WOODMAN, Lafayette, son of Samuel, d. Nov. 3, 1915, aged 91, m. (pub. Feb. 18, 1851, in Haverhill, Mass.), Sarah Carr, both of Alton.

WOODMAN, James M., son of Joseph, b. Nov. 9, 1821, d. Aug. 28, 1868, m. Mar. 11, 1855, by Rev. Thomas J. Greenwood, Maria P. Brewster, both of Great Falls.

WOODMAN, Moses Gilman, son of Moses, b. Nov. 3, 1830, m. July 31, 1856, by Elder Elias Hutchins, Hannah F. Chesley, d. May 2, 1894, aged 62, dau. of Stephen P., both of Durham

WOODS, Leonard, m. (pub. May 16, 1826, in Berwick, Me.), Adeline Emery.

WORSTER, Thomas, son of Thomas, m. Jan. 20, 1738, Anne Spinney, b. Apr. 12, 1719, dau. of John.

WORSTER, John, son of Thomas, m. July 15, 1751, Lydia Remick, bpt. Aug. 28, 1720, dau. of Joshua.

WORSTER, Lemuel, son of John, m. Dec. 12, 1769, by Rev. Matthew Merriam, Mercy Woodsum.

WORSTER, Alexander, son of John, m. Jan. 25, 1796, by Rev. Matthew Merriam, Molly Libbey.

WORSTER, Ezekiel, son of Ezekiel, b. Sept. 4, 1768, d. Nov. 15, 1841, m. July 3, 1797, by Rev. Jacob Foster, Anne Pray, of Lebanon, Me.

WORSTER, Isaac, son of Lemuel, b. Apr. 11, 1772, d. Mar. 11, 1838, aged 66, m. July 19, 1797, by Rev. Jacob Foster, Tampson Frost, d. May 18, 1855, aged 81.

WORSTER, Mark, son of George, b. Jan. 7, 1770, d. Sept. 8, 1842, aged 73, m. Apr. 29, 1798, by Rev. Joseph Hilliard, Dorcas Gowel, d. May 8, 1834, aged 61.

WORSTER, Samuel, son of Samuel, b. July 28, 1780, d. Sept. 20, 1805, m. Oct. 14, 1802, by Rev. Joseph Hilliard, Patty Brown.

WORSTER, Lemuel, son of Lemuel, m. July 4, 1805, by Rev. Joseph Hilliard, Betsey Wentworth.

WORSTER, Col. Alexander, m. Oct. 25, 1836, Abra (Applebee) Remick, wid. of John, dau. of Thomas.

WRIGHT, Enoch G., d. Aug. 3, 1869, m. Mar. 22, 1859, Eliza A. Chesley, b. Apr. 2, 1822, d. Mar. 15, 1907, dau. of Thomas.

WRIGHT, James, m. May 15, 1867, in Dover, Sarah F. Twombly.

WYMAN, Charles A., July 10, 1862, in Dover, Lilla S. Steel.

YEATON, Richard, of Somersworth, d. Sept. 8, 1785, m. Feb. 5, 1759, by Rev. John Morse, Experience Pray, of Portsmouth, dau. of John.

YEATON, Thomas B., m. Feb. 7, 1866, in Dover, Lorinda N. Hall.

2) **YORK**, Samuel, b. 1645, d. Mar. 17, 1718, m. Hannah -----, d. Nov. 28, 1724, aged 70.

6) YORK, Thomas, of Lee, son of Eliphalet, d. Nov. 11, 1857, aged 70, m. (1) in 1811, by Rev. John Osborne, Polly Chapman, of Newmarket, d. June 19, 1815, aged 36, m. (2) in 1817, by Rev. John Osborne, Mrs. Deborah (Elkins) Hanscom, of Lee, d. July 21, 1827, aged 34, m. (3) Harriet Bartlett, d. Dec. 17, 1840, aged 29.

6) YORK, Elijah, son of Eliphalet, d. Feb. 18, 1861, aged 71, m. in 1813, by Rev. John Osborne, Comfort Chapman, of Lee, d. Apr. 13, 1883, aged 92.

YORK, Jonathan, m. Nov. 13, 1814, by Rev. Isaac Smith, Nancy Wilson.

6) YORK, Daniel, son of Eliphalet, b. July 15, 1791, d. in 1867, m. Feb. 11, 1817, by Rev. John Osborne, Elizabeth Langley, b. Apr. 3, 1794, d. in 1872, both of Lee.

6) YORK, Deac. Eliphalet, son of Eliphalet, d. Jan. 31, 1887, aged 90, m. Feb. 7, 1820, by Rev. John Osborne, Mary Frost Durgin, d. Aug. 12, 1877, aged 76, dau. of Josiah, both of Lee.

YORK, Jeremiah, son of George, d. June 2, 1888, aged 85, m. int. Nov. 20, 1824, in New Durham, Hannah B. Nason, d. Mar. 28, 1899, aged 91, both of New Durham.

YORK, David, son of Eliphalet, d. Aug. 24, 1859, aged 65, m. int. Mar. 26, 1825, in Lee, Hannah Durrell, b. Nov. 7, 1800, d. Aug. 1, 1886, dau. of Joseph, both of Lee.

YORK, Thomas, of Lee, m. int. Mar. 9, 1828, in Lee, Mary Bennett, of Newmarket.

YORK, John Langdon, Jr., son of John, b. Dec. 25, 1807, d. Apr. 7, 1873, m. Mar. 12, 1829, by Elder Enoch Place, Hannah Bickford, d. July 2, 1833, aged 35, both of Rochester.

YORK, David D., son of John, d. Apr. 18, 1884, aged 70, m. (1) int. Apr. 28, 1839, in Lee, Mary Bartlett, b. Sept. 28, 1814, d. Sept. 19, 1846, dau. of Josiah, both of Lee, m. (2) May 9, 1852, in Lee, Susan G. Blanchard, of Lee.

YORK, James M., son of Daniel, b. June 12, 1818, m. (1) Dec. 7, 1842, by Rev. John Parkman, Catharine Dockham, d. Sept. 28, 1843, aged 20, m. (2) Oct. 28, 1846, Lucy A. Willey, d. Mar. 2, 1879, aged 58, both of Dover.

YORK, John B., of Portsmouth, aged 26, m. Dec. 23, 1851, in Dover, Lydia Kenniston, of Durham, aged 27.

YORK, William B., of Lee, b. 1835, m. July 15, 1858, in Lee, Mary J. Currier, of Manchester, b. 1831.

YORK, Israel G., son of John, b. 1840, d. Apr. 21, 1882, m. Oct. 11, 1862, in Lee, Lizzie A. Dow, b. Jan. 10, 1846, d. June 1, 1920, both of Lee.

YORK, Elbridge G., b. 1815, m. Apr. 22, 1863, in Lee, Mrs. Mary Jane York, b. 1836, both of Lee.

YORK, George T., m. June 16, 1866, by Rev. James Rand, Martha E. Young.

YORK, Simeon D., d. Apr. 7, 1927, aged 85, m. (1) Nov. 28, 1866, in Dover, Mary E. Keith, b. Feb. 26, 1847, d. Dec. 10, 1885, m. (2) Aug. 7, 1894, in Dover, Josephine McGroty.

YORK, George, son of William, d. Mar. 22, 1889, aged 46, m. May 18, 1870, by Rev. James Drummond, Mary Thompson.

YORK, Fred B., m. Dec. 31, 1873, in Lee, Olivia J. Otis, both of Lee.

YORK, George H., of Newfield, Me., m. Oct. 22, 1874, by Rev. Asa Piper, Hattie M. Lord, of Limerick, Me.

YORK, Josiah, m. Aug. 30, 1875, in Rochester, Nancy P. Hayes.

YOUNG, Job, of York, Me., son of Rowland, m. Nov. 17, 1727, Patience King, dau. of Richard.

3) YOUNG, Eleazer, son of Jonathan, d. Sept. 1798, m. near 1745, Mary Ham, b. Oct. 8, 1723.

YOUNG, Timothy, d. Mar. 1820, aged 71, m. Nov. 11, 1773, by Dr. Belknap, Lydia Demeritt, both of Madbury, d. Mar. 5, 1838, aged 88, dau. of Ebenezer.

YOUNG, Stephen, of Barrington, d. 1826, aged 80, m. Apr. 4, 1775, by Dr. Belknap, Kezia Hanson, of Madbury, b. Dec. 27, 1757, dau. of Timothy.

YOUNG, Eleazer, m. Dec. 1, 1778, by Rev. Isaac Smith, Hannah Bayley.

YOUNG, Joseph, son of Capt. Thomas, m. Nov. 1791, by Rev. William Hooper, in Madbury, Sarah Pinkham, both of Dover.

YOUNG, Ephraim, d. Aug. 1825, m. near 1800, Diadana Coffin.

YOUNG, John, of Dover, son of William and Susanna, b. Dec. 12, 1776, d. Sept. 27, 1854, in Tuftonboro, m. (pub. Nov. 26, 1803, in Dover), Hannah Ham, b. Mar. 3, 1780, d. July 1, 1875.

YOUNG, Jonathan, m. (pub. May 19, 1804, in Portsmouth), Lucy Loud.

YOUNG, Josiah, m. Aug. 14, 1806, in Wakefield, by Rev. Asa Piper, Nancy Young, of Wakefield.

YOUNG, Thomas, of Wakefield, b. 1784, d. 1864, m. Dec. 23, 1813, by Rev. Joseph Haven, Mary Nute, b. Dec. 23, 1783, d. Jan. 9, 1861, dau. of Samuel[5].

YOUNG, John, m. Sept. 28, 1817, in Berwick, Me., Esther Hall, d. Oct. 10, 1873, aged 83.

YOUNG, Stephen F., son of Jonathan, b. 1806, d. Dec. 4, 1893, m. Nov. 11, 1824, by Rev. Thomas C. Upham, Lydia W. Main, of Strafford, b. 1802, d. Nov. 21, 1881.

YOUNG, Charles, of Dover, b. Nov. 22, 1799, d. Oct. 5, 1882, m. (1) Ruth -----, d. May 3, 1827, aged 28, m. (2) May 6, 1829, in Wakefield, Mary Ann Hanson, b. July 6, 1806, d. Apr. 23, 1885.

YOUNG, Benjamin, of Strafford, m. (pub. Feb. 14, 1826, in Farmington), Deborah Furber, of Farmington.

YOUNG, Jonathan, of Milton, son of Levi, d. Aug. 4, 1891, aged 86, m. July 27, 1830, by Rev. Nathaniel Berry, Alice Knox, of Alton.

YOUNG, Hollis, m. near 1835, Betsey A. Drew, b. Feb. 17, 1814, dau. of John.

YOUNG, Jonathan, of Barrington, son of Eleazer and Alice, b. Sept. 28, 1807, d. Aug. 1873, m. Sept. 20, 1835, by Rev. William Demeritt, Sophia Maria Ricker, of Madbury, b. 1815, d. 1889.

YOUNG, Capt. Joseph, Jr., d. Apr. 10, 1868, aged 57, m. int. July 23, 1837, in Dover, Caroline Spurlin, d. Feb. 22, 1890, aged 75, dau. of Thomas.

YOUNG, John B., son of Jonathan, b. Apr. 13, 1819, m. Jan. 19, 1845, by Rev. John Parkman, Mary Jane Buzzell, d. Jan. 27, 1886, aged 64, both of Barrington.

YOUNG, Moses C., son of Joseph, d. Feb. 9, 1890, aged 81, m. (pub. July 1, 1845, in Ossipee), Mary K. Tibbets, both of Ossipee.

YOUNG, Stephen E., of Barrington, son of Jonathan, d. Oct. 27, 1860, aged 37, m. (pub. Nov. 30, 1847, in Nashua), Mary Jane Drowne, of Nashua, dau. of Ezra.

YOUNG, William H., m. (1) Sarah -----, d. Mar. 22, 1848, aged 34, m. (2) Jan. 24, 1849, in Barrington, Sophia Locke Hall, d. Oct. 21, 1898, aged 70, dau. of Jacob.

YOUNG, Joseph H., of Lawrence, Mass., m. Mar. 6, 1850, in Newmarket, Abby H. Dame, of Lee.

YOUNG, William C., m. Sept. 20, 1852, in Madbury, Climena M. (Chesley) Meserve, wid. of George, d. July 25, 1855, aged 31, dau. of Paul.

YOUNG, Lt. Col. Andrew H., of Barrington, son of Aaron, b. June 16, 1827, d. Dec. 10, 1890, aged 63, m. May 12, 1853, by Rev. Alvin

Tobey, Susan E. Miles, of Madbury, b. Aug. 27, 1832, d. Nov. 15, 1915, aged 83, dau. of Tichenor.

YOUNG, Abiel, b. 1833, d. 1909, m. (pub. Feb. 14, 1854, in Haverhill, Mass.), Sarah E. Roles, d. Feb. 12, 1913, aged 80, both of Durham.

YOUNG, Moses N., d. Sept. 12, 1879, aged 40, m. Apr. 10, 1858, by Rev. Thomas J. Greenwood, Mary Jane Bolo, b. 1842, d. 1930, dau. of Rufus.

YOUNG, Moses F., m. Oct. 4, 1862, in Dover, Anna L. Varney.

YOUNG, Ezra D., m. Nov. 25, 1863, in Dover, Hattie M. Rogers.

YOUNG, Joseph, m. July 19, 1865, in Dover, Lizzie E. Spurlin.

YOUNG, James M., m. Nov. 28, 1865, by Rev. John Winkley, Sarah Thompson, both of Barrington.

YOUNG, Theodore L., m. Aug. 5, 1867, by Rev. Robert S. Stubbs, Anna McLin.

YOUNG, Jacob W., m. Oct. 12, 1867, by Rev. Robert S. Stubbs, Mrs. Betsey A. Harris.

YOUNG, Samuel, of Middleton, m. Jan. 4, 1874, in Middleton, Sarah M. Stevens.

INDEX

----, Abbie 56 Abigail 100 156
Adaline 189 Alice 27 Almira
211 Ann 149 Anna 24 Avis 1
Betsey 37 76 131 Caroline
198 Clara E 122 Deborah 11
119 Eleanor 3 Elizabeth 5 11
13-14 98 136 142 149-150
165 208 Emma 201 Eunice T
120 Hannah 24 33 35 94 104
145 152 165 171 213
Hannah H 197 Harriet D 13
Jane 24 Joanna 149 Johanna
149 Judith 94 Lois 81 Lucy A
188 Lucy S 191 Lydia 137
Maria 193 199 Martha 45
186 Mary 17 80 85 101 103
142 186 Mary Ann 183 Mary
C 83 Mary E 153 Mary H 198
Matilda 52 Mehitable 196
206 Nancy D 101 Olive 103
Olive C 207 Patience 185
Phebe 63 Polly 144 192
Rachel 98 211 Ruth 215
Sarah 165 184 215 Sarah A
25 105 Susan 4 115 202
Susan E 18 102 Susan H 139
ABBOTT, Anna 81 Betsey 103
Esther F 186 Olive L 158
ACKERMAN, Lydia J 103
ADAMS, Annie B 143 Elizabeth
21 Lois 149 Louise R 182
Martha 97 Orris E 53
Rosamond P 16 Sally 26

ADAMS (cont.)
Susan 16 Temperance P 110
AKERMAN, Rachel 10
ALLARD, Sally 55
ALLEN, ----- 203 Abigail 121
Deborah 65 Florence 99
Hannah 87 Harriet 33 Helen
40 Lauretta 37 Lizzie 91
Martha 127 Mary 53 108
Nancy 46 Nancy Mahaley 152
Olive 206 Sarah 197
ALVISIO, Ellen Teressa 138
ALVORD, Della P 73
AMBLER, Hannah 60 Mary 119
AMBROSE, Anna 134 Betsey
156 Cordelia N 41
AMES, Lydia 20 Lydia S 20
ANDERSON, Ann C 138
ANDREWS, Experience 53 Jane
M 6 Molly 92
APPLEBEE, Abra 158 213
Eunice A 150 Hannah 162
Sarah E 155 Sophia 102
ARLIN, Emily 170 Mary J 118
ASH, Judith 61
ASHTON, Elizabeth E 209
ASPINWALL, Melinda M 183
ATHERTON, Fanny 124
ATKINS, Abigail 86
ATKINSON, Charlotte King 40
Susan Sparhawk 125
AUSTIN, Caddie 102 Catharine
104 Keziah 113 Sarah 93 201
AVERILL, Sarah 181

AVERY, Bridget 60 Mary 35 Rebecca 73 Sally 136
AYER, Betsey 76
AYERS, Abbie K 18 Elizabeth 183 Emily 125 Jane 18 Lucy I 187 Mary S 164 Mattie E 7 Orinda 154 Temperance 115
BABB, Abigail 97 Alice 68 Betsey 68 153 Charlotte 5 Eleanor 117 Elizabeth 91 Etta C 118 Hannah 148 Lizzie S 125 Margaret 68 Maria 127 Mary 19 Mary A 121 Mary Esther 167 Sarah 158 Sarah J 74
BABCOCK, Abigail Stanton 13
BACON, Emily 66
BADGER, Hannah 143 Judith 36 144 185 Mary S 36
BAGLEY, Anna A 109
BAKER, Abby F 122 Adeline F 154 Eunice 152 Fannie E 5 Lois 5 Mary Ann 44 Mehitable 184
BALCH, Dolla K 26 Joanna 180 Martha 84
BALL, Maria 159
BALLARD, Abigail 81 Betsey 176 Lydia 6 Sarah 166
BAMFORD, Eleanor 63 Mary 94
BANCROFT, Sarah 180
BANKS, Julia M 72
BARBER, Maria D 170
BARKER, Louisa Ann 28
BARNES, Anne 88 Mary Elizabeth 66 Rebecca 14
BARTLETT, Anna M 114 Dorcas 36 Harriet 213 Mary 213 Mary D 47 Sally 126 Sally I 127 Sarah C 191 Susan F 157
BATCHELDER, Abigail 40 Deborah 13 Eunice 67 Hannah 39 59 Lorinda P 50 Olive 89

BATEMAN, Lizzie 111
BATES, Anna 38
BATSON, Sarah L 37
BATTLES, Mary 203
BAYLEY, Hannah 214
BEACHER, Fanny 5
BEAN, Jemmima 132 Lizzie A 117 Lydia 82 Mary 120 Olive 51 Ruth 93
BEARD, Esther 85 Mary 101
BEARDSLEE, Hannah M 208
BEDELL, Nancie C 83 Sarah F 202
BEEDE, Anna 197
BEEDLE, Mary Ann 154
BELL, Charlotte 202 Polly 173
BENN, Eliza A 198
BENNETT, Abigail 175 Cordelia A 154 Dolly 36 59 Eliza G 10 Elizabeth 209-210 Hannah C 36 Lydia A 67 Lydia Jane 151 Martha 83 Mary 11 42 204 213 Matilda A 208 Mehitable L 86 Ruth 29 126 Sarah 192 Sarah C 174
BERRY, Abigail 69 71 105 157 195 Abigail Ann 31 Anna 210 Carrie 28 Eliza 9 Elizabeth 24 Emma J 106 Jane 81 Jane M 131 Joan 82 Judith 19 Julia 138 Lucy Hannah 17 Lydia 5 Marcy 68 Margaret 10 Mary A 45 Mary Ann 107 Mary F 59 Mary Jane 209 Mehitable 18 Melissa Ann 18 Miriam 12 Nellie S 184 Rosanna 84 Sally 69 Sarah 95 129 Sarah A 8 Sarah M 161
BICKFORD, Abigail 145 Catharine W 174 Charlotte 141 Elizabeth 45 90 103 192 Esther F 39 Eveline 66 Hannah 44 202 213 Hannah J 131 Love 111 Lucia 44 Lucy 170 Lydia H 127 Martha

BICKFORD (cont.)
  9 Mary 12 93 151 163 Mary E
  5 19 Peggy 67 Sarah 12 159
  Sarah Ann 204 Susannah 9
BIGELOW, Susan 136
BILLINGS, Addie 175
BINGER, Emeline 71
BLAISDELL, Allie W 165 Betsey
  197 Ella J 83 Harriet I 13
  Lydia 39 Mary 115 Sarah
  Ann 198
BLAKE, Elizabeth 29 Hannah
  67-68 Laura A 181 Nancy
  136
BLANCHARD, Cynthia E 178
  Susan 55 Susan G 213
BLANE, Mary F H 88
BOARDMAN, Ruth A 31
BOBBOTT, Hannah 131
BODGE, Avis Jane 163 Betsey
  69 Lydia C 147 Sarah 134
BODWELL, Joanna 102 Molly
  161
BOICE, Lydia 145
BOLO, Mary Jane 216
BOLTER, Ida F 29
BOND, Ada J 191
BOODEY, Ariana E 71 Asenath
  Abigail 26 Hannah 199
  Martha 26 Martha Ann 212
  Mary S 95 Sarah 199
  Susanna M 101
BOOKER, Nellie 81
BORTON, Costilla 138
BOSTON, Milisse 162
BOURNE, Matilda T 60
BOUTWELL, Harriet N 21
BOWEN, Martha 36
BOYNTON, Nancy 167 Sally 86
BRACKETT, Eleanor 9 Elizabeth
  63 Emily W 6 Experience D
  78 Jennie 106 Martha 167
  Miriam 96 Sarah Cuthbert 83
BRADEEN, Sarah F 58
BRAGDON, Annie S 138 Betsey

BRAGDON (cont.)
  124 Electra J 81 Isabella 80
  Sarah 172
BRAGG, Elizabeth 113
BRANSCOMB, Helen M 1
BRAWN, Alice N 44 Mary 84
BREWSTER, Abigail 129 Eliza
  11 Maria P 212 Tamson 10
BRIERLEY, Frances W 167
BROCK, Betsey 86 Betsey D 10
  Caroline L 171 Drusilla 205
  Harriet A 161 Jane 42 Lavina
  171 Lizzie H 179 Lydia 33
  Lydia A 64 Marcia O 199
  Margaret 28
BROOKS, Anne 196 Caroline
  128 Letitia 158 Nellie 34
BROUGHTON, Persis B 163
BROWN, Abigail 134 195 Alice A
  127 Annie E 131 171 Betsey
  171 Eliza J 67 Eliza Jane 205
  Elizabeth 100 Etta 159
  Eugenia F 144 Grace E 93
  Hannah 38 Hannah S 91
  Irena 2 Judith 153 Lucy 72
  Lucy M 183 Lydia 21 Martha
  63 Mary 10 55 118 Mary S 90
  Matha Abiah 145 Melissa 157
  Olive A 174 Patience 155
  Patty 212 Peggy 6 Sabra 28
  Sally 75 154 Sarah 166
  Sarah L 177
BROWNE, Margaret 183
BROWNELL, Mary A 152
BRYANT, Isabella 19 Polly 112
BUCK, Sarah E 72
BUCKNELL, Mehitable 112
BUFFUM, Elizabeth 37
  Mehitable 196 Zerviah 197
BUNCE, Louisa 73
BUNKER, Anna 181 Deborah
  195 Hannah 10 Hannah J 71
  Lillis 104 Love 11 Martha A
  134 Mary 150 Mary Ann 70
  Mary Jane C 64 Mary M 62

BUNKER (cont.)
  Mehitable 78 Melvina A 96
  Prudence 62 Rebecca K 119
  Sarah Ann 176 Sophia 158
  Susan J 127
BURBANK, Mary 160
BURKE, Hannah J 40
BURLEIGH, Anna Hilton 32
  Dolly 23 Drusilla 147 Judith
  168 Lucy 101 Martha 187
  Mary 94 Melissa J 196 Sarah
  L 111
BURLEY, Augusta 150 Elizabeth
  30 Elizabeth J 74 Mary Jane
  137 Sally 114 Sarah 94
  Sarah L 111 Susan 41
BURNAM, Alice Ellen 41
BURNHAM, Deborah 206 Eliza
  42 Elizabeth 21 23 Hannah
  132 Mary 33 175 Mary E 79
  Sally 28
BURNS, Emeline 148
BURROWS, Abigail 139
  Charlotte Ann 139 Dolly 158
  Louise 40 Nelly 80
BUSBY, Sarah G 140
BUSS, Hannah 29
BUSWELL, Abigail 123 Betsy
  169 Lydia 134
BUTLER, Etta M 48 Martha A 93
  Mary 17 98 158 Ruth 36
  Sally 118 Sarah A 84
BUZZELL, Abigail 126 211
  Adaline M 92 Ann 181 Avis
  50 Celissa A 11 Dorothy 27
  Eliza 211 Esther N 61
  Frances R 5 Hannah 23
  Joanna 140 Lydia 22 158
  Mary 3 Mary A 179 Mary
  Jane 215 Mary S 193 Nancy
  171 173 Sakey 113 Sarah
  152 Susan 172
BUZZY, Catron 4
CADY, Salome C 91
CALDWELL, Deliverance 116

CALDWELL (cont.)
  Mary Jane 95
CAMPERNELL, Mae F 164
CANAVAN, Bridget 66
CANNEY, Abigail 158 Anne 147
  Delaime 55 Elizabeth 33
  Izetta 130 Laura Isabelle 65
  Lavinia 148 Lydia 98 Mary
  109 Sally 66 Sarah Abbie 210
CARBERRY, Mary 177
CARD, Abbie L 59 Abby F 38
  Abigail 35 149 Elizabeth F
  158 Maria 148 Sarah J 22
CARLE, Lizzie T 177
CARLETON, Clara A 203
CARLISLE, Hannah 19
CARLTON, Sarah 64
CARPENTER, Eliza 199 Fannie
  205
CARR, Anne 150 Caroline
  Peabody 112 Hannah 165
  Jemina 142 Mary 5 Sarah
  212
CARTER, Annie M 179 Betsey F
  167 Eliza J 14 Mary 44 Mary
  W 107 Sarah M 150
CARTLAND, Caroline 171 Ellen
  G 189 Emily Jane 126
  Hannah 50
CARY, Emma C 209
CASEY, Jane 194
CASWELL, Jennie 194 Mary 92
  Mary Burnham 172 Pauline S
  201
CATE, Abby Y 143 Abigail 129
  210 Hannah 51 Susanna 86
CATER, Amanda A 152 Mahala
  W 26
CATON, Sarah 59
CAVERLY, Abba A 26 Charlotte
  88 Clarissa 193 Comfort 16
  Elizabeth 33 Elizabeth O 71
  Florence E 9 Harriet Adeline
  195 Lydia 20 Lydia Ann 17
  Mary 145 Mary S 26 Polly

CAVERLY (cont.)
  144 Sally 195 Sally H 35
CAVERNO, Mercy F 151
CHADBOURNE, Abigail 194
  Hattie A 87 Sarah 15
CHADWICK, Sarah C 180
CHAMBERLAIN, Abby D 57 Ada
  B 180 Almira B 60 Clarissa
  143 Comfort 12 Dorothy 61
  Elizabeth Jane 42 102
  Experience 113 Mary E 123
  Rebecca 191 Sally 178
CHAMPION, Elizabeth A 153
  Olive A 102
CHANDLER, Dorothy 183
  Harriet B 76
CHANEY, Matilda 166
CHAPMAN, Bessie 96 Betsy 80
  Comfort 213 Eliza 176 Eliza F
  30 Etta E 95 Judith G 100
  Lizzie M 87 Lucy A 81 Mary
  35 Nancy 182 Olive 68 Polly
  213
CHASE, Abby D 168 Anne 4
  Annie L 73 Clara 141 Flavia
  59 Hannah 92 Harriet Louise
  65 Louisa H 82 Lydia 161
  Mary 89 Mary A 65 Mary C
  84 Mary R 53 Mary Yeaton 56
  Polly 204 Sarah 43
CHESLEY, Abigail F 19 Abigail
  H 211 Annette Elizabeth 35
  Augusta A 125 Calista A 208
  Climena 131 Climena M 215
  Deborah 188 Eliza A 213
  Elizabeth 108 181 Elizabeth
  A 130 Emeline S 126 Hannah
  22 85 143 145 187 Hannah F
  212 Laura A 158 Loretta
  Sullivan 8 Louisa J 30 103
  Lydia 21 207 Mary 17 26 85
  Mary Elizabeth 56 Nancy P
  50 Priscilla Adams 116
  Rosetta Marie 164 Sarah 60
  114 Sarah E 31 Sarah

CHESLEY (cont.)
  Elizabeth 140 Sarah J 102
  Sophia 205 Susannah 169
CHESWELL, Mehitable 175
CHICK, Abbie H 113 Anna 203
  Anne 74 Caroline M 112
  Cynthia 163 Delia P 107
  Elizabeth 121 Georgia B 135
  Mary 157 Nellie F 177 Statira
  134
CHOATE, Abby C 74
CHRISTENSON, Sarah 141
CHRISTIE, Emma J 96 Sarah J
  66
CHURCH, Abigail 210 Charity
  185 Eunice 63 Martha 1
  Prudence 188
CHURCHILL, Sarah E 174 Zelia
  124
CILLEY, Louisa M 188 Sally 58
CLANCY, Mary E 22 90
CLARK, Abigail 32 Ann 14 Anne
  88 Arabella M 122 Charlotte
  23 186 Deliverance 76 113
  Eliza Jane 20 Elizabeth 82
  114 196 Elizabeth C 161
  Eunice 84 Jane 73 Joanna
  112 Lois 195 Mary 40 43 50
  88 154 Mary Ann 70 Mary H
  196 Mary J 13 Mary Jane
  190 Meriah 204 Molly 65
  Nabby 138 Nancy 66 Polly 98
  Priscilla 203 Rebecca 211
  Ruth 170 S F 184 Sally 82
  Sarah 8 60 104 141 Sarah E
  165 Sukey 120 Susan 5
  Susan F 184 Susan W S 170
  Susannah 23
CLARKE, Ellen A 128 Mary 199
CLAY, Hannah 50 115 Jane 156
  Lydia 101 156 Martha 151
  Mary 168 Sally 33
CLEAVES, Carrie N 36
CLEMENT, Esther 102 Jennie P
  182

CLEMENTS, Anna 80 Arvilla S 210 Betsey 15 Elizabeth L 181 Lydia 15 Martha A 38 Mary 98 Sarah E 154
CLEVELAND, Mehitable 7
CLIFFORD, Annie A 144 Peace 7
CLOUGH, Betsey 67 Betsy 186 Hannah L 95 Judith 155 Louisa Victoria 20 Lovey 8 Mary P 211 Polly 186 Rebecca 35 Sarah E 200 Susan A 34
CLOUTMAN, Anna 125 Mary D 210 Sarah E 11 Sophia D 181
COBB, Ellen D 14
CODDINGTON, Mary 142
COE, Anne 10 Mary 85
COFFIN, Abigail 186 Deborah 170 Diadana 214 Hannah 87 Jane 133 Lydia 57 Nancy N 161
COGSWELL, Abigail 175 Judith 118 196 Polly 141 Sophia 43
COLBATH, Belinda E 32 Elizabeth 4 Elvira 187 Statira 32 Susan H 195
COLBEY, Elizabeth 76
COLBY, Hattie R 137 Louisa M 192 Rosamond W 195
COLCORD, Sarah H 26
COLE, Betsey 136 Clara A 142 Eleanor A 178 Eliza Ann 73 Eunice 102 Jane 92 114 Jerusha 178 Lydia 197 Maria D 6 Martha Jane 178 Mary E 150 Polly 65 Susannah 158
COLEMAN, Abby 182 Abigail 171 Belle 49 Emily 78 Mehitable 130
COLLINS, Jennie 114
COLOMY, Emily S 157
COMINGS, Carrie W 203
CONACKER, Hannah 80
CONANT, Abigail 196
CONNER, Amanda J 37 Dorothy

CONNER (cont.) 53 Elizabeth 52 Harriet 75 Judith 170 Mary 74
COOK, Anna E 113 Anna V 3 Clarissa P 54 Hannah 116 Hannah J 180 Lavina 139 Mary 152 Mary A 34 Mary E 159 Mary Eliza 178 Mary H 179 Mary S 89 Nancy 162 Nellie P 201 Penelope 8
COOMES, Abigail 4
COOPER, Eleanor 178 Esther A 80 Mary 194 Mary E 14 Nancy 84 Nancy J 77 Sarah Smith 27 Susan L 189
COPP, Caroline 28 Esther 74 Ida 182 L 177 Lucy 207 Polly 60 Sally 61 Sarah 80
CORLISS, Emily 152 Lydia J 109
CORSON, Caroline 28 Delia 202 Elizabeth 161 Ellen J 28 Hannah J 52 Harriet N 27 Mary L 47 Susan A 161
COTTON, Abby 187 Charlotte B 159 Eliza 41 Elizabeth 149 Melissa M 107 Nancy D 150 Salome A 38
COURSON, Mehitable 210
COUSENS, Mary E 127
COUSINS, Emily I 172
COWAN, Susan Ellen 170
COWELL, Maria 49 Sarah 108
COX, Henrietta 152 Lucy 160
CRAM, Abigail 184 Hannah 110 Mary 43 Polly 14
CRAWFORD, Hannah 120 Mary 120 Sally 44
CRITCHERSON, Mary A 155 Susan 124
CRITCHET, Abigail 17
CRITCHETT, Martha Susan 188
CROMMETT, Elizabeth 45 55 Margaret 57 Polly 111
CROMWELL, Elizabeth 29 Love

CROMWELL (cont.)
  12 Lucy 160 Sarah 27
CROOK, Nellie 203
CROSBY, Elizabeth 205 Lizzie W
  18 Sarah 111
CROWELL, Statira 46
CUMMINGS, Nettie G 194
CURRIER, Judith 59 184 Lydia
  47 Mary 97 Mary J 214
CURTIS, Harriet 3 Martha Ann
  137 Mary J 135
CUSHING, Caroline 93 Charlotte
  108 Eliza 13 Elizabeth
  Hanson 44 Hannah 208
CUSHMAN, Lizzie J 1 Louisa 38
CUTLER, Susan W 210
CUTT, Sarah 29
CUTTER, Sarah Ann 124
CUTTS, Elizabeth 44 Mary 152
DACY, Lydia A 110
DALTON, Hannah 136
DAME, Abby H 215 Adriana 171
  Alice 46 Anna 21 Betsey 42
  Eliza S 45 Elizabeth 207
  Hannah 129 Hannah L 105
  Hannah M 12 Josephine A
  174 Lois 163 Lydia A 139
  Mary Ann 84 Mary Helen 132
  Nancy 161 Sarah P 120
  Sophia 136 Sophronia 18
  Temperance 62
DAMON, Ann 76
DANA, Olive A 88
DANFORTH, Anne 166 Cornelia
  C 164 Mary 10
DANIEL, Ann 29
DANIELS, Abigail 22 Christine
  90 Eliza 14 Eliza J 34
  Elizabeth 135 Emma M 18
  Lovey 199 Maria S 97 Mary
  Ann 207 Mary J 162
  Mehitable 45 Rebecca 26
  Sarah 207 Susan 28
DANIELSON, Sally 16
DARLING, Sarah 94

DAVIS, Abigail D 190 193
  Adaline E P 95 Amanda M 36
  Ann M 81 Anna 45 Caroline
  179 Clara A 13 Clara E 164
  Deborah 188 Dorrinda M 204
  Eliza 105 Elizabeth 45 55
  Elizabeth S 34 Ellen R 182
  Elzira 3 Emily M 118 Emma
  38 Emma F 117 Gracie 95
  Hannah 89 Hannah J 83
  Hannah L 187 Hannah M
  169 Judith 13 Laura P 117
  Louisa 17 Louisa F 126
  Louisa J 189 Love 81
  Lucinda 98 Marianna 36
  Martha 99 Mary 31 93 Mary
  Ann 59 Mary E 127 177 Mary
  Elizabeth 47 Mary Jane 151
  Melissa F 100 Nancy 169
  Patty 180 Polly 163 Rhoda
  189 Rhoda O 204 Sally 13 16
  Sarah E 72 Sarah F 127
  Sarah J 46 Susan 147 Susan
  E 189 Susanna 57 Susannah
  108 Tryphena 167 Vienna M
  136
DAY, Mahala M 96 Melissa A 68
  Susan 147
DEAN, Elizabeth 104
DEARBORN, Anna 2 Annie M 84
  Charlotte M 78 Hannah P 42
  Lena 11 Mary 178 Sarah 115
DECATUR, Jennie N 211
DEERING, Martha H 164
DELAND, Leonora A 90
DELANEY, Hattie 96
DEMERITT, Anna 33 Betty 144
  Deborah 49 Eliza H 55
  Elizabeth A 90 Elizabeth B
  173 Emma E 189 Eunice 46
  Frances W 50 Hannah 29
  Hannah Y 49 Lois 49 Louisa
  W 76 Lydia 214 Lydia M 86
  Martha Abigail 47 Mary Jane
  20 Polly 29 Sally 153 Sarah

NEW HAMPSHIRE MARRIAGES SUPPLEMENT

DEMERITT (cont.)
   158 Sarah Ann 154 212
   Sophia 17 114 Sophia T 108
   Sukey 119 Susan 8 97
DENNETT, Catherine 64 Lydia
   153 171
DEXTER, Eliza A 1
DICEY, Abbie 107 Victoria E 204
DICKEY, Jemima 141 Lydia A
   67
DILL, Lucretia W 72
DIXON, Charlotte 109 Ellen M
   170 Hannah 155
DOCKHAM, Catharine 214
   Lydia Ann 52 Sarah 46
DOE, Deborah 75 Elizabeth 61
   211 Hannah 205 Mary A 202
   Mary E 97 Mehitable M 110
   Nancy 21 Sally G 209
DOICK, Mary I 59
DOLLIVER, Georgia A 34
DOLLOFF, Nancy L 17
DOOR, Elizabeth 64 Lydia 103
DORE, Adaline 19 Eunice 118
   Julia F 88 Livona 78 Lydia
   113 Sarah Jane 18 Sophia
   200
DORMAN, Carrie A 50
DORR, Mary E 121
DOTEN, Hannah 207
DOW, Annie 94 Elizabeth 180
   Elizabeth A 47 Hannah 132
   Helen A 123 Lizzie A 214
   Lydia 15 Mary 175 Mary Jane
   138 Olive 187 Sally 175
   Sukey C 62
DOWELL, Hattie M 148
DOWNES, Susan 147
DOWNING, Elizabeth 140
DOWNS, Abbie F 82 Abigail A
   176 Amanda 3 Ann 80 122
   Charlotte 122 Diadamia 122
   Elizabeth 75 122 Lavinia 71
   Love 5 Mary 53 Mary E 56
   204 Mercy 121 180 Olive 204

DOWNS (cont.)
   Polly 122 Rebecca 91 130
   Rebecca H 39 Sally 94 Sarah
   87 94 Sarah Ann 161 Sophia
   156
DREW, Abbie A 52 Abby J 25
   Anna 181 Betsey 206 Betsey
   A 215 Charlotte 195
   Charlotte B 93 Clarinda 56
   Elizabeth 111 116 161 176
   Elizabeth L 54 Ellen K 113
   Emma C 111 Evelina B 48
   Hannah 94 Helen A 150
   Isabella 19 Jane 68 Joanna
   114 Joanna H 191 Julia Ann
   107 182 Lavina 9 Lucinda 92
   Lucy Chesley 203 Lydia J
   207 Martha 199 Martha Ann
   150 Mary 15 75 Mary Ellen
   72 Melvina R 101 Nancy 65
   174 Patience 94 Rebecca 19
   Salina 156 Sally 209 Sara
   210 Sarah 192 Sarah Abigail
   47 Sarah L 175 Sophia 151
   Susan A 14
DRISCOLL, Sophia 158
DROWNE, Mary Jane 215
DUDLEY, Anna 144 168
   Dorothy 4 Hannah 135 Mary
   144 Sarah 104 166
DUNLAP, Martha T 196
DUNN, Elizabeth 45
DUNNELL, Hannah 3
DUNNELLS, Nancy 116
DUNNELS, Helen 8 Mary 211
DUNTLEY, Emily P 54 Mary 130
DURANT, Carrie S 148 Eliza 209
DURGIN, Annie M 156 Deborah
   12 Dolly 28 Elizabeth J 78
   Hannah 44 Hannah A 52
   Hannah F 138 Lydia 8 Lydia
   C 160 Mary A 191 Mary Frost
   213 Melissa A 93 Sophronia
   D 60 Susan P 114
DURRELL, Hannah 213 Lydia

DURRELL (cont.)
 Augusta 154 Rebecca P 9
DUTTON, Elizabeth 38
DYER, Emeline 57 Hannah 204
 Mary E 202 Thankful V 86
EARL, Lizzie M 88
EASTMAN, Eunice 66 Lydia Ann
 141 Mary F 194 Sally 185
EDGECOMB, Amelia 58
EDGERLY, Alice 151 Elizabeth
 91 108 Hannah 110 Lydia
 108 Molly 14 Polly 55 Sally
 59 104
EHLISHER, Sophia J 143
ELA, Edner 67 Hannah 190
ELKINS, Deborah 213 Hannah
 154 Kezia 62 Rebecca 19
 Sally 7
ELLIOT, Comfort 209 Hannah
 57 Nancy 188 Susan 130
ELLIOTT, Mary M 123
ELLIS, Abigail 198 Grace 166
 Mariah 61 Mary J 132
ELLISON, Anna 68 Lydia S 181
 Mehitable 53 Molly 52 Nancy
 52 Sarah 12 Sarah A 41
EMBRY, Sarah J 177
EMERSON, Abigail 21 Anna 15
 Annie E 23 Avis 23 Deborah
 50 Elizabeth 46 Ellen F 24
 Ellen Sophia 90 Hannah 76
 146 200 Huldah D 18 Lois
 146 Lydia Jane 119 Mary 176
 Mary Ann 47 Mary Jane 127
 Mary Ridgway 182 Nabby 49
 Sally 108 Sarah E 110
EMERY, Adeline 212 Elizabeth
 98 Hannah 79 Lizzie H 179
 Lydia A 179 Lydia Ann 58
 Melissa 168 Olive 2 Olive J
 111 Polly 118
ENGLAND, Martha J 72
ESTES, Hannah 173 Joanna 59
 Mary 162 Olive Ann 12-13
EVANS, Almira 5 Anna 4

EVANS (cont.)
 Elizabeth 43 Elizabeth D 25
 Fanny 199 Hannah 49 125
 Lydia 25 Mary J 103 Sally 25
 Sarah 22 Sarah Bell 152
 Susan M 17
EVERETT, Helen F 148
FABYAN, Olive 51
FAIRBANKS, Emma C 57
FALL, Abigail 176 Angeline 180
 Judith 82 Mary 162 Mary
 Ann 42 Mary E 27 Sarah F 81
FARNHAM, Hannah 149
 Lucinda J 22
FARRAR, Jettie 160
FARRELL, Jane 64
FAXON, Nellie N 72
FELCH, C 165
FELKER, Augusta Ann 72
 Elizabeth Hannah 71 Martha
 H 25 Rachel 197
FELLOWS, Hannah 207
FERGUSON, Mary 91 Shuah
 172
FERNALD, Abby 64 Hannah 122
 Joanna 147 Josie M 23
 Margaret 41 Mary 13 Nancy
 H 53 Sally 41 155 Sarah 19
 Sarah P 170
FIELD, Abigail 128 Elizabeth
 202
FIELDS, Maria 169 Mary Jane
 78 Nellie O 23
FIFE, Emma 56 Mary 67
FIFIELD, Hannah 175 Nabby
 133
FISH, Hannah 139
FISHER, Susanna 207
FITCH, Martha 129
FITTS, Dolly 17
FITZGERALD, Mary A 114
FLACK, Mary E 184
FLAGG, Abbie E 106 Nettie J
 202
FLANDERS, Eliza 150 Isabel A

FLANDERS (cont.)
  57 Mary Anna 72
FLETCHER, Joanna 42
FLORENCE, Elizabeth 61
FLOYD, Elizabeth Walton 86
FOGG, Elizabeth 190 Emma A 4
  Esther 114 Mary J 124
FOLLET, Abigail 206
FOLLETT, Abigail 103 Deborah
  118 Susannah 12
FOLSOM, Anna 7 Betty 190
  Elaine 77 Elizabeth 7 17 29
  Hannah 125 145 Jemima 137
  Joanna 30 Lydia 168
  Margaret Friend 7 Mary 208
  Mehitable 103 Molly 64
FOOTE, Nellie J 158
FOOTMAN, Susanna 197
FORD, Amanda M 128 Caroline
  54 Flora E 140 Sarah 137
FOSS, Abigail 192 Alice J 152
  Almira N 198 Anna 181
  Betsey 144 Betsey C 92
  Betsey M 25 Caroline E 36
  Clarissa Ann 89 Eleanor 182
  Eliza 69 Eliza A 198 Eliza
  Jane 97 Emily A 22 Emma
  130 Emma F 182 Hannah 6
  70 Hannah Jane 203 Hannah
  S 173 Harriet 70 Harriet L
  163 Jane 10 Lorinia N 173
  Lucy Y 188 Lydia 70 Lydia D
  70 Martha M 92 Mary 10 197
  Mary A 144 Mary R 178
  Nancy L 148 Olive Ann 177
  Rebecca 83 155 Sally 197
  Samson 69 Sarah 69 132
  Sarah A 71 95 Sarah E 7
  Sarah F 28 Sarah M 36 Sena
  39
FOSTER, Frances Ellen 205
  Hannah 36 Sarah 190
FOWLER, Mary 51
FOX, Sally T 91 Susan 12 Susan
  M 106

FOYE, Addie S 126 Louisa 108
  Sarah 195 Sarah A 206
FRANCIS, Elizabeth B 15
FREEMAN, Abby 178 Betsey
  157 Emma D 206 Mary O 1
FREESE, Rachel 206
FRENCH, Adaline 182 Betty 34
  Elizabeth B 136 Hannah 23
  Jane C 54 Katharine 176
  Lavina 26 Lizzie J 73 Lucy A
  132 Lucy Maria 72 Mary 4 62
  Mary J 130 Mary Jane 182
  Mary M 168 Mehitable 32
  Olive 119 Polly 112 Priscilla
  S 3 Sally 184
FROST, Carrie A 72 Dorothy 106
  Eliza 135 Emma 205 Jane 16
  Louisa 88 Lydia A 90
  Margaret 100 Mary 160 Mary
  S 150 Mehitable S 129 Polly
  122 Sarah 9 29 Tampson 212
FRYE, Abigail 128 Gertrude 206
  Matilda J 156 Ruth 104
FULLER, Caroline E 97
FULLERTON, Ann C 134
  Elizabeth 57
FURBER, Betsey 127 Deborah
  215 Elizabeth 11 44
  Elizabeth A 122 Hannah 7
  Hannah M 189 Lavina 17
  Mary M 6 Sarah 192
FURBISH, Sarah Ann 2 Sarah F
  31
FURBUSH, Sarah 136
GAGE, Carrie C 156 Lydia 43
  Maria A 163 Sarah 66 Sarah
  Jane 39
GALE, Hannah 35 Martha A 77
  Mary 156 Mary S 77 Sally 4
  Shuah 155 Susannah 189
GALLAGER, Margaret 164
GAMBLE, Mary 11
GANNET, Sarah 202
GARLAND, Dorcas 53 Elizabeth
  43 Elizabeth Ann 24

GARLAND (cont.)
  Elizabeth H 159 Elizabeth J
  108 Lydia 201 Polly 115
  Sarah A 111
GARMON, Olive 57
GARVIN, Sally 155
GEAR, Abigail 187 Emily F 23
  Mary Ann 14 Olive 177
GEORGE, Abby S 31 Hannah R
  173
GERALD, Lizzie M 208
GERRISH, Anabel 11 Eleanor
  172 Elizabeth 12 Hannah 46
  Lucy 165 Margery 88 Mary
  121 Mary A 98 Mary D 124
  Mary Morrill 211 Sarah 130
GETCHELL, Dolly 89 Jennie A
  112 Martha A 152 Mary 73
GILBERT, Mary E 132
GILE, Jane 91 Lydia Ann 85
GILES, Isabella F 97 Lois 6
  Maria 187
GILL, Susanna 111
GILMAN, Abigail 46 Alice 76 175
  Anna 61 Annette 201 Apphia
  123 Betsy 77 141 Betty 60
  135 Bridget 85 Dolly 78
  Elizabeth 34 Ella 180 Emma
  38 Hannah 2 111 190
  Hannah J 17 Joanna 144
  Judith 157 Lydia 8 Mary 111
  155 172 Mary M 193 Mary T
  78 Molly 57 Polly 77 85
  Rebecca 142 Sally 36 134
  Sarah 35 52 Sarah Phillips
  185 Susan 77
GILMORE, Emily 46 Mary S 73
GILPATRICK, Sarah Ellen 51
GLASS, Elizabeth 31 Lois D 200
GLEASON, Frances Jane 134
  Mary 52 Molly 52
GLIDDEN, Drusilla 45 Elma P
  81 Jerusha 176 Lydia 20 61
  Lydia S 20 Mary 73 135 168
  Mary A 45 Mary W 133

GLIDDEN (cont.)
  Meriam 175 Phebe 174
  Susanna 78
GLINES, Corisand S 159 Mary A
  182
GLOVER, Caroline 123-124
  Eliza 73 Lucinda 34 Polly 114
  Sarah F 42
GOLDSMITH, Mary A 139
GOOCH, Elizabeth 32
GOODALE, Mary A 166
GOODALL, Almira N 71
GOODRICH, Lydia D 208
GOODWIN, Abby J 148 Abigail
  84 Aline C 100 Ann 133
  Betsey 163 Caroline 117
  Eliza A 81 Elizabeth 82 Eva F
  122 Hannah 44 Hattie S 91
  Isabel 159 Leah Helen 51
  Margaret 96 Maria 150
  Martha 196 Martha J 93
  Mehitable 79 139 Molly 3
  Myra 143 Olive 18 82 91
  Olivia Jane 141 Paulina 35
  Pheobe S 102 Polly 118
  Rhoda 54 Susan 139
GORDON, Anna 19 Frances 199
GOSS, Abigail 17 Delia H 62
GOULD, Anna H 73 Bethiah 31
  Elizabeth 128 Julia A 72
  Laura 179
GOVE, Mary Page 24
GOWEL, Dorcas 212
GOWELL, Elizabeth 37 Emma
  183 Lydia 88
GOWEN, Helen E 80
GRANT, Emily O 62 Emma J
  131 Esther 73 Martha A 42
  Rebecca 129 Sarah 78 Sarah
  O 7 Theodosha 126
GRANVILLE, Eliza J 22
GRAY, Betsey 202 Ellen J 5
  Maria L 169 Martha F 146
  Mary Jane 141 Mary W 183
  Polly 82 Sarah 189 Sarah E D

GRAY (cont.)
  58
GREELEY, Betsy 22 Deborah 59
  Nancy 22
GREEN, Mary A 145 S---- 118
GREENOUGH, Sally 145
GRIFFIN, Emma A 206 Hannah
  J 188 Nancy 188
GRIFFITH, Mary Ann 2
GROVER, Henrietta 103 Mahala
  Jane 40 Martha Murray 75
  Mary 86
GROVESNOR, Lucy 115
GUNNISON, Polly 7
GUPPEY, Abigail 44
GUPTILL, Alice 119 Annie D 95
  Hannah 194 Lydia 167
  Martha 186 Mary 79 Nabby
  85 Nancy 140 Sally 94 194
  Sarah 74
HAGGINS, Mary 148
HAINES, Abbie 14 Abigail 58
  Angelissa 166 Hannah 61 93
  Sally 79
HALE, Caroline 191 Elizabeth
  112 187 Elizabeth White 112
  Mary Ann 124 Mary Elizabeth
  191
HALEY, Abby A 7 Betsey 164
  Martha 167 Mary Ann 159
HALL, Abby F 96 Abigail 9
  Abigail G 91 Betsey 22
  Charity 85 Deborah Jane C
  89 Elizabeth 160 Ellen A 178
  Ellen P 86 Esther 196 215
  Georgio A 16 Hannah 94
  Jennie M 208 Joanna 15
  Lorinda N 213 Lucinda 86
  Maribah 14 Mary Augusta 86
  Mindwell A 55 Nancy 176
  Patience 15 Sally 43 58 146
  Sarah 9 Sarah A F 18 Sophia
  67 Sophia Locke 215
HAM, Abigail 107 130 149
  Almira 186 Aramantha E 88

HAM (cont.)
  Betsey 157 Deborah 143 190
  Eleanor 64 Eleanor A 57
  Eliza 21 Elizabeth 87 Ellen A
  65 Hannah 122 214 Joanna
  107 Lucy 183 Lydia 145 151
  Margaret 86 Margaret J 156
  Maria M 191 Mary 66 214
  Mary E 106 141 Nabby 51
  Patience 151 Phebe H 146
  Phebe L 16 Rebecca 23
  Rosalie A 22 Susan M 56
  Susanna 153 199
HAMILTON, Betsey 32 Hannah
  24 Mary 27 Sarah 189 Sarah
  W 135
HAMLIN, Caroline W 75
HAMMETT, Abigail 4 Lizzie P 6
HAMMON, Patience T 88
HAMPSEN, Ellen 99
HANKS, Bell 14
HANNAFORD, Sally 152
HANSCOM, Deborah 213
  Emeline S 205 Katharine 27
  Mehitable C 163 Polly 206
  Sarah 145
HANSCOMB, Love 209
HANSON, Abbie P 7 Caroline
  137 Christine H 58 Cordelia
  134 Dorcas 123 Eliza 88-90
  Elizabeth 37 194 Elvira R 177
  Emma F 55 Hannah 43 190
  193 Ida S 26 Irene F 31 Kezia
  214 Lydia 169 196 Margaret
  89 145 Maria A 31 Martha A
  116 Mary 32 45 62 100 128
  Mary A 56 Mary Ann 190 215
  Mary Dame 64 Mary J C 45
  Mary S 103 Mehitable 87
  Miriam S 159 Nancy G 184
  Nancy H 96 Orissa O 14
  Pamelia 6 Patience 32 199
  Rebecca 74 Ruth 98 Sarah
  140 Sarah A 137 Sarah E 129
  Susan 90 Susan F 135

HANSON (cont.)
 Susanna 113 Viannah M 123
HARDISON, Emma D 109
HARDY, Elizabeth 118
HARFORD, Elizabeth 124
HARMON, Louise D 65 Nancy J
 52 Susan M 158
HARRIS, Betsey A 216 Rebecca
 205
HART, Ann E 96 Elmira 30
 Lydia A 159 Mary 120 Sarah
 R 195
HARTFORD, Bridget 147 Ellen F
 63 Jennie B 50 Keziah 92
 Patience 179 Sarah 92
HARTY, Rebecca 87
HARVEY, Hannah Frank 47
 Sarah E 194
HASELL, Caroline H 2
HASEY, Sally 95
HASK, Catharine 38
HASTY, Laura 96
HATCH, Abigail F 116 Huldah
 165 Mary J 3 Submit B 190
HAVEN, Ruth 1 Sarah F 81
HAWKINS, Betsey 19 Betsey B
 71 Betsey M 210 Eliza Jane
 105 Nancy M 132 Nellie M
 179
HAYES, Abigail 170 Abra 68
 Anna 196 Carrie J 88
 Clarissa 39 Elizabeth 59 68-
 69 162 Elizabeth Lucy 25
 Elizabeth M 175 Ellen G 73
 Evengline 121 Freelove J 16
 Hannah 40 Leonora L 182
 Lizzie K 85 Lydia R 26
 Mahala W 26 Mahalia 91
 Martha 70 Mary 10 Mary
 Ham 198 Mary Jane 205
 Mehitable 87 Nancy P 214
 Polly 10 Sally 129 Sarah 9 49
 103 110 Sarah C 3 10 Sarah
 E 1 Sarah Ellen 38 Sophia
 Elizabeth 80 Susan R 41

HAYES (cont.)
 Tamson 92 Tamson M 163
HAYMAN, Olive 3
HEAD, Nabby 34
HEARD, Abigail 100 199 Dorcas
 63 191 Elizabeth 175
 Hannah 98 Jane 36 Joanna
 179 Judith 64 Lydia 165
 Mary 15 26 Phebe 139 Sarah
 140
HEATH, Martha 58 Nancy D 166
HENDERSON, Delia A 137
 Elizabeth 119 Ellen 169
 Margaret E 150 Mary E 45
 Susan 131 Susan M 25
HERRING, Mary E 52
HERSEY, Clarissa H 77 Drusilla
 C 72 Frances A 93 Hannah R
 126 Nancy M 60
HERSOM, Lucretia 187
HEWITT, Merriam 68 Susan 181
HICKS, Deborah 190 Elizabeth
 110 Martha 201
HIGGINS, Elizabeth 143 Sally G
 14
HIGHT, Mary 155
HILL, Abby A 131 Abigail 103
 Betsey Horney 125 Catharine
 69 Charlotte 114 Darinda A 6
 Eleanor 81 Eliza A 95
 Elizabeth 80 Etta C 148
 Eunice 52 Frances M 162
 Hannah 14 42 Hannah A 100
 Hannah Abbie 101 Hannah
 W 53 Huldah 169 Judith 69
 113 Julia E 129 Lydia 86
 Lydia Gove 54 Mary 29 50
 146 Mary Ellen 34 Mary
 Margaret 185 Mary
 Underwood 65 Olive 90 Polly
 157 185 Roxanna A 68 Ruth
 M 46 Sally 173 193 Sarah 32
 202 Sarah E 161 Sarah F 102
HILLER, Emma J 131
HILLIARD, Anna 67 Rachel 180

HILTON, Abigail 95 Elizabeth 201 Lovey 150 Mary G 167 Sarah 76 Susan L 19 Syrena O 10
HINKSON, Abigail 133 Phebe 78
HINMAN, Sylvinia J 15
HITCHCOCK, Jane A 200
HOAG, Lydia 8 Phebe 104
HOBBS, ----- 141 Abbie 61 Abigail 41 Mary A 40
HODGDON, Abby H 77 Abigail 75 101 187 Ann W 186 Anne 88 Elizabeth 12 162 202 Hannah L 149 Jennie E 198 Kezia 80 Lydia 21 Martha 113 Mary 138 Mary Ann 147 Nellie J 194 Patience C 105 Priscilla 203 Rebecca G 158 Sarah 68 Sarah M 131 Tamsin 40
HODGKINS, Henrietta 36
HODSDON, Mary 81
HODSON, Olive 122
HOITT, Alvina A 146 B A 107 Judith 21 Lydia 92 Maggie I 201 Martha A 148 Martha J 67 Mary E 33 Mercy J 30
HOLBROOK, Hattie H T 61
HOLDEN, Elizabeth 208 Jane A 107
HOLEY, Alice 184
HOLLAND, Rebecca 200
HOLMES, Eleanor 43 Mary 32 Sally L 4 Sarah 32 Sarah E 106 Shuah 82
HOLT, Lucy A 11
HOOK, Sarah 75
HOOPER, Fanny M 97 Jennie H 206 Julia M 30 Mary 160 Sally 29
HOPE, Mary 15 Susan A 57
HOPKINSON, Lydia 174
HORN, Alice 110 Alice W 151 Angeline 177 Camilla A 99 Eleanor 205 Josephine A 27

HORN (cont.) Judith 22 Lydia J 16 Patience 69
HORNE, Abra 40 Camela 37 Charlotte W 140 Eleanor 111 Elizabeth 38 89 Ella J 61 Fanny H 72 Hannah 167 Harriet 33 Lucy 82 Lydia 133 Martha J 179 Mary 87 Mary E 201 Mehitable 87 Mercy 67 Olive 99 Ruth 118 Sarah 39 Sarah E 119 Sophia 123 Susanna Y 87
HORSUM, Hannah 73
HOSMER, Mary A 92
HOWARD, Deborah H 193 Elizabeth Ann 166 Emma A 145 Mahala 193 Sarah 89 Sarah E 100
HOWE, Abby 53 Almira C 83 Charlotte 13 Julia A J 161 Lucy J 98 Sarah 112
HOY, Agnes 14
HUBBARD, Abigail 79 Catherine 169 Comfort 203 Harriet A 64 Jemima 130 Mary 63 Mary Elizabeth 174
HUCKINS, Abigail 157 Ellen J 135 Hannah 153 Josephine 204 Lucy C 27 Margery 153 Martha Jane 211 Mary 181 Molly 15 Olive 119 Sally 46 Welthean 178
HUGGINS, Polly 38
HUGHES, Catherine 42
HULL, Abigail 100 Love 29
HUNKIN, Mary 115
HUNTOON, Cynthia A 24
HUNTRESS, Margaret 135 Phebe Ann 134 Susanna Thompson 51
HURD, Alma L 52 Emma J 11 Georgie H 107 Laura A 157 Mary 121 Mary F 129 Olive A 152 Roxanna B 179 Sarah 82

HUSSEY, Adelaid 5 Amanda M 25 Anna 210 Annie L 171 Eliza W 11 Elizabeth Jane 42 Emily C 66 Hannah 52 196 Hulda 142 Lavina S 119 Martha F 37 Mary 192 Mercy 129 Nellie A 204 Rosanna A 102 Ruth 197 Sarah E 87
HUTCHINS, Laura E 203 Lois C 14 Lucy A 29 Nellie D 201 Phymelia A 156
HUTCHINSON, Betsy 156 Emma T 120 Hannah 66 Harriet M 90 Joanna 104 Susanna 15 Theodate 138
HYDE, Frances A 204
INGRAHAM, Fannie M 146
IRVIN, Mary 211
JACKSON, Abby T 105 Abigail 115 Emma L 97 Hannah 115 Lydia 103 133 Martha 92 Mary 115 Viola 65
JACOBS, Mary T 100 Nancy 123 180
JAMES, Anne 132 Elizabeth S 144 Ellen M 185 Lizzie J 90 Ruth 25
JAMESON, S A 48
JASPER, Fannie 50
JEFFERS, Lydia 140
JELLISON, Molly 136 Sarah 84
JENKINS, Catherine 141 Elizabeth 196 Hannah 140 Hannah M 114 Keziah 83 Sarah Jane 30
JENNESS, Hannah 120 Josephine S 76 Lucy 153 Lydia M 196 Mary 153 Mary V 189 Patience 12 Patience S 114 Sarah B 208 Sarah J 147
JEROLD, Ellen S 118
JEWETT, Addie 156 Eliza G 40 Eliza S 106 Lydia M 44 Nancy R 174 Sarah 150
JOHNSON, Abbie M 110 Anna

JOHNSON (cont.) M 129 Catherine 107 Ellen B 163 Elvira 18 Elvira A 48 Mary E 166 Molly 178 Sally 181 Sarah 139
JOICE, Mary L 57
JONES, Alice Ann 207 Ann 149 Betsey 176 Charlotte Cushing 1 Comfort 117 Eliza J 151 Eliza W 70 Elizabeth 109 113 Elizabeth E 46 Ella Adelia 66 Emily J 144 Eunice 82 Hannah 51 179 Hannah T 116 Henrietta 199 Lucinda 143 Lydia 101 124 Lydia Mcduffee 163 Martha A 22 93 Mary 8 39 51 190 Mary E 198 Mary Howard 145 Mary Susan 151 Mehitable 210 Sally 77 126 152 Sarah 88 189 Sarah A 97 Sarah H 206 Sarah J 52 Sarah M 97 Sophia G 69 Suky 82 Susan A 205
JORDAN, Adelia A 164 Ida E 18 Jane 172 Louisa S 175 Mary Eliza 91
JOY, Eliza H 131 201 Emeline L 185 Fanny A 50 Mary 176 Mary Ann 167 Mary S 5 Polly 147 Sally 144 Sarah 211 Sarah E 83 Susanna 52 128
JUDKINS, Dorcas 2 Nancy 121
KEAY, Lydia 121 Nettie 186 Sarah 88
KEITH, Mary E 214
KELLEY, Abigail 186 Adaline 112 Anne 49 Deborah 166 Diana 53 Eunice 36 Hannah 87 Lois 46 Mary 46 77 Mary J 60 Nancy 17 Sally 134 168 184
KELLY, Anna 33 Elizabeth 173 Lucretia 198
KELSEY, Eliza 138 Jane 188

KELSEY (cont.)
  Sukey 188
KENDALL, Hattie C 131 Nancy J
  133 Phebe F 105
KENISON, Harriet A 47
KENISTON, Rhoda 200
KENNARD, Hannah 203
KENNEY, Julia E 61
KENNISON, Lois E 18 Polly 111
KENNISTON, Elizabeth 136
  Hannah 58 116 Lydia 214
  Sally 111 Sarah E 79
KENT, Eliza 126 Elizabeth 11 33
  Hannah 115 Mary 52 60
  Polly 157
KERBY, Anna 194
KEYES, Eliza J 174
KIDDER, Lizzie 22
KIELLEY, Frances 116
KILLEY, Lydia 147
KIMBALL, Dorothy 59 Ella E 36
  Ellen A 164 Hannah L 64
  Joanna 123 Lydia 53 Mary
  129 134 Sally 123 Sarah E
  166 Sarah W 177 Susanna
  112 Tryphina 42
KING, Patience 214
KINGSBURY, Nancy 42
KINSMAN, Mary 16
KITTREDGE, Abby W 204
KNAPP, Martha Knight 6
KNIGHT, Debbey 128 Deborah 1
  Kezia 153 Lois 111 Lydia 179
  Nancy C 76 Rebecca F 76
  Rosamond 29
KNIGHTS, Mary A 78
KNOWLES, Abbie D 155 Abigail
  37 Elizabeth Jane 169 Mary
  114
KNOX, Adah 76 Alice 215
  Catherine L 153 Lydia 79
  Lydia A 60 Mercy 121 Nancy
  D 199 Rosella 139 Sarah 75
LADD, Betsey 165 Lucinda 210
  Mehitable 145 Sophia 122

LAKE, Elizabeth 100
LAMOS, Betsey 79 Deliverance
  128 Esther 34 Mary A 79
  Phebe T 210 Polly 34 Sarah
  189
LAMPER, Lucy 190
LAMPREY, Hannah 114 Nancy
  172
LANDLEY, Mary Ann 45
LANE, Charlotte 115 Eliza A 1
  Henrietta C 25 Mary Ann 115
LANG, Abbie M 204 Deliverance
  149 Martha 200
LANGDON, Martha 183 Sarah
  197
LANGLEY, Abigail 207 Betsey
  Jane 122 Delia F 206
  Elizabeth 213 Ellen M 3
  Esther 12 Hannah 12 Keziah
  46 Maria Jane 210 Martha A
  178 Mary 205 Mary Ann 21
  Sadie A 37 Sally 14 23 Sarah
  62 Sarah L 194 Sarah R 99
LANGMAID, Susan 113
LAPISH, Mehitable 24
LAPSLEY, Ann J 172
LAWRENCE, Eliza 147
LEACH, Augusta 199
LEAR, Martha Ann 137
LEATHERS, Abigail 49 Lydia
  177 Martha 68 Sarah 79
LEAVITT, Ann M 185 J Abbie 53
  Lydia 32 Mattie E 119
LEE, Clarissa 50 Hannah 180
  Joanna 183 Mary Ann 152
LEGG, Sarah A 153
LEGRO, Ann 122 Julia Ann 119
LEIGH, Sabra 79
LEIGHTON, Abbie M 84 Augusta
  3 Belinda O 113 Clara B 156
  Eliza C 141 Elizabeth 29 159
  Fannie 164 Hannah 85
  Hannah E 120 Jennie 38
  Lucinda T 6 Lydia 164 Mary
  157 Mary M 60 Olive J 75

LEIGHTON (cont.)
  Patience M 33 Phebe 57
  Rhoda A 121 Sarah 4 32 165
  Sarah C 2 Sarah Jane 70
  Susanna 55
LELAND, Harriet E 48
LEONARD, Deborah 79
LESLIE, Hannah F 144
LEWIS, Lydia J 30 Sarah
  Carpenter 129
LIBBEY, Abigail 13 Adah 9 Alice
  I 81 Belinda 134 Eleanor 115
  Fanny C 83 Lydia 26 Martha
  S 25 Mary 113 155 Mary Ann
  16 Mehitable 92 Molly 212
  Olive Esther 2 Phebe P 128
  Rachael A 27 Rhoda B 204
  Sally 41 Sarah M 85
  Susannah 23
LINSCOTT, Rebecca 84
LITTLE, Eliza 172 Mary 206
  Sarah 152
LITTLEFIELD, Annie H 191 Jane
  92 Louisa 99
LOCK, Margaret Ann 20 Mary A
  117 Mary F E 34 Prudence 4
LOCKE, Abigail P 97 Alice 49
  Caroline H 199 Carrie J 73
  Emeline 75 Hannah 9
  Mehitable B 20 Meribah 4
  Sarah B 120 Sarah E 187
  Sarah H 135 Vienna O 95
LOCKETT, Minnie 140
LOMBARD, Mary A 90
LONG, Catherine 36 Electra J
  34 Emily 60
LORD, Amy 200 Anna 64
  Elizabeth 32 106 Emily 198
  Georgio A 16 87 Hannah 22
  31 Hattie M 214 Lizzie F 204
  Lydia 41 Martha 31 108 153
  Mary 100 161 Phebe 196
  Polly 122 Rebecca 54 Sally 80
  Sarah 32 80 Susan 28
LOUD, Lucy 214

LOUGEE, Charlotte 167 Eliza B
  55 Jennie M 113 Lydia 155
  Molly 180 Nancy 180 Sally
  142 Sarah M 61
LOUGER, Sally 142
LOVERING, Anna M 45
LOW, Lydia H 84
LOWE, Martha Hale 73
LOWELL, Mary L 99
LUCAS, Hannah F 40 Mary M
  79 Sarah J 74
LUCY, Mary E 26 Sally 75
LUNT, Mary 8
LYFORD, Almira 151 Betsey 102
  Eunice 113
LYMAN, Lovey 170
LYTLE, Maggie H 155
MACK, Elizabeth C 49 Ellen 94
  Isabelle A 59 Roena Chick
  117
MADDOX, Hannah S 99 Julia A
  116
MAIN, Elizabeth 43 Lydia 205
  Lydia W 215 Mary 139
MALEHAM, Susan 169
MANCER, Mary E 28
MANNING, Caroline 104 Sarah
  Ann 87
MARCH, Eliza W 6 Elizabeth
  150
MARDEN, Judith 71 Olive 192
  Olivia B 191 Susan 29
MARKS, Marilla 102
MARSH, Betsey 123 Hannah E
  142
MARSTON, Jennie S 125
MARTIN, Addie E 43 Elizabeth L
  141 Hepzibath 13 Molly 98
MASON, Charlotte W 18
  Deborah 35 Eliza D 99 Mary
  196
MATHES, Ann 33 Elizabeth 33
  Elizabeth C 7 Ella M 135
  Frances 126 Judith Matilda
  146 Martha Ann 56 Ruth 182

MATHES (cont.)
    Sally 8 Sarah Ida B 43
MATHEWS, Elizabeth C 6
    Martha A 155
MATTHEWS, Martha 177 Ruth
    94
MAXFIELD, Betty 53
MAXWELL, Martha L 50
MCCANN, Lucy E 95
MCCARREL, Abigail 138 Rachel
    155
MCCHARLES, Annie 121
MCCOY, Huldah 166 Margery
    118
MCCRILLIS, Mary 49
MCDANIEL, Irena 83 Polly 21
MCDANIELS, Susan J 40
MCDUFFEE, Ellen L 4 Lydia 44
    Martha A 179 Mary 112 164
    Nancy 153 Sally 30
MCGOOCH, Elizabeth 202
MCGOUGH, Mary 20
MCGROTY, Josephine 214
MCINTIRE, Mary 188
MCLIN, Anna 216
MCNEAL, Mary 67 Susannah 9
MEADER, Hannah 162 Hannah
    D 209 Love 35 Mary E 6
    Nellie 87 Sarah F 5
MEGAN, Catherine 136
MELCHER, Esther 103
MERRILL, Annie S 178 Cora E
    57 Elizabeth 21 Frances
    Marion 71 Hannah L 149
    Hephzibah H 92 Lizzie S 64
    Mary E 157 Miranda O 76
MERROW, Elizabeth A 103
    Lovina Elizabeth 208 Maria
    130
MERSERVE, Lois G 55
MESERVE, Abigail 194 Carrie F
    194 Climena M 215 Eunice
    46 Louisa F 46 Mary Jane 30
    Polly 126 Sarah Ann 49
MIDDLETON, Mary Jane 181

MILES, Eliza H 201 Mary Ann
    149 Sarah F 105 Susan E
    216
MILLER, Abby 174 Abigail 165
    Joyce 13 Judith Abbie 117
    Sarah E 136 Susan 3
MILLS, Deborah 150 Polly 75
    Shore 40 Susan Jane 56
MITCHELL, Lizzie 183 Peggy 12
MIX, Julia A 34
MONTGOMERY, Emily A 145
    Susan 119 Tamson H 50
MOODY, Betsey 7 Dolly 133
    Hannah 203 Maria E 96 Mary
    27 109 Mary H 154 Mehitable
    108 206 Sarah 130
MOONEY, Mary Jane 58
MOORE, Abigail 198 Agnes 168
    Augusta S 133 Elizabeth 190
    Emma S 139 Hannah E 158
    Jane E 134 Lucy 189 Polly
    138 Sarah A 125
MOOTREY, Mary 77
MORDOUGH, Susan A 20
MORGAN, Betsey 93 Mary 189
    Nancy 143 Sarah C 52 Sarah
    F 84
MORRILL, Hannah 141 Molly
    175 Rachel W 125 Sally 166
    Sarah 84 Sarah Jane 20
    Sarah M 184
MORRIS, Amanda C 32 Rachael
    61
MORRISON, Addie 95 Betsey
    152 Hannah E 48 Sarah M
    43
MORSE, Annie M 15 Betsey 77
    Eliza 66
MORTON, Elizabeth 61
MOSES, Abigail 134 Elizabeth
    135 Jenny 169 Mary 131
    Sarah Ann 199
MOSLEY, Ann E 190
MOTT, Lizzie C 122
MOULTON, Abby J 22 Abra 59

MOULTON (cont.)
  Alta A 75 Betsey 156
  Catherine L 140 Dolly B 160
  Dorothy S 39 Elizabeth 189
  Hannah 7 172 Lucy 189
  Margaret F 9 Mary Fogg 126
  Mary Jane 1 Molly 134 Nancy
  C 16 Nancy E 135 Nellie L
  112 Polly 101 Sarah A 64
MUDGE, ----- 129
MUDGETT, Hannah 101 Mary
  34
MUGRIDGE, Lizzie M 63
MULLEN, Alice 81 Elizabeth 82
  Pamelia A 161
MURPHY, Jane 39
MURRAY, Annie E 43 Rebecca
  43
MURROW, Emma 161
NALTY, Agnes A 81
NASON, Clara L 131 Elizabeth
  79 82 98 Hannah 104
  Hannah B 213 Keziah 66
  Mary 27 Precilla 47 Sarah E
  16
NAY, Abigail 173 Sarah 41
NEAL, Hannah 85 Hannah E 81
  Kezia 89 Lydia 16 Nellie 102
  Nellie A 155 Patience 153
  Sarah 85
NEALLEY, Harriet 117
NEIL, Elizabeth 205 Margaret
  202
NELSON, Abigail 16 115 Addie
  M 102 Mehitable 147 S A 112
  Sally 183 Sarah 24 42
NEWBURY, Annie 188
NEWCOMB, Maria B 185
NEWELL, Emma P 161
NICHOLS, Elizabeth B 2 Eunice
  37 Helen L 48
NISBETT, Judith 28
NOBLE, Abigail 52 Dorothy 6
  Eliza 191 Sarah 122 Tirzah
  199

NOCK, Abigail 54
NORRIS, Betsy 154 Lydia 28
  165 Polly 165
NORWOOD, Abigail 124
NOWELL, Nancy 143 Patience
  96
NUDD, Adeline 139 Sally 158
NUTE, Achsah 202 Amanda J
  166 Anne 192 Bridget 66
  Clara D 152 Elizabeth 33 151
  192 Hannah 139 Isadore V
  74 Julia A 35 Lydia A 100
  Maria L 176 Martha A 132
  Mary 128 215 Mary A 139
  Mary J 204 Melissa B 128
  Nancy 99 Sarah 2 28 Sophia
  99 182 Sophia J 198 Susan
  15 Tamson 179
NUTTER, Ann 107 Betsey D 37
  Betsey N 66 Clara A 171 E
  Jennie 206 Elizabeth 90
  Flora B 142 Harriet 149
  Lucinda 83 Marie S 153
  Martha P 54 Mary 150 Mary
  M 164
O'BRIEN, Joanna 6
O'CONNER, Lydia E 5
ODIORNE, Mehitable 183
  Rebecca H 24 Susanna 23
ODLIN, Sarah 66
ORDWAY, Dorothy 151 Martha
  13
ORNE, Anna 5 Mary Ann 99
OSBORNE, Abigail Smith 145-
  146 Adeline Elizabeth 126
  Angie A 208 Eliza 32 Mary A
  27 Sally 59
OSGOOD, Alice M 42 Betsy 141
  165 Clara A 142 Nancy 167
  Polly 9 Rachel 167
OTIS, Abigail G 47 Dorothy 82
  Jemima 141 Maria 105
  Martha A 107 Mary Jane 70
  Nellie E 68 Olivia J 214
  Rebecca 82 Sarah 144 Sarah

OTIS (cont.)
  Ann 100 Susan 210 Susanna 45
OXFORD, Ellen E 136
PAGE, Abigail 120 Adino 142 Almira 130 Ann E 131 Anna 104-105 142 Anne 104 Betsy 173 Betty 191 Deborah 111 Eleanor 67 Eleanor H 101 Eliza 41 Elizabeth 78 137 142 Emily A 178 Hannah 59 168 Hannah F 125 Josephine W 139 Judith 119 Mary 35 77 142 Mary A 176 Mary Ann 103 Mary S 199 Meribah 120 Rebecca 46 Sarah 142
PAINE, Hannah 1 Mary 112 182 Sarah 182
PALMER, Abbie M 75 Jennie 72 Lydia M 116
PARCHER, Annie M 24
PARKER, Ann 117 Elizabeth 1 Jerusha 102 Laura A 83 Sarah O 140
PARKS, Mary 130
PARSHLEY, Alice 70 Emeline S 200 Lydia C 95 Mary Ann 177
PARSLEY, Polly 144
PARSONS, Abby E 128 Almira S 147 Annie L 140 Hannah 176 Harriet 109 Martha A 135 Ruth 22 Sally 156
PARTRIDGE, Harriet A 203
PASHO, Augusta 91
PATCH, Susan A 48
PATRICK, Mary 165 Olive 118
PATTEN, Hannah 89 Rebecca 165
PATTERSON, Hannah 98
PAUL, Arabelle E 209 Caroline H 194 Emily J 208 Eunice 184 Lydia 178
PEARL, Elizabeth 9 Sarah 70
PEARSON, Elizabeth 101

PEASE, Sarah F 117
PEASLEE, Clara J 64
PEASLEY, Mary 24
PEAVEY, Elizabeth 39 Mary E 200 Nancy 54 Patience 204 Rachel 50 Sarah Ann 132
PECK, Nellie M 67
PEIRCE, Abigail 210 Elizabeth 88 Elizabeth B 88 Harriet H 112 Olive W 50 Sarah 138
PENDERGAST, Abigail J 154 Jane 155 Mehitable 147 Permelia A 166 Rachel 19 Sophia 207
PENDEXTER, Ann Mary 212 Deborah 178 Hannah C 30 Margaret Jane 112 Mary 37 Sophia 136
PERCY, Nellie G 81
PERKINS, Abbie 68 Alfarata M 174 Charlotte 101 Elizabeth 53 Ellen F 209 Emma A 129 Esther 121 Fannie M C 65 Hannah 169 Hannah R 107 Jane W 72 Jennie A 81 Judith 123 Lucy A 101 Lydia 83 Lydia A 169 Mary 157 Mercie R 45 Nancy 138 Nancy E 191 Nettie C 105 Rebecca 126 Rosebell 78 Sarah Ann 193 Susan 10 148 Susan A 93
PERMAT, Judith 41
PERRY, Elmira 71 Mary 176
PERVIER, Betsy 207
PETERSON, M A 17
PEVERLY, Abigail 32 Ann Elizabeth 172 Elizabeth 94 136 153 Joanna 98 Louisa E 148 Mary 101 Sarah 96 Susanna 51 Temperance 200
PHILBRICK, Abigail 157 Betty 76 Katharine 66 Sarah A 47
PHILBROOK, Deb. 36 Lydia 125
PHILLIPS, Hannah 19

PHILPOT, Clara M 178
PICKERING, Abbie E 3 Abigail 63 Betsey 97 Mary E 62 Sarah 110
PIER, Hannah T 147
PIERCE, Atsy L 120 Hannah M 178 Harriet King 179 Julia E 203 Sarah A 63 Susan J 23
PIKE, Abigail 85 Annie Bell 22 Dolly 77 Eliza 68 Mary A 65 Nancy W 124 Sarah A 20 Sarah P 135
PINDER, Elizabeth 57 Mary C 112
PINKHAM, Anne A 75 Catherine 141 Eliza B 187 Evelyn F 63 Hannah 50 63 Hannah M 56 Lucretta 22 Lucy D 112 Mary J 131 Mary Jane 129 Minerva E 124 Sarah 214 Sarah A 113
PIPER, Abigail 185 Amanda 127 Betsey 4 Catherine Redman 125 Elizabeth Gerrish 207 Judith 76 Patience O 2 Sarah Little 48
PITMAN, Elizabeth 104 Mary 174 Sarah 11 Susanna 58
PITTS, Elizabeth 98
PLACE, Abigail 160 Elizabeth L 6 Emily Y 71 Mary E 5 Olive W 60 Sarah E 66 Sarah H 198 Sophia 62 Susan 211
PLUMER, Annie M 131 Caroline H 164 Olive 195 Sarah 108
PLUMMER, Dorcas 147 Elizabeth 108 Hannah 89 100 124 Lucinda G 187 Lydia 118 Mary 125 Mary Ann 80 Sarah 137 Sarah H 67
POLAND, Rebecca 131
POOLE, Mary E 28
POOR, Jenny L 9
PORCHER, Lizzie 3
PORTER, Hannah 63 Harriet M 96 Jane S 42

POTTER, Catherine E 146 Lydia Warner 137
POWERS, Celestia E 124 Eliza Olivia 90
PRAY, Abby 112 Abigail 104 Alice 90 Ann 201 Anne 212 Experience 213 Joanna 147 Mary 53 Mehitable 92 Polly 2 Sarah 119 200 Susan L 131
PREBLE, Mary F 186 Sarah 139
PRENTISS, Rebecca 129 Ruth 136
PRESCOTT, Ann 72 Leah 141 Lucy 73 Martha 143 Mittee Leavitt 167 Rachel 113
PRESTON, Jennie M 110
PRICE, Elizabeth Story 94 Lucy 48 Mary 39
PROCTOR, Mary S 116
PUFFER, Jennie 116
PUGSLEY, Fannie 39
PULSIFER, Hannah 20
PURINTON, Elizabeth 165
PUSBECK, L Etta 170
PUTNAM, Harriet 154 Minnie A 120 Rebecca Page 156
QUARLES, Belinda K 48
QUIMBY, Ellen A 84 Elvira B 106 Hannah 63 Kesiah F 160 Mary S 90 Ruth 158 Sarah C 2
QUINT, Rebecca 117
RAINS, Ellen C 3
RAITT, Isabelle 24
RAMSBOTTOM, Nancy C 39
RANCES, Sarah 8
RAND, Abigail 172 Anna S 79 Betsey 19 Betsy 156 Cynthia D 72 Elizabeth 1 120 Martha 86 Mary 196 Molly 160 Phebe 201 Polly 160 Sarah 123 Theodate S 124
RANDALL, Abigail 157 Deborah 115 Hannah 29 Hattie C 134 Lizzie S 157 Martha 127 Mary

RANDALL (cont.)
  7-8 98 117 Mary Beck 107
  Sarah 76 Sarah M 83
  Sophronia A 70
RANDLETT, Mary A 62
RANKINS, Betty 95 Clara A 54
RANSOM, Lydia M 205
RAYNER, Eliza Ann 193
READ, Nancy 147
READE, Lydia 184
REDFORD, Mary 166
REED, Ellen A 170
REMICK, Abigail 125 Abra 213
  Alpha 40 Anne 67 Eliza L 40
  Lillie G 14 Lydia 158 212
  Lydia Staples 142 Mary 79
  181 Nancy 200 Olive 162
  Sally 162 Sarah 51 Susan
  162
RENDALL, Lydia 85
RENSHAW, Mary M 186
REYNOLDS, Augusta T 181 Avis
  126 Elvina A 159 Josephine
  M 11 Martha 139
RICE, Augusta M W 106 Marcia
  A 160 Mary 106 Sarah 103
RICHARDS, Abigail 61 Lois 61
  Louisa A 109 Mary 33 194
  Mary Ann 106 Mehitable 77
  Nancy 195 Sarah 68
RICHARDSON, Abigail 130
  Abigail P 33 Elizabeth 78
  Jennie 7 Lydia 38 Mary 183
  Sarah 77 Sarah E 93 Susan
  83 97
RICKER, Abigail 33 113-114
  Annie A 140 Asenath 202
  Betsey 13 15 Eliza 84 Emma
  64 Hannah 98 Joanna 166
  Lankis 27 Lizzie A 152
  Martha 108 Martha A 127
  Mary 32 53 57 89 130
  Phoebe F 61 Rebecca 39
  Rhoda 114 Sarah D 99
  Sophia Maria 215 Theodate

RICKER (cont.)
  37
RIDLEY, Fanny 8
RILEY, Catherine 203 Isabella
  91 Lucretia 177
RINES, Judith 3 Mary Ann 181
  198 Mary B 36 Mary E 187
  Sally 3 Sarah E 173
ROBERTS, Abigail 40 Addie A
  45 Charlotte 109 Elizabeth J
  18 Elizabeth R 62 Emeline 60
  Eunice J 160 Hannah 42 123
  Hattie S 187 Irene 48 Laura A
  48 Lydia 28 130 Maria 30
  Martha Jane 28 Mary 5 39
  Mary Ann 80 154 Mary E P
  109 Mercy Ann 209 Molly
  121 Roesa A 104 Ruth 107
  Ruth T 54 Sarah 85 93 155
  196 Sarah F 81 Susan F 164
  Susanna 202
ROBERTSON, Polly 135
ROBIE, Sarah 208
ROBINSON, Christiana B C 193
  Eliza Ann 203 Sarah 7
ROBY, Mary E 144
ROGERS, Elizabeth 59 Hattie E
  208 Hattie M 216 Jane 21
  Lydia 196 Mahala 148
  Martha A 90 Mary 201 Nancy
  106 Ruth 162 Sally 27 64
  167 Susan Ann 208
ROLES, Elizabeth 193 Sarah E
  216
ROLFE, Jennie 101
ROLLINS, Abigail 167 Alice
  Osborne Williams 127 Anne
  Weeks 85 Augusta M 138
  Betsey B 127 Dorcas 8
  Elizabeth 38 Emily Ann 62
  Lucinda J 18 Lucy 103 Maria
  J 8 Martha 193 Mary 33
  Mary P 109 Nancy 17 Olive A
  186 Patience 48 Sarah 59
  Sarah A 68

ROSE, Sarah E 133
ROSS, Anna 206 Deborah 77 Esther 12 115 Hannah 144 Polly 122 Sarah H 11
ROTHWELL, Alice 191 Lizzie A 148 Mary J 160 Rachel 5
ROWE, Elizabeth 71 Sally 35 Sarah 138
ROWELL, Judith Ann 52 Molly 74
RUNDLET, Dolly 28
RUNDLETT, Abigail P 176 Betsy 175 Eliza F 51 Nancy 4 Susan L 136
RUNNELS, Abigail 173 Francenia 191 Hannah 9 24 Polly 101 Susanna 35 187
RUSSELL, Olive 20
RUST, Betsey S 118 Hannah Horne 143 Ida M 13 Jane 98 Martha C 174 Mary 67
RYAN, Caroline M 24 Deborah 205
SALMON, Emma T 74
SAMPSON, Hannah P 161
SANBORN, ----- 59 Addie Nancy 31 Betsy 168 Betty 1 Caroline 208 Deborah 35 Elizabeth 149 Elvira M 85 Georgianna 206 Hannah G 85 Hannah S 142 Jean 32 Lois 184 Lovey 151 Lydia 118 Molly 180 Nancy 122 Polly 13 Rebecca 78 Sarah 137 190 Sarah J 162 Susan R 76
SANDERS, Betsey Y 26 Jane H 10 Jennie 95 Lavina 148
SARGENT, Judith 13 Margaret 53 Molly 155 Phebe 83 Sarah 84
SAUNDERS, Eunice 107
SAVAGE, Clarrie A 157
SAVORY, Lydia A 121 Sophia 54
SAWYER, Abigail 110 Adaline 72 Almira F 7 Elizabeth H 157

SAWYER (cont.)
  Emma R 4 Francena J 59 Hannah 29 168 M Ellen 109 Mary E 97 Mary P 57 Sarah Ann 69
SAYWARD, Hannah 96 Margaret Ann 70
SCALES, Elizabeth A 7 Nancy 192
SCAMMON, Elizabeth 94
SCATES, Lydia 25 Lydia J 163 Mary 188 Sarah 40
SCEGGEL, Adelia F 63
SCOTT, Annie E 206
SCRIBNER, Huldah 170 Mary 96
SCRIGGINS, Fannie 48
SCRUTON, Betsey 43 Hannah E 171 Mary F 11 Nancy 25 Patience 70 Sarah A 106
SCULLY, Sarah J 38 202
SEAVEY, Abigail A 135 Dorothy 171 Eliza 101 Frederica 125 Jennie 7 Jennie A 91 Julia A 171 Lydia Ann 65 Mary 57 149
SEAWARD, Joanna 14
SENTER, Lavinia T 36 Mary Elizabeth 171
SEVERANCE, Lydia 140
SEWARD, Lizzie A 26
SEWELL, Georgia M 34
SHACKFORD, Elizabeth 51 Nancy 173 Susanna 140
SHACKLEY, Louise 121 Patty 82
SHANNON, Nancy 114
SHAPLEIGH, Catherine 95 Martha J 170
SHATTUCK, Sophia 54
SHAW, Eliza L 97 Elizabeth 115 Octavia Adams 30 Rachel 125
SHEAFE, Emily 146
SHEARDEN, Mary 65
SHEPARD, Lois 77 Phebe W 96

SHEPPARD, Harriet P 188 Phebe 37
SHERBURNE, Elizabeth 2 149 Jane Colbath 149 Rebecca 146 Sarah 149 Susannah 206
SHERIDAN, Julia A C 158
SHERMAN, Florence L 95
SHIELDS, Catherine E 204
SHOREY, Abigail 187 Amy 81 Eliza A 203 Lucy J 174 Mary E 201
SHORTRIDGE, Mary 122
SIAS, Mary 44 Welthern 209
SIBLEY, Abigail 183 Lydia 15
SILVERA, Elizabeth 146
SIMES, Ann 175 Eliza Ann 145
SIMMONS, Mary 67
SIMPSON, Ellen L 189 Fanny 8 Martha 183 Mary G 167
SINNOTT, Mary A 26
SLOPER, Anna 144 Deborah Jane 70 Hannah S 181 Meribah 144 Sally 27
SMALL, Joanna 133 Joanna E 142 Mary 31
SMALLCORN, Lucy M 121
SMART, Alice Ann 207 Charlotte 146 Mary A 97 Susan D 110
SMITH, Anna 32 123 Betsy 133 Betty 77 165 Catherine L 18 Comfort 29 Deborah 52 Dolly 74 Dorcas 202 Eliza A 11 95 Emily A 72 Eunice 63 Fannie C 201 Hannah 36 Hannah L 133 Hannah P 27 Ida L 106 Joanna 123 130 Lucinda 71 Lydia 141 Lydia M 108 Maria M 172 Martha 5 119 Martha B 208 Martha G 177 Mary 43 57 89 176 Mary Amanda 179 Mary J 34 Mary J S 180 Mary Jane 24 103 Molly 34 Rosamond 182 Rufina 144 Ruth 140 Sally 35 168 205

SMITH (cont.) Sarah 14 74 76 133 Sarah C 145 Susanna 117 Tamson 162
SNELL, Abby H 208 Abby Mary 62 Deliverance 23 Eliza C 195 Elizabeth 211 Elizabeth J 31 Linda A 109 Lydia A 16 Mary 164 Susan 96 Temperance 102
SOUTHWICK, Martha 175
SPENCER, Elizabeth 75 Mary 107 Sarah 151 Welthen 84
SPINNEY, Alice 185 Anne 212 Esther D 37 Martha 174 Mary 145 Patience 37 Sarah A 179 Susan R 124 Temperance 16
SPOKEFIELD, Kezia 76
SPRAGUE, Elizabeth 59
SPRINGER, Ann 34 Joanna 128
SPURLIN, Caroline 215 Lizzie E 216
SPURLING, Sabrina 56
STACKPOLE, Lucy 98 Mary A 148 Mary Jane 131 Sabra 79
STACY, Joanna 88 Sally 151
STANTON, Abby D 142 Hannah 33 133 Maria A 87 Nellie E 34
STANWOOD, Elizabeth M 176
STAPLES, Elizabeth L 110 Margaret 51
STARBARD, Mary 192
STARBIRD, Angeline 123
STAVERS, Ann Maria 136 Martha 191 Mary 191
STEEL, Lilla S 213
STEVENS, Abbie E 107 Abigail 142 Abigail E 31 Betsey 119 Catherine T 8 Elizabeth 187 Elizabeth A 127 Etta 110 Frances 53 Hannah 58 Lucinda 74 Lydia Ann 126 Mary 45 51 Mary P 99

STEVENS (cont.)
　Rebecca A 159 Sarah J 46
　Sarah M 216 Shuah 134
STEVENSON, Joanna 11 Mary 45
STEWART, Hattie M 169
STICKNEY, Almira 106
STILES, Clara R 122 Louisa 204
　Sarah E 132 Susan P 48
STILLINGS, Anna 15 Elizabeth A 90 Emeline 139
STILSON, Ann Carr 188 Carrie G 73 Elizabeth 115 Sarah 80 Susan C 142
STIRLING, Elzira 98
STOCKBRIDGE, Peggy 42
STOCKER, Nancy 38
STOKES, Abigail 192
STONE, Dorcas 84 Mary 84
STOYLES, Mary 148
STRAW, Jane 110
STREETER, Julia Ann 107
STURTEVANT, Elizabeth V 161
STYLES, Clara 20 Mary 161
SWAIN, Abigail 183 Ann M 121 Annie E 49 Elizabeth 173 Elizabeth A 63 Lydia 177 Malvina A 155 Mary E 31 56 Mary S 24 Rebecca 169 Sally 53 Sarah E 34
SWAINE, Elizabeth 191
SWASEY, Elizabeth 51 Eunice C 19 Joann 164 Sally 152
SWEAT, Dorothy 206 Mary 24 183
SWEATT, Deborah 2
SWETT, Abigail 132
TABOR, Eliza-ann 100
TANNER, Mary F 133 Mary G 25
TAPPAN, Adah B 54
TASKER, Abigail 16 115 137 Eliza 26 Lavina M 97 Lois 85 Mary 25 154 Mary Ann 201 Sally 192 Sarah E 123
TAYLOR, Elizabeth T 140 Judith

TAYLOR (cont.)
　83 Lavinia 155 Lydia S 55 Martha B 176 Mary J 18 Olive L 193 Phebe 209 Sarah 13
TEAGUE, Caroline 179
TEBBETS, Abigail 38 Debby 12 Elizabeth 137 Hannah 186 Judith 186
TEBBETTS, Abigail 153 Hannah 105 Lydia 177 Patience 52 Sarah 151 Susan 27
TEED, Elizabeth 41
TETHERLY, Mary E 37 Mary K 37 Nancy B 182 Rhoda P 199 Sarah A 37
THAYER, Emma V 48
THING, Abigail 96 Betsy 77 Hannah 130
THOMAS, Abigail 55 Georgiana D 112 Sarah 12 Sobriety 43
THOMPKINS, Lizzie K 144
THOMPSON, Abby Jane Augusta 20 Abigail 103 207 Ada M 164 Betsy 35 Cynthia A 158 Delania 201 Dora J 20 Hannah 69 168 Hannah R 62 Harriet N 212 Hattie A 209 Jane M 190 Kesiah R 188 Lavina 64 Lavina Perkins 194 Lovey 110 115 Lucy 98 Lucy A 34 Mary 125 214 Nancy S 20 Rebecca 165 Sarah 184 216 Sarah A F 65 Susan 23 Susanna 187 Temperance 12
THURLIN, Temperance 76
THURLOW, Linna H 166
THURSTON, Elizabeth 175 Elvira 120 Lucy 168 Melissa E 105 Nancy M 110 Phebe 92
TIBBETS, Elizabeth S 201 Mary K 215
TIBBETTS, Abbie 165 Abbie M 81 Abigail 11 209 Charity 6 Charlotte 23 Deborah 74

TIBBETTS (cont.)
　Hannah 93 Jennie L 65
　Joanna 30 Laura J 166 Mary
　Frances 42 Minerva A 43
　Nancy D 137 Sally 49 Sarah
　172 Sarah E 95 208
TILDEN, Abigail 95
TILTON, Abbie I 57 Betty 76
　Elizabeth 211 Eva 208
　Hannah 59 Isabel A 47
　Judith 168 Polly 143 Sarah F
　177
TITCOMB, Eliza 68 Elizabeth
　153 Elizabeth W 7 Mary 210
　Sarah 200
TOMPSON, Betsey 80
TORR, Caroline 43 93 Eunice
　130 Sarah 49
TORREY, Eliza 122
TOWLE, Dolly 111 Elizabeth 210
TOWN, Emma A 53
TOWNSEND, Elizabeth M 175
TOZIER, Anne 104
TRAFTON, Abbie L 160
TRASK, Sarah A 182 Sarah E
　124
TREDICK, Lucretia B 133
TREMILLS, Adeline 163
TREWORGIE, Catherine 95
TRICKEY, Clarissa 46 Eliza G 4
　Lydia J 198 Mary 11 Mary
　Ann 149 Sarah 115 Sarah H
　161
TRIPE, Anna 200 Nancy 200
TRUE, Lucy S 191
TUCKER, Esther 201 Mary E
　178 Mary N 75 Meriam 180
　Molly 142 Sarah M 101
　Sophronia R 131
TUFTS, Anna Louisa 3 Eliza 75
　Nancy 87
TURNER, Annie 37 Mary 164
TUTTLE, Abigail 86 142 196
　Augusta M 19 Bessie E 15
　Comfort 74 Delia A 83

TUTTLE (cont.)
　Elizabeth 56 Ellen E 86
　Esther 70 119 Esther G 45
　Fannie L 194 Frances 48
　Georgianna 22 Hannah 60
　118 Hope 192 Judith 37
　Katherine 38 Lavina 192 Love
　132 Lucy 138 Lydia 117 202
　Maria 54 Martha Ella 23
　Mary J 143 Mary Jane 191
　Peggy 106 Sally 9 Sarah 56
　Sarah E 99 Sarah R 193
　Sarah S 1 Susan M 73
TWOMBLEY, Louisa 66 Martha
　S 155 Sarah 63
TWOMBLY, Ann 61 Ann M 195
　Anna 3 Eleanor 160 Eliza 40
　Eunice 89 Helen C 134 Lois 5
　Martha 1 Martha Ann 195
　Martha H 25 65 Mary 103
　Mary A 91 Mehitable 100
　Mercy 67 Nancy 17 29 Polly
　82 169 Rachel 1 Rhoda 63
　Sally 136 Sarah 47 194
　Sarah F 213 Susanna 143
　Tamson 44 154
VANDUZZA, Phoebe 156
VARNEY, Abbie 198 Abby Ann
　204 Abigail 28 104 112 128
　161 Almira 99 Anna L 216
　Betsey 197 C M 133 Caroline
　137 Charlotte 197
　Deliverance 128-129
　Elizabeth 13 Esther 21
　Hannah 68 197 Hannah
　Hurd 1 Hannah M 58 Jane H
　173 Leonora 99 Lucy Jane
　109 Lydia 129 197 Lydia J 16
　Maria 50 Martha 192 195
　Martha J 87 Martha M 136
　Mary 98 Mary E 52 72 Mary
　Jane 93 Mercy 74 94 105
　Mercy Hanson 44 Nancy J 48
　Patience 69 Ruth 140 Sarah
　A 97 198

VEDION, Emma 8
VERY, Lydia 156
VICCAR, Joanna 149
VICKERY, Abby E 28 Amanda 174 Azella A 65 Emma L 142 Mahala 156
VINALL, Sarah Abby 117
WADE, Mary E 20
WADLEIGH, Mary A 56
WAKEFIELD, Sarah Elizabeth 73
WALDRON, Anna P 47 Anne 167 Celia C 200 Hannah 101 194 Jane N 141 Mary 101 172 208 Sally 85 Sarah 69 101 Susan 85
WALFORD, Jane 148
WALKER, Abigail 73-74 170 Anna 171 Betsey 135 Elizabeth 186 Ella 78 Emeline 198 Harriet 115 159 Lucy Maria 184 Lydia 15 Mary A 97 175 Olive 106
WALLACE, Anna 21 Comfort 175 Emma B 164 Hannah A 173 Mary E 201 Octavie 48
WALLINGFORD, Abra 59 Betsey 80 Elizabeth 37 Hannah 17 Lydia 41 Lydia R 74 Margaret 185 Martha A 171 Mary 185 Nancy 100 Sarah 108
WALLIS, Comfort 113
WARD, Martha C 50
WARREN, Addie 83 Carrie M 118 Lucinda W 125 Margaret 92 Mary 88 Rachel 172 Sarah J 129
WATERHOUSE, Alice 56 Mary 69 Mary A 121
WATERMAN, Clarissa 135
WATSON, Abigail 75 190 Abigail J 165 Anna M 105 Betsey 206 Betsey J 94 Clara L 87 Clarissa 126 Elizabeth 2 132 Hannah 193 Harriet 55 210

WATSON (cont.) Lucy 87 98 Lydia 126 Mary Fogg 135 Mary J 145 Nancy 110 132 198 Sally 106 Sarah 89 159
WEAVER, Louisa 81
WEBBER, Alma J 90 Almeda 120 Mary 166 Mary Ann 22
WEBSTER, Eliza J 185 Hannah M 177 Harriet J 120 Marianna 185 Mary C 13 Mary E 81 Nancy A 2 Sarah F 171
WEDGEWOOD, Betsey 185
WEED, Anna 133 Dorothy 133 Hannah 164
WEEKS, Elizabeth 132 Hannah 76 Julia A 196 Martha 41 Mary 187 Sarah 37
WELCH, Finette 50 Georgia A 111 Mahala 70 Sarah 105
WENTWORTH, Abby C 184 Abia D 137 Abigail 2 Abigail M 190 Almira P 58 Augusta M 189 Betsey 212 Clara A 102 Clara E 204 Clara L 62 Clarissa 159 Dorothy F 91 Estella J 143 Frances D 109 Hannah 15 38 Jennie M 40 Joanna 20 194 Judith 54 Lois A 90 Louisa 109 Lucretia S 100 Lydia 179 Martha 196 Mary 17 160 196 Mary A 184 209 Mary Ann 199 Mary E 42 Mary F 31 Mercy 163 Molly 15 121-122 Olive A 54 Philena 72 Ruth 99 Ruth P 190 Sally 111 181 Sarah 207 Sarah E 19 Sarah Knox 40 Susan 109 120
WEST, Frances K 38
WESTMAN, Elizabeth 1
WEYMOUTH, Betsy 132 Mary 52 Tabitha 104
WHIDDEN, Catharine E R 184

NEW HAMPSHIRE MARRIAGES SUPPLEMENT

WHIDDEN (cont.)
   Lavinia 148
WHITE, Elizabeth 132 Margaret
   51 Martha Dodge 159 Mary
   100 Susan A 172
WHITEHOUSE, Abigail 63
   Arabell 72 Elizabeth 120 128
   Elmira 51 Emma E 124
   Hannah S 26 Louisa G 21
   Lydia 178 Mary E 181 Nancy
   Ann 178 Sarah Ann 31
   Susan 41 Tamson 55
WHITING, Sarah Jane 9
WHITMAN, Hannah 190
WHITTEN, Hannah A 5 Nancy
   Frances 138 Sarah A 60
WHITTIER, Ruth 174 Salome 91
   Sarah 197
WIGGIN, Abigail 192 Ann L 150
   Anna 102 Annie 188 Augusta
   109 Belle 9 Dorothy 143 Eliza
   105 Eliza A 41 Elizabeth 185
   Elizabeth A 79 Emily C 180
   Fanny A 168 Hannah 186
   189 Harriet N 18 Hattie S 127
   Lucy A 111 Lydia 146
   Mabelle F 78 Maria 141
   Martha 162 Mary 118 Mary A
   88 Mary Hannah 179 Mary
   Jane 154 Mehitable H 174
   Mercy 173 Olive 207 Rachel
   33 Rosannah 49 Sally 19 41
   183 Sarah Ann 119 Sophia
   136 Susannah C 16
   Temperance 9 Zetta W 117
WIGGLESWORTH, Mary S 157
WILKINS, Carrie 39
WILLARD, Ann 39 Marjory 207
WILLEY, Abigail 117 Alvira 118
   Betsey 173 Christian 202
   Clara A 180 Clara J 93
   Frances E 22 Hannah 35 127
   Keziah 171 Lucy A 214
   Martha 8 Mary 19 55 62 94
   116 Mary Ann 180 Mary D

WILLEY (cont.)
   180 Mary E 209 Polly 200
   Susan W 193
WILLIAMS, Abigail 150 157 Alice
   166 Avis 177 Eliza D 211
   Elizabeth A 61 Louisa 116
   Mary 146 Sarah L 93
WILLOWBY, Patience 79
WILMOT, Sarah 12
WILSON, Abigail 207 Martha 99
   Nancy 213 Rebecca 14
   Ursula A 127
WINBURN, Susannah 1
WING, Sophronia W 78
WINGATE, Abigail 163 Lydia 69
   125 Mary 188 Polly 74 Sarah
   121 125
WINKLEY, Lavina 11 Martha
   179 Mary Ann 132 Mary F
   185
WINN, Dorcas A 72
WISE, Sarah 82
WITHAM, Betsy 172 Eliza A 48
   151 Emeline S 82 Lydia M 83
   Martha 123 Mary C 4 Mary
   Ellen 142 Mehitable 168
   Nancy E 45
WITHER, Ellen 145
WITHERELL, Amelia C 154
WOOD, Annie A 60 Charlotte D
   116 Sally 143 Sarah A 73
   Sarah J 72
WOODBURY, Elizabeth 56
WOODMAN, Elizabeth 116
   Elizabeth P 30 Emily 22
   Eunice 1 Hannah 58 Hannah
   R 173 Lizzie A 110 Loella 198
   Martha 49 Mary 28 211
   Rachel A 38 Sarah 200 Sarah
   A 146
WOODSUM, Mercy 212
WOODUS, Jennie 48
WORCESTER, Nancy 195
WORMWOOD, Jerusha 128
WORSTER, Betsey 170 Mary

WORSTER (cont.)
170 197 Sarah 201
WORTHING, Olivia 209
WORTMAN, Caroline E 186
WRIGHT, Josephine 97
YEATON, Elizabeth 27 58 Mary 39 171 183
YORK, Abigail 30 Comfort 176 Elizabeth F 181 Hattie E 48 Julia 65 Mary 47 Mary Jane 214 Mrs Mindwell A 87 Sarah 58 159
YOUNG, Abigail 78 Annie 65 Annie E 203 Coridle 9 Deborah 148

YOUNG (cont.)
Drusilla 207 Druzilla E 109
Eleanor M 71 Ellen 184 Ellen E 187 Ellen T 210 Emma I 148 Hannah 57 119 145 151 Hannah C 170 Hannah D 139 Harriet A 206 Lucy W 17 Martha E 214 Martha F 146 Mary 35 89 185 Mary A 83 Mary Ann 6 Mehitable C 114 Melissa 107 Nancy 215 Olive J 23 Patience 157 Rebecca A 198 Sally B 46 Sarah 39 128 Sophia 49 Sophronia Jane 80

www.ingramcontent.com/pod-product-compliance
Lightning Source LLC
Chambersburg PA
CBHW060118170426
43198CB00010B/937